YOU ARE NOT DISQUALIFIED FROM RECEIVING GOD'S FAVOR AND GOODNESS

Adam was a snitch.
Jacob was a thief.
Jonah was defiant.
Noah was a drunk.
Elijah was suicidal.
Mark was a quitter.
Joseph was abused.
Miriam was a racist.
Hannah was barren.
Lot committed incest.
Gideon was a coward.
Simon was a sorcerer.
Zaccheus was corrupt.
Moses was a murderer.
Thomas was a doubter.
Abram pimped his wife.
Rahab was a prostitute.
David was an adulterer.
Nathaniel was a skeptic.
Onesimus was a fugitive.
Ruth was an illegal alien.
Solomon worshiped idols.
Saul persecuted Christians.
Matthew was a collaborator.
Mary Magdalene was possessed.
The Samaritan woman was an outcast.
All 11 of Jesus' 12 disciples deserted him,
and Peter denied having ever even known him,
because
JESUS CHRIST WAS A CONVICTED FELON.

Psalm 107
(vv. 9-16)

He satisfies the thirsty,
and fills the hungry with good things.

Some sat in darkness and deep gloom,
bound fast in misery and iron;

Because they rebelled against the words of God,
and despised the counsel of the Most High.

So he humbled their spirits with hard labour;
they stumbled, and there was none to help.

Then they cried to the Lord in their trouble,
and he delivered them from their distress.

He led them out of darkness and deep gloom
and broke their bonds asunder.

Give thanks to the Lord for his mercy,
and the wonders he does for his children.

For he shatters the doors of bronze,
and breaks in two the iron bars.

Daily Light on the Prisoner's Path

Second Edition

J. R. Woodgates

Milestones

Entry Date _____

Location _____

My Baptism Date _____

   Location _____

   By Whom _____

Transfer Date _____

To _____

Transfer Date _____

To _____

Transfer Date _____

To _____

Release Date/EOS _____

Copyright © 2015, 2020 J. R. Woodgates.

All rights reserved. No part of this book may be used or reproduced by any means, graphic, electronic, or mechanical, including photocopying, recording, taping or by any information storage retrieval system without the written permission of the author except in the case of brief quotations embodied in critical articles and reviews.

WestBow Press books may be ordered through booksellers or by contacting:

WestBow Press
A Division of Thomas Nelson & Zondervan
1663 Liberty Drive
Bloomington, IN 47403
www.westbowpress.com
1 (866) 928-1240

Because of the dynamic nature of the Internet, any web addresses or links contained in this book may have changed since publication and may no longer be valid. The views expressed in this work are solely those of the author and do not necessarily reflect the views of the publisher, and the publisher hereby disclaims any responsibility for them.

Any people depicted in stock imagery provided by Getty Images are models, and such images are being used for illustrative purposes only.
Certain stock imagery © Getty Images.

ISBN: 978-1-4908-6415-0 (sc)
ISBN: 978-1-4908-6416-7 (hc)
ISBN: 978-1-4908-6414-3 (e)

Library of Congress Control Number: 2014922859

Printed in the United States of America.

WestBow Press rev. date: 03/13/2020

Morning and evening Scripture selections from the King James Version compiled by Johnathan Bagster and family, first published by his son, Robert, in England, 1875, under the title, *Daily Light on the Daily Path*. P.D.

No One Asked by Robert L. Hambrick. Re-printed by permission from Prisoner Express, a program of the Durlan Alternative Library, a project of the Center for Transformative Action at Cornell University, Ithaca, NY.

Broken Dreams from *Mother's Legacy* by Lauretta P. Burns. Copyright © 1991. Used by permission.

Never Came to Me from an unpublished collection, *Trapped in the Mirror: Reflective Convictions* by Deon C. Nowell. Used by permission of the author.

Who Am I? from *Letters and Papers from Prison, Enlarged Ed.*, by Dietrich Bonhoeffer, translated from the German by R. H. Fuller, Frank Clark, et al. Copyright © 1953, 1967, 1971 by SCM Press, Ltd. Reprinted with the permission of Scribner, a division of Simon & Schuster, Inc. All rights reserved.

Forgive Our Sins As We Forgive by Rosamond E. Herklots (1905-1987). Reproduced by permission of Oxford University Press. All rights reserved.

C. S. Lewis quotation from *The Great Divorce* by C. S. Lewis. Copyright © C. S. Lewis Pte., Ltd. 1946. Extract reprinted by permission.

Oswald Chambers quotations from the October 6, October 12, December 7 and December 31 readings in *My Utmost for His Highest*. Used by kind permission of Oswald Chambers Publications Association, Ltd., administered by Discovery House Publishers, Grand Rapids, MI.

D. A. Carson quotation from the January 23 reading in *For the Love of God: A Daily Companion for Discovering the Riches of God's Word*, Vol. 2 by D. A. Carson. Copyright © 1999 Crossway, Wheaton, IL. Used by permission.

Nancy R. Pearcey and Michael J. Wilkins quotations from the DVD, *Jesus: Man, Messiah or More?* Copyright © 2009 RBC Ministries, Grand Rapids, MI 49501. Used by permission. All rights reserved.

Gordon Robertson quotation copyright © 2014 Gordon Robertson. Reprinted with permission. All rights reserved.

Robert Farrar Capon quotation from *The Third Peacock: A Book About God and the Problem of Evil* by Robert Farrar Capon. Copyright © 1971, 1986.

All Scripture quotations are from the King James Version of the Bible. P.D.

Prayers on pages 24, 28 and 54, Psalms 25, 32 and 107 (vv. 9-16), and The Lord's Prayer adapted from *The Book of Common Prayer for The Episcopal Church*. P.D.

Cover design by Larry Smith, LSDesign@aol.com

TABLE OF CONTENTS

About This Book 1
Four Truths About God and Yourself 2
Dread, Despair and Defiance 6
Do Your Time in God's Time 7
Experience God's Presence 9
All-the-Time Anger 10
I Believe in God. Why is Jesus So Special? 15
A Divine Plea Agreement 17
What is True Repentance? 25
A Formal Prayer of Repentance 28
A Hearty Sinner's Prayer 30
Now What? 33
Forgiveness 35
My (Former) Enemies List 37
Forget About It! 39
I've Confessed All to God. Must I Confess All to the Police? 41
How to Pray 42
The Lord's Prayer 44
The 23rd Psalm 45
The Ten Commandments (Plus One) 46
The Apostles' Creed 47
Will God Really Protect Me? 55
Spiritual Warfare 56
Doing Good Time 61
Altering the Atmosphere 62
Me, Myself and I 65
Promises for Prisoners 68
Daily Light for Every Morning and Evening 72

I'm Still in a Gang 444
I'm Stuck in Solitary 446
I'm Down for Life 449
Can I Lose My Salvation? 454
Get Me Outta Here! 457
When It's Finally Time to Leave 461

HYMNS

In Anger, Lord, Rebuke Me Not 8
Amazing Grace 19
Come, Ye Sinners, Poor and Needy 21
Forgive Our Sins As We Forgive 34
All the Way My Savior Leads Me 38
Before the Throne of God Above 40
What a Friend We Have in Jesus 48
Be Still, My Soul 50
How Firm a Foundation 52
St. Patrick's Breastplate 58
A Mighty Fortress is Our God 60
If Thou But Suffer God to Guide Thee 456
Whate'er My God Ordains is Right 458

POEMS

How'd You Lose Your Kingdom? 5
A Hymn to God the Father 24
Never Came to Me 64
Broken Dreams 64
No One Asked 448
The Serenity Prayer 451
Who Am I? 452
Thank You, God 463

*Thy word is a lamp unto my feet,
and a light unto my path...
I am afflicted very much:
quicken me, O Lord,
according unto thy word.*
— Psalm 119:105,107

**Dedicated to
The Butner Brotherhood
and to all prisoners ready
to make their path one of
faith, hope and restoration**

*When thou goest, it shall lead thee;
when thou sleepest, it shall keep thee; and
when thou wakest, it shall talk with thee.
For the commandment is a lamp;
and the law is light.*
— Proverbs 6:22

*Let all those that put their trust in thee rejoice:
Let them ever shout for joy, because thou defendest them...
For thou, Lord, wilt bless the righteous;
With favour wilt thou compass him as with a shield.*
— Psalm 5:11-12

About This Book

This is a spiritual survival guide for men living in confinement.

It's also about how to become a fully blessed son of the Father.

Although this book is for men, women inmates also benefit from reading it.

It's useful whether you are new to the system or have been down for decades.

Each selection of morning and evening Bible verses relates to a general theme, identified by the banner verse in italics. As you read, mark, learn and inwardly digest God's living Word, the Holy Spirit will use it to influence your thinking and reach into your heart (see 2 Timothy 3:16-17). These verses will ease your mind and reassure you of God's control and concern for your welfare. They will also inspire you to learn more about his supernatural power that can make you a new man (or woman) and improve the spiritual atmosphere around you.

Don't keep this book to yourself. Read it out loud to your bunkie, a cellie and others who might be interested in it but do not read. Talk about its teachings and try out its methods. Before long, things will begin to change.

I've included some classic expressions of Christian belief, as well as a few psalms, really old hymns, prayers and poems. They will assure you that any anger, fear, sadness or frustration you are feeling is not unusual or permanent. Other prisoners have felt just as awful, drawn close to God and enjoyed immediate relief. Instead of feeling totally upset, isolated or intimidated, you'll soon be able to walk tall as a son of the Father, bearing his authority and strength.

That will make all the difference during your remaining time behind bars.

I hope that one day, along with the repentant psalmist, you will be able to say, *Before I was afflicted, I went astray: but now have I kept thy word... It is good for me that I have been afflicted; that I might learn thy statutes* (Psalm 119:67,71).

I too was briefly afflicted in prison (BOP 28626-016) and now walk the path of freedom in Christ. So can you. It may take a while before you're ready to follow all of my suggestions (and those in the Recommended Readings), but as you do so, you will gradually be able to live at peace with your enemies (and yourself), improve the spiritual atmosphere around you and even be a blessing to others.

The more you apply God's Word while walking in the wisdom and power he wants to give you, the more you will know for real that he is faithful in keeping every one of his many good promises (see Numbers 23:19 and pp. 68-71).

J. R. Woodgates
Washington, DC

Four Truths About God and Yourself

This is a people robbed and spoiled;
they are all of them snared in holes,
and they are hid in prison houses:
they are for a prey, and none delivereth;
for a spoil, and none saith, Restore.
— Isaiah 42:22

God has followed every step of your downward path from youthful delinquency or deviancy all the way to this human stockyard where you must now live inside a razor wire fence perimeter, stripped of your individuality, tagged with a number, culled, corralled and herded by handlers who care less about your welfare than whether you stray out of bounds.

Despite knowing all the facts about you (including what you think about him), God has never stopped caring about your welfare. Even if you've deliberately done very bad things, he wants to help you. Whether you're already doing time in a detention center, jail or prison or are waiting to be charged, tried, sentenced or transferred, God knows how bad (or good) things may yet get for you.

When my spirit was overwhelmed within me,
then thou knewest my path (Psalm 142:3).

God wants to bring you through whatever lies ahead, because he can change whatever lies ahead. He can also change you. If you'll let him lead, he has an amazing upward path of faith, hope – and, yes, restoration – for you to walk.

#1 - God is not against you.

He does not hate you and he is not angry with you, despite all that you've done.

Actually, he wants to bless you (see 2 Chronicles 16:9a).

No matter who you are or what you've done to get here, you can receive free forgiveness and mercy from God – you don't have to suffer for it or earn it.

God takes no pleasure in your unhappiness. He is more interested in correcting the sinfulness that has gotten you into this much trouble.

It's easier than you may think to let God straighten out your life and set you on a path of restoration. He has *already* forgiven your sins; now he's just waiting for you to *accept* his forgiveness. He *already* has a plan to make your life purposeful and even enjoyable; now he's just waiting for you to let him show you the way.

Although it's too late to avoid being judged by a court for your crimes, *you can still avoid being judged by God for your sins.* If you don't avoid that (by accepting his forgiveness and committing to turn away from sin), after you die you will face divine punishment far worse than any sentence from an earthly court.

Because God loves you, *he's made a way for you to avoid getting that punishment.*

#2 - God wants you to avoid divine punishment.

God can prevent you from receiving your well-deserved divine punishment by *cancelling* all of your sins (even the really bad ones no one else is willing to forgive). All your guilt and shame can be scrubbed clean, too.

God says, *Though your sins be as scarlet, they shall be as white as snow* (Isaiah 1:18) – not because they don't matter, but because God's only Son, Jesus, has already taken the punishment for you (see John 3:16, Colossians 1:21-22). What a break!

Thou, Lord, art good, and ready to forgive; and plenteous in mercy unto all them that call upon thee.
— Psalm 86:5

Because God truly loves you, he wants to protect you from being punished by him for your sins. Now is the time to receive his total immunity from divine judgment (see 2 Corinthians 6:2).

#3 - God is not getting even with you.

Maybe you're a Christian who fears God's judgment because you knew better but did bad things anyway (see Jeremiah 2:13,17,19-22).

Don't let self-reproach keep you from returning to your Father.

He is waiting to restore you (see Luke 15:11-32)!

I will be his father, and he shall be my son. If he commit iniquity, I will chasten him with the rod of men, and with the stripes of the children of men: But my mercy shall not depart away from him (2 Samuel 7:14-15).

Criminal behavior by Christians does not disqualify them from again enjoying the Father's favor and goodness
(see Psalm 103:8-14).

As a wayward son, honestly confess your willful disobedience and again accept your Father's full forgiveness. Then sincerely recommit to walking with him along whatever good path he chooses for you (see Psalm 16:11, Proverbs 3:5-6).

#4 - God can be trusted with your future.

God has a much larger purpose for you than just being a shifty ex-con. If eventually you do get released, you can go back to the streets not as a harder criminal or broken-down victim but as a truly new man (or woman) with divinely inspired ideas for an honest future (see Proverbs 8:12,21,35).

Getting out happy, whole and restored really is possible for you – unless you refuse to believe that God is offering you any positive changes or you refuse to accept them on his terms (see Psalm 68:6, Isaiah 61:1-3,6-7, Zechariah 9:12).

Decide now to put your trust in God, accept his forgiveness, and choose to believe that he has a good purpose and destiny for you. You will soon stop dreading the future and what may be waiting for you just around the corner.

O taste and see that the Lord is good:
blessed is the man that trusteth in him.
— Psalm 34:8

If you cooperate with God, he will:

- Clear your guilty conscience
- Give you a positive new identity as a fully loved son
- Break curses or childhood vows that may be holding you back
- Expose the destructive lies of Satan that may be deceiving you
- Deal with your anger, resentments and grief
- Give you hope and ideas for a good future (see Proverbs 8:12,21,35)
- Perform spiritual heart surgery on you (see Mark 7:21-23, Ezekiel 36:26), and
- Make you a blessing to others

The God of all grace...after that ye have suffered a while,
make you perfect, stablish, strengthen, and settle you.
— 1 Peter 5:10

The Father's blessings can surprise you.

With men this is impossible;
but with God all things are possible.
— Matthew 19:26

Your case is closed...then it's reopened.
Your kids won't visit...then they show up.
Your fears won't ease...then they go away.
Your appeal is denied...then it's reconsidered.
Your harassers won't shut up...then they let up.
Your transfer stays on hold...then it goes through.
Your classification won't change...then it's lowered.

Of course, I can't promise that God will do any of these things for you, but he's done them all for countless other prisoners who have put their trust in him. There is no reason to think he won't make good things happen for you, too.

God *wants* to bless you – starting now, if you'll let him – but only on his terms.

God really can improve your current situation, give you steady peace of mind, self-control and a new positive outlook (see Isaiah 26:3, Psalm 146:5-9).

Isn't that what you need right now?

As the best Father you could ever hope to have, God can assure you of his love and care, beginning right now. Then he can renew your mind and heart to make you the successful son you still can become (see Romans 12:2, Hebrews 10:16), and inspire you with good ideas for an honest, satisfying future – regardless of what others may think or say about you (see Psalm 31:20, Isaiah 54:17, Proverbs 8:12,21,35).

No matter how bad your past is or how unworthy your spiritual condition seems to be, God wants you to become one of his forgiven, blessed sons. Do that and then he can enable you to get through the rest of your time safely and purposefully – even if you never leave prison.

Does that interest you?

Then keep reading and step onto the path of faith, hope and restoration!

> No matter what happens, we are going to have to wander around down here in the dark of badness as long as we live. Why not take a chance on the invisible Guide?
>
> If he's for real, you win hands down; if not, you only lose what you had to lose anyway.
>
> It's a proposition no betting man would refuse.
>
> The worst thing you can do is break even.
>
> —*Robert Farrar Capon*
> *(based on Pascal's Wager)*

How'd You Lose Your Kingdom?

For want of a nail, a shoe was lost,
For want of a shoe, a horse was lost,
For want of a horse, a rider was lost,
For want of a rider, a message was lost,
For want of a message, a battle was lost,
For want of a battle, a war was lost,
For want of a war, a kingdom was lost.
And all for want of a horseshoe nail.

Dread, Despair and Defiance

Whether you're wearing stripes, whites, blues, grays, greens, reds, khakis or a carrot suit, you're under pressure to conform. The system, society and other inmates want to eventually push you into a state of dread, despair or defiance:

Dread It's every man for himself in here; I can't trust anyone. The system is rigged to either break me down or wear me down. Other inmates only want to play me (or maybe even slay me). I must live by the convict code, or else.

Despair This place is just a human animal control facility. My life has lost its significance. Even if I'm released tomorrow, my future is ruined: I am now and forever a disgraced social outcast who can never expect to be fully forgiven or trusted, only shamed, shunned and suspected as a public safety risk.

Defiance The system thinks it took my identity along with my street clothes. I'm not supposed to be anything more than a compliant little inmate. Well, I'm not like all the clueless losers locked up in here with me; I'm proud of who and what I am, and everybody else needs to know it too.

You can rebel, retreat or be renewed.

You can loudly reject the labels others try to hang on you, adopt a boldly belligerent attitude, cover yourself with grotesque tattoos, dominate weaker men, join an aggressive gang or sullenly keep to yourself.

On the other hand, if you feel like a luckless idiot or a vulnerable victim, you can retreat into depression or a fearful basic survival mode.

Such feelings and reactions are yours to choose; no one can force them on you.

Unless you actually enjoy feeling awful, let God replace your dread, despair or defiance with genuine peace of mind (even inner joy) as you begin trusting in his favor and goodness, as well as his protection (see Psalm 5:11-12, Hebrews 13:5-6).

Let God make himself real to you, renew your mind and heart, then give new meaning to your life with a positive sense of purpose and personal significance.

Isn't that what you've always wanted?

Now unto him that is able to keep you from falling,
and to present you faultless before the presence of his glory
with exceeding joy,
To the only wise God our Saviour,
be glory and majesty, dominion and power,
both now and ever.
Amen.
— Jude 24-25

Do Your Time in God's Time

> **_Counting time_**
> **_is not as important_**
> **_as making time count._**

The Bible talks about "the fullness of time," when all sorts of different things finally come together to accomplish God's will.

It may take a while, but it does come.

Here's what God told his own chosen people who were so disobedient that he allowed them to become captives of an enemy nation for 70 years:

> *I know the thoughts that I think toward you, saith the Lord,*
> *thoughts of peace, and not of evil, to give you an expected end....*
> *Ye shall seek me, and find me, when ye shall search for me*
> *with all your heart. And I will be found of you, saith the Lord:*
> *and I will turn away your captivity....*
> *For I am with thee, saith the Lord, to save thee....*
> *But I will correct thee in measure,*
> *and will not leave thee altogether unpunished.*
> — *Jeremiah 29:11,13-14, 30:11*

In the fullness of time God can end your captivity and bring you to an expected end – if you seek him with all your heart and keep trusting him with both your current situation and your future, come what may (see Psalms 69, 130, 55:22).

God has a special love for prisoners
(see Psalm 102:19-20)
– BUT –
There is a special place in divine wisdom for discipline ("chastening") in the lives of his disobedient creatures.

> *Now no chastening for the present seemeth to be joyous,*
> *but grievous: nevertheless, afterward it yieldeth*
> *the peaceable fruit of righteousness...*
> — *Hebrews 12:11*

Right now, things may look grim. Even in the best joint incarceration is no picnic and a daily sense of danger, intimidation or futility can be very real.

But God is *more* real than anything you're experiencing.

Let him begin to show you what that means.

In Anger, Lord, Rebuke Me Not;

Withdraw the dreadful storm;
Nor let thy fury grow so hot
Against a feeble worm.

My soul's bowed down with heavy cares,
My flesh with pain oppressed;
My couch is witness to my tears,
My tears forbid my rest.

Sorrow and pain wear out my days,
I waste the night with cries,
Counting the minutes as they pass,
Till the slow morning rise.

Shall I be still tormented more?
Mine eye consumed with grief?
How long, my God, how long before
Thine hand afford relief?

He hears when dust and ashes speak,
He pities all our groans;
He saves us for his mercy's sake,
And heals our broken bones.
The virtue of his sovereign word
Restores our fainting breath;
For silent graves praise not the Lord,
Nor is he known in death.

—Isaac Watts (1719), age 45
(Based on Psalm 6)

Experience God's Presence

If you've never related to God personally (or aren't even sure if he exists), try this experiment: Open your door to him and see what happens.

> *Behold, I stand at the door and knock:*
> *if any man hear my voice, and open the door, I will come in to him, and will sup with him, and he with me (Revelation 3:20).*

No matter how bad you've been or how unworthy you feel, the Bible says, *Draw near to God and He will draw near to you (James 4:8)*. Even if your background is hostile to Christianity, God will respond generously if you reach out to him sincerely (see Romans 10:12-13).

God will meet you just as you are, without demanding that you first "get right" with him (you can decide to do that later). He is a divine spirit who *will* reveal his love for you in an obvious manner if you really want him to.

Just ask him to "show up."

Ask God to prove he is real and that he cares about you by revealing himself right now in some unmistakable way in your current situation.

Because God unconditionally loves everyone ("any man" includes you), he will reveal himself to the most guilty, hostile or skeptical sinner (is that you?) if he's just *willing to be willing to believe* that God is real and will really answer him (see Job 33:15-18, Matthew 7:7-8, Hebrews 11:6).

Talk to God any time – sitting up or lying down, out loud or silently, alone on your bunk, on your knees or while walking the track (even around a "dog pen").

It might happen tonight or next week, but once God shows up and proves to you that he has heard you *and is on your side*, you might want to tell him that you appreciate his help (and need his forgiveness (read Psalm 38)).

That's what he's waiting for (see 2 Chronicles 16:9a, Romans 2:4).

After we die, we all must answer to God for how we've chosen to live (see Jeremiah 32:18-19, 2 Corinthians 5:10, Hebrews 9:27). When that happens, if we've accepted his full forgiveness, we won't have anything to worry about; if not, we will. The sooner you open your door and let God reach you, then accept his forgiveness and start operating in the power and wisdom he wants to give you, the better things will go for you. Otherwise, as time goes by you'll probably get into more legal, financial and social troubles, have to do more damage control and face even more serious setbacks. Why put yourself through that?

> *A wise man feareth, and departeth from evil:*
> *but the fool rageth and is confident.*
> — Proverbs 14:16

All-the-Time Anger

Anger is good. The Father gets angry. Jesus expresses anger. It's a temporary state of mind that warns others and gives you pushback strength when you need it.

All-the-time anger is bad (see Ecclesiastes 7:9).

Inmates with all-the-time anger don't just get into trouble; they make trouble, often interpreting as displays of disrespect what they might ignore on the street.

All it takes is a wrong look, gesture or body bump. Even if a fistfight or stabbing doesn't occur, a heated display of "mouth-to-mouth combat" may break out, with every kind of high-decibel accusation, insult and threat getting thrown in place of punches. The convict code exists because of men like that.

Are you a human IED about to go off?

Feeling shafted by society or the system can make us angry before we even arrive.

Maybe you're facing a "three strikes" sentence.

Are you the victim of a lowdown stop-and-frisk sweep or deportation dragnet?

Did you catch a charge carrying a mandatory minimum of heavy time and a fine, even though more violent or financially destructive criminals routinely get lesser sentences or walk away with only probation? Perhaps you've got a grudge against the snitch who ratted you out, the pitiless prosecutor who railroaded you, the lame lawyer who didn't defend you, the co-defendant who flipped on you or the judge who sentenced you.

No matter what your rage mechanism is, God can defuse it and make you much safer to be around.

Is your case so serious or scandalous that friends and loved ones have turned their backs on you? Maybe you've been jilted just because you're in jail.

Prison frustrations and fears produce anger.

Most of us don't come into the system already angry and ready to "go off" on others, but it doesn't take long for many of us to *get* angry and stay that way.

Prison frustrations stem from powerlessness.

You have no say about your classification or with whom you're assigned to live. Every morning, noon and night you're told when and where you may walk, how to dress, make up your bunk, stand up for count, line up for chow, behave on the rec yard, watch TV and even talk on the phone.

Unless there's money coming in to your commissary or canteen account (or you've got a good hustle), you can't even choose what to eat or wear. At the very least, there's no comfortable seating, very little quiet and almost no privacy.

Even shot callers must submit to the will of the wardens.

Believing that they've had their masculinity stolen by other inmates or the system, the loss of so much personal control makes many prisoners overly frustrated. Eventually, some feel like the biblical strongman, Samson, who was betrayed, blinded and bound behind prison walls, then made an object of public mockery. He got so angry that he asked God to make him strong just once more so he could kill his enemies and himself in a crashing display of suicidal revenge (read Judges 16).

> *I have roared by reason of the disquietness of my heart.*
> — *Psalm 38:8*

Prison fears stem from violence.

Too many frustrated men try to look and feel powerful by preying on the weak or less clever. Money and food shakedowns, forced labor and sex are used, with threats of a beat-down, rape or even murder employed to enforce their will.

Figuring that a good offense is the best defense against such dangers, you might decide to work out, get buff, then tough, fake a hard look and form alliances with the right men, then hit back hard if you're assaulted. That should keep the head-busters at bay, but it could also turn you into one and make you constantly wary of revenge attacks.

Many convicts believe that just to survive they must go against their true nature and turn vicious. They regret making themselves so dangerous.

Your anger may be more personal.

You may deeply resent not being the man you could have become had your mother or father not died or disappeared, been locked up, showed no interest in you or kept you from growing up right. Grief over what you've lost (or never had) may have made you so bitter about life that you now feel cheated out of a good future and resent other peoples' successes.

Were you belittled as a boy, called names or roughed up physically and emotionally by bullies? Now you may have a chip on your shoulder and start fights just to prove to others (and yourself) that you're a real man.

God does not disapprove of rightful anger, so you don't have to apologize for hating what's happened in your life or for how you feel about it.

Were you taken advantage of sexually by someone who then got away with it? Maybe you've never quit hating him for it (and yourself for not stopping it). Now your anger flares up against anyone who reminds you of him or of what happened to you.

If you're a gangbanger, nobody forced you to become a thug or to express your racial pride hatefully; you adopted those values. Naturally, you wanted strength, bravery and respect. You looked around and saw that gang members had all that, so you acted like them and got accepted. Now the gang is your main family and its violent methods are all you have to help you get by.

For any of these or other reasons, you may be carrying some heavy anger about what has happened to you (and how you let yourself get into this mess).

Sin makes you do things you never thought you'd do.

Sin takes you farther than you ever thought you'd go.

Sin keeps you longer than you ever thought you'd stay.

Sin costs you more than you ever thought you'd pay.

You can decide now whether to let anger continue ruling your life – and ruining it – or let God make you the successful son you still can become.

Let God fix your feelings.

Unresolved hatreds, resentments and griefs easily lead to all-the-time anger, big-time trouble and long-term lockup.

If you're trying to cope with all-the-time anger, God can help you quit being controlled by it and making other people upset – without losing your self-respect or personal safety (see Ephesians 4:26,31, Colossians 3:21).

> *He that is slow to anger is better than the mighty;*
> *and he that ruleth his spirit than he that taketh a city.*
> *— Proverbs 16:32*

Jesus was betrayed by a close friend, falsely accused by lying witnesses, suffered severe police brutality, unfair judicial treatment and merciless public humiliation (see Isaiah 53:3-4, Matthew 26:60), yet with God's help (see Luke 22:43) he endured all of it without once reacting in anger (see Isaiah 53:7, 1 Peter 2:21-23).

That way he fulfilled the Father's good will and purpose for his life.

By helping you to control your temper, God can help you fulfill his good will and purpose for your life, too (he really does have a higher calling for you than just being a jailbird).

You can't undo your crimes, but you can overcome the angry disposition that may be causing you to commit them. In time, God can help you to stop being so easily stirred up by rages, hatreds and resentments, and instead gain control over your emotions and your environment – if you're willing to cooperate with him.

The alternative is to stay angry, unhappy and alienated forever.

Recommended Readings

Redeemed Unredeemable, Thomas Horn & Donna Howell (Defense Publishing). It can happen to you: When Manson Family murderers Susan Atkins and Charles "Tex" Watson, Karla Faye Tucker and serial killers Ted Bundy, Jeffrey Dahmer and "Son of Sam" all asked God for mercy, he gave each of them a full pardon.

The Shot Caller: A Latino Gangbanger's Miraculous Escape from a Life of Violence to a New Life in Christ, Casey Diaz (Thomas Nelson). Diaz came to Los Angeles from El Salvador at age two. At 11 he joined the Rockwood Street Locos gang. At 16, he was sent to New Folsom State Prison to spend more than 12 years in solitary confinement. What happened there can only be described as a divine miracle.

Time of Grace: Thoughts on Nature, Family, and the Politics of Crime and Punishment, Ken Lamberton (University of Arizona Press). The former high school biology teacher, convicted of a sex offense with a student, writes frankly and eloquently about his struggles to keep his wife and daughters, while maintaining his faith and sanity, during 12 years inside the Arizona prison system.

Law Man: My Story of Robbing Banks, Winning Supreme Court Cases, and Finding Redemption, Shon Hopwood (Crown). After a decade in federal prisons, he earned a JD degree, a federal judge clerkship and a full professorship at Georgetown University School of Law, where he now advocates for criminal justice reform.

The Other Wes Moore: One Name, Two Fates, Wes Moore (Spiegel & Grau). Two "Wes Moores," born just months apart in nearby Baltimore neighborhoods; both fatherless, running the streets with their crews; both in trouble with the law. One Wes Moore became a Rhodes Scholar, decorated veteran and White House Fellow; the other is a convicted murderer still serving life. What happened?

Street God: The Explosive True Story of a Former Drug Boss on the Run from the Hood – and the Courageous Mission That Drove Him Back, Dimas Salaberrios (Tyndale). On the streets of New York he was called "Daylight," but he was a nightmare: selling drugs at 11; by 15, facing time on Rikers Island; eventually becoming a Bronx drug boss driven by angry ambition – until an experience of God's presence brought him to his senses and a new purpose on those same streets.

Taming of a Villain: A Message of Hope, Allen Langham (Monarch). How this top English rugby league player slid into a career of crime, drink, drugs and angry violence. Then, in a prison cell he had a surprise encounter with Jesus Christ.

One Day in the Life of 179212 (Lantern) and *The Convict Christ* (Orbis), Jens Soering. This Christian convict, paroled in 2019 after serving 33 years of a double-life murder sentence in the Virginia prison system, has an eye-opening understanding of convict realities and true biblical justice.

*We ourselves were sometimes
foolish, disobedient, deceived, serving divers lusts
and pleasures, living in malice and envy,
hateful, and hating one another.
But then the kindness and love of
God our Saviour toward man appeared...*
— Titus 3:3-4

Back in the 1st Century, when there were lots of different "masters" in the world of Judaism and the wider Greco-Roman world, one finally had to make a determination as to which was the right one, the good one.

When Jesus came on the scene, he did not offer himself as just another option. He said, "You are either with me or you are against me" (Matthew 12:30).

He was not just one of many choices.

In our day we likewise have many, many choices of where we can place our allegiance, but Jesus calls us to himself personally.

He says, "I'm not just another rabbi, I'm not just a revolutionary leader, I'm not just a great teacher [although he is all of those] (see Matthew 23:8-10, John 1:49, Hebrews 3:3-4)."

Jesus made a claim that is virtually unheard of: the claim to be sent by the Father as the one way to know the Father. And he made the claim that he was not just a prophet, or a priest, or a king, but that he was Lord; he was God in flesh.

Now that's a radical claim that really deserves all of us to sit up and say, "Whoa, I'd better at least look into this."
—*Michael J. Wilkins*

---

*God, having raised up his son Jesus, sent him to bless you,
in turning away every one of you from his iniquities.*
— Acts 3:26

I Believe in God.
Why is Jesus So Special?

The Bible says Jesus is special for many reasons. For us sinners he is special because he has blazed the only pathway to eternal life with the Father in heaven.

Our Problem: Sinful Disobedience

God created us Earthlings to be his righteous children, share his holiness, worship him and enjoy happy fellowship with him as our heavenly Father. But God's most important heavenly creature, Lucifer (aka Satan, the Devil, the Tempter, the Evil One), became jealous of both God and mankind and rebelled (see Isaiah 14:12-15). He was expelled, came to Earth and corrupted humanity's hearts and minds, turning us into natural-born sinners, rebels, and violators of God's holy will.

All have sinned and come short of the glory of God (Romans 3:23).
They are all gone aside, they are all together become filthy: there is none that doeth good, no, not one (Psalm 14:3).

Now, due to the Devil's dirty work, our Creator cannot have natural fellowship with any of us unrighteous creatures – not because he hates us, but because the white-hot purity of his holiness (his "wrath" against sin) will just burn us up (see Deuteronomy 4:24, Psalm 97:3,5).

Your iniquities have separated between you and your God,
and your sins have hid his face from you, that he will not hear.
For your hands are defiled with blood, and your
fingers with iniquity; your lips have spoken lies,
your tongue has muttered perverseness.
— Isaiah 59:2-3

As natural-born sinners (unrighteous creatures), our only spiritual destiny after physical life ends is to be eternally separated from God (in hell).

The soul that sinneth, it shall die (Ezekiel 18:20a).

But our Father doesn't want that to happen to us (see Exodus 33:20, Ezekiel 33:11).

The glory of the Father (our Creator) is that he is just as merciful towards us as he is a hater of sin (see Psalm 85:10, Isaiah 44:22, Romans 3:26). So he has made a way for us to get back into fellowship with him as our Father – but on his terms.

God's Solution: Merciful Justice

God's terms meet the demands of his justice (by punishing unrighteous humanity's sinful corruption) *and* his mercy (by restoring his fellowship with humanity). Those who accept his terms are considered by him to be righteous; as a result they get total immunity from future divine judgment (see Romans 3:26).

God is able to do all that by having substituted his own punishment for ours.

To restore our human nature and open a way for us to have fellowship with him as our Father, God sent his only son, Jesus, to Earth on a supernatural assignment (see John 3:13,16, 1 John 4:8-10).

Jesus had to live as a human, fully tempted by evil, but never sin (see Hebrews 4:15) – without relying on divine superpowers (he'd given those up (see Philippians 2:6-7)). Instead, he had to remain in constant prayer contact with the Father for instructions and apply the knowledge he learned from the scriptures with insights from the Holy Spirit (see Isaiah 11:2, Matthew 26:53, Luke 2:40,52, Hebrews 5:7-9).

Ultimately, Jesus had to bravely allow all of the guilt, blame, shame, sickness and fatal divine punishment (wrath) for all of humanity's sins – past, present and future – to be laid on himself as a self-sacrifice for those sins (see Isaiah 53:6).

If Jesus could do all that, then Satan's dirty work could be undone (see 1 John 3:8).

He hath made him who knew no sin to be sin for us; that we might be made the righteousness of God in him (2 Corinthians 5:21).

Jesus did it all, in obedience to the Father, suffering and dying as a sinner, even though he had never committed any sins (see Isaiah 53:7-12, Hebrews 2:14, 10:11-14).

Christ hath once suffered for sins, the just for the unjust, that he might bring us to God, being put to death in the flesh, but quickened by the Spirit: by which he went and preached unto the spirits in prison (1 Peter 3:18-19).

We are sanctified [made righteous] through the offering of the body of Jesus Christ once for all (Hebrews 10:10).

The Father then resurrected Jesus and raised him to new life and glory back in heaven where he now sits at the Father's right hand as the King of kings and the Lord of lords (see Philippians 2:8-11, Hebrews 1:1-4, Revelation 17:14).

We see Jesus, who was made a little lower than the angels for the suffering of death, crowned with glory and honour; that he by the grace of God should taste death for every man (Hebrews 2:9).

Most people believe that if they just "try to be good" and "be a nice person," then God will accept their humane works and forgive their sinfulness.

But the Bible's clear message is that good deeds and being "nice" do not obtain divine forgiveness. Only a sacrificial payment of blood can do that (see Leviticus 17:11, Hebrews 9:22).

A Divine Blood Payment

When Jesus was tortured and then nailed to a wood cross to hang naked in public and die in the hot sun, it was not his wrecked body that he mainly offered up to the Father as a sacrifice for humanity's sins; it was his uniquely pure blood.

Jesus' sinless blood was so potent that it alone satisfied the payment required by divine justice for all human sins – past, present and future (see Hebrews 9:12-15).

God commendeth his love towards us, in that, while we were yet sinners, Christ died for us. Much more then, being now justified by his blood, we shall be saved from wrath through him (Romans 5:8-9).

Christ sacrificed himself for all our sins, they all are forgiven.

"So if God has forgiven all our sins," you may ask, "why is he still threatening us with divine judgment and eternal damnation?" Because Christ's punishment hasn't given humanity a blanket pardon that overrides everyone's free will; no one can personally benefit from Christ's sacrifice unless he personally *accepts* God's forgiveness and repents. God's forgiveness (pardon) must be consciously received by each Earthling individually (by his own free choice). Only then can he be made a righteous son (or daughter) of the Father with total immunity from divine judgment (see John 1:12, 3:17-19, Romans 6:23, Hebrews 8:12, 9:13-14, 10:19-20,22). That's why it is said, "God has no grandchildren."

A Divine Plea Agreement

In the afterlife the mandatory minimum sentence for *unrepentant* sinners is exile from heaven in hell (where the horrors are far worse than those in any prison).

Jesus says he is coming back soon to judge us all, alive and dead (see John 5:22,25-29, Matthew 25:31-33, 1 John 2:28).

When that happens, your future will depend on whether you ever became a *repentant* sinner and accepted a divine plea agreement.

If you did, Jesus will recognize you as an adopted righteous brother and son of the Father,

We must all appear before the judgment seat of Christ; that every one may receive the things done in the body, according to that he hath done, whether it be good or bad.
— 2 Corinthians 5:10

then welcome you into heaven for a happy eternity of joyous fellowship with God and with all other "saved" sinners (see Matthew 25:34,46, John 5:22-24).

If you didn't, a divine detainer will be waiting for you: You will be judged as an *unrepentant* sinner – an unrighteous alien and stranger to God – and receive the mandatory sentence from Jesus: unhappy eternal exile to hell (see Matthew 7:21-23, 25:41). All your "niceness" and good deeds will have had no influence.

No appeals will be heard. That's why it's called The Last Judgment.

These are the terms of the divine plea agreement the Father offers to every one of us sin-corrupted creatures:

If you agree to:

- **Admit** your guilt (make a confession to God of all your known sins)
- **Plead** for mercy (so that you may receive God's forgiveness)
- **Acknowledge** Jesus' suffering and death as being his punishment on your behalf (to "save" you from the experience of God's holy wrath)
- **Renounce** (reject) Satan and all his evil works, sincerely asking for God's help to repent (turn away) from all future sinful behavior, **and**
- **Follow** Jesus as your Lord and King (giving him control of your life)

Then the Father agrees to:

- **Accept** and apply the Blood of Jesus as sufficient payment for your sins
- **Declare** you to be fully forgiven and without personal guilt
- **Expunge** all your past sins from his records (his divine memory)
- **Give** you his Holy Spirit to help you live as a follower of Jesus, and
- **Adopt** you into his eternal family (giving you everlasting life), and naming you a righteous son (or daughter) and heir of the Kingdom of God

The Bible says there is no other way for us unrighteous sin-corrupted *creatures* of God to become righteous *children* of God and thereby enjoy fellowship with the Father, Son and Holy Spirit, with total immunity from future divine judgment and punishment for our sins (see John 1:12, 3:36, 5:24, 14:6, Acts 4:12, 1 John 5:12).

A Divine Promise

We are "saved" from God's judgment and holy wrath (see Romans 8:1-2,33-34, John 5:24) by grace through our faith in Jesus (see Galatians 3:26, Ephesians 2:8-9), whose blood sacrifice removed our sin guilt, making us righteous in the Father's sight.

> *Blotting out the handwriting of ordinances that was against us, which was contrary to us, and took it out of the way, nailing it to his cross (Colossians 2:14).*

Your victim(s), the court, society, your family and other convicts may still call you a criminal (or worse) but your heavenly Father won't. Whatever others may still think or say about you will not matter to him (see Psalm 31:20, Isaiah 54:17).

Every child of God in Christ is entitled to receive every divine blessing and protection (see Deuteronomy 28:2-10, Psalm 5:11-12, Galatians 3:29) — even in prison.

Behold, what manner of love
the father hath bestowed upon us,
that we should be called the sons of God.
— 1 John 3:1

Recommended Readings

What's God Up To on Planet Earth?, Mark J. Keown (Wipf and Stock). Restoration!

Who is This Jesus?, Michael Green (Regent College). Traces the short, significant life of the construction worker from Nazareth executed by the Romans because Jewish religious leaders condemned him for calling God "Father" (see John 5:18).

Basic Christianity, John Stott (IVP). Probably the most complete yet concise explanation of what Jesus came to do and of what modern Christianity is about.

Amazing Grace,

How sweet the sound,
That saved a wretch like me.
I once was lost but now am found,
Was blind, but now I see.
'Twas Grace that taught my heart to fear
And Grace, my fears relieved.
How precious did that Grace appear
The hour I first believed.
Through many dangers, toils and snares
I have already come;
'Tis Grace that brought me safe thus far
and Grace will lead me home.
The Lord has promised good to me.
His Word my hope secures.
He will my shield and portion be,
As long as life endures.
Yea, when this flesh and heart shall fail,
And mortal life shall cease,
I shall possess within the veil,
A life of joy and peace.
When we've been there ten thousand years
Bright shining as the sun.
We've no less days to sing God's praise
Than when we've first begun.
—*John Newton (1725-1807), et al.*

I have blotted out, as a thick cloud,
thy transgressions, and, as a cloud, thy sins.
— Isaiah 44:22

Every religion basically says that there's some kind of problem – that there's a gap between us and the Divine, that we need to become "enlightened" – there's some problem that we face. And they all give you a set of rules on how to fix it:

You need to do this kind of meditating...

You need to have this diet...

You need to follow these rules...

You need to do these rituals...

You need to *do*, you need to *do*, you need to *do*.

They all tell you what *you* need to do.

They pile responsibility and tasks on top of you.

Christianity is the only religion that tells you what God has done to cross the gap, to fix the problem, to repair the relationship.

It's the only religion where God takes on himself the task of coming and fixing it *for* us, so that we don't have to be the ones who solve the problem.

That's what's unique about Christianity, and *that's what's so uniquely special about Jesus.*

We all kind of know The Golden Rule – and we all know we don't keep it. We all have our own sense of inadequacy and guilt, inferiority, failure, and so on. We know we don't do what we should do. We've got plenty of people telling us that.

We don't need that.

What's unique about Christianity is that it's not about one more set of rules; it's about God's own solution. It's not up to what *you* do; it's what God has done *for* you, through Jesus, on the cross.

—*Nancy R. Pearcey*

Come, Ye Sinners, Poor and Needy,

Weak and wounded, sick and sore;
Jesus ready stands to save you,
Full of pity, love and power.
He is able, He is able;
He is willing; doubt no more.

Come, ye thirsty, come, and welcome,
God's free bounty glorify;
True belief and true repentance,
Every grace that brings you nigh.
Without money, without money,
Come to Jesus Christ and buy.

Come, ye weary, heavy laden,
Bruised and broken by the fall;
If you tarry till you're better,
You will never come at all.
Not the righteous, not the righteous;
Sinners Jesus came to call!

Let not conscience make you linger,
Nor of fitness fondly dream;
All the fitness He requires
Is to feel your need of Him.
This He gives you, this He gives you,
Let your hopes no more be dim.

I will arise and go to Jesus,
He will embrace me in His arms;
In the arms of my dear Savior,
Oh, there are ten thousand charms.

—Joseph Hart (1759), age 47

> ### *People Do Not Drift Toward Holiness*
>
> Apart from grace-driven effort, people do not gravitate toward godliness, prayer, obedience to Scripture, faith and delight in God.
>
> We drift toward **compromise**
>   ...and call it tolerance.
>
> We drift toward **disobedience**
>   ...and call it freedom.
>
> We drift toward **superstition**
>   ...and call it faith.
>
> We cherish the indiscipline of **lost self-control**
>   ...and call it relaxation.
>
> We slouch toward **prayerlessness**
>   ...and say we've escaped legalism.
>
> We slide toward **godlessness**
>   ...and believe we have been liberated.
>
> —D. A. Carson

Psalm 25
(For any Sinner Seeking God's Mercy)

TO YOU, O LORD, I lift up my soul;
O my God, I put my trust in you;
   let me not be humiliated,
   nor let my enemies triumph over me.
Let none who look to you be put to shame; but let
   the treacherous be disappointed in their schemes.

Show me your ways, O Lord,
   and teach me your paths.
Lead me in your truth, and teach me,
   for you are the God of my salvation;
in you have I trusted all the day long.

Remember, O Lord, your compassion and love,
   for they have always existed from days of old.

Remember not the sins of my youth and my transgressions,
   but remember me according to your love
   and for the sake of your goodness, O Lord.

Good and upright is the Lord,
   therefore he teaches sinners the way to go.
He guides the humble in doing right
   and teaches his way to the lowly.
All the paths of the Lord are love and faithfulness
   to those who keep his covenant and his
      testimonies.

For your Name's sake, O Lord,
   forgive my sin, for it is great.

What man is he that fears the Lord?
God will teach him the way he should choose.
His soul shall dwell at ease
   and his children shall inherit the earth.

The Lord is a friend to those who fear him
   and he will fulfil for them his covenant.

My eyes are ever turned toward the Lord,
   for he alone can pluck my feet out of this net.

Turn to me and have pity on me,
   for I am left alone and in misery.
The sorrows of my heart have increased;
   O bring me out of all my troubles.

Look upon my pain and misery
   and forgive me all my sin.
Look upon my enemies, for they are many,
   and they have violent hatred of me.
Protect my life and deliver me;
   let me not be ashamed, for I have trusted in you.

Let integrity and uprightness preserve me,
   for I wait on you to help me.

Deliver me, O God, out of all my troubles.

ALMIGHTY GOD,
to you all hearts are open,
all desires are known,
and from you no secrets are hid:
Cleanse the thoughts of my heart
by the inspiration of your Holy Spirit,
that I may perfectly love you, and
worthily make known the greatness of your Name;
through Jesus Christ my Lord.
Amen.

A Hymn to God the Father

Wilt Thou forgive that sin where I begun,
   which was my sin, though it were done;
Wilt Thou forgive that sin through which I run,
   and do run still, though still I do deplore?
When Thou hast done, Thou hast not done;
   For I have more.

Wilt Thou forgive that sin which I have won
   others to sin, and made my sins their door?
Wilt Thou forgive that sin which I did shun
   a year or two, but wallow'd in a score?
When Thou hast done, Thou hast not done;
   For I have more.

I have a sin of fear, that when I've spun
   my last thread, I shall perish on the shore;
But swear by Thyself that at my death Thy Son
   shall shine as He shines now and heretofore:
And having done that, Thou hast done;
   I fear no more.

—John Donne (1623), age 51

What is True Repentance?

Repentance always brings a man to this point: I have sinned.
The surest sign that God is at work is when a man says that, and means it. Anything less than this is remorse for having made blunders, the reflex action of disgust at himself.
—*Oswald Chambers*

All of us feel remorse and even disgust after getting caught and locked up. That's normal, but it's not true repentance. Many go from feeling remorse to resentment, depression, despair and even suicide.

Godly sorrow worketh repentance to salvation...
but the sorrow of the world worketh death (2 Corinthians 7:10).

It's a healing process.

When we act in true repentance, we go from simply regretting the tactical errors we've made to feeling real sorrow for the sinful behavior that's brought us here. Instead of just saying that we've "made some mistakes," we take moral responsibility for our willful misconduct, fully confess it all to God, seek and receive his full forgiveness, then move on with a sincere desire to stop sinning.

That's all we have to do; *God does everything else.*

His amazing grace causes changes to occur in and around us as we gradually stop thinking and acting like a natural-born sinner and start enjoying life with new purpose as a blessed son of the Father (see Ephesians 2:1-10, Colossians 1:10-14).

It's not jailhouse religion.

Some men fake it: They may go to Chapel, bow their head or cross themselves before meals, leave a Bible in plain view on top of their locker or a rosary draped across their pillow. But unlike real Christians, they only do it to avoid getting robbed, assaulted or suspected of illicit activities by deputies or COs, their counselor, case manager, bunkie or cellies.

Hypocrisy is the compliment vice pays to virtue.
—*La Rochefoucauld*

Inmates who practice jailhouse religion are only imitating true repentance; they are still willful sinners (or plan to go back to being such once they get released).

They profess that they know God;
but in works they deny him,
being abominable, and disobedient,
and unto every good work reprobate.
— *Titus 1:16*

Make sure Jesus' blood sacrifice applies fully.

You cannot be saved "mostly." Saying a sinner's prayer once or twice but from then on trying to get away with hidden sins puts you in serious danger of being judged and sentenced by Jesus as a hypocrite (see Jeremiah 17:5, Psalm 50:16-22, Romans 8:5-8, 2 Corinthians 5:10-11, Galatians 6:7-8). You don't want that to happen.

Trying to have it both ways with God is never good. Not confessing to him fully the things you've recently done (or are planning to do) *that you know are sinful*, makes you an unrepentant sinner all over again (see James 4:17).

Because moral choices have eternal consequences, use your free will wisely. God honors choices – for better and for worse (see 1 Chronicles 28:9, Acts 5:1-11).

There are only two kinds of people in the end:
those who say to God, "Thy will be done,"
and those to whom God says, in the end, "Thy will be done."
All that are in Hell, choose it.
Without that self-choice there could be no Hell.
—*C. S. Lewis*

Don't think that since God sees and hears everything, anyway, there's no need for you to tell him what he already knows (see Psalms 11:4, 90:8, Hebrews 4:13).

Regular confession to God is for your benefit, not his: If you knowingly keep hidden sins on your conscience, you will never enjoy a guilt-free relationship with him (see Titus 1:15-16), receive all of his blessings (see Proverbs 28:13) or even know for sure that you are really saved (see 1 Corinthians 6:9-10, Revelation 21:7-8).

Why live like that?

If we sin willfully after that we have received the knowledge
of the truth, there remaineth no more sacrifice for sins, But
a certain fearful looking for of judgement and fiery indignation,
which shall devour the adversaries (Hebrews 10:26-27).

God can help you make an honest, full confession to him of *all* your sins and so be at peace (see Psalms 51:2-10,14-17, 86:5, 139:23-24, James 4:7-8,10, 1 John 1:6-9).

Without becoming neurotically obsessed with it, regularly confess to him any willful sinfulness in your thoughts and behavior, seek and receive the Father's forgiveness, and ask the Holy Spirit for the grace to help you willingly turn away from sin and live with integrity (see Ezekiel 18:30-32, Proverbs 3:34, Galatians 5:16).

He will gladly do it!

Psalm 32

Happy is the man whose transgressions are forgiven,
and whose sin is put away!

Happy is the man to whom the Lord imputes no guilt,
and in whose spirit there is no guile!

While I held my tongue, my bones withered away,
because of my groaning all day long.

For your hand was heavy upon me day and night;
my moisture was dried up as in the heat of summer.

Then I acknowledged my sin to you;
I did not conceal my guilt.

I said, "I will confess my transgressions to the Lord."
Then you forgave me the guilt of my sin.

Therefore all the faithful will make their prayers to you
in time of trouble; when the great waters overflow,
they shall not reach them.

You are my hiding-place; you preserve me from trouble;
you surround me with shouts of deliverance.

"I will instruct you and teach you in the way that you should
go; I will guide you with my eye.
Do not be like horse or mule,
which have no understanding;
who must be fitted with bit and bridle,
or else they will not stay near you."

Great are the tribulations of the wicked;
but mercy embraces those who trust in the Lord.

Be glad, you righteous, and rejoice in the Lord;
shout for joy, all who are true of heart!

A Formal Prayer of Repentance
(In each section be specific about your sins.)

Most holy and merciful Father: I confess to you and to the whole communion of saints in heaven and on earth that
I have sinned by my own fault in thought, word, and deed;
by what I have done, and by what I have left undone.

I have not loved you with my whole heart and mind and strength. I have not loved my neighbor as myself.
I have not forgiven others, as I have been forgiven.
Have mercy on me, Lord.

I have been deaf to your call to serve, as Christ served me.
I have not been true to the mind of Christ.
I have grieved your Holy Spirit.
Have mercy on me, Lord.

I confess to you, Lord, all my past unfaithfulness:
The pride, hypocrisy, and impatience of my life.
My self-indulgent appetites and ways,
and my exploitation of other people.

My anger at my own frustration,
and my envy of those more fortunate than I.
My love of worldly goods and comforts.
My dishonesty in daily life and work.
My negligence in prayer and worship, and
my failure to commend to others the faith that is in me.

Accept my repentance, Lord, for the wrongs I have done:
For my blindness to human need and suffering, and
my indifference to injustice and cruelty,
Accept my repentance, Lord.

For all false judgments:
For uncharitable thoughts toward my neighbors, and
for my prejudice and contempt
toward those who differ from me,
Accept my repentance, Lord.

For my waste and pollution of your creation, and
my lack of concern for those who come after me,
Accept my repentance, Lord.

Restore me, good Lord, and let your anger depart from me;
Favorably hear me, for your mercy is great.

Accomplish in me the work of your salvation,
that I may show forth your glory in the world.
By the cross and passion of your Son, my Lord,
bring me with all your saints to the joy of His resurrection.

Amen.

A Hearty Sinner's Prayer
(Be specific about your sins and needs, as appropriate.)

O God, though I know I don't deserve it,
 I want the forgiveness you're offering me (see Psalm 86:5).
Please forgive me for what I've done with my life.
I know I've blown it too many times.
I know that what I've *been* doing is wrong and that what I *was* doing was wrong.
That's why I'm here.
I am truly sorry for every sin I've committed against you...
 against other people...
 and against myself.
I've committed so many sins that I can't even remember them all, but I know you can.
O God, please have mercy on me!
I'm ready to make things right with you, with other people and with myself.
Today/tonight I'm saying "yes" to you.
Thank you, Jesus, for taking the punishment I deserve and for sacrificing your own sinless blood for me.
I believe the Father raised you from the grave with some kind of power that's still operating today and available to a broken man/woman like me who's willing to trust you.
O God, I need to know you better!
I need you to be my Father.
I want to know why you created me and let me be born, and what I'm here for...especially in this place.
O God, protect me from my enemies!
I admit that without you guiding me my life is meaningless and dangerous. All the things driving me (resentment, anger, fear, hatred, envy, lust, addiction) are out of control.
I give up!

O Jesus, be Lord of my life!
Show me how to live right.
Lead me on the right path in this place.
I don't really know how to behave myself...
   how to think straight...
   how to love other people or myself properly...
   or how to let other people love me.

I need you to change who I am and help me stop giving in to my sinful desires. I need that "new beginning" you talk about (see 2 Corinthians 5:17).

[Sometimes I've acted like a Christian, but I was just faking it. Now I am so sorry for being such a rebellious phony. I've never really given you control of my life before, but I mean it now. I'm asking for real this time for you to please come into my heart as Lord of my life.]

I'm giving myself to you – every bit of it (even the part that still likes getting away with stuff).

I'm ready to be straightened out by you and turned into the successful son/daughter you say you want me to be.

I know that soon I'll be much happier.

From this moment on I'm giving you my life and asking you to take full control of it, for my own good and for your glory, for as long as I live.

And please, God, fill me right now – even as I pray this – with the presence and power of your Holy Spirit to help me resist evil, inspire me and keep me focused on you.

Thank you!
In your name, Jesus, I pray.
Amen.

If any man be in Christ,
he is a new creature:
old things are passed away;
behold, all things are become new.
— 2 Corinthians 5:17

How the New Life in Christ Works

If Jesus Christ is to regenerate me, what is the problem He is up against?

I have a heredity I had no say in;

I am not holy, nor likely to be;

If all Jesus Christ can do is to tell me I must be holy, His teaching plants despair.

But if Jesus Christ is a Regenerator, One Who can put into me His own heredity of holiness, then I begin to see what He is driving at when He says that I have to be holy. Redemption means that Jesus Christ can put into any man the hereditary disposition that was in Himself, and all the standards He gives are based on that disposition:

His teaching is for the life He puts in.

The moral transaction on my part is agreement with God's verdict on sin in the Cross of Jesus Christ....

The moral miracle of Redemption is that God can put into me a new disposition whereby I can live a totally new life.

Redemption means that I can be delivered from my heredity of sin and through Jesus Christ can receive an unsullied heredity; that is, the Holy Spirit.

—*Oswald Chambers*

Be blameless and harmless,
the sons of God, without rebuke,
in the midst of a crooked and perverse nation,
among whom ye shine as lights in the world.
— Philippians 2:15

Now What?

*With the heart man believeth unto righteousness;
and with the mouth confession is made unto salvation.*
— Romans 10:10

Although your relationship with the Father is personal, if you have said a sinner's prayer all by yourself, you must now tell others (see Matthew 5:14-16).

Try to meet fellow Christians. Talk to a chaplain (even if you're in solitary); identify yourself as a new Christian and ask for help, including an easy-to-read Bible and information about baptism (see Acts 22:16, Mark 16:16).

You may still feel strong urges to speak or react sinfully, but God can enable your mind and heart to resist them (see Romans 12:2, Hebrews 10:16).

Stand fast therefore in the liberty wherewith Christ hath made us free, and be not entangled again with the yoke of bondage.
— Galatians 5:1

Don't get upset when you are tempted by evil thoughts, selfish desires or immoral impulses (it's not a sin to feel tempted). Just don't nurture them in your head or act on them for real (see James 1:12-16). Instead, resist temptation by letting God's grace work inside of you, as well as in your immediate situation (see Psalm 73, Romans 6:6-14).

Victory over all the circumstances of life comes not by might nor by power but by a practical confidence in God, and by allowing his Spirit to dwell in our hearts and control our actions and emotions (see Zechariah 4:6). *—Eric Liddell*

The world, the flesh and the Devil will always try to pull you back as a natural-born sinner who "just can't help it." Overcome that by walking tall as a born-again son/daughter of the Father, believing that you can do all things well with the strength God gives you (see Isaiah 40:29-31, 1 Corinthians 10:13, Philippians 4:13).

If possible, obtain some of the Recommended Readings (either through the library or a friend on the outside who will buy them online). Study them and apply their teachings (ideally, with others). Continue confessing and repenting of any new sinfulness and keep asking the Holy Spirit to lead you (see 1 John 1:6-7).

Read these morning and evening scriptures (and a daily devotional, if you can get one), asking the Holy Spirit to give you understanding. Join a Bible study and attend Chapel, even if it's not your favorite worship style (see Hebrews 3:13, 10:25).

Memorize God's scriptural promises (see pp. 68-71). From now on, they will be a strong comfort and encouragement to you and those you share them with.

Pray to God throughout the day, expecting to get answers and clear guidance.

"Forgive Our Sins As We Forgive,"

You taught us, Lord, to pray;
But you alone can grant us grace
To live the words we say.

How can your pardon reach and bless
The unforgiving heart
That broods on wrongs
And will not let old bitterness depart?

In blazing light your Cross reveals
The truth we dimly knew:
How small the debts men owe to us,
How great our debt to you.

Lord, cleanse the depths within our souls,
And bid resentments cease;
Then, reconciled to God and man,
Our lives will spread your peace.

—Rosamond E. Herklots (1969), age 64

Forgiveness

It's normal to nurse grudges against those who've done you wrong: your parents (or their nasty friends), abusive siblings, wives or girlfriends; the crooked business partner, dishonest detective, aggressive prosecutor, lying co-defendant, hard-hearted judge or mean probation officer responsible for your being here.

Enemies find *you* behind bars. They hate you for your background, your race, your manners, your looks or your offense.

You soon get challenged, sized up and often scorned.

Why shouldn't you hate people like that?

Because your unforgiveness of others – even when justified – acts like a curse. It makes you so unhappy, self-pitying and preoccupied with revenge fantasies that you cannot enjoy all the benefits of being forgiven by God.

Unforgiveness is like drinking poison,
hoping the other guy dies.

God's Word clearly says that you cannot enjoy his full forgiveness until you show him some willingness to forgive others (see Matthew 18:23-35).

Your Forgiveness of Others is Non-Negotiable
(see Mark 11:25-26 and The Lord's Prayer)
Forgiving others reflects your having become a "new creature" in Christ and an imitator of his generous mercy towards unworthy sinners like yourself
(see Matthew 5:44-45, 2 Corinthians 5:17, Colossians 3:13).

The hardest thing about following Jesus as Lord is agreeing to obey his commands before you fully understand their wisdom or purpose. Often, it's only *after* you obey that understanding comes.

Jesus' hardest command is that you show mercy to your unrepentant enemies (see Luke 6:27-28). That seems unfair since, to receive God's forgiveness, you first had to apologize to him and say a sinner's prayer accepting it.

But remember: God forgave your sins *before* you asked, not *because* you asked.

God expects you to forgive your abuser(s), double-crossing friend(s) and others who haven't asked for it, and then let God deal with them if they never repent. That's his job, not yours (see Deuteronomy 32:35, Romans 12:19, 2 Thessalonians 1:6-10).

Of course, your letting them off the hook like that goes against human nature and logic; nobody can do that and really mean it, right?

If you're a "new creature" in Christ, you *can* do it (and really mean it).

If you're willing to lay aside your hard feelings and ask God for some of *his own divine ability to forgive*, you can receive it and use it. Then you'll understand.

Granting your enemies unconditional forgiveness immediately calms you down (no more revenge fantasies); then, unexpected blessings may appear in the form of a physical healing, a relationship breakthrough or just better sleep and a welcome sense of serenity (see 1 Corinthians 2:9-10).

Jesus came to heal the broken-hearted (see Luke 4:18), including those who still feel the pains of childhood neglect or abuse, adult betrayal or bitter judgments against God as an indifferent, unjust or hateful Father.

Because unforgiveness also blocks God's healing power, your forgiveness of others enables him to start healing your own inner wounds.

> *[Jesus] made peace through the blood of his cross,*
> *by him to reconcile all things unto himself (Colossians 1:20).*

Your peace with God is made possible by your faith in Christ's sacrifice (which broke Satan's power to forever alienate you from the Father (see Romans 5:1-2, Ephesians 2:13-18)); it also makes you able to have peace with others.

> **Your Forgiveness of Others**
> **releases supernatural grace like almost nothing else.**
> **Other than becoming a righteous son of the Father,**
> **forgiveness is the most significant step you can take**
> **on the prisoner's path of faith, hope and restoration.**

Recommended Readings

Total Forgiveness, R. T. Kendall (Charisma House). How to forgive all of your enemies (including yourself) and humbly seek others' forgiveness of you.

The Way of the Prisoner: Breaking the Chains of Self Through Centering Prayer and Centering Practice, Jens Soering (Lantern). How centering yourself twice daily on God's Word, with prayer, can help you overcome feelings of anxiety, resentment and ungodly personal judgments against yourself and others.

Set Free: Discover Forgiveness Amidst Murder and Betrayal, Stephen Owens with Ken Abraham (B&H). When Owens was 12, his mother hired a hit man to murder his father. After 25 years, God opened a door to set Owens free from his prison of unforgiveness and his mother free from her Tennessee death row cell.

> **As I walked out the door**
> **toward the gate that would lead to my freedom,**
> **I knew that if I didn't leave my bitterness**
> **and hatred behind, I'd still be in prison.**
> **—*Nelson Mandela***

My (Former) Enemies List

Name(s) or Initials _____

    When I Forgave _____

    Results _____

Name(s) or Initials _____

    When I Forgave _____

    Results _____

Name(s) or Initials _____

    When I Forgave _____

    Results _____

Name(s) or Initials _____

    When I Forgave _____

    Results _____

Name(s) or Initials _____

    When I Forgave _____

    Results _____

Name(s) or Initials _____

    When I Forgave _____

    Results _____

All the Way My Savior Leads Me,

What have I to ask beside?
Can I doubt His tender mercy,
Who through life has been my Guide?
Heav'nly peace, divinest comfort,
Here by faith in Him to dwell!
For I know, whate'er befall me,
Jesus doeth all things well;
For I know, whate'er befall me,
Jesus doeth all things well.

All the way my Savior leads me,
Cheers each winding path I tread;
Gives me grace for every trial,
Feeds me with the living Bread.
Though my weary steps may falter,
And my soul athirst may be,
Gushing from the Rock before me,
Lo! A spring of joy I see;
Gushing from the Rock before me,
Lo! A spring of joy I see.

All the way my Savior leads me,
O the fullness of His love!
Perfect rest to me is promised
In my Father's house above.
When my spirit, clothed immortal,
Wings its flight to realms of day,
This my song through endless ages:
Jesus led me all the way;
This my song through endless ages:
Jesus led me all the way.

—*Fanny Crosby (1875), age 55*

Forget About It!

In God's eyes you're now as clean as a clam (see Romans 8:1, Hebrews 8:12). Your standing with the Father as a righteous son or daughter is all-good. As long as you continue confessing to God and repenting of any new sins, you can forget about having to face divine judgment for them. As your faith matures, he will even help you eventually forget about having to sin so compulsively (see Romans 6:20-23).

This one thing I do,
forgetting those things which are behind,
and reaching forth unto those things which are before,
I press toward the mark for the prize of
the high calling of God in Christ Jesus.
— Philippians 3:13-14

Your Father forgives and forgets.
You must forgive and forget.
Must your victim(s), the court, society
and your family also forgive and forget?

Your confessed crimes, though forgiven and forgotten by your Father (see Isaiah 43:25), are still very real to other people. Some may go on feeling justifiable anger towards you for the injuries you caused them. That's their free choice to make. You may face years of hostility, fear, suspicion or even retribution – in addition to any court-ordered restitution, supervision, testing, tracking or treatment.

Just accept that, trusting God to guide you through it all and take care of you.

Don't waste time regretting the past, resenting the present or fearing the future (those are dead-end distractions). Instead, maintain an obedient attitude of outspoken praise and thanksgiving to God at all times, come what may, whether or not you feel like it (see Psalms 69, 130, 55:22, 59:16-17, Colossians 1:10-14).

Then watch his amazing grace work breakthroughs and miracles for you!

Recommended Readings

Prison to Praise, *Power in Praise* and *Praise Works!*, Merlin R. Carothers (Foundation of Praise). You *must* read these three classics that tell how, in response to obedient praise, God often miraculously turns around "impossible" legal, health, and relationship problems for all kinds of folks (including those living behind bars).

Fresh Faith and *Fresh Power*, Jim Cymbala with Dean Merrill (Zondervan). The Brooklyn Tabernacle pastor tells stories of repentant sinners like NYC's once-infamous serial killer, David Berkowitz, aka "Son of Sam." All have been restored by their expectant faith in God's promises and reliance on the Holy Spirit.

Before the Throne of God Above

I have a strong and perfect plea.
A great high Priest whose Name is Love
Who ever lives and pleads for me.
My name is graven on His hands,
My name is written on His heart.
I know that while in Heaven He stands
No tongue can bid me thence depart.

When Satan tempts me to despair
And tells me of the guilt within,
Upward I look and see Him there
Who made an end of all my sin.
Because the sinless Savior died
My sinful soul is counted free.
For God the just is satisfied
To look on Him and pardon me.

Behold Him there the risen Lamb,
My perfect spotless righteousness,
The great unchangeable I AM,
The King of glory and of grace,
One in Himself I cannot die.
My soul is purchased by His blood,
My life is hid with Christ on high,
With Christ my Savior and my God!
—*Charitie L. Bancroft (1863), age 22*

I've Confessed All to God. Must I Confess All to the Police?

You must clean up all of your old business with God – and keep it clean.

That doesn't necessarily mean you must also come clean with everyone else.

Although the criminal justice system operates under God's authority to enforce rules and punish evildoers (see Romans 13:1-7), there are too many crooked investigators, incompetent attorneys, overzealous prosecutors and biased judges.

It's not smart to expose yourself to the system unnecessarily or unwisely.

The Bible does not say that a Christian must *always* divulge every piece of self-incriminating information – only if the Holy Spirit stirs up a strong feeling (a conviction) to do so in his own conscience (see Romans 14:23, 1 John 3:18-21).

If you committed a crime that an innocent man has been convicted of, you should think about coming forward to clear him (as well as your conscience).

If you pleaded "not guilty" to a crime you actually committed, you should think about changing your plea to "guilty" (ideally, with a plea agreement).

If the Holy Spirit convicts your conscience to come clean about a crime you've previously denied committing or have never been caught for, you may face a new charge for it. But God honors obedient truthfulness (see Psalm 31:5); your Father will go before you, give you favor with the authorities and bring you through it.

The same is true if you feel led not to report a previously undisclosed offense but then approach your victim(s) asking for forgiveness or to make restitution. That could trigger a criminal investigation. Still, God will honor your integrity.

Self-reporting a previously undisclosed crime is a very serious matter. Ask the Holy Spirit to guide your thinking (through Bible study and prayer, alone or with others) before making any decision you might regret for the rest of your life.

Your heavenly Father, not the legal establishment or anybody else, is the only one looking out for your best interests, safety and long-term welfare.

In all of your decisions, let your conscience be influenced by the Holy Spirit. He will direct your thinking and your next steps (see Proverbs 3:5-6).

His is the only guidance you can fully depend on (see Proverbs 10:22).

Recommended Reading

Coming Clean: The True Story of a Cocaine Drug Lord and His Unexpected Encounter with God, Jorge Valdés (WaterBrook). The Cuban immigrant raised in poverty became head of U.S. operations for the Medellín drug cartel, with a direct connection to presidents, generals, Hollywood celebrities, hired killers and kidnappers. Then came 11 years in federal prison...and a new conscience.

How to Pray

All that Scripture requires is that you believe.

Don't have faith in your prayer or some ritual, or how much you've fasted or even your knowledge of Scripture (those are all good and in their own way can help your mind and spirit be receptive and confident about what you're doing).

But Jesus says it clearly in Mark 11:22:

Have faith in God.

Put all your faith there and in what Jesus has already done for you. If you don't think you have much faith, let Jesus be your faith – he lives in all born-again Christians and he's full of faith!

Look to him, because it's by his atoning blood and by his stripes (wounds) that we're healed. It's not by prayers (what we think) but by what Jesus has already done.

When you immerse yourself in that, you get all the faith you need.

That's the key.

—*Gordon Robertson*

Christians have direct access to the Father only through the work of Jesus Christ: His sacrificial blood payment for all of our sins (see Ephesians 1:7), his physical suffering for all of our sicknesses (see Isaiah 53:5), his abiding in us (see John 15:7) and his continuing prayers to the Father on our behalf (see 1 John 2:1, Hebrews 7:25).

Study the morning scriptures for December 3.

Pray directly to God (see Jeremiah 33:3, Hebrews 10:19).

Pray to the Father in Jesus' name. He is the "author and finisher" of your faith (see Hebrews 12:2); he wants you to experience joy in praying (see John 16:24).

Pray with a clear conscience. Own up to any recent sins, confessing them honestly, then seek and receive the Father's full forgiveness plus any loving correction he may apply (see Psalm 66:18, Mark 11:2, 1 John 1:7-9, 3:21-22).

Pray with the Holy Spirit's guidance, either in your own language or in an unknown prayer language (tongues) that God may give you, letting him direct your prayers according to his perfect will (see Romans 8:26-27, Ephesians 6:18).

Pray for what you truly need, not for selfish gain or materialistic pleasures (see James 4:2-3).

Pray thankfully, believing in God's total control, favor and promises to always take good care of you as you trust him, come what may (see Philippians 4:61, 1 Thessalonians 5:16-18, Psalm 62:8, Hebrews 11:6).

Pray positively for God's good will to be done in you, your loved ones, enemies, fellow prisoners, and in the midst of every kind of personal challenge you are facing (see 1 Timothy 2:8 and The Lord's Prayer).

Pray from your gut. A pure prayer motive influences God more than pretty words (see 1 Samuel 16:7). If you like, use Bible verses, a prayer book, prayer card, rosary or memorized prayers, but keep it real with prayers and praises in your own words, too.

Pray with persistence and patience. God certainly answers our sincere prayers (see James 5:16) but according to his own will and on his own schedule. The sinner's prayer and some emergency and healing prayers can get results in 60 seconds. All others are only answered in the fullness of time after other things happen that must take place first (see the morning scriptures for October 30).

Recommended Readings

Breakthrough Prayer: The Power of Connecting with the Heart of God, Jim Cymbala (Zondervan). Explains the spiritual laws and principles governing answered prayer; how to cooperate with God to get results in the fullness of time according to his will and promises; dramatic examples from Cymbala's NYC congregation.

Prayer 101: Experiencing the Heart of God, Warren W. Wiersbe (David Cook). Explores God's will, how our relationships with God and others affect our prayers (and vice versa); what it means to pray for our enemies; points away from legalism toward joy in practicing the daily rhythm of conversation with God; includes questions for individual reflection or small group discussion.

How to Pray for the Release of the Holy Spirit, Dennis Bennett (Bridge-Logos). How to receive the Pentecostal "baptism" that involves much more than just speaking in tongues. The Episcopal priest, called "the father of the charismatic movement," helped more than 25,000 believers release God's spirit in their lives.

Trusting God, Jerry Bridges (NavPress). Because untested faith is no faith at all, only in threatening circumstances can you learn to trust God completely. Bridges will persuade you of God's love for you, his total control over every challenge you are facing (and everyone involved in it), and of his willingness to help you.

The Sword of the Spirit—The Word of God, Joy Lamb (Lamb's Books). Scriptures rephrased as declarations; strong prayers for spiritual protection, deliverance, blessing, binding, cutting, renouncing, more.

The Lord's Prayer

OUR FATHER,
who art in heaven,
hallowed be thy name.

Thy kingdom come,
thy will be done on earth as it is in heaven.

Give us this day our daily bread,
and forgive us our trespasses,
as we forgive those who trespass against us.

And lead us not into temptation,
but deliver us from evil.

[For thine is the kingdom,
and the power,
and the glory,
for ever and ever.]

Amen.

*You can personalize this prayer by inserting
your name or another person's name:
(Hallowed be thy name in *...
Thy will be done for *...
Give * this day...
Deliver * from evil..., etc.)*

The 23rd Psalm

THE LORD IS MY SHEPHERD;
I shall not want.
He maketh me to lie down in green pastures:
He leadeth me beside the still waters.
He restoreth my soul:
He leadeth me in the paths of righteousness
for his name's sake.

Yea, though I walk through
the valley of the shadow of death,
I will fear no evil:
for thou art with me;
Thy rod and thy staff they comfort me.

Thou preparest a table before me
in the presence of mine enemies:
Thou anointest my head with oil;
My cup runneth over.

Surely goodness and mercy
shall follow me all the days of my life:
and I will dwell in the house of the Lord for ever.

You can make this a powerful prayer for someone else by inserting his or her name wherever "I," "my," "me" or "mine" appears.

The Ten Commandments (Plus One)

Exodus 20:1-17
John 13:34

1. **You shall have no other gods before me.**
2. **You shall not make for yourself any carved image...you shall not bow down to them nor serve them.**
3. **You shall not take the name of the Lord your God in vain.**
4. **Remember the Sabbath day, to keep it holy.** Six days you shall labor and do all your work, but the seventh day is the Sabbath of the Lord your God. In it you shall do no work.
5. **Honor your father and your mother**, that your days may be long upon the land which the Lord your God is giving you.
6. **You shall not commit murder.**
7. **You shall not commit adultery.**
8. **You shall not steal.**
9. **You shall not bear false witness against your neighbor.**
10. **You shall not covet** your neighbor's house; you shall not covet your neighbor's wife, or his manservant, or his maidservant, or his ox, or his donkey, or anything that is your neighbor's.
11. **Love others as Christ has loved you.**

The Apostles' Creed

I BELIEVE IN GOD, the Father almighty,
   creator of heaven and earth.

I believe in Jesus Christ,
   his only Son, our Lord.

He was conceived by the power of
   the Holy Spirit and born of
   the Virgin Mary.

He suffered under Pontius Pilate,
   was crucified, died, and was buried.

He descended to the dead.

On the third day he rose again.

He ascended into heaven,
   and is seated at the right hand of the Father.

He will come again, in glory,
   to judge the living and the dead.

I believe in the Holy Spirit,
   the holy catholic Church,
   the communion of saints,
   the forgiveness of sins,
   the resurrection of the body,
   and the life everlasting.

   Amen.

What a Friend We Have in Jesus,

All our sins and griefs to bear!
What a privilege to carry
Everything to God in prayer!
Oh, what peace we often forfeit,
Oh, what needless pain we bear,
All because we do not carry
Everything to God in prayer.

Have we trials and temptations?
Is there trouble anywhere?
We should never be discouraged;
Take it to the Lord in prayer.
Can we find a friend so faithful
Who will all our sorrows share?
Jesus knows our every weakness;
Take it to the Lord in prayer.

Are we weak and heavy laden,
Cumbered with a load of care?
Precious Savior, still our refuge,
Take it to the Lord in prayer.
Do your friends despise, forsake you?
Take it to the Lord in prayer!
In his arms he'll take and shield you;
You will find a solace there.

—Joseph Scriven (1848), age 29

Answers To Prayer

Date _____

Need _____ I asked God to "show up." _____

Results _____

Date _____

Need _____

Results _____

Date _____

Need _____

Results _____

Date _____

Need _____

Results _____

Date _____

Need _____

Results _____

Date _____

Need _____

Results _____

Be Still, My Soul,

The Lord is on thy side;
Bear patiently the cross of grief or pain;
Leave to thy God to order and provide;
In every change He faithful will remain.
Be still, my soul; thy best, thy heavenly, Friend
Through thorny ways leads to a joyful end.

Be still, my soul; thy God doth undertake
To guide the future as He has the past.
Thy hope, thy confidence, let nothing shake;
All now mysterious shall be bright at last.
Be still, my soul; the waves and winds still know
His voice, who ruled them while He dwelt below.

Be still, my soul, though dearest friends depart
And all is darkened in the vale of tears;
Then shalt thou better know His love, His heart,
Who comes to soothe thy sorrows and thy fears.
Be still, my soul; thy Jesus can repay
From His own fulness all He takes away.

Be still, my soul; the hour is hastening on
When we shall be forever with the Lord,
When disappointment, grief, and fear are gone,
Sorrow forgot, love's purest joys restored.
Be still, my soul; when change and tears are past,
All safe and blessed we shall meet at last.

—*Catharina von Schlegel (1752), age 55*

Answers To Prayer

Date _____

Need _____

Results _____

Date _____

Need _____

Results _____

Date _____

Need _____

Results _____

Date _____

Need _____

Results _____

Date _____

Need _____

Results _____

Date _____

Need _____

Results _____

How Firm a Foundation,

Ye saints of the Lord,
Is laid for your faith in his excellent Word!
What more can he say than to you he hath said,
To you that for refuge to Jesus have fled?

"Fear not, I am with thee; O be not dismayed!
For I am your God, and will still give thee aid;
I'll strengthen thee, help thee,
And cause thee to stand,
Upheld by my righteous, omnipotent hand.

"When through the deep waters I call thee to go,
The rivers of woe shall not thee overflow;
For I will be with thee, thy troubles to bless,
And sanctify to thee thy deepest distress.

"When through fiery trials thy pathway shall lie,
My grace, all-sufficient, shall be thy supply;
The flame shall not hurt thee; I only design
Thy dross to consume, and thy gold to refine.

"The soul that to Jesus hath fled for repose,
I will not, I will not desert to his foes;
That soul, though all hell shall endeavor to shake,
I'll never, no, never, no, never forsake!"

—*Attributed to John Rippon (1787), age 36*

Answers To Prayer

Date _____

Need _____

Results _____

Date _____

Need _____

Results _____

Date _____

Need _____

Results _____

Date _____

Need _____

Results _____

Date _____

Need _____

Results _____

Date _____

Need _____

Results _____

Waters flowed over mine head;
then I said, I am cut off.
I called upon thy name, O Lord, out of the low dungeon.
Thou hast heard my voice:
Hide not thine ear at my breathing, at my cry!
Thou drewest near in the day that I called upon thee:
thou saidst, Fear not.
— Lamentations 3:54-57

ALMIGHTY GOD,
you know I have no power in myself to help myself:
Keep me safe both outwardly in my body
and inwardly in my soul, that I may be defended
from any attacks that may come upon my body,
and from all evil thoughts
that may try to assault and harm my soul.
I pray this in the name of Jesus Christ my Lord,
living and reigning with you and the Holy Spirit,
one God, for ever and ever.
Amen.

Whoso hearkeneth unto me shall dwell safely,
and shall be quiet from fear of evil.
— Proverbs 1:33

In the day when I cried thou answeredst me,
and strenthenedst me with strength in my soul...
Though I walk in the midst of trouble,
thou wilt revive me:
thou shalt stretch forth thine hand
against the wrath of mine enemies,
and thy right hand shall save me.
— Psalm 138:3,7

Will God Really Protect Me?

Divine protection results from renouncing evil and sincerely desiring to do God's will (see Psalm 66:17-20, Matthew 6:33). He can tell if you're just sweet-talking him into giving you free bodyguard services (you may be disappointed). God wants you to become so dependent on himself for your protection that you always give him the credit for being safe (see Psalm 59:16).

Depend on God alone and he will use his strong influence on your behalf (though always at his discretion (see Deuteronomy 31:8, Proverbs 21:1)), as well as give you the right words to say.

Be Careful and Behave Yourself
Don't get played and don't play others (see Matthew 10:16). You may get a little roughed up, hassled and nervous (even very scared), but God promises to deliver his righteous sons and daughters out of serious trouble (see 1 Samuel 2:9, Psalms 34:17, 91:9-16).

Lean hard on God at all times (see Proverbs 1:33).

Thank God for giving you favor with deputies or COs, staff, and other inmates (see Psalm 5:11-12), and for giving you spiritual understanding about what's really going on and how to pray (see James 1:5).

Memorize the morning scriptures for March 28.

I give unto you power...over all the power of the enemy: and nothing by any means shall hurt you (Luke 10:19).

You can take authority against any spirit of anger, panic, fear, dread, sickness or hopelessness that may try to disturb your peace of mind. Just bind it *in Jesus' name* (out loud, if possible), commanding it to leave and not bother anyone else, then thank the Holy Spirit for controlling the spiritual atmosphere around you and for keeping you steady (see Isaiah 26:3).

Ask God for boldness to pray with strong belief for his will to be done. God honors even a little faith and gives more to those who ask for it (see Mark 9:23-24)

The Lord is good, a strong hold in the day of trouble; and he knoweth them that trust in him (Nahum 1:7).

Walking under divine protection is a sign of God's favor and goodness towards you – as long as you walk along the right path and follow his leading. If you decide on your own to go into dangerous territory, you may get hurt. Just as stepping out of bounds physically can get you into trouble, so stepping out of bounds spiritually or morally can instantly expose you to evil hazards.

Spiritual Warfare

Every detention center, city or county jail, state prison and federal correctional institution (civilian and military) is a Devil's playground for men deeply corrupted by evil and active in sin. All inmate hostility, violence, despair and depravity can be traced to evil influences (see Ephesians 6:12).

Prisons truly can be hell on Earth (see Psalm 74:20). Even if you are not in a joint run by violent gangs or in a savage "gladiator school" where blood crews are kept busy and fresh fish are picked out and turned out, Satan is still at work.

Evil spirits stalk every cellblock and rec yard, looking for any kind of vulnerable inmate, emotionally charged situation or hopeless condition (see 1 Peter 5:8). They prey on men's minds, planting evil thoughts that spew from their mouths. They torment sleepers, whose anguished cries in the night disturb their neighbors.

Jesus' authority is supreme, so use it!

God's righteous sons and daughters can actually repel evil. Christians have Jesus' full permission to use his authority to run off any evil spirit(s) that may come near or interfere with their immediate environment (see James 4:7, 1 Peter 5:8-9).

**The perils around you are real.
God's power and presence are more real.**

~

**Evil cannot overwhelm you
when the Most High overshadows you.**

~

**Your path cannot lead to personal destruction
when you have personal intimacy with the Father.**

On your bunk or cot, mattress, pillow, the walls of your cell, cubicle or just the floor area around you, make an invisible sign of the cross with a bare finger in the name of the Father, Son and Holy Spirit. Declare *in Jesus' name* (out loud, if possible) that they are now cleansed of any evil associations or past defilements and are now out of bounds to all evil spirits. In this manner, quietly and privately spiritually decontaminate every living space to which you are assigned, asking the Holy Spirit to remain present with you there at all times.

If any demonic activity has occurred in your living area (killing, suicide, rape, torture, beating, occult ritual) bind the spirit associated with it, commanding it *in the name of Jesus* to get out and stay out. Ask the Holy Spirit to prevail.

Every day, quietly pray a blessing over yourself, your bunkie or cellie, cellblock, tier or housing unit, compound and institution. Ask the Holy Spirit to make God's truth and peace the main influences (see John 8:32).

Be cautious but unafraid of others.

Frequently thank God (out loud, if possible) for going before you as your "vanguard" and behind you as your "rearguard."

The effectual fervent prayer of a righteous man availeth much.
— James 5:16

As a regular precaution, *in Jesus' name* forbid evil spirits from stirring up misunderstandings between you and your bunkie, cellies, staff or others. Then thank the Holy Spirit for maintaining an atmosphere of truthfulness and honesty and for always giving you the right words to say (see Luke 12:11-12, 21:14-15).

Develop situational awareness by asking the Holy Spirit for insights into what's really going on around you and how to pray about it (see James 1:5).

Claim divine protection from psychological, verbal and physical intimidation, thanking God for keeping you at peace with others, including those who hate you (see Proverbs 16:7 and St. Patrick's Breastplate).

Be strong and of a good courage, [do not] be afraid of them:
for the Lord thy God, he it is that doth go with thee;
he will not fail thee nor forsake thee.
— Deuteronomy 31:6

When you see haters, silently forgive them, asking the Holy Spirit to bless them and minister healing and release to their angry, troubled souls. Then ask Jesus to give you his love for them, despite their willful sinfulness (see Psalm 64).

Recommended Readings

Satan Fears You'll Discover Your True Identity, Charles H. Kraft (Chosen). Most Christians don't know about the authority they have been given from Jesus to expel evil. Satan knows and works hard to keep us ignorant. Kraft explains our unique identity in Creation and how we can walk tall as God's son and daughters.

Armed and Dangerous: The Ultimate Battle Plan for Targeting and Defeating the Enemy, John Ramirez (Chosen). This former NYC satanic cult priest has personal knowledge of evil and 20+ years' experience helping fellow Christians repel it. How to recognize and defeat evil influences, yourself – wherever you are.

The Shadow of His Wings, Gereon Goldmann, O.F.M. (Ignatius Press). A German Franciscan's astounding chronicle of inconceivable ordeals and accomplishments during and after the Nazi era: youth, seminary, conscription into Himmler's SS, irregular ordination, covert ministry to *Wehrmacht* infantry, French imprisonment in North Africa, and much more. How, against all odds, God fulfilled a nun's unbelievable prophecy about him, answered his prayers and supernaturally rescued him from death more than once. A great read – and it all really happened!

St. Patrick's Breastplate

I bind unto myself today
The strong name of the Trinity,
By invocation of the same,
The Three in One and One in Three.

I bind this day to me for ever,
By power of faith, Christ's Incarnation;
His baptism in the Jordan River;
His death on cross for my salvation;
His coming at the day of doom;
I bind unto myself today.

I bind unto myself today
The power of God to hold and lead,
His eye to watch, His might to stay,
His ear to hearken to my need.
The wisdom of my God to teach,
His hand to guide, his shield to ward,
The word of God to give me speech,
His heavenly host to be my guard.

Against the demon snares of sin,
The vice that gives temptation force,
The natural lusts that war within,
The hostile men that mar my course;
Or few or many, far or nigh,
In every place and in all hours
Against their fierce hostility,
I bind to me these holy powers.

Against all Satan's spells and wiles,
Against false words of heresy,
Against the knowledge that defiles,
Against the heart's idolatry,
Against the wizard's evil craft,
Against the death-wound and the burning
The choking wave and the poisoned shaft,
Protect me, Christ, till thy returning.

Christ be with me, Christ within me,
Christ behind me, Christ before me,
Christ beside me, Christ to win me,
Christ to comfort and restore me,
Christ beneath me, Christ above me,
Christ in quiet, Christ in danger,
Christ in hearts of all that love me,
Christ in mouth of friend and stranger.

I bind unto myself the name,
The strong name of the Trinity;
By invocation of the same.
The Three in One, and One in Three,
Of whom all nature hath creation,
Eternal Father, Spirit, Word:
Praise to the Lord of my salvation,
Salvation is of Christ the Lord!

—Patrick of Ireland (c. 430), age 58

A Mighty Fortress is Our God,

A bulwark never failing;
Our helper He amid the flood
Of mortal ills prevailing.
For still our ancient foe
Doth seek to work us woe;
His craft and power are great,
And armed with cruel hate,
On earth is not his equal.
Did we in our own strength confide,
Our striving would be losing,
Were not the right Man on our side,
The Man of God's own choosing.
Dost ask who that may be?
Christ Jesus, it is He;
Lord Sabaoth, His name,
From age to age the same,
And He must win the battle.
And tho' this world, with devils filled,
Should threaten to undo us,
We will not fear, for God hath willed
His truth to triumph through us.
The prince of darkness grim,
We tremble not for him;
His rage we can endure,
For lo! his doom is sure;
One little word shall fell him.
That Word above all earthly powers,
No thanks to them, abideth;
The Spirit and the gifts are ours,
Through Him who with us sideth.
Let goods and kindred go,
This mortal life also;
The body they may kill;
God's truth abideth still;
His Kingdom is forever!
—*Martin Luther (1528), age 45*

Doing Good Time

It is not God's will for any of us to get locked up. He wants us all to "walk in the light" and stay out of trouble (see Isaiah 2:5, John 8:12). But while too many innocent men and women are locked up behind bars (you may be one of them), if we get caught breaking certain laws there are consequences, including incarceration.

God's original good will and purpose for us can get overtaken by our sinfulness.

God wants to set the captives free (see Isaiah 42:7, 61:1).

What does *that* mean? Immediate release? Acquittal? Parole? Deportation? For some it might, but the rest of us must remain locked up for a while longer.

God can set us free another way: by transforming us from victims to victors. You can quit being a victim of your sins and circumstances and gain spiritual control over yourself and even your environment.

If you faithfully "abide" in Jesus (and he in you), he will not only make you righteous before the Father, he will equip you spiritually to help others get free. He has good things for you to do while you "redeem the time" (see Colossians 4:5).

You can minister in every way Jesus did.

Anyone who "abides" in Jesus and faithfully obeys his commands can not only eventually stop thinking and acting sinfully (see Romans 6:14-22, 1 John 3:6,9) but also minister in the same ways Jesus did – even more so (see John 14:12, 15:4-5).

Your faith should not stand in the wisdom of men,
but in the power of God.
— 1 Corinthians 2:5

The Bible calls this doing "signs and wonders" with the authority and power Jesus gives to his faithful followers (see Hebrews 2:3-4, Luke 9:1-2, Mark 16:17-18). The disciples advanced God's Kingdom through preaching and teaching, conversions, healings and deliverances (see Mark 6:12 13).

So too, should modern believers – including prisoners.

The convict code says, "Do your own time; mind your own business; don't be a snoop, a sneak or a snitch; don't see anything or say anything." Even so, Christians are to be "salt" and "light," bringing glory to God by having a strong positive influence on the spiritual atmosphere (see Ephesians 5:8-10, Colossians 4:5-6).

> **Spiritual truth is learned by atmosphere, not by intellectual reasoning. God's Spirit alters the atmosphere of our way of looking at things, and things begin to be possible which never were possible before.**
>
> **—Oswald Chambers**

Altering the Atmosphere

Satan stays busy distracting natural-born sinners from God's influence. He plants lies in our heads (often in childhood) about who we are and what we are, and wrong ideas about how to behave in order to "make it."

He also warps our thinking about God and other people (see John 8:43-45).

God has given us free will to choose for ourselves whether to trust him or to keep following our corrupted natural instincts. For that reason, the Devil stirs up spiritual and emotional "static" around sinners to keep them from recognizing God's presence and thinking clearly about their options (see 2 Corinthians 4:4).

By supernaturally reducing that static, you can frustrate Satan's plans and help your unrepentant fellow prisoners consider the restoration God is offering them.

Using the prayer power and command authority Jesus has given you, the atmosphere in your housing unit, pod, tier or compound can actually be altered from one of anger, chaos or intimidation to one of relative order and even peace (see James 3:16-18).

Though shalt also decree a thing, and it shall be established unto thee: and the light shall shine upon thy ways (Job 22:28).

Alone or with others during controlled movements and as you walk the yard or common areas, declare God's sovereignty and control over your facility and everyone in it. *In Jesus' name* decree that God's truth is exposing and removing demonic strongholds of intimidation and fear; that Satan's efforts to corrupt and control both inmates and staff are being frustrated (see Psalm 140:8), and that God's Word is being confirmed by signs and wonders (see Mark 16:20, Acts 4:30).

Death and life are in the power of the tongue: and they that love it shall eat the fruit thereof (Proverbs 18:21).

In a spiritual atmosphere less jammed by Satanic static, you can start showing off God's power to unrepentant unbelievers (see Acts 14:3, 1 Peter 2:12) with authoritative commands for their healing and with supernatural words of knowledge or wisdom when you pray for their legal, family and personal needs.

Undeserved blessings give unbelieving inmates an unexpected experience of God's mercy, opening their hearts and minds to his love (see Romans 2:4). Then perhaps for the first time they can make a clear-headed decision to stop being corrupted creatures of God and become sons of the Father and followers of Jesus.

Sinners often come to repentance after being unexpectedly blessed by God, once he's altered the spiritual atmosphere in which they freely think and act.

That's how you can destroy the Devil's works (see 1 John 3:8), make new disciples (see Matthew 28:18-19) and advance God's Kingdom (see Matthew 5:14-16).

Use your prayer power and command authority.

Working together, you and your fellow Christian convicts can exert a strong positive influence on your jail or prison environment (see Philippians 2:15).

As the spiritual atmosphere changes, God will guide your prayer and ministry activities among unrepentant unbelievers (see Matthew 18:19-20, James 1:5). Expect to see physical healings, legal and relationship breakthroughs, conversions and even deliverances. Eventually, gradual reductions in gang violence and racial tensions may result, as well as positive policy and staffing changes (see James 3:18).

These may occur slowly (and with some setbacks) but they really can happen. The Recommended Readings describe actual methods for achieving them.

Once you become assured of the Lord's favor and goodness, it's liberating to no longer feel forsaken and forgotten, as though you've been left to just rot in a human landfill or survive at the mercy of brutal psychos. Instead, energized by positive expectations and a firm sense of divine protection and purpose, you can praise God every day as you watch in amazement how his love gradually brightens the dark atmosphere (and people) around you (see 1 John 3:8).

Jesus warned his disciples that they would minister "as lambs among wolves." Prisons are full of wolves, so be sure to *walk [cautiously], not as fools...because the days are evil...understanding what the will of the Lord is* (Ephesians 5:15-17).

Recommended Readings

The Supernatural Power of a Transformed Mind, Bill Johnson (Destiny Image). How to routinely witness the miraculous, receive direct revelation from God and operate in Christian signs and wonders as a minister of his mercy to others.

Snapshots of Time: Stories of Heaven Invading a Texas Prison, Jeff Hale (CreateSpace). Still serving a 40-year sentence on a wrongful conviction, Hale, with his fellow Christians, are witnessing amazing miracles and breakthroughs as God alters the spiritual atmosphere and they minister to inmates in God's supernatural power.

Do What Jesus Did, Robby Dawkins (Chosen). How to follow the examples of Chicagoland Christians bringing God's supernatural healing and restoration to all kinds of hurting people, including witches, addicts and violent Latin Kings.

The Essential Guide to Healing: Equipping All Christians to Pray for the Sick, Bill Johnson & Randy Clark (Chosen). How to minister using Jesus' authority with words of knowledge from the Holy Spirit, employing a simple five-step method.

Speak Life: Creating Your World With Your Words, Katherine Ruanola (Ruanola Ministries). Know how God is totally with you, in you, and for you; how much power your words have and how the promises of God can be released by them.

Never Came to Me

I wonder where your love went,
Because it never came to me.
I wonder, if things were different,
How would they be?
We are one but I can't understand what you see.
To abandon your son and allow me to be
Raised in the streets.
I wonder what you feel at night,
The thoughts that cross as you envision your life.
Do you toss and turn in your sleep,
Or are you cold-hearted?
Do you rest in peace?
You were a father to all the rest of your kids,
So I wonder where your love went.
Because it never came to me.

—*Deon C. Nowell (2012), age 31*
FCI Butner Low

Broken Dreams

As children bring
their broken toys
with tears for us to mend,
I brought my broken dreams to God,
because He is my Friend.

But then, instead of leaving Him
in peace to work alone,
I hung around and tried to help
with ways that were my own.

At last I snatched them back and
cried, "How can you be so slow?"
"My child," He said, "what could I do?
You never did let go."

—*Lauretta P. Burns (1957), age 39*

Me, Myself and I

Walking the prisoner's path of faith, hope and restoration isn't just about getting saved and staying out of trouble. There's unconditional forgiveness to work through and spiritual warfare to wage in a dark place full of evil dangers.

> *The way of the wicked is as darkness:*
> *They know not at what they stumble.*
> *But the path of the just is as the shining light,*
> *that shineth more and more unto the perfect day.*
> *— Proverbs 4:19,18*

This is a good place for you to start learning to walk on "the path of the just" in the "shining light" as a loved son of the Father. Living away from the distractions of the street, you can spend more time correcting a lifetime of bad choices.

> *My people have committed two evils:*
> *They have forsaken me, the fountain of living waters,*
> *and hewed them out cisterns, broken cisterns,*
> *that can hold no water.*
> *— Jeremiah 2:13*

Things don't get easier – you just get better.

Among your most satisfying achievements behind bars can be overcoming the spiritual and psychological effects of sins that may have been committed against you and the destructive lies of Satan that may have deceived you (see John 8:44b).

Now you really can become "a new creature in Christ" (see 2 Corinthians 5:17).

The Recommended Readings offer insights and answers about all kinds of issues.

> *When my father and my mother forsake me,*
> *then the Lord will take me up.*
> *— Psalm 27:10*

If you are like most convicts, your bad behavior got started, in part, because something was wrong with your family. Most likely what spoiled things for you early on was a missing, abusive, deadbeat or otherwise inadequate dad.

Every son needs an admired father figure to guide him away from his mother's overprotective influence and tell him that he's successfully becoming a man.

Boys need to hear that and believe it.

If they never do – or worse, if they hear (and believe) belittling or insulting words said to them – they can become prone to discouragement and self-doubt.

A damaged self-image can lead to low self-esteem, even self-hatred, resentments, aching envies, sexual frustrations, confused relationships, violent impulses, depression, substance abuse, self-injury and an early death.

There's Satan's plan for your life.

Maybe you enjoyed a happy boyhood but unchecked adolescent rebelliousness or irresponsibility led to reckless social behavior and drug or thug activity.

Maybe you're now a missing, abusive, deadbeat or otherwise inadequate dad.

Because of what you've been through (and have put others through), you may be scarred psychologically, emotionally, spiritually, physically or sexually.

On top of all that, if every day you dread being attacked (or can't shake the trauma of having already been assaulted), your nerves may be shot, leaving you in continual fear of lurking enemies and predators. You may think your only choice is to become a vicious head-buster, yourself, or just give up and endure tortuous isolation in protective custody.

The Father has better options for you.

Read, pray, listen, respond and receive.

As a "new creature" in Christ, you can relax and trust God to engineer all of your circumstances (see Psalm 37:23-24). As a loved son of the best Father you could ever hope to have, you can start enjoying his blessings (see John 10:10), let him renew your heart and mind (see Romans 12:2, Hebrews 10:16) and quit believing Satan's awful lies about yourself and others (see Ephesians 4:17-32, Titus 2:11-12, 3:3-7).

No matter how screwed up you are (or think you are), God can fix everything.

Eventually, you will develop a new self-image, creative ideas for an honest future, and a sense of godly purpose, inspired by a love for others (and for yourself) you never thought you could ever enjoy (see Proverbs 1:33, 8:12,21,35, 16:3, Isaiah 54:17, 2 Timothy 1:7, Hebrews 13:5-6).

The name for this kind of personal restoration is "inner healing."

Sometimes, deliverance is also needed. That's the binding and banishing of a troublesome evil spirit that may oppress you with self-sabotaging thoughts or sick fantasies. It's not the same as exorcism, which is the ritual expulsion of a demon that has taken over ("possessed") a person's active will. That is very rare.

Recommended Readings

Growing Pains, John & Paula Sandford (Charisma House). How to let God free you from disturbing childhood experiences or perceptions that have left you feeling ashamed, angry, confused, inadequate or just empty inside.

Battlefield of the Mind, Joyce Meyer (Warner Faith). How to recognize and renounce the lies of Satan and break the mental strongholds they produce.

The Search for Significance, Robert S. McGee (Thomas Nelson). How to refute lies about yourself; God's answers to the performance trap, approval addiction, the blame game, and shame; understanding godly conviction versus sin guilt, more.

Before You Get Here: Baggage to Drop On Your Way to Heaven, Michael Evans (Wholeness Ministries). A useful DIY guide to getting right with God, yourself, and others; includes forgiveness, self-acceptance, renunciation of evil, more.

Killing Lions: A Guide Through the Trials Young Men Face, John & Samuel Eldredge (Thomas Nelson). Answering the haunting boyhood question, "Do I have what it takes?" often leads to unsatisfying, even dangerous, efforts to "be a man." How to instead humbly walk tall as a self-confident and blessed son of the Father.

Healing the Hidden Self, Barbara Shlemon Ryan (Ave Maria Press). This simple DIY prayer review through your sequential life stages can reveal and relieve the sources of all kinds of unresolved present-day inner struggles.

Blessing or Curse, Derek Prince (Chosen). Identify curses placed on you by others (or yourself). How to end family patterns of occult activity, chronic illness, child abuse, suicide, addiction, violence, infidelity, divorce and/or criminality.

After the Trauma the Battle Begins, Nigel W. D. Mumford (Troy). The former British marine commando suffered severe PTSD before God restored his mind and soul. Now an Episcopal priest, he tells how God can cure you of "shell shock," whether combat-related or more personal (rape, assault and other traumas).

Tempted and Tried, Russell D. Moore (Crossway). The Baptist leader says, "You cannot triumph over temptation. Only Jesus can." Satan counterfeits the Father's blessings, but Jesus can keep you from being deceived. Lots of good insights here.

The Masculine Mandate, Richard D. Phillips (Reformation Trust). The Presbyterian pastor, father and former West Point instructor explains the biblical masculinity code for single and married men, contrasting it to what secular society dictates.

How to Forgive Ourselves —Totally, R. T. Kendall (Charisma House). For anyone carrying shame and guilt because of immoral things done to or with others in school, young adulthood or the military, or feeling defeated by a failed marriage, wayward children or a ruined future because of one's own wrongdoing.

The Red Sea Rules, Robert J. Morgan (Thomas Nelson). How to get through an "impossible" situation with patience, faith and trust in God's supernatural power to deliver you; based on the Exodus story (Genesis 14-15).

> *I will praise thee, O Lord my God, with all my heart:*
> *and I will glorify thy name for evermore.*
> *For great is thy mercy toward me:*
> *thou hast delivered my soul*
> *from the lowest hell.*
> *— Psalm 86:12-13*

✢ Promises for Prisoners ✢

HE HATH LOOKED DOWN from the height of his sanctuary; from heaven did the Lord behold the earth; to hear the groaning of the prisoner; to loose those that are appointed to death (Psalm 102:19-20).

THE LORD WILL NOT CAST OFF FOR EVER: Though he cause grief, yet will he have compassion according to the multitude of his mercies. For he does not afflict willingly nor grieve the children of men. To crush under his feet all the prisoners of the earth, to turn aside the right of a man before the face of the Most High, to subvert a man in his cause, the Lord approveth not (Lamentations 3:31-36).

HE HATH SAID, I WILL NEVER LEAVE THEE, nor forsake thee. So that we may boldly say, The Lord is my helper, and I will not fear what man shall do unto me (Hebrews 13:5-6).

FEAR THOU NOT; FOR I AM WITH THEE: be not dismayed; for I am thy God: I will strengthen thee; yea, I will uphold thee with the right hand of my righteousness (Isaiah 41:16).

WHOSO HEARKENETH UNTO ME shall dwell safely, and shall be quiet from fear of evil (Proverbs 1:33).

NO WEAPON THAT IS FORMED AGAINST THEE shall prosper; and every tongue that shall rise against thee in judgment thou shalt condemn. This is the heritage of the servants of the Lord, and their righteousness is of me, saith the Lord (Isaiah 54:17).

THOU SHALT HIDE THEM in the secret of thy presence from the pride of man: thou shalt keep them secretly in a pavilion from the strife of tongues (Psalm 31:20).

I WILL SEEK THAT WHICH WAS LOST, and bring again that which was driven away, and will bind up that which was broken, and will strengthen that which was sick (Ezekiel 34:16).

COMMIT THY WORKS UNTO THE LORD, and thy thoughts shall be established (Proverbs 16:3).

THE GOD OF ALL GRACE, who hath called us unto his eternal glory by Christ Jesus, after that ye have suffered awhile, make you perfect, stablish, strengthen, settle you (1 Peter 5:10).

WITH GOD NOTHING SHALL BE IMPOSSIBLE (Luke 1:37).

RESIST THE DEVIL and he will flee from you (James 4:7).

THE NAME OF THE LORD IS A STRONG TOWER; the righteous runneth into it, and is safe (Proverbs 18:10).

GOD HATH NOT GIVEN US THE SPIRIT OF FEAR; but of power, and of love, and of a sound mind (2 Timothy 1:7).

THE ANGEL OF THE LORD ENCAMPETH ROUND ABOUT them that fear him, and delivereth them... The righteous cry, and the Lord heareth, and delivereth them out of all their troubles (Psalm 34:7,17).

GOD IS OUR REFUGE AND STRENGTH, a very present help in trouble (Psalm 46:1).

CALL UPON ME IN THE DAY OF TROUBLE: I will deliver thee, and thou shalt glorify me (Psalm 50:15).

HE SHALL CALL UPON ME, and I will answer him: I will be with him in trouble, I will deliver him (Psalm 91:15).

IF WE SAY WE HAVE NO SIN, we deceive ourselves, and the truth is not in us. If we confess our sins, he is faithful and just to forgive us our sins, and to cleanse us from all unrighteousness (1 John 1:8-9).

THERE IS THEREFORE NOW NO CONDEMNATION to them which are in Christ Jesus, who walk not after the flesh, but after the Spirit (Romans 8:1).

AS FAR AS EAST IS FROM WEST, so far hath he removed our transgressions from us. Like as a father pitieth his children, so the Lord pitieth them that fear him (Psalm 103:12-13).

THOU SHALT NOT BE FORGOTTEN OF ME. I have blotted out, as a thick cloud, thy transgressions, and, as a cloud, thy sins (Isaiah 44:21-22).

THOU WILT KEEP HIM IN PERFECT PEACE, whose mind is stayed on thee: because he trusteth in thee (Isaiah 26:3).

PRAY ONE FOR ANOTHER: the effectual fervent prayer of a righteous man availeth much (James 5:16).

WHATSOEVER THOU SHALT BIND on earth shall be bound in heaven: and whatsoever thou shalt loose on earth shall be loosed in heaven (Matthew 16:19).

IF TWO OF YOU SHALL AGREE on earth as touching any thing that they shall ask, it shall be done for them of my Father in heaven. For where two or three are gathered together in my name, there am I in the midst of them (Matthew 18:19-20).

IF YE CONTINUE IN MY WORD, then are ye my disciples indeed; and ye shall know the truth, and the truth shall make you free (John 8:31-32).

THIS IS THE CONFIDENCE THAT WE HAVE IN HIM, that, if we ask anything according to his will, he heareth us: and if we know that he hear us, whatsoever we ask, we know that we have the petitions that we desired of him (1 John 5:14-15).

THE EYES OF THE LORD RUN TO AND FRO throughout the whole earth, to shew himself strong in the behalf of them whose heart is perfect toward him (2 Chronicles 16:9a).

BEHOLD, THE EYE OF THE LORD IS UPON THEM that fear him, upon them that hope in his mercy; to deliver their soul from death (Psalm 33:18-19).

THE LORD IS NIGH UNTO THEM that are of a broken heart; and saveth such as be of a contrite spirit. The Lord redeemeth the soul of his servants: and none of them that trust in him shall be desolate (Psalm 34:18,22).

THE LORD IS NIGH UNTO ALL THEM that call upon him, to all that call upon him in truth. He will fulfil the desire of them that fear him: he also will hear their cry, and will save them. The Lord preserveth all them that love him: but all the wicked will he destroy (Psalm 145:18-20).

TURN YOU AT MY REPROOF: behold, I will pour out my spirit unto you, I will make known my words unto you (Proverbs 1:23).

THE LORD SHALL GUIDE THEE CONTINUALLY, and satisfy thy soul in drought (Isaiah 58:11).

THE STEPS OF A GOOD MAN are ordered by the Lord: and he delighteth in his way. Though he fall, he shall not be utterly cast down: for the Lord upholdeth him with his hand (Psalm 37:23-24).

TRUST IN THE LORD with all thine heart; and lean not unto thine own understanding. In all thy ways acknowledge him, and he shall direct thy paths (Proverbs 3:5-6).

BE [ANXIOUS] FOR NOTHING; but in every thing by prayer and supplication with thanksgiving let your requests be made known unto God. And the peace of God, which passeth all understanding, shall keep your hearts and minds through Christ Jesus (Philippians 4:6-7).

THOUGH I WALK IN THE MIDST OF TROUBLE, thou wilt revive me: thou shalt stretch forth thine hand against the wrath of mine enemies, and thy right hand shall save me (Psalm 138:7).

Other Personal Scriptures:

_____

_____

_____

_____

_____

Psalm 121

I will lift up mine eyes unto the hills,
from whence cometh my help.

My help cometh from the Lord,
which made heaven and earth.

He will not suffer thy foot to be moved:
he that keepeth thee will not slumber.

Behold, he that keepeth Israel
shall neither slumber nor sleep.

The Lord is thy keeper:
the Lord is thy shade upon thy right hand.

The sun shall not smite thee by day,
nor the moon by night.

The Lord shall preserve thee from all evil:
he shall preserve thy soul.

The Lord shall preserve thy going out
and thy coming in from this time forth,
and even for evermore.

JANUARY 1 MORNING

This one thing I do,
forgetting those things which are behind,...
I press toward the mark
for the prize of the high calling of God in Christ Jesus.
— PHILIPPIANS 3:13,14

Father, I will that they...whom thou hast given me, be with me where I am; that they may behold my glory, which thou hast given me. — I know whom I have believed, and am persuaded that he is able to keep that which I have committed unto him against that day. — He which hath begun a good work in you will perform it until the day of Jesus Christ. — Know ye not that they which run in a race run all, but one receiveth the prize? So run, that ye may obtain. And every man that striveth for the mastery is temperate in all things. Now they do it to obtain a corruptible crown; but we an incorruptible. — Let us lay aside every weight, and the sin which doth so easily beset us, and let us run with patience the race that is set before us, looking unto Jesus.

John 17:24   2 Timothy 1:12   Philippians 1:6
1 Corinthians 9:24,25   Hebrews 12:1,2

JANUARY 1 EVENING

The Lord, he it is that doth go before thee;
he will be with thee, he will not fail thee.
— DEUTERONOMY 31:8

If thy presence go not with me, carry us not up hence. — O Lord, I know that the way of man is not in himself: it is not in man that walketh to direct his steps. — The steps of a good man are ordered by the Lord: and he delighteth in his way. Though he fall, he shall not be utterly cast down: for the Lord upholdeth him with his hand. — I am continually with thee: thou hast holden me by my right hand. Thou shalt guide me with thy counsel, and afterward receive me to glory. — I am persuaded, that neither death, nor life, nor angels, nor principalities, nor powers, nor things present, nor things to come, nor height, nor depth, nor any other creature, shall be able to separate us from the love of God, which is in Christ Jesus our Lord.

Exodus 33:15   Jeremiah 10:23
Psalms 37:23,24, 73:23,24   Romans 8:38-39

JANUARY 2 MORNING

Sing unto the Lord a new song.
— ISAIAH 42:10

Sing aloud unto God our strength; make a joyful noise unto the God of Jacob. Take a psalm, and bring hither the timbrel, the pleasant harp with the psaltery. — He hath put a new song in my mouth, even praise unto our God: many shall see it, and fear, and shall trust in the Lord. — Be strong and of a good courage; be not afraid, neither be thou dismayed: for the Lord thy God is with thee whithersoever thou goest. — The joy of the Lord is your strength. — Paul...thanked God, and took courage. — Knowing the time, that now it is high time to awake out of sleep: for now is our salvation nearer than when we believed. The night is far spent, the day is at hand: let us therefore cast off the works of darkness, and let us put on the armour of light. Let us walk honestly, as in the day; not in rioting and drunkenness, not in chambering and wantonness, not in strife and envying. But put ye on the Lord Jesus Christ, and make not provision for the flesh, to fulfil the lusts thereof.

Psalms 81:1,2, 40:3   Joshua 1:9
Nehemiah 8:10   Acts 28:15   Romans 13:11-14

JANUARY 2 EVENING

Let my prayer be set forth before thee as incense;
and the lifting up of my hands as the evening sacrifice.
— PSALM 141:2

Thou shalt make an altar to burn incense upon:...and thou shalt put it before the veil that is by the ark of the testimony, before the mercy seat that is over the testimony, where I will meet with thee. And Aaron shall burn thereon sweet incense every morning:...and when Aaron lighteth the lamps at even, he shall burn incense upon it, a perpetual incense before the Lord throughout your generations. — [Jesus] is able to save them to the uttermost that come unto God by him, seeing he ever liveth to make intercession for them. — The smoke of the incense, which came with the prayers of the saints, ascended up before God out of the angel's hand. — Ye also, as lively stones, are built up a spiritual house, an holy priesthood, to offer up spiritual sacrifices, acceptable to God by Jesus Christ. — Pray without ceasing.

Exodus 30:1,6-8   Hebrews 7:25   Revelation 8:4
1 Peter 2:5   1 Thessalonians 5:17

JANUARY 3 MORNING

He led them forth by the right way.
— PSALM 107:7

He found [Jacob] in a desert land, and in the waste howling wilderness; he led him about, he instructed him, he kept him as the apple of his eye. As an eagle stirreth up her nest, fluttereth over her young, spreadeth abroad her wings, taketh them, beareth them on her wings: so the Lord alone did lead him. — Even to your old age I am he; and even to hoar hairs will I carry you: I have made, and I will bear; even I will carry, and will deliver you. — He restoreth my soul: he leadeth me in the paths of righteousness for his name's sake. Yea, though I walk through the valley of the shadow of death, I will fear no evil: for thou art with me; thy rod and thy staff they comfort me. — The Lord shall guide thee continually, and satisfy thy soul in drought, and make fat thy bones: and thou shalt be like a watered garden, and like a spring of water, whose waters fail not. — For this God is our God for ever and ever: he will be our guide even unto death. — Behold, God exalteth by his power: who teacheth like him?

Deuteronomy 32:10-12   Isaiah 46:4   Psalm 23:3,4
Isaiah 58:11   Psalm 48:14   Job 36:22

JANUARY 3 EVENING

What wilt thou that I shall do unto thee...
Lord, that I may receive my sight.
— LUKE 18:41

Open thou mine eyes, that I may behold wondrous things out of thy law. — Then opened he their understanding, that they might understand the scriptures. — The Comforter, which is the Holy Ghost, whom the Father will send in my name...shall teach you all things. — Every good gift and every perfect gift is from above, and cometh down from the Father of lights. — The God of our Lord Jesus Christ, the Father of glory...give unto you the spirit of wisdom and revelation in the knowledge of him: the eyes of your understanding being enlightened; that ye may know what is the hope of his calling, and what the riches of the glory of his inheritance in the saints, and what is the exceeding greatness of his power to us-ward who believe, according to the working of his mighty power.

Psalm 119:18   Luke 24:45   John 14:26
James 1:17   Ephesians 1:17-20

JANUARY 4 MORNING

Ye are not as yet come to the rest and to the inheritance,
which the Lord your God giveth you.
— DEUTERONOMY 12:9

This is not your rest. — There remaineth therefore a rest to the people of God. — Within the veil; whither the forerunner is for us entered, even Jesus. — In my Father's house are many mansions: if it were not so, I would have told you. I go to prepare a place for you. And if I go and prepare a place for you, I will come again, and receive you unto myself; that where I am, there ye may be also. — With Christ; which is far better. — God shall wipe away all tears from their eyes; and there shall be no more death, neither sorrow, nor crying, neither shall there be any more pain; for the former things are passed away. — There the wicked cease from troubling: and there the weary be at rest. — Lay up for yourselves treasures in heaven. For where your treasure is, there will your heart be also. — Set your affection on things above, not on things on the earth.

Micah 2:10   Hebrews 4:9, 6:19,20   John 14:2,3
Philippians 1:23   Revelation 21:4   Job 3:17
Matthew 6:20,21   Colossians 3:2

JANUARY 4 EVENING

O death, where is thy sting?
O grave, where is thy victory?
— 1 CORINTHIANS 15:55

The sting of death is sin. — But now once in the end of the world hath he appeared to put away sin by the sacrifice of himself. And as it is appointed unto men once to die, but after this the judgment: so Christ was once offered to bear the sins of many; and unto them that look for him shall he appear the second time without sin unto salvation. — As the children are partakers of flesh and blood, he also himself likewise took part of the same; that through death he might destroy him that had the power of death, that is, the devil; and deliver them who through fear of death were all their lifetime subject to bondage. — I am now ready to be offered, and the time of my departure is at hand. I have fought a good fight, I have finished my course, I have kept the faith: henceforth there is laid up for me a crown of righteousness.

1 Corinthians 15:56   Hebrews 9:26-28, 2:14,15
2 Timothy 4:6-8

JANUARY 5 MORNING

We which have believed do enter into rest.
— HEBREWS 4:3

They weary themselves to commit iniquity. — I see another law in my members, warring against the law of my mind, and bringing me into captivity to the law of sin which is in my members. O wretched man that I am! Who shall deliver me from the body of this death? — Come unto me, all ye that labour and are heavy laden, and I will give you rest. — Being justified by faith, we have peace with God through our Lord Jesus Christ: by whom also we have access by faith into this grace wherein we stand, and rejoice in hope of the glory of God. — He that is entered into his rest, he also hath ceased from his own works. — Not having mine own righteousness, which is of the law, but that which is through the faith of Christ, the righteousness which is of God by faith. — This is the rest wherewith ye may cause the weary to rest; and this is the refreshing.

Jeremiah 9:5   Romans 7:23,24   Matthew 11:28
Romans 5:1,2   Hebrews 4:10
Philippians 3:9   Isaiah 28:12

JANUARY 5 EVENING

Set a watch, O Lord, before my mouth;
keep the door of my lips.
— PSALM 141:3

If thou, Lord, shouldest mark iniquities, O Lord, who shall stand? — They provoked his spirit, so that he spake unadvisedly with his lips. — Not that which goeth into the mouth defileth a man; but that which cometh out of the mouth, this defileth a man. — A whisperer separateth chief friends. — There is that speaketh like the piercings of a sword: but the tongue of the wise is health. The lip of truth shall be established for ever: but a lying tongue is but for a moment. — The tongue can no man tame; it is an unruly evil, full of deadly poison. Out of the same mouth proceedeth blessing and cursing. My brethren, these things ought not so to be. — Put off...anger, wrath, malice, blasphemy, filthy communication out of your mouth. Lie not one to another, seeing that ye have put off the old man with his deeds. — This is the will of God, even your sanctification. — In their mouth was found no guile.

Psalms 130:3, 106:33   Matthew 15:11   Proverbs 16:28, 12:18,19   James 3:8,10
Colossians 3:8,9 1   Thessalonians 4:3   Revelation 14:5

JANUARY 6 MORNING

Let the beauty of the Lord our God be upon us:
and establish thou the work of our hands.
— PSALM 90:17

Thy renown went forth among the heathen for thy beauty: for it was perfect through my comeliness, which I had put upon thee, saith the Lord GOD. — We all, with open face beholding as in a glass the glory of the Lord, are changed into the same image from glory to glory, even as by the Spirit of the Lord. — The Spirit of glory and of God resteth upon us. — Blessed is every one that feareth the Lord; that walketh in his ways. For thou shalt eat the labour of thine hands: happy shalt thou be, and it shall be well with thee. — Commit thy works unto the Lord, and thy thoughts shall be established. — Work out your own salvation with fear and trembling. For it is God which worketh in you both to will and to do of his good pleasure. — Our Lord Jesus Christ himself, and God, even our Father, which hath loved us, and hath given us everlasting consolation and good hope through grace, comfort your hearts, and stablish you in every good word and work.

Ezekiel 16:14 2 Corinthians 3:18 Psalm 128:1,2 Proverbs 16:3
Philippians 2:12,13 2 Thessalonians 2:16,17

JANUARY 6 EVENING

The apostles gathered themselves together unto Jesus,
and told him all things they had done.
— MARK 6:30

There is a friend that sticketh closer than a brother. — The Lord spake unto Moses face to face, as a man speaketh unto his friend. — Ye are my friends, if ye do whatsoever I command you. Henceforth I call you not servants; for the servant knoweth not what his lord doeth: but I have called you friends; for all things that I have heard of my Father I have made known unto you. — When ye shall have done all those things which are commanded you, say, We are unprofitable servants. — Ye have not received the spirit of bondage again to fear; but ye have received the Spirit of adoption, whereby we cry, Abba, Father. — In every thing by prayer and supplication with thanksgiving let your requests be made known unto God. — The prayer of the upright is his delight.

Proverbs 18:24 Exodus 33:11 John 15:14,15
Luke 17:10 Romans 8:15 Philippians 4:6 Proverbs 15:8

JANUARY 7 MORNING

Think upon me, my God, for good.
— NEHEMIAH 5:19

Thus saith the Lord; I remember thee, the kindness of thy youth, the love of thine espousals, when thou wentest after me in the wilderness. — I will remember my covenant with thee in the days of thy youth, and I will establish unto thee an everlasting covenant. — I will visit you, and perform my good word toward you. — For I know the thoughts that I think toward you, saith the Lord, thoughts of peace, and not of evil, to give you an expected end. — As the heavens are higher than the earth, so are my ways higher than your ways, and my thoughts than your thoughts. — I would seek unto God, and unto God would I commit my cause: which doeth great things and unsearchable; marvellous things without number. — Many, O Lord my God, are thy wonderful works which thou hast done, and thy thoughts which are to us-ward: they cannot be reckoned up in order unto thee: if I would declare and speak of them they are more than can be numbered.

Jeremiah 2:2   Ezekiel 16:60   Jeremiah 29:10,11
Isaiah 55:9   Job 5:8,9   Psalm 40:5

JANUARY 7 EVENING

I will not fail thee, nor forsake thee.
— JOSHUA 1:5

There failed not ought of any good thing which the Lord had spoken unto the house of Israel; all came to pass. — God is not a man, that he should lie; neither the son of man, that he should repent: hath he said, and shall he not do it? or hath he spoken, and shall he not make it good? — The Lord thy God, he is God, the faithful God, which keepeth covenant and mercy with them that love him. — He will ever be mindful of his covenant. — Can a woman forget her sucking child, that she should not have compassion on the son of her womb? Yea, they may forget, yet will I not forget thee. Behold, I have graven thee upon the palms of my hands. — The Lord thy God in the midst of thee is mighty; he will save, he will rejoice over thee with joy; he will rest in his love, he will joy over thee with singing.

Joshua 21:45   Numbers 23:19   Deuteronomy 7:9
Psalm 111:5   Isaiah 49:15,16   Zephaniah 3:17

JANUARY 8 MORNING

*They that know thy name will put their trust in thee:
for thou, Lord, hast not forsaken them that seek thee.*
— PSALM 9:10

The name of the Lord is a strong tower: the righteous runneth into it, and is safe. — I will trust, and not be afraid: for the Lord JEHOVAH is my strength and my song; he also is become my salvation. — I have been young, and now am old; yet have I not seen the righteous forsaken, nor his seed begging bread. — For the Lord loveth judgment, and forsaketh not his saints, they are preserved for ever: but the seed of the wicked shall be cut off. — The Lord will not forsake his people for his great name's sake: because it hath pleased the Lord to make you his people. — Who delivered us from so great a death, and doth deliver: in whom we trust that he will yet deliver us. — Be content with such things as ye have: for he hath said, I will never leave thee, nor forsake thee. So that we may boldly say, The Lord is my helper, I will not fear what man shall do unto me.

Proverbs 18:10   Isaiah 12:2   Psalm 37:25,28
1 Samuel 12:22 2   Corinthians 1:10   Hebrews 13:5,6

JANUARY 8 EVENING

They are without fault before the throne of God.
— REVELATION 14:5

The iniquity of Israel shall be sought for, and there shall be none; and the sins of Judah, and they shall not be found: for I will pardon them whom I reserve. — Who is a God like unto thee, that pardoneth iniquity, and passeth by the transgression of the remnant of his heritage? He retaineth not his anger forever, because he delighteth in mercy. He will turn again, he will have compassion upon us; he will subdue our iniquities; and thou wilt cast all their sins into the depths of the sea. — He hath made us accepted in the beloved. — To present you holy and unblameable and unreproveable in his sight. — Now unto him that is able to keep you from falling, and to present you faultless before the presence of his glory with exceeding joy, to the only wise God our Saviour, be glory and majesty, dominion and power, both now and ever. Amen.

Jeremiah 50:20   Micah 7:18,19   Ephesians 1:6
Colossians 1:22 Jude 24,25

JANUARY 9 MORNING

Thou hast given a banner to them that fear thee,
that it may be displayed because of the truth.
— PSALM 60:4

Jehovah Nissi (The Lord my banner). — When the enemy shall come in like a flood, the Spirit of the Lord shall lift up a standard against him. — We will rejoice in thy salvation, and in the name of our God we will set up our banners. — The Lord hath brought forth our righteousness: come, and let us declare in Zion the work of the Lord our God. — We are more than conquerors through him that loved us. — Thanks be to God, which giveth us the victory through our Lord Jesus Christ. — The captain of our salvation. — My brethren, be strong in the Lord, and in the power of his might. — Valiant for the truth. — Fight the Lord's battles. — Be strong, all ye people of the land, saith the Lord, and work: fear ye not. — Lift up your eyes, and look on the fields; for they are white already to harvest. — Yet a little while, and he that shall come will come, and will not tarry.

Exodus 17:15   Isaiah 59:19   Psalm 20:5   Jeremiah 51:10
Romans 8:37   1 Corinthians 15:57   Hebrews 2:10   Ephesians 6:10   Jeremiah 9:31
Samuel 18:17   Haggai 2:4,5   John 4:35   Hebrews 10:37

JANUARY 9 EVENING

One thing is needful.
— LUKE 10:42

There be many that say, Who will shew us any good? Lord, lift thou up the light of thy countenance upon us. Thou hast put gladness in my heart, more than in the time that their corn and their wine increased. — As the hart panteth after the water brooks, so panteth my soul after thee, O God. My soul thirsteth for God, for the living God. — O God, thou art my God; early will I seek thee: my soul thirsteth for thee, my flesh longeth for thee in a dry and thirsty land, where no water is. — I am the bread of life: he that cometh to me shall never hunger; and he that believeth on me shall never thirst. Lord, evermore give us this bread. — Mary...sat at Jesus' feet, and heard his word. — One thing have I desired of the Lord, that will I seek after; that I may dwell in the house of the Lord all the days of my life, to behold the beauty of the Lord, and to enquire in his temple.

Psalms 4:6,7, 42:1,2, 63:1   John 6:35,34   Luke 10:39   Psalm 27:4

JANUARY 10 MORNING

I pray God your whole spirit and soul and body
be preserved blameless
unto the coming of our Lord Jesus Christ.
— 1 THESSALONIANS 5:23

Christ loved the church, and gave himself for it; that he might present it to himself a glorious church, not having spot, or wrinkle, or any such thing; but that it should be holy and without blemish. — Whom we preach, warning every man, and teaching every man in all wisdom; that we may present every man perfect in Christ Jesus. — The peace of God which passeth all understanding. — Let the peace of God rule in your hearts, to the which also ye are called in one body. — Our Lord Jesus Christ himself and God, even our Father, which hath loved us, and hath given us everlasting consolation and good hope through grace, comfort your hearts, and stablish you in every good word and work. — Who shall also confirm you unto the end, that ye may be blameless in the day of our Lord Jesus Christ.

Ephesians 5:25,27   Colossians 1:28   Philippians 4:7
Colossians 3:15 2   Thessalonians 2:16,17 1   Corinthians 1:8

JANUARY 10 EVENING

Will God in very deed dwell with men on the earth?
— 2 CHRONICLES 6:18

Let them make me a sanctuary; that I may dwell among them. — I will meet with the children of Israel, and the tabernacle shall be sanctified by my glory. And I will dwell among the children of Israel, and will be their God. — Thou hast ascended on high, thou hast led captivity captive: thou hast received gifts for men; yea, for the rebellious also, that the Lord God might dwell among them. — Ye are the temple of the living God; as God hath said, I will dwell in them, and walk in them; and I will be their God, and they shall be my people. — Your body is the temple of the Holy Ghost which is in you. — Ye...are builded together for an habitation of God through the Spirit. — The heathen shall know that I the Lord do sanctify Israel, when my sanctuary shall be in the midst of them for evermore.

Exodus 25:8, 29:43,45   Psalm 68:18 2   Corinthians 6:16
1 Corinthians 6:19   Ephesians 2:22   Ezekiel 37:28

JANUARY 11 MORNING

Praise waiteth for thee, O God, in Zion.
— PSALM 65

To us there is but one God, the Father, of whom are all things, and we in him; and one Lord Jesus Christ, by whom are all things, and we by him. — All men should honour the Son, even as they honour the Father. He that honoureth not the Son honoureth not the Father which hath sent him. — By him therefore let us offer the sacrifice of praise to God continually, that is, the fruit of our lips giving thanks to his name. — Whoso offereth praise glorifieth me: and to him that ordereth his conversation aright will I shew the salvation of God. — I beheld, and, lo, a great multitude, which no man could number, of all nations, and kindreds, and peoples, and tongues, stood before the throne, and before the Lamb, clothed with white robes, and palms in their hands; and cried with a loud voice, saying, Salvation to our God which sitteth upon the throne, and unto the Lamb. Amen: Blessing, and glory, and wisdom, and thanksgiving, and honour, and power, and might, be unto our God for ever and ever. Amen.

1 Corinthians 8:6   John 5:23   Hebrews 13:15
Psalm 50:23   Revelation 7:9,10,12

JANUARY 11 EVENING

Who redeemeth thy life from destruction.
— PSALM 103:4

Their Redeemer is strong; the Lord of hosts is his name. — I will ransom them from the power of the grave; I will redeem them from death: O death, I will be thy plagues; O grave, I will be thy destruction. — As the children are partakers of flesh and blood, he also himself likewise took part of the same; that through death he might destroy him that had the power of death, that is, the devil; and deliver them who through fear of death were all their lifetime subject to bondage. — He that believeth on the Son hath everlasting life: and he that believeth not the Son shall not see life; but the wrath of God abideth on him. — Ye are dead, and your life is hid with Christ in God. When Christ, who is our life, shall appear, then shall ye also appear with him in glory. — When he shall come to be glorified in his saints, and to be admired in all them that believe.

Jeremiah 50:34   Hosea 13:14   Hebrews 2:14,15
John 3:36   Colossians 3:3,4   2 Thessalonians 1:10

JANUARY 12 MORNING

The only wise God our Saviour
— JUDE 25

Christ Jesus, who of God is made unto us wisdom, and righteousness, and sanctification, and redemption. — Canst thou by searching find out God? Canst thou find out the Almighty unto perfection? It is as high as heaven; what canst thou do? Deeper than hell; what canst thou know? — We speak the wisdom of God in a mystery, even the hidden wisdom, which God ordained before the world unto our glory. — The mystery, which from the beginning of the world hath been hid in God, who created all things by Jesus Christ: to the intent that now unto the principalities and powers in heavenly places might be known, by the church, the manifold wisdom of God. — If any of you lack wisdom, let him ask of God, that giveth to all men liberally, and upbraideth not; and it shall be given him. — The wisdom that is from above is first pure, then peaceable, gentle, and easy to be intreated, full of mercy and good fruits, without partiality, and without hypocrisy.

1 Corinthians 1:30   Job 11:7,8   1 Corinthians 2:7
Ephesians 3:9,10   James 1:5, 3:17

JANUARY 12 EVENING

When shall I arise, and the night be gone?
— JOB 7:4

Watchman, what of the night? The watchman said, The morning cometh. — Yet a little while, and he that shall come will come, and will not tarry. — He shall be as the light of the morning, when the sun riseth, even a morning without clouds. — I go to prepare a place for you. And if I go and prepare a place for you, I will come again, and receive you unto myself; that where I am, there ye may be also. Let not your heart be troubled, neither let it be afraid. Ye have heard how I said unto you, I go away, and come again unto you. — Let all thine enemies perish, O Lord; but let them that love him be as the sun when he goeth forth in his might. — Ye are all the children of light, and the children of the day: we are not of the night, nor of darkness. — There shall be no night there.

Isaiah 21:11,12   Hebrews 10:37   2 Samuel 23:4
John 14:2,27,28   Judges 5:31
1 Thessalonians 5:5   Revelation 21:25

JANUARY 13 MORNING

Thou wilt keep him in perfect peace,
whose mind is stayed on thee:
because he trusteth in thee.
— ISAIAH 26:3

 Cast thy burden upon the Lord, and he shall sustain thee; he shall never suffer the righteous to be moved. — I will trust, and not be afraid: for the Lord JEHOVAH is my strength and my song; he also is become my salvation. — Why are ye fearful, O ye of little faith? — Be careful for nothing; but in every thing by prayer and supplication with thanksgiving let your requests be made known unto God. And the peace of God, which passeth all understanding, shall keep your hearts and minds through Christ Jesus. — In quietness and in confidence shall be your strength. — The effect of righteousness [shall be] quietness and assurance for ever. — Peace I leave with you, my peace I give unto you: not as the world giveth, give I unto you. Let not your heart be troubled, neither let it be afraid. — Peace, from him which is, and which was, and which is to come.

Psalm 55:22 Isaiah 12:2 Matthew 8:26 Philippians 4:6,7
Isaiah 30:15, 32:17 John 14:27 Revelation 1:4

JANUARY 13 EVENING

Let not the sun go down upon your wrath.
— EPHESIANS 4:26

 If thy brother shall trespass against thee, go and tell him his fault between thee and him alone: if he shall hear thee, thou hast gained thy brother...Lord, how oft shall my brother sin against me, and I forgive him? Till seven times? Jesus saith unto him, I say not unto thee, Until seven times: but, Until seventy times seven. — When ye stand praying, forgive, if ye have ought against any: that your Father also which is in heaven may forgive you your trespasses. — Put on, therefore, as the elect of God, holy and beloved, bowels of mercies, kindness, humbleness of mind, meekness, longsuffering; forbearing one another, and forgiving one another, if any man have a quarrel against any: even as Christ forgave you, so also do ye. — Be ye kind one to another, tenderhearted, forgiving one another, even as God for Christ's sake hath forgiven you. — The apostles said unto the Lord, Increase our faith.

Matthew 18:15,21,22 Mark 11:25
Colossians 3:12,13 Ephesians 4:32 Luke 17:5

JANUARY 14 MORNING

My Father is greater than I.
— JOHN 14:28

When ye pray, say, Our Father which art in heaven. — My Father, and your Father...my God and your God. As the Father gave me commandment, even so I do. — The words that I speak unto you I speak not of myself: but the Father that dwelleth in me, he doeth the works. — The Father loveth the Son, and hath given all things into his hand. — Thou hast given him power over all flesh, that he should give eternal life to as many as thou hast given him. — Lord, shew us the Father, and it sufficeth us. Jesus saith unto him, Have I been so long time with you, and yet hast thou not known me, Philip? He that hath seen me hath seen the Father; and how sayest thou then, Shew us the Father? Believest thou not that I am in the Father, and the Father in me? — I and my Father are one. — As the Father hath loved me, so have I loved you: continue ye in my love. If ye keep my commandments, ye shall abide in my love; even as I have kept my Father's commandments, and abide in his love.

Luke 11:2   John 20:17, 14:31,10, 3:35, 17:2, 14:8-10, 10:30, 15:9,10

JANUARY 14 EVENING

[The woman's seed] shall bruise thy head,
and thou shalt bruise his heel.
— GENESIS 3:15

His visage was so marred more than any man, and his form more than the sons of men. — He was wounded for our transgressions, he was bruised for our iniquities: the chastisement of our peace was upon him; and with his stripes we are healed. — This is your hour, and the power of darkness. — Thou couldest have no power at all against me, except it were given thee from above. — The Son of God was manifested, that he might destroy the works of the devil. — He cast out many devils; and suffered not the devils to speak, because they knew him. — All power is given unto me in heaven and in earth. — In my name shall they cast out devils. — The God of peace shall bruise Satan under your feet shortly.

Isaiah 52:14, 53:5   Luke 22:53   John 19:11
1 John 3:8   Mark 1:34   Matthew 28:18
Mark 16:17   Romans 16:20

JANUARY 15 MORNING

*My soul cleaveth unto the dust:
quicken thou me according to thy word.*
— PSALM 119:25

If ye...be risen with Christ, seek those things which are above, where Christ sitteth on the right hand of God. Set your affection on things above, not on things on the earth. For your life is hid with Christ in God. — Our conversation is in heaven; from whence also we look for the Saviour, the Lord Jesus Christ: who shall change our vile body, that it may be fashioned like unto his glorious body, according to the working whereby he is able even to subdue all things unto himself. — The flesh lusteth against the Spirit, and the Spirit against the flesh; and these are contrary the one to the other: so that ye cannot do the things that ye would. — Brethren, we are debtors, not to the flesh, to live after the flesh. For if ye live after the flesh, ye shall die: but if ye through the Spirit do mortify the deeds of the body, ye shall live. — Dearly beloved, I beseech you as strangers and pilgrims, abstain from fleshly lusts, which war against the soul.

Colossians 3:1-3   Philippians 3:20,21
Galatians 5:17   Romans 8:12,13 1   Peter 2:11

JANUARY 15 EVENING

The measure of faith.
— ROMANS 12:3

Him that is weak in the faith. — Strong in faith, giving glory to God. — O thou of little faith, wherefore didst thou doubt? — Great is thy faith: be it unto thee even as thou wilt. — Believe ye that I am able to do this? They said unto him, Yea, Lord... According to your faith be it unto you. — Lord, increase our faith. — Building up yourselves on your most holy faith. — Rooted and built up in him, and established in the faith. — He which stablisheth us with you in Christ...is God. — The God of all grace...after that ye have suffered a while, make you perfect, stablish, strengthen, settle you. — We...that are strong ought to bear the infirmities of the weak, and not to please ourselves. — Let us not... judge one another...but judge this rather, that no man put a stumblingblock or an occasion to fall in his brother's way.

Romans 14:1,20   Matthew 14:31, 15:28, 9:28,29   Luke 17:5 Jude 20
Colossians 2:7 2   Corinthians 1:21 1   Peter 5:10   Romans 15:1, 14:13

JANUARY 16 MORNING

It pleased the Father, that in him should all fulness dwell.
— COLOSSIANS 1:19

The Father loveth the Son, and hath given all things into his hand. — God hath highly exalted him, and given him a name which is above every name: that at the name of Jesus every knee should bow, of things in heaven, and things in earth, and things under the earth; and that every tongue should confess that Jesus Christ is Lord, to the glory of God the Father. — Far above all principality, and power, and might, and dominion, and every name that is named, not only in this world, but also in that which is to come. — By him were all things created, that are in heaven, and that are in earth, visible and invisible, whether they be thrones, or dominions, or principalities, or powers: all things were created by him, and for him. — Christ both died, and rose, and revived, that he might be Lord both of the dead and living. — And ye are complete in him, which is the head of all principality and power. — Of his fulness have all we received.

John 3:35   Philippians 2:9-11   Ephesians 1:21
Colossians 1:16   Romans 14:9   Colossians 2:10   John 1:16

JANUARY 16 EVENING

Write the things which thou hast seen,
and the things which are,
and the things which shall be hereafter.
— REVELATION 1:19

Holy men of God spake as they were moved by the Holy Ghost. — That which we have seen and heard declare we unto you, that ye also may have fellowship with us: and truly our fellowship is with the Father, and with his Son Jesus Christ. — Behold my hands and my feet, that it is I myself: handle me, and see; for a spirit hath not flesh and bones, as ye see me have. And when he had thus spoken, he shewed them his hands and his feet. — He that saw it bare record, and his record is true: and he knoweth that he saith true, that ye might believe. — We have not followed cunningly devised fables, when we made known unto you the power and coming of our Lord Jesus Christ, but were eyewitnesses of his majesty. — That your faith should not stand in the wisdom of men, but in the power of God.

2 Peter 1:21   1 John 1:3   Luke 24:39,40
John 19:35   2 Peter 1:16   1 Corinthians 2:5

JANUARY 17 MORNING

Thou hast in love to my soul
delivered it from the pit of corruption.
— ISAIAH 38:17

God sent his only begotten Son into the world, that we might live through him. Herein is love, not that we loved God, but that he loved us, and sent his Son to be the propitiation for our sins. — Who is a God like unto thee, that pardoneth iniquity, and passeth by the transgression of the remnant of his heritage? He retaineth not his anger for ever, because he delighteth in mercy. He will turn again, he will have compassion upon us; he will subdue our iniquities; and thou wilt cast all their sins into the depths of the sea. — O Lord my God, I cried unto thee, and thou hast healed me. O Lord, thou hast brought up my soul from the grave: thou hast kept me alive, that I should not go down to the pit. — When my soul fainted within me I remembered the Lord: and my prayer came in unto thee, into thine holy temple. — I waited patiently for the Lord. He brought me up...out of an horrible pit, out of the miry clay, and set my feet upon a rock.

1 John 4:9,10   Micah 7:18,19   Psalm 30:2,3   Jonah 2:7   Psalm 40:1,2

JANUARY 17 EVENING

The things which are.
— REVELATION 1:19

Now we see through a glass, darkly. — Now we see not yet all things put under him. — We have...a more sure word of prophecy; whereunto ye do well that ye take heed, as unto a light that shineth in a dark place, until the day dawn, and the day star arise in your hearts. — Thy word is a lamp unto my feet, and a light unto my path. — Beloved, remember ye the words which were spoken before of the apostles of our Lord Jesus Christ; how that they told you there should be mockers in the last time, who should walk after their own ungodly lusts. — The Spirit speaketh expressly, that in the latter times some shall depart from the faith, giving heed to seducing spirits, and doctrines of devils. — Little children, it is the last time. — The night is far spent, the day is at hand: let us therefore cast off the works of darkness, and let us put on the armour of light.

1 Corinthians 13:12   Hebrews 2:8 2   Peter 1:19   Psalm 119:105
Jude 17,18 1   Timothy 4:1 1   John 2:18   Romans 13:12

JANUARY 18 MORNING

Him that was to come.
— ROMANS 5:14

Jesus...made a little lower than the angels for the suffering of death...that he by the grace of God should taste death for every man. — One died for all. — As by one man's disobedience many were made sinners, so by the obedience of one shall many be made righteous. — The first man Adam was made a living soul; the last Adam was made a quickening spirit. — That was not first which is spiritual, but that which is natural; and afterward that which is spiritual. — God said, Let us make man in our image, after our likeness. So God created man in his own image, in the image of God created he him. — God...hath in these last days spoken unto us by his Son, the brightness of his glory, and the express image of his person. — Thou hast given him power over all flesh. — The first man is of the earth, earthy: the second man is the Lord from heaven. As is the earthy, such are they also that are earthy: and as is the heavenly, such are they also that are heavenly.

Hebrews 2:9 2 Corinthians 5:14 Romans 5:19 1 Corinthians 15:45,46 Genesis 1:26,27 Hebrews 1:1-3 John 17:2 1 Corinthians 15:47,48

JANUARY 18 EVENING

Things which shall be hereafter.
— REVELATION 1:19

As it is written, Eye hath not seen, nor ear heard, neither have entered into the heart of man, the things which God hath prepared for them that love him. But God hath revealed them unto us by his Spirit. — The Spirit of truth...will shew you things to come. — Behold, he cometh with clouds; and every eye shall see him, and they also which pierced him: and all kindreds of the earth shall wail because of him. Even so, Amen. — I would not have you to be ignorant, brethren, concerning them which are asleep, that ye sorrow not, even as others which have no hope. For if we believe that Jesus died and rose again, even so them also which sleep in Jesus will God bring with him. For the Lord himself shall descend from heaven, with a shout, with the voice of the archangel, and with the trump of God: and the dead in Christ shall rise first: then we which are alive and remain shall be caught up together with them in the clouds, to meet the Lord in the air: and so shall we ever be with the Lord.

1 Corinthians 2:9,10 John 16:13 Revelation 1:7 1 Thessalonians 4:13,14,16,17

JANUARY 19 MORNING

Serving the Lord with all humility of mind.
— ACTS 20:19

Whosoever will be great among you, let him be your minister; and whosoever will be chief among you, let him be your servant: even as the Son of man came not to be ministered unto, but to minister, and to give his life a ransom for many. — If a man think himself to be something, when he is nothing, he deceiveth himself. — I say, through the grace given unto me, to every man...not to think of himself more highly than he ought to think; but to think soberly, according as God hath dealt to every man the measure of faith. — When ye shall have done all those things which are commanded you, say, We are unprofitable servants: we have done that which was our duty to do. — Our rejoicing is this...that in simplicity and godly sincerity, not with fleshly wisdom, but by the grace of God, we have had our conversation in the world. — We have this treasure in earthen vessels, that the excellency of the power may be of God, and not of us.

Matthew 20:26-28   Galatians 6:3   Romans 12:3
Luke 17:10 2   Corinthians 1:12, 4:7

JANUARY 19 EVENING

We have turned every one to his own way.
— ISAIAH 53:6

Noah...planted a vineyard: and he drank of the wine, and was drunken. — Abram...said unto Sara his wife...Say, I pray thee, thou art my sister: that it may be well with me for thy sake. — Isaac said unto Jacob...Art thou my very son Esau? And he said, I am. — Moses...spake unadvisedly with his lips. — The men took of their victuals, and asked not counsel at the mouth of the Lord. And Joshua made peace with them. — David did that which was right in the eyes of the Lord, and turned not aside from any thing that he commanded him all the days of his life, save only in the matter of Uriah the Hittite. — These all...obtained a good report through faith. — Being justified freely by his grace through the redemption that is in Christ Jesus. — The Lord hath laid on him the iniquity of us all. — Not for your sakes do I this, saith the Lord GOD, be it known unto you: be ashamed and confounded for your own ways.

Genesis 9:20,21, 12:11,13, 27:21,24   Psalm 106:32,33   Joshua 9:14,15
1 Kings 15:5   Hebrews 11:39   Romans 3:24   Isaiah 53:8   Ezekiel 36:32

JANUARY 20 MORNING

His name shall be called Wonderful.
— ISAIAH 9:6

The Word was made flesh, and dwelt among us, (and we beheld his glory, the glory as of the only begotten of the Father) full of grace and truth. — Thou hast magnified thy word above all thy name. — They shall call his name Emmanuel, which being interpreted is, God with us. — JESUS: for he shall save his people from their sins. — All men should honour the Son, even as they honour the Father. — God...hath highly exalted him, and given him a name which is above every name. — Far above all principality, and power, and might, and dominion, and every name that is named, not only in this world, but also in that which is to come; and hath put all things under his feet. — He had a name written, that no man knew, but he himself...KING OF KINGS, AND LORD OF LORDS. — Touching the Almighty, we cannot find him out. — What is his name, and what is his son's name, if thou canst tell?

John 1:14   Psalm 138:2   Matthew 1:23,21   John 5:23   Philippians 2:9
Ephesians 1:21,22   Revelation 19:12,16   Job 37:23   Proverbs 30:4

JANUARY 20 EVENING

The Lord's portion is his people.
— DEUTERONOMY 32:9

Ye are Christ's; and Christ is God's. — I am my beloved's, and his desire is toward me. — I am his. — The Son of God...loved me, and gave himself for me. — Ye are not your own, ye are bought with a price: therefore glorify God in your body, and in your spirit, which are God's. — The Lord hath taken you, and brought you forth out of the iron furnace, even out of Egypt, to be unto him a people of inheritance, as ye are this day. — Ye are God's husbandry, ye are God's building. — Christ as a son over his own house; whose house are we, if we hold fast the confidence and the rejoicing of the hope firm unto the end. — A spiritual house, an holy priesthood. — They shall be mine, saith the Lord of hosts, in that day when I make up my jewels. — All mine are thine, and thine are mine; and I am glorified in them. — The glory of his inheritance in the saints.

1 Corinthians 3:23   Song of Solomon 7:10, 2:16
Galatians 2:20   1 Corinthians 6:19,20   Deuteronomy 4:20   1 Corinthians 3:9
Hebrews 3:6   1 Peter 2:5   Malachi 3:17   John 17:10   Ephesians 1:18

JANUARY 21 MORNING

Every branch that beareth fruit, he purgeth it.
— JOHN 15:2

He is like a refiner's fire, and like fullers' soap: and he shall sit as a refiner and purifier of silver: and he shall purify the sons of Levi, and purge them as gold and silver, that they may offer unto the Lord an offering in righteousness. — We glory in tribulations: knowing that tribulation worketh patience; and patience, experience; and experience, hope: and hope maketh not ashamed; because the love of God is shed abroad in our hearts by the Holy Ghost which is given unto us. — If ye endure chastening, God dealeth with you as with sons, for what son is he whom the Father chasteneth not? But if ye be without chastisement, whereof all are partakers, then are ye bastards, and not sons. Now no chastening for the present seemeth to be joyous, but grievous: nevertheless afterward it yieldeth the peaceable fruit of righteousness unto them which are exercised thereby. Wherefore lift up the hands which hang down, and the feeble knees.

Malachi 3:2,3   Romans 5:3-5   Hebrews 12:7,8,11,12

JANUARY 21 EVENING

Now we call the proud happy.
— MALACHI 3:15

Thus saith the high and lofty One that inhabiteth eternity, whose name is Holy; I dwell in the high and holy place, with him that is of a contrite and humble spirit, to revive the spirit of the humble, and to revive the heart of the contrite ones. — Better it is to be of an humble spirit with the lowly, than to divide the spoil with the proud. — Blessed are the poor in spirit for theirs is the kingdom of heaven. — These six things doth the Lord hate: yea, seven are an abomination unto him: a proud look.... — Every one that is proud of heart is an abomination to the Lord. — Search me, O God, and know my heart: try me, and know my thoughts: and see if there be any wicked way in me, and lead me in the way everlasting. — Grace be unto you, and peace, from God our Father, and the Lord Jesus Christ. I thank my God upon every remembrance of you. — Blessed are the meek: for they shall inherit the earth.

Isaiah 57:15   Proverbs 16:19   Matthew 5:3
Proverbs 6:16,17, 16:5   Psalm 139:23,24
Philippians 1:2.3   Matthew 5:5

JANUARY 22 MORNING

This God is our God for ever and ever:
he will be our guide even unto death.
— PSALM 48:14

    O Lord, thou art my God; I will exalt thee, I will praise thy name; for thou hast done wonderful things; thy counsels of old are faithfulness and truth. — The Lord is the portion of mine inheritance, and of my cup. — He leadeth me in the paths of righteousness, for his name's sake. Yea, though I walk through the valley of the shadow of death, I will fear no evil: for thou art with me; thy rod and thy staff they comfort me. — Thou hast holden me by my right hand. Thou shalt guide me with thy counsel, and afterward receive me to glory. Whom have I in heaven but thee? And there is none upon earth that I desire beside thee. My flesh and my heart faileth: but God is the strength of my heart, and my portion for ever. — Our heart shall rejoice in him, because we have trusted in his holy name. — The Lord will perfect that which concerneth me: thy mercy, O Lord, endureth for ever: forsake not the works of thine own hands.

    Isaiah 25:1   Psalms 16:5, 23:3,4. 73:23-26, 33:21, 138:8

JANUARY 22 EVENING

In the multitude of my thoughts within me
thy comforts delight my soul.
— PSALM 94:19

    When my heart is overwhelmed: lead me to the rock that is higher than I. — O Lord, I am oppressed; undertake for me. — Cast thy burden upon the Lord, and he shall sustain thee. — I am but a little child: I know not how to go out or come in. — If any of you lack wisdom, let him ask of God...and it shall be given him. — Who is sufficient for these things? — I know that in me (that is, in my flesh,) dwelleth no good thing. — My grace is sufficient for thee: for my strength is made perfect in weakness. — Son, be of good cheer; thy sins be forgiven thee...Daughter, be of good comfort; thy faith hath made thee whole. — My soul shall be satisfied as with marrow and fatness...when I remember thee upon my bed, and meditate on thee in the night watches.

    Psalm 61:2   Isaiah 38:14   Psalm 55:22   1 Kings 3:7   James 1:5
    2 Corinthians 2:16   Romans 7:18
    2 Corinthians 12:9   Matthew 9:2,22   Psalm 63:5,6

JANUARY 23 MORNING

Hope maketh not ashamed.
— ROMANS 5:5

I am the Lord:...they shall not be ashamed that wait for me. — Blessed is the man that trusteth in the Lord, and whose hope the Lord is. — Thou wilt keep him in perfect peace, whose mind is stayed on thee: because he trusteth in thee. Trust ye in the Lord for ever: for in the Lord JEHOVAH is everlasting strength. — My soul, wait thou only upon God; for my expectation is from him. He only is my rock and my salvation: he is my defence; I shall not be moved. — I am not ashamed, for I know whom I have believed. — God, willing more abundantly to shew unto the heirs of promise the immutability of his counsel, confirmed it by an oath: that by two immutable things, in which it was impossible for God to lie, we might have a strong consolation, who have fled for refuge to lay hold upon the hope set before us; which hope we have as an anchor of the soul, both sure and stedfast, and which entereth into that within the veil; whither the forerunner is for us entered, even Jesus.

Isaiah 49:23   Jeremiah 17:7   Isaiah 26:3,4
Psalm 62:5,6   2 Timothy 1:12   Hebrews 6:17-20

JANUARY 23 EVENING

The offence of the cross.
— GALATIANS 5:11

If any man will come after me, let him deny himself, and take up his cross, and follow me. — Know ye not that the friendship of the world is enmity with God? Whosoever therefore will be a friend of the world is the enemy of God. — We must through much tribulation enter into the kingdom of God. Whosoever believeth on him shall not be ashamed. — Unto you therefore which believe he is precious: but unto them which be disobedient, the stone which the builders disallowed, the same is made the head of the corner, and a stone of stumbling, and a rock of offence. — God forbid that I should glory, save in the cross of our Lord Jesus Christ, by whom the world is crucified unto me, and I unto the world. — I am crucified with Christ. — They that are Christ's have crucified the flesh with the affections and lusts. — If we suffer, we shall also reign with him: if we deny him, he also will deny us.

Matthew 16:24   James 4:4   Acts 14:22   Romans 9:33   1 Peter 2:7,8
Galatians 6:1, 2:20, 5:24   2 Timothy 2:12

JANUARY 24 MORNING

The Lord is at hand.
— PHILIPPIANS 4:5

The Lord himself shall descend from heaven with a shout, with the voice of the archangel, and with the trump of God: and the dead in Christ shall rise first: then we which are alive and remain, shall be caught up together with them in the clouds, to meet the Lord in the air: and so shall we ever be with the Lord. Wherefore comfort one another with these words. — He which testifieth these things saith, Surely I come quickly; Amen. Even so, come, Lord Jesus. — Wherefore, beloved, seeing that ye look for such things, be diligent that ye may be found of him in peace, without spot, and blameless. — Abstain from all appearance of evil. And the very God of peace sanctify you wholly; and I pray God your whole spirit and soul and body be preserved blameless unto the coming of our Lord Jesus Christ. Faithful is he that calleth you, who also will do it. — Be ye also patient; stablish your hearts; for the coming of the Lord draweth nigh.

1 Thessalonians 4:16-18   Revelation 22:20
2 Peter 3:14 1   Thessalonians 5:22-24   James 5:8

JANUARY 24 EVENING

The choice vine.
— GENESIS 49:11

My wellbeloved hath a vineyard in a very fruitful hill: and he fenced it, and gathered out the stones thereof, and planted it with the choicest vine...and he looked that it should bring forth grapes, and it brought forth wild grapes. — Yet I had planted thee a noble vine, wholly a right seed: how then art thou turned into the degenerate plant of a strange vine unto me. — The works of the flesh are manifest, which are these; adultery, fornication, uncleanness... envyings, murders, drunkenness, revellings, and such like:...but the fruit of the Spirit is love, joy, peace, longsuffering, gentleness, goodness, faith, meekness, temperance. — I am the true vine, and my Father is the husbandman. Every branch in me that beareth not fruit he taketh away: and every branch that beareth fruit, he purgeth it, that it may bring forth more fruit. Abide in me, and I in you... Herein is my Father glorified, that ye bear much fruit; so shall ye be my disciples.

Isaiah 5:1,2   Jeremiah 2:21   Galatians 5:19,21-23   John 15:1,2,4,8

JANUARY 25 MORNING

*The righteousness of God
which is by faith of Jesus Christ
unto all and upon all them that believe.*
— ROMANS 3:22

He hath made him who knew no sin to be sin for us; that we might be made the righteousness of God in him. — Christ hath redeemed us from the curse of the law, being made a curse for us. — Who of God is made unto us wisdom, and righteousness, and sanctification, and redemption. — Not by works of righteousness which we have done, but according to his mercy he saved us, by the washing of regeneration, and renewing of the Holy Ghost; which he shed on us abundantly through Jesus Christ our Saviour. — I count all things but loss for the excellency of the knowledge of Christ Jesus my Lord: for whom I have suffered the loss of all things, and do count them but dung, that I may win Christ, and be found in him, not having mine own righteousness, which is of the law, but that which is through the faith of Christ, the righteousness which is of God by faith.

2 Corinthians 5:21   Galatians 3:13
1 Corinthians 1:30   Titus 3:5,6   Philippians 3:8,9

JANUARY 25 EVENING

The spirit of adoption, whereby we cry, Abba, Father.
— ROMANS 8:15

Jesus...lifted up his eyes to heaven, and said, Father...Holy Father...O righteous Father. — He said, Abba, Father. — Because ye are sons, God hath sent forth the Spirit of his Son into your hearts, crying, Abba, Father. — For through him we both have access by one Spirit unto the Father. Now therefore ye are no more strangers and foreigners, but fellow citizens with the saints and of the household of God. — Doubtless thou art our father...thou, O Lord, art our father, our redeemer; thy name is from everlasting. — I will arise and go to my father, and will say unto him, Father, I have sinned against heaven, and before thee, and am no more worthy to be called thy son: make me as one of thy hired servants. And he arose, and came to his father. — Be ye therefore followers of God, as dear children.

John 17:1,11,25 Mark. 14:36   Galatians 4:6   Ephesians 2:18,19
Isaiah 63:16   Luke 15:18-20   Ephesians 5:1

JANUARY 26 MORNING

Let us go forth unto him without the camp,
bearing his reproach.
For here have we no continuing city,
but we seek one to come.
— HEBREWS 13:13,14

Beloved, think it not strange concerning the fiery trial which is to try you, as though some strange thing happened unto you: but rejoice, inasmuch as ye are partakers of Christ's sufferings; that, when his glory shall be revealed, ye may be glad also with exceeding joy. — As ye are partakers of the sufferings, so shall ye be also of the consolation. — If ye be reproached for the name of Christ, happy are ye; for the Spirit of glory and of God resteth upon you: on their part he is evil spoken of, but on your part he is glorified. — They departed from the presence of the council, rejoicing that they were counted worthy to suffer shame for his name. — Choosing rather to suffer affliction with the people of God, than to enjoy the pleasures of sin for a season; esteeming the reproach of Christ greater riches than the treasures in Egypt: for he had respect unto the recompence of the reward.

1 Peter 4:12.13   2 Corinthians 1:7   1 Peter 4:14   Acts 5:41   Hebrews 11:25,26

JANUARY 26 EVENING

The Lord Jesus Christ...shall change our vile body,
that it may be fashioned like unto his glorious body.
— PHILIPPIANS 3:20,21

Upon the likeness of the throne was the likeness as the appearance of a man above upon it. And I saw as the colour of amber, as the appearance of fire round about within it, from the appearance of his loins even upward, and from the appearance of his loins even downward, I saw as it were the appearance of fire, and it had brightness round about. This was the appearance of the likeness of the glory of the Lord. — We all, with open face, beholding as in a glass the glory of the Lord, are changed into the same image from glory to glory, even as by the Spirit of the Lord. — It doth not yet appear what we shall be: but we know that, when he shall appear, we shall be like him; for we shall see him as he is. — They shall hunger no more, neither thirst any more. — They sing the Song of Moses the servant of God, and the Song of the Lamb.

Ezekiel 1:26-28   2 Corinthians 3:18   1 John 3:2   Revelation 7:16, 15:3

JANUARY 27 MORNING

Ye know that he was manifested to take away our sins:
and in him is no sin.
— 1 JOHN 3:5

God...hath in these last days spoken unto us by his Son, who being the brightness of his glory, and the express image of his person, and upholding all things by the word of his power, when he had by himself purged our sins, sat down on the right hand of the Majesty on high. — He hath made him to be sin for us, who knew no sin; that we might be made the righteousness of God in him. — Pass the time of your sojourning here in fear: forasmuch as ye know that ye were not redeemed with corruptible things, as silver and gold;...but with the precious blood of Christ, as of a lamb without blemish and without spot: who verily was foreordained before the foundation of the world, but was manifest in these last times for you. — The love of Christ constraineth us; because we thus judge, that if one died for all, then were all dead: and that he died for all, that they which live should not henceforth live unto themselves, but unto him which died for them, and rose again.

Hebrews 1:13 2 Corinthians 5:21 1 Peter 1:17-20 2 Corinthians 5:14,15

JANUARY 27 EVENING

I have set before you life and death,
blessing and cursing:
therefore choose life.
— DEUTERONOMY 30:19

For I have no pleasure in the death of him that dieth, saith the Lord God: wherefore turn yourselves, and live ye. — If I had not come and spoken unto them, they had not had sin: but now they have no cloke for their sin. — That servant, which knew his lord's will, and prepared not himself, neither did according to his will, shall be beaten with many stripes. — The wages of sin is death; but the gift of God is eternal life through Jesus Christ our Lord. — He that believeth on the Son hath everlasting life: and he that believeth not the Son shall not see life; but the wrath of God abideth on him. — Know ye not, that to whom ye yield yourselves servants to obey, his servants ye are to whom ye obey; whether of sin unto death, or of obedience unto righteousness? — If any man serve me, let him follow me; and where I am, there shall also my servant be: if any man serve me, him will my Father honour.

Ezekiel 18:32 John 15:22 Luke 12:47
Romans 6:23 John 3:36 Romans 6:16 John 12:26

JANUARY 28 MORNING

As thy days, so shall thy strength be.
— DEUTERONOMY 33:25

When they shall lead you, and deliver you up, take no thought beforehand what ye shall speak, neither do ye premeditate: but whatsoever shall be given you in that hour, that speak ye: for it is not ye that speak, but the Holy Ghost. — Take no thought for the morrow: for the morrow shall take thought for the things of itself. Sufficient unto the day is the evil thereof. — The God of Israel is he that giveth strength and power unto his people. Blessed be God. — He giveth power to the faint; and to them that have no might he increaseth strength. — My grace is sufficient for thee: for my strength is made perfect in weakness. Most gladly therefore will I rather glory in my infirmities, that the power of Christ may rest upon me. Therefore I take pleasure in infirmities, in reproaches, in necessities, in persecutions, in distresses for Christ's sake: for when I am weak, then am I strong. — I can do all things through Christ which strengtheneth me. — O my soul, thou hast trodden down strength.

Matthew 13:11, 6:34   Psalm 68:35   Isaiah 40:29
2 Corinthians 12:9,10   Philippians 4:13   Judges 5:21

JANUARY 28 EVENING

Awake, O north wind, and...blow upon my garden,
that the spices thereof may flow out.
— SONG OF SOLOMON 4:16

No chastening for the present seemeth to be joyous, but grievous: nevertheless afterward it yieldeth the peaceable fruit of righteousness unto them which are exercised thereby. — The fruit of the Spirit. — He stayeth his rough wind in the day of the east wind. — Like as a father pitieth his children, so the Lord pitieth them that fear him. — Though our outward man perish, yet the inward man is renewed day by day. For our light affliction, which is but for a moment, worketh for us a far more exceeding and eternal weight of glory; while we look not at the things which are seen, but at the things which are not seen. — Though [Jesus] were a Son, yet learned he obedience by the things which he suffered. — In all points tempted like as we are, yet without sin.

Hebrews 12:11   Galatians 5:22   Isaiah 27:8
Psalm 103:13 2   Corinthians 4:16-18   Hebrews 5:8, 4:15

JANUARY 29 MORNING

Thou God seest me.
— GENESIS 16:13

O Lord, thou hast searched me, and known me. Thou knowest my downsitting and mine uprising, thou understandest my thought afar off. Thou compassest my path and my lying down, and art acquainted with all my ways. For there is not a word in my tongue, but, lo, O Lord, thou knowest it altogether... Such knowledge is too wonderful for me: it is high, I cannot attain unto it. — The eyes of the Lord are in every place, beholding the evil and the good. — The ways of man are before the eyes of the Lord, and he pondereth all his goings. — God knoweth your hearts: for that which is highly esteemed among men is abomination in the sight of God. — The eyes of the Lord run to and fro throughout the whole earth, to shew himself strong in the behalf of them whose heart is perfect toward him. — Jesus...knew all men, and needed not that any should testify of man; for he knew what was in man. — Lord, thou knowest all things; thou knowest that I love thee.

Psalm 139:1-4,6   Proverbs 15:3, 5:21   Luke 16:15
2 Chronicles 16:9   John 2:24,25, 21:17

JANUARY 29 EVENING

I will praise thee, O Lord my God, with all my heart:
and I will glorify thy name for evermore.
— PSALM 86:12

Whoso offereth praise glorifieth me. — It is a good thing to give thanks unto the Lord, and to sing praises unto thy name, O most High: to shew forth thy lovingkindness in the morning, and thy faithfulness every night. — Let every thing that hath breath praise the Lord. — I beseech you...brethren, by the mercies of God, that ye present your bodies a living sacrifice, holy, acceptable unto God, which is your reasonable service. — Jesus...that he might sanctify the people with his own blood, suffered without the gate. By him therefore let us offer the sacrifice of praise to God continually, that is, the fruit of our lips giving thanks to his name. — Giving thanks always for all things unto God and the Father in the name of our Lord Jesus Christ. — Worthy is the Lamb that was slain to receive power, and riches, and wisdom, and strength, and honour, and glory, and blessing.

Psalms 50:23, 92:1,2, 150:6   Romans 12:1
Hebrews 13:12,15   Ephesians 5:20   Revelation 5:12

JANUARY 30 MORNING

*Let us run with patience the race that is set before us,
looking unto Jesus the author and finisher of our faith.*
— HEBREWS 12:1,2

If any man will come after me, let him deny himself, and take up his cross daily, and follow me. — Whosoever he be of you that forsaketh not all that he hath, he cannot be my disciple. — Let us therefore cast off the works of darkness. — Every man that striveth for the mastery is temperate in all things. Now they do it to obtain a corruptible crown; but we an incorruptible. I therefore so run, not as uncertainly; so fight I, not as one that beateth the air: but I keep under my body, and bring it into subjection: lest that by any means, when I have preached to others, I myself should be a castaway. — Brethren, I count not myself to have apprehended: but this one thing I do, forgetting those things which are behind, and reaching forth unto those things which are before, I press toward the mark for the prize of the high calling of God in Christ Jesus. — Then shall we know, if we follow on to know the Lord.

Luke 9:23, 14:33   Romans 13:12
1 Corinthians 9:25,27   Philippians 3:13,14   Hosea 6:3

JANUARY 30 EVENING

It is good for a man that he bear the yoke in his youth.
— LAMENTATIONS 3:27

Train up a child in the way he should go: and when he is old, he will not depart from it. — We have had fathers of our flesh, which corrected us; and we gave them reverence: shall we not much rather be in subjection unto the Father of spirits, and live? For they verily for a few days chastened us after their own pleasure; but he for our profit, that we might be partakers of his holiness. — Before I was afflicted I went astray: but now have I kept thy word. It is good for me that I have been afflicted; that I might learn thy statutes. — I know the thoughts that I think toward you, saith the Lord, thoughts of peace, and not of evil, to give you an expected end. — Humble yourselves, therefore under the mighty hand of God, that he may exalt you in due time.

Proverbs 22:6   Hebrews 12:9,10   Psalm 119:67,71
Jeremiah 29:11 1   Peter 5:6

JANUARY 31 MORNING

*If ye will not drive out the inhabitants of the land
from before you...those which ye let remain of them
shall be pricks in your eyes, and thorns in your sides,
and shall vex you in the land wherein ye dwell.*
— NUMBERS 33:55

Fight the good fight of faith. — The weapons of our warfare are not carnal, but mighty through God to the pulling down of strongholds; casting down imaginations...and bringing into captivity every thought to the obedience of Christ. — Brethren, we are debtors, not to the flesh, to live after the flesh. For if ye live after the flesh, ye shall die; but if ye through the Spirit do mortify the deeds of the body, ye shall live. — The flesh lusteth against the Spirit, and the Spirit against the flesh; and these are contrary the one to the other: so that ye cannot do the things that ye would. — I see another law in my members, warring against the law of my mind, and bringing me into captivity to the law of sin which is in my members. — We are more than conquerors through him that loved us.

1 Timothy 6:12 2 Corinthians 10:4,5
Romans 8:12,13 Galatians 5:17 Romans 7:23, 8:37

JANUARY 31 EVENING

*If a man sin against the Lord,
who shall intreat for him?*
— 1 SAMUEL 2:25

If any man sin, we have an advocate with the Father, Jesus Christ the righteous: and he is the propitiation for our sins: and not for ours only, but also for the sins of the whole world. — Whom God hath set forth to be a propitiation through faith in his blood, to declare his righteousness for the remission of sins that are past, through the forbearance of God; to declare, I say, at this time his righteousness: that he might be just, and the justifier of him which believeth in Jesus. — He is gracious unto him, and saith, Deliver him from going down to the pit: I have found a ransom. — What shall we then say to these things? If God be for us, who can be against us? It is God that justifieth. Who is he that condemneth? It is Christ that died, yea, rather, that is risen again, who is even at the right hand of God, who also maketh intercession for us.

1 John 2:1,2 Romans 3:25,26 Job 33:24 Romans 8:31,33,34

FEBRUARY 1 MORNING

Whom having not seen, ye love.
— 1 PETER 1:8

We walk by faith, not by sight. — We love him, because he first loved us. — And we have known and believed the love that God hath to us. God is love; and he that dwelleth in love dwelleth in God, and God in him. — In whom ye trusted, after that ye heard the word of truth, the gospel of your salvation: in whom also after that ye believed, ye were sealed with that Holy Spirit of promise. — God would make known what is the riches of the glory of this mystery among the Gentiles; which is Christ in you, the hope of glory. — If a man say, I love God, and hateth his brother, he is a liar: for he that loveth not his brother whom he hath seen, how can he love God whom he hath not seen? — Jesus saith unto him, Thomas, because thou hast seen me, thou hast believed: blessed are they that have not seen, and yet have believed. — Blessed are all they that put their trust in him.

2 Corinthians 5:7   1 John 4:19,16   Ephesians 1:13
Colossians 1:27   1 John 4:20, 20:29   Psalm 2:12

FEBRUARY 1 EVENING

THE LORD OUR RIGHTEOUSNESS.
— JEREMIAH 23:6

We are all as an unclean thing, and all our righteousnesses are as filthy rags. — I will go in the strength of the Lord God: I will make mention of thy righteousness, even of thine only. — I will greatly rejoice in the Lord, my soul shall be joyful in my God; for he hath clothed me with the garments of salvation, he hath covered me with the robe of righteousness, as a bridegroom decketh himself with ornaments, and as a bride adorneth herself with her jewels. — Bring forth the best robe, and put it on him. — To her was granted that she should be arrayed in fine linen, clean and white: for the fine linen is the righteousness of saints. — I count all things but loss for the excellency of the knowledge of Christ Jesus my Lord...that I may win Christ, and be found in him, not having mine own righteousness, which is of the law, but that which is through the faith of Christ, the righteousness which is of God by faith.

Isaiah 64:6   Psalm 71:16   Isaiah 61:10
Luke 15:22   Revelation 19:8   Philippians 3:8-9

FEBRUARY 2 MORNING

Oh that thou wouldest keep me from evil.
— 1 CHRONICLES 4:10

Why sleep ye? Rise and pray, lest ye enter into temptation. — The spirit indeed is willing, but the flesh is weak. — Two things have I required of thee; deny me them not before I die: remove far from me vanity and lies: give me neither poverty nor riches, feed me with food convenient for me: lest I be full and deny thee, and say, Who is the Lord? or lest I be poor, and steal, and take the name of my God in vain. — The Lord shall preserve thee from all evil: he shall preserve thy soul. — I will deliver thee out of the hand of the wicked, and I will redeem thee out of the hand of the terrible. — He that is begotten of God keepeth himself, and that wicked one toucheth him not. — Because thou hast kept the word of my patience, I also will keep thee from the hour of temptation, which shall come upon all the world, to try them that dwell upon the earth. — The Lord knoweth how to deliver the godly out of temptations.

Luke 22:46   Matthew 26:41
Proverbs 30:7-9   Psalm 121:7   Jeremiah 15:21
1 John 5:18   Revelation 3:10   2 Peter 2:9

FEBRUARY 2 EVENING

One star differeth from another star in glory.
— 1 CORINTHIANS 15:41

By the way they had disputed among themselves, who should be the greatest. And he sat down, and called the twelve, and saith unto them, If any man desire to be first, the same shall be last of all. — Be clothed with humility: for God resisteth the proud, and giveth grace to the humble. Humble yourselves therefore under the mighty hand of God, that he may exalt you in due time. — Let this mind be in you, which was also in Christ Jesus: who made himself of no reputation, and took upon him the form of a servant, and was made in the likeness of men. Wherefore God also hath highly exalted him, and given him a name which is above every name: that at the name of Jesus every knee should bow. — They that be wise shall shine as the brightness of the firmament; and they that turn many to righteousness as the stars for ever and ever.

Mark 9:34,35   1 Peter 5:5,6
Philippians 2:5-7,9,10   Daniel 12:3

FEBRUARY 3 MORNING

Be strong, and work;
for I am with you, saith the Lord of hosts.
— HAGGAI 2:4

I am the vine, ye are the branches: he that abideth in me, and I in him, the same bringeth forth much fruit: for without me ye can do nothing. — I can do all things through Christ which strengtheneth me. — Strong in the Lord, and in the power of his might. — The joy of the Lord is your strength. — Thus said the Lord of hosts; Let your hands be strong, ye that hear in these days these words by the mouth of the prophets. — Strengthen ye the weak hands, and confirm the feeble knees. Say to them that are of a fearful heart, Be strong, fear not. — The Lord looked upon him, and said, Go in this thy might. — If God be for us, who can be against us? — Therefore seeing we have this ministry, as we have received mercy, we faint not. — Let us not be weary in well doing: for in due season we shall reap, if we faint not. — Thanks be to God, which giveth us the victory through our Lord Jesus Christ.

John 15:5   Philippians 4:13   Ephesians 6:10   Nehemiah 8:10   Zechariah 8:9
Isaiah 35:3,4   Judges 6:14   Romans 8:31   2 Corinthians 4:1   Galatians 6:9
1 Corinthians 15:57

FEBRUARY 3 EVENING

The darkness hideth not from thee.
— PSALM 139:12

His eyes are upon the ways of man, and he seeth all his goings. There is no darkness, nor shadow of death, where the workers of iniquity may hide themselves. — Can any hide himself in secret places that I shall not see him?... Do not I fill heaven and earth? saith the Lord. — Thou shalt not be afraid for the terror by night...nor for the pestilence that walketh in darkness...Because thou hast made the Lord, which is my refuge, even the Most High, thy habitation; there shall no evil befall thee, neither shall any plague come nigh thy dwelling. — He that keepeth thee will not slumber. The Lord is thy keeper: the Lord is thy shade upon thy right hand. The sun shall not smite thee by day, nor the moon by night. The Lord shall preserve thee from all evil. — Yea, though I walk through the valley of the shadow of death, I will fear no evil, for thou art with me.

Job 34:21,22   Jeremiah 23:24
Psalms 91:5,6,9,10, 121:3,5-7, 23:4

FEBRUARY 4 MORNING

*The Lord hath said unto you,
Ye shall henceforth return no more that way.*
— DEUTERONOMY 17:16

Truly if they had been mindful of that country from whence they came out, they might have had opportunity to have returned. But now they desire a better country, that is a heavenly. Choosing rather to suffer affliction with the people of God, than to enjoy the pleasures of sin for a season; esteeming the reproach of Christ greater riches than the treasures in Egypt. — The just shall live by faith: but if any man draw back, my soul shall have no pleasure in him. But we are not of them who draw back unto perdition, but of them that believe to the saving of the soul. — No man, having put his hand to the plough, and looking back, is fit for the kingdom of God. — God forbid that I should glory, save in the cross of our Lord Jesus Christ, by whom the world is crucified unto me, and I unto the world. — Come out from among them, and be ye separate, saith the Lord, and touch not the unclean thing; and I will receive you. — He which hath begun a good work in you, will perform it until the day of Jesus Christ.

Hebrews 11:15,16,25,26, 10:38,39   Luke 9:62
Galatians 6:14 2 Corinthians 6:17   Philippians 1:6

FEBRUARY 4 EVENING

They talk to the grief of those whom thou hast wounded.
— PSALM 69:26

I was but a little displeased, and they helped forward the affliction. — Brethren, if a man be overtaken in a fault, ye which are spiritual, restore such an one in the spirit of meekness; considering thyself, lest thou also be tempted. — He which converteth the sinner from the error of his way shall save a soul from death, and shall hide a multitude of sins. — Comfort the feebleminded, support the weak, be patient toward all men. — Let us not...judge one another any more: but judge this rather, that no man put a stumblingblock or an occasion to fall in his brother's way. — We...that are strong ought to bear the infirmities of the weak and not to please ourselves. — Charity... rejoiceth not in iniquity. — Let him that thinketh he standeth take heed lest he fall.

Zechariah 1:15   Galatians 6:1   James 5:20
1 Thessalonians 5:14   Romans 14:13, 15:1
1 Corinthians 13:4,6, 10:12

FEBRUARY 5 MORNING

*I am come that they might have life,
and that they might have it more abundantly.*
— JOHN 10:10

In the day that thou eatest thereof thou shalt surely die. — She took of the fruit thereof, and did eat, and gave also unto her husband with her; and he did eat. — The wages of sin is death; but the gift of God is eternal life through Jesus Christ our Lord. — If by one man's offence death reigned by one; much more they which receive abundance of grace and of the gift of righteousness shall reign in life by one, Jesus Christ. — Since by man came death, by man came also the resurrection of the dead. For as in Adam all die, even so in Christ shall all be made alive. — Our Saviour Jesus Christ...hath abolished death, and hath brought life and immortality to light through the gospel. — God hath given to us eternal life, and this life is in his Son. He that hath the Son hath life; and he that hath not the Son of God hath not life. — For God sent not his Son into the world to condemn the world; but that the world through him might be saved.

Genesis 2:17, 3:6   Romans 6:23, 5:17 1   Corinthians 15:21,22
2 Timothy 1:10 1   John 5:11,12   John 3:17

FEBRUARY 5 EVENING

The judgment-seat.
— 1 CORINTHIANS 5:10

We are sure that the judgment of God is according to truth. — When the Son of man shall come in his glory, and all the holy angels with him, then shall he sit upon the throne of his glory: and before him shall be gathered all nations: and he shall separate them one from another, as a shepherd divideth his sheep from the goats. — Then shall the righteous shine forth as the sun, in the kingdom of their Father. — Who shall lay any thing to the charge of God's elect? It is God that justifieth. Who is he that condemneth? It is Christ that died, yea, rather, that is risen again, who is even at the right hand of God, who also maketh intercession for us. — There is therefore now no condemnation to them which are in Christ Jesus. — We are chastened of the Lord, that we should not be condemned with the world.

Romans 2:2   Matthew 25:31,32, 13:43
Romans 8:33,34,1 1   Corinthians 11:32

FEBRUARY 6 MORNING

*The grace of our Lord was exceeding abundant
with faith and love which is in Christ Jesus.*
— 1 TIMOTHY 1:14

Ye know the grace of our Lord Jesus Christ, that, though he was rich, yet for your sakes he became poor, that ye through his poverty might become rich. — For where sin abounded, grace did much more abound. — That in the ages to come he might shew the exceeding riches of his grace in his kindness toward us through Christ Jesus. For by grace are ye saved through faith; and that not of yourselves: it is the gift of God: not of works, lest any man should boast. — Knowing that a man is not justified by the works of the law, but by the faith of Jesus Christ, even we have believed in Jesus Christ, that we might be justified by the faith of Christ, and not by the works of the law: for by the works of the law shall no flesh be justified. — According to his mercy he saved us, by the washing of regeneration, and renewing of the Holy Ghost; which he shed on us abundantly through Jesus Christ our Saviour.

2 Corinthians 8:9   Romans 5:20   Ephesians 2:7-9   Galatians 2:16   Titus 3:5,6

FEBRUARY 6 EVENING

I am...the bright and morning Star.
— REVELATION 22:16

There shall come a star out of Jacob. — The night is far spent, the day is at hand: let us therefore cast off the works of darkness, and let us put on the armour of light. — Until the day break, and the shadows flee away, turn, my beloved, and be thou like a roe or a young hart upon the mountains of Bethel. — Watchman, what of the night? The watchman said, The morning cometh, and also the night: if ye will enquire, enquire ye: return, come. — I am the light of the world. — I will give him the morning star. — Take ye heed, watch and pray: for ye know not when the time is. For the Son of man is as a man taking a far journey, who left his house, and gave authority to his servants, and to every man his work, and commanded the porter to watch. Watch ye therefore...lest coming suddenly he find you sleeping. And what I say unto you I say unto all, Watch.

Numbers 24:17   Romans 13:12   Song of Solomon 2:17
Isaiah 25:11,12   John 8:12   Revelation 2:28   Mark 13:33,37

FEBRUARY 7 MORNING

When thou has eaten and are full...
thou shalt bless the Lord thy God
for the good land which he hath given thee.
— DEUTERONOMY 8:10

Beware that thou forget not the Lord thy God. — One of them, when he saw that he was healed, turned back, and with a loud voice glorified God, and fell down on his face at his feet, giving him thanks: and he was a Samaritan. And Jesus answering said, Were there not ten cleansed? But where are the nine? There are not found that returned to give glory to God, save this stranger. — Every creature of God is good, and nothing to be refused, if it be received with thanksgiving: for it is sanctified by the word of God and prayer. — He that eateth, eateth to the Lord, for he giveth God thanks. — The blessing of the Lord, it maketh rich, and he addeth no sorrow with it. — Bless the Lord, O my soul: and all that is within me, bless his holy name. Bless the Lord, O my soul... who forgiveth all thine iniquities...who crowneth thee with lovingkindness and tender mercies.

Deuteronomy 8:11   Luke 17:15-18   1 Timothy 4:4,5
Romans 14:6   Proverbs 10:22   Psalm 103:1-4

FEBRUARY 7 EVENING

Jesus...was moved with compassion toward them.
— MATTHEW 14:14

Jesus Christ the same yesterday, and today, and for ever. — We have not an high priest which cannot be touched with the feeling of our infirmities; but was in all points tempted like as we are, yet without sin. — Who can have compassion on the ignorant, and on them that are out of the way. — He cometh, and findeth them sleeping, and saith unto Peter, Simon, sleepest thou? Couldest not thou watch one hour? Watch ye and pray, lest ye enter into temptation. The spirit truly is ready, but the flesh is weak. — Like as a father pitieth his children, so the Lord pitieth them that fear him. For he knoweth our frame; he remembereth that we are dust. — Thou, O Lord, art a God full of compassion, and gracious, longsuffering, and plenteous in mercy and truth. O turn unto me, and have mercy upon me; give thy strength unto thy servant, and save the son of thine handmaid.

Hebrews 13:8, 4:15, 5:2   Mark 14:37,38   Psalms 103:13,14, 86:15,16

FEBRUARY 8 MORNING

Henceforth I call you not servants;
for the servant knoweth not what his lord doeth:
but I have called you friends.
— JOHN 15:15

The Lord said, shall I hide from Abraham that thing which I do? — It is given unto you to know the mysteries of the kingdom of heaven. — God hath revealed them unto us by his Spirit: for the Spirit searcheth all things, yea, the deep things of God. — Even the hidden wisdom, which God ordained before the world unto our glory. — Blessed is the man whom thou choosest, and causest to approach unto thee, that he may dwell in thy courts: we shall be satisfied with the goodness of thy house, even of thy holy temple. — The secret of the Lord is with them that fear him: and he will shew them his covenant. — I have given unto them the words which thou gavest me; and they have received them, and have known surely that I came out from thee, and they have believed that thou didst send me. — Ye are my friends, if ye do whatsoever I command you.

Genesis 18:17   Matthew 13:11   1 Corinthians 2:10,7
Psalms 65:4, 25:14   John 17:8, 15:14

FEBRUARY 8 EVENING

Thou shalt call thy walls Salvation,
and thy gates Praise.
— ISAIAH 60:18

The wall of the city had twelve foundations, and in them the names of the twelve apostles of the Lamb. — Ye are no more strangers and foreigners, but fellow citizens with the saints, and of the household of God, and are built upon the foundation of the apostles and prophets, Jesus Christ himself being the chief corner stone; in whom all the building fitly framed together groweth unto an holy temple in the Lord: in whom ye also are builded together for an habitation of God through the Spirit. — If so be ye have tasted that the Lord is gracious. To whom coming, as unto a living stone, disallowed indeed of men, but chosen of God, and precious, ye also, as lively stones, are built up a spiritual house, an holy priesthood, to offer up spiritual sacrifices, acceptable to God by Jesus Christ. — Praise waiteth for thee, O God, in Zion.

Revelation 21:14   Ephesians 2:19-22   1 Peter 2:3-5   Psalm 65:1

FEBRUARY 9 MORNING

Now he is comforted.
— LUKE 16:25

Thy sun shall no more go down; neither shall thy moon withdraw itself: for the Lord shall be thine everlasting light, and the days of thy mourning shall be ended. — He will swallow up death in victory; and the Lord God will wipe away tears from off all faces; and the rebuke of his people shall he take away from off all the earth. — These are they which name out of great tribulation, and have washed their robes, and made them white in the blood of the Lamb. Therefore are they before the throne of God, and serve him day and night in his temple: and he that sitteth on the throne shall dwell among them. They shall hunger no more, neither thirst any more; neither shall the sun light on them, nor any heat. For the Lamb which is in the midst of the throne shall feed them, and shall lead them unto living fountains of waters. — God shall wipe away all tears from their eyes; and there shall be no more death, neither sorrow, nor crying, neither shall there be any more pain: for the former things are passed away.

Isaiah 60:20, 25:8   Revelation 7:14-17, 21:4

FEBRUARY 9 EVENING

The night cometh when no man can work.
— JOHN 9:4

Blessed are the dead which die in the Lord…they…from their labours; and their works do follow them. — There the wicked cease from troubling; and there the weary be at rest. — Samuel said to Saul, Why hast thou disquieted me, to bring me up? — Whatsoever thy hand findeth to do, do it with thy might; for there is no work, nor device, nor knowledge, nor wisdom, in the grave, whither thou goest. — The dead praise not the Lord, neither any that go down into silence. — I am now ready to be offered, and the time of my departure is at hand. I have fought a good fight, I have finished my course, I have kept the faith: henceforth there is laid up for me a crown of righteousness, which the Lord, the righteous judge, shall give me at that day. — There remaineth therefore a rest to the people of God. For he that is entered into his rest, he also hath ceased from his own works, as God did from his.

Revelation 14:13   Job 3:17   1 Samuel 28:15
Ecclesiastes 9:10   Psalm 115:17   2 Timothy 4:6-8   Hebrews 4:9,10

FEBRUARY 10 MORNING

*The light of the body is the eye:
therefore when thine eye is single
thy whole body also is full of light.*
— LUKE 11:34

    The natural man receiveth not the things of the Spirit of God: for they are foolishness unto him: neither can he know them, because they are spiritually discerned. — Open thou mine eyes, that I may behold wondrous things out of thy law. — I am the light of the world: he that followeth me shall not walk in darkness, but shall have the light of life. — We all, with open face beholding as in a glass the glory of the Lord, are changed into the same image...even as by the Spirit of the Lord. — God, who commanded the light to shine out of darkness, hath shined in our hearts, to give the light of the knowledge of the glory of God in the face of Jesus Christ. — The God of our Lord Jesus Christ, the Father of glory, give unto you the spirit of wisdom and revelation in the knowledge of him...that ye may know what is the hope of his calling, and what the riches of the glory of his inheritance in the saints.

1 Corinthians 2:14   Psalm 119:18   John 8:12
2 Corinthians 3:18, 4:6   Ephesians 1:17,18

FEBRUARY 10 EVENING

*He smote the rock,
that the waters gushed out,
and the streams overflowed.*
— PSALM 78:20

    All our fathers were under the cloud, and all passed through the sea; and were all baptized unto Moses in the cloud and in the sea; and did all eat the same spiritual meat; and did all drink the same spiritual drink: for they drank of that spiritual Rock that followed them: and that rock was Christ. — One of the soldiers with a spear pierced his side, and forthwith came there out blood and water. — He was wounded for our transgressions, he was bruised for our iniquities: the chastisement of our peace was upon him; and with his stripes we are healed. — Ye will not come to me, that ye might have life. — My people have committed two evils; they have forsaken me the fountain of living waters, and hewed them out cisterns, broken cisterns, that can hold no water. — If any man thirst, let him come unto me, and drink. — Whosoever will, let him take the water of life freely.

1 Corinthians 10:1-4   John 19:34   Isaiah 53:5   John 5:40
Jeremiah 2:13   John 7:37   Revelation 22:17

FEBRUARY 11 MORNING

They that feared the Lord spake often one to another:
and the Lord harkened, and heard it,
and a book of remembrance was written before him
for them that feared the Lord,
and that thought upon his name.
— *MALACHI 3:16*

It came to pass that, while they communed together and reasoned, Jesus himself drew near, and went with them. — Where two or three are gathered together in my name, there am I in the midst of them. — My fellow labourers, whose names are in the book of life. — Let the word of Christ dwell in you richly in all wisdom; teaching and admonishing one another in psalms and hymns and spiritual Song, singing with grace in your hearts to the Lord. — Exhort one another daily, while it is called to day; lest any of you be hardened through the deceitfulness of sin. — Every idle word that men shall speak, they shall give account thereof in the day of judgment. For by thy words thou shalt be justified, and by thy words thou shalt be condemned. — Behold, it is written before me.

Luke 24:15   Matthew 18:20   Philippians 4:3
Colossians 3:16   Hebrews 3:13   Matthew 12:36,37   Isaiah 65:6

FEBRUARY 11 EVENING

The trees of the Lord are full of sap.
— *PSALM 104:16*

I will be as the dew unto Israel: he shall grow as the lily, and cast forth his roots as Lebanon. His branches shall spread, and his beauty shalt be as the olive tree, and his smell as Lebanon. — Blessed is the man that trusteth in the Lord, and whose hope the Lord is. For he shall be as a tree planted by the waters, and that spreadeth out her roots by the river, and shall not see when heat cometh, but her leaf shall be green; and shall not be careful in the year of drought, neither shall cease from yielding fruit. — I the Lord have brought down the high tree, have exalted the low tree, have dried up the green tree, and have made the dry tree to flourish. — The righteous shall flourish like the palm tree: he shall grow like a cedar in Lebanon. Those that be planted in the house of the Lord shall flourish in the courts of our God. They shall still bring forth fruit in old age; they shall be fat and flourishing.

Hosea 14:5,6   Jeremiah 17:7,8   Ezekiel 17:24   Psalm 92:12-14

FEBRUARY 12 MORNING

They shall be mine, saith the Lord of hosts,
in that day when I make up my jewels.
— MALACHI 3:17

I have manifested thy name unto the men which thou gavest me out of the world: thine they were, and thou gavest them me; and they have kept thy word. I pray for them: I pray not for the world, but for them which thou hast given me; for they are thine. And all mine are thine, and thine are mine; and I am glorified in them. Father, I will that they also, whom thou hast given me, be with me where I am: that they may behold my glory, which thou hast given me: for thou lovedst me before the foundation of the world. — I will come again, and receive you unto myself. — He shall come to be glorified in his saints, and to be admired in all them that believe...in that day. — We which are alive and remain shall be caught up together with them in the clouds, to meet the Lord in the air: and so shall we ever be with the Lord. — Thou shalt also be a crown of glory in the hand of the Lord, and a royal diadem in the hand of thy God.

John 17:6,9,10,24, 14:3   2 Thessalonians 1:10   1 Thessalonians 4:17   Isaiah 62:3

FEBRUARY 12 EVENING

I beseech thee, shew me thy glory.
— Exodus 33:18

God, who commanded the light to shine out of darkness, hath shined in our hearts, to give the light of the knowledge of the glory of God in the face of Jesus Christ. — The Word was made flesh and dwelt among us, (and we beheld his glory, the glory as of the only begotten of the Father,) full of grace and truth... No man hath seen God at any time; the only begotten Son, which is in the bosom of the Father, he hath declared him. — My soul thirsteth for God, for the living God: when shall I come and appear before God? — When thou saidst, Seek ye my face; my heart said unto thee, Thy face, Lord, will I seek. — We all, with open face beholding as in a glass the glory of the Lord, are changed into the same image from glory to glory, even as by the Spirit of the Lord. — Father, I will that they also, whom thou hast given me, be with me where I am; that they may behold my glory, which thou hast given me: for thou lovedst me before the foundation of the world.

2 Corinthians 4:6   John 1:14,18   Psalm 42:2, 27:8
2 Corinthians 3:18   John 17:24

FEBRUARY 13 MORNING

*Upon the likeness of the throne was the likeness
as the appearance of a man above upon it.*
— EZEKIEL 1:26

The man Christ Jesus. — Made in the likeness of men...found in fashion as a man. — Forasmuch...as the children are partakers of flesh and blood, he also himself likewise took part of the same; that through death he might destroy him that had the power of death. — I am he that liveth, and was dead; and, behold, I am alive for evermore. — Christ being raised from the dead dieth no more; death hath no more dominion over him. For in that he died, he died unto sin once: but in that he liveth, he liveth unto God. — What and if ye shall see the Son of Man ascend up where he was before?— He raised him from the dead, and set him at his own right hand in the heavenly places. — In him dwelleth all the fulness of the Godhead bodily. — Though he was crucified through weakness, yet he liveth by the power of God. For we also are weak in him, but we shall live with him by the power of God.

1 Timothy 2:5   Philippians 2:7,8   Hebrews 2:14   Revelation 1:18   Romans 6:9,10   John 6:62   Ephesians 1:20   Colossians 2:9 2   Corinthians 13:4

FEBRUARY 13 EVENING

Thy word hath quickened me.
— PSALM 119:50

The first man Adam was made a living soul; the last Adam was made a quickening spirit. — As the Father hath life in himself; so hath he given to the Son to have life in himself. — I am the resurrection, and the life: he that believeth in me though he were dead, yet shall he live: and whosoever liveth and believeth in me shall never die. — In him was life; and the life was the light of men...As many as received him, to them gave he power to become the sons of God, even to them that believe on his name: which were born, not of blood, nor of the will of the flesh, nor of the will of man, but of God. — It is the spirit that quickeneth; the flesh profiteth nothing: the words that I speak unto you, they are spirit, and they are life. — The word of God is quick and powerful, and sharper than any two-edged sword, piercing even to the dividing asunder of soul and spirit and of the joints and marrow, and is a discerner of the thoughts and intents of the heart.

1 Corinthians 15:45   John 5:26, 11:25,26, 1:4,12,13, 6:63   Hebrews 4:12

FEBRUARY 14 MORNING

*Suffer it to be so now:
for thus it becometh us to fulfil all righteousness.*
— MATTHEW 3:15

I delight to do thy will, O my God: yea, thy law is within my heart. — Think not that I am come to destroy the law, or the prophets: I am not come to destroy, but to fulfil. For verily I say unto you, till heaven and earth pass, one jot or one tittle shall in no wise pass from the law, till all be fulfilled. — The Lord is well pleased for his righteousness' sake; he will magnify the law, and make it honourable. — Except your righteousness shall exceed the righteousness of the scribes and Pharisees ye shall in no case enter into the kingdom of heaven. — What the law could not do, in that it was weak through the flesh, God sending his own Son in the likeness of sinful flesh, and for sin, condemned sin in the flesh: that the righteousness of the law might be fulfilled in us, who walk not after the flesh, but after the Spirit. — Christ is the end of the law for righteousness to every one that believeth.

Psalm 40:8   Matthew 5:17,18   Isaiah 42:2   Matthew 5:20   Romans 8:3,4, 10:4

FEBRUARY 14 EVENING

I am thy part and thine inheritance.
— NUMBERS 18:20

Whom have I in heaven but thee? And there is none upon earth that I desire beside thee. My flesh and my heart faileth: but God is the strength of my heart, and my portion for ever. — The LORD is the portion of mine inheritance and of my cup: thou maintainest my lot. The lines are fallen unto me in pleasant places; yea, I have a goodly heritage. — The Lord is my portion, saith my soul; therefore will I hope in him. — Thy testimonies have I taken as an heritage for ever: for they are the rejoicing of my heart. — O God, thou art my God; early will I seek thee: my soul thirsteth for thee, my flesh longeth for thee in a dry and thirsty land, where no water is...Because thou hast been my help, therefore in the shadow of thy wings will I rejoice. — My beloved is mine, and I am his.

Psalms 73:25,26, 16:5,6   Lamentations 3:24
Psalms 119:111, 63:1,7 Song of Solomon 2:16

FEBRUARY 15 MORNING

Who can say, I have made my heart clean?
— PROVERBS 20:9

The Lord looked down from heaven upon the children of men, to see if there were any that did understand, and seek God. They are all gone aside, they are all together become filthy: there is none that doeth good, no, not one. — They that are in the flesh cannot please God. — To will is present with me; but how to perform that which is good I find not. For the good that I would I do not: but the evil which I would not, that I do. — We are all as an unclean thing, and all our righteousnesses are as filthy rags: and we all do fade as a leaf: and our iniquities, like the wind, have taken us away. — The scripture hath concluded all under sin, that the promise by faith of Jesus Christ might be given to them that believe. — God was in Christ, reconciling the world unto himself, not imputing their trespasses unto them. — If we say that we have no sin, we deceive ourselves, and the truth is not in us. If we confess our sins, he is faithful and just to forgive us our sins, and to cleanse us from all unrighteousness.

Psalm 14:2,3   Romans 8:8, 7:18,19   Isaiah 64:6
Galatians 3:22 2   Corinthians 5:19 1   John 1:8,9

FEBRUARY 15 EVENING

The floods lift up their waves.
— PSALM 93:3

The Lord on high is mightier than the noise of many waters, yea, than the mighty waves of the sea. — O Lord God of hosts, who is a strong Lord like unto thee? Or to thy faithfulness round about thee? Thou rulest the raging of the sea: when the waves thereof arise, thou stillest them. — Fear ye not me? saith the Lord: will ye not tremble at my presence, which have placed the sand for the bound of the sea by a perpetual decree, that it cannot pass it? — When thou passest through the waters, I will be with thee; and through the rivers, they shall not overflow thee. — Peter...walked on the water, to go to Jesus. But when he saw the wind boisterous, he was afraid; and beginning to sink, he cried, saying, Lord, save me. And immediately Jesus stretched forth his hand, and caught him, and said unto him, O thou of little faith, wherefore didst thou doubt? — What time I am afraid, I will trust in thee.

Psalms 93:4, 89:8,9   Jeremiah 5:22   Isaiah 43:2
Matthew 14:29-31   Psalm 56:3

FEBRUARY 16 MORNING

Thy name is as ointment poured forth.
— SONG OF SOLOMON 1:3

Christ...hath loved us, and hath given himself for us, an offering and a sacrifice to God for a sweetsmelling savour. — Unto you therefore which believe he is precious. — God also hath highly exalted him, and given him a name which is above every name: that at the name of Jesus every knee should bow. — In him dwelleth all the fulness of the Godhead bodily. — If ye love me, keep my commandments. — The love of God is shed abroad in our hearts by the Holy Ghost which is given unto us. — The house was filled with the odour of the ointment. — They took knowledge of them, that they had been with Jesus. — O Lord our Lord, how excellent is thy name in all the earth! who hast set thy glory above the heavens. — Emmanuel...God with us. — His name shall be called Wonderful, Counsellor, The Mighty God, The Everlasting Father, The Prince of Peace. — The name of the Lord is a strong tower: the righteous runneth into it, and is safe.

Ephesians 5:2 1 Peter 2:7 Philippians 2:9 Colossians 2:9 John 14:15 Romans 5:5 John 12:3 Acts 4:13 Psalm 8:1 Matthew 1:23 Isaiah 9:6 Proverbs 18:10

FEBRUARY 16 EVENING

We that are in this tabernacle do groan, being burdened.
— 2 CORINTHIANS 5:4

Lord, all my desire is before thee; and my groaning is not hid from thee... Mine iniquities are gone over mine head: as an heavy burden they are too heavy for me. — O wretched man that I am! Who shall deliver me from the body of this death? — The whole creation groaneth and travaileth in pain together until now. And not only they, but ourselves...which have the firstfruits of the Spirit... groan within ourselves waiting for the adoption, to wit, the redemption of our body. — Now for a season, if need be, ye are in heaviness through manifold temptations. — Shortly I must put off this my tabernacle. — For this corruptible must put on incorruption and this mortal must put on immortality. So when this corruptible shall have put on incorruption, and this mortal shall have put on immortality, then shall be brought to pass the saying that is written, Death is swallowed up in victory.

Psalm 38:9,4 Romans 7:24, 8:22,23 1 Peter 1:6 2 Peter 1:14 1 Corinthians 15:53,54

FEBRUARY 17 MORNING

The whole bullock shall he carry forth without the camp unto
a clean place, where the ashes are poured out,
and burn him on the wood with fire.
— LEVITICUS 4:12

They took Jesus, and led him away. And he bearing his cross went forth into a place called the place of a skull, which is called in the Hebrew Golgotha: where they crucified him. — The bodies of those beasts, whose blood is brought into the sanctuary by the high priest for sin, are burned without the camp. Wherefore Jesus also, that he might sanctify the people with his own blood, suffered without the gate. Let us go forth therefore unto him without the camp, bearing his reproach. — The fellowship of his sufferings. — Rejoice, inasmuch as ye are partakers of Christ's sufferings: that, when his glory shall be revealed, ye may be glad also with exceeding joy. — Our light affliction, which is but for a moment, worketh for us a far more exceeding and eternal weight of glory.

John 19:16,18   Hebrews 13:11-13   Philippians 3:10
1 Peter 4:13   2 Corinthians 4:17

FEBRUARY 17 EVENING

God created man in his own image.
— GENESIS 1:27

Forasmuch then as we are the offspring of God, we ought not to think that the Godhead is like unto gold, or silver, or stone, graven by art and man's device. — God, who is rich in mercy, for his great love wherewith he loved us, even when we were dead in sins, hath quickened us together with Christ. We are his workmanship, created in Christ Jesus unto good works, which God hath before ordained that we should walk in them. — For whom he did foreknow, he also did predestinate to be conformed to the image of his Son, that he might be the firstborn among many brethren. — We know that, when he shall appear, we shall be like him; for we shall see him as he is. — I shall be satisfied, when I awake, with thy likeness. — He that overcometh shall inherit all things; and I will be his God, and he shall be my son. — If children, then heirs; heirs of God, and joint-heirs with Christ.

Acts 17:29   Ephesians 2:4,5,10   Romans 8:29
1 John 3:2   Psalm 17:15   Revelation 21:7   Romans 8:17

FEBRUARY 18 MORNING

Thou art my hope in the day of evil.
— JEREMIAH 17:17

There be many that say, Who will shew us any good? Lord, lift thou up the light of thy countenance upon us. — I will sing of thy power; yea I will sing aloud of thy mercy in the morning; for thou hast been my defence and refuge in the day of my trouble. — In my prosperity I said, I shall never be moved. Thou didst hide thy face, and I was troubled. I cried to thee, O Lord: and unto the Lord I made supplication. What profit is there in my blood, when I go down to the pit? Shall the dust praise thee? Shall it declare thy truth? Hear, O Lord, and have mercy upon me: Lord, be thou my helper. — For a small moment have I forsaken thee; but with great mercies will I gather thee. In a little wrath I hid my face from thee for a moment; but with everlasting kindness will I have mercy on thee, saith the Lord thy Redeemer. — Sorrow shall be turned into joy. — Weeping may endure for a night, but joy cometh in the morning.

Psalms 4:6, 59:16, 30:6-10   Isaiah 54:7,8   John 16:20   Psalm 30:5

FEBRUARY 18 EVENING

Adam...begat a son in his own likeness.
— GENESIS 5:3

Who can bring a clean thing out of an unclean? — Behold, I was shapen in iniquity; and in sin did my mother conceive me. — Dead in trespasses and sins... by nature the children of wrath, even as others. — I am carnal, sold under sin. That which I do I allow not; for what I would, that do I not; but what I hate, that do I. I know that in me (that is, in my flesh,) dwelleth no good thing. — By one man sin entered into the world...by one man's disobedience many were made sinners. — If through the offence of one many be dead, much more the grace of God, and the gift by grace, which is by one man, Jesus Christ, hath abounded unto many. — The law of the Spirit of life in Christ Jesus hath made me free from the law of sin and death. — Thanks be to God, which giveth us the victory through our Lord Jesus Christ.

Job 14:4   Psalm 51:5   Ephesians 2:1,3
Romans 7:14,15,18, 5:12,19, 5:15, 8:2
1 Corinthians 15:57

FEBRUARY 19 MORNING

The Lord giveth wisdom:
out of his mouth cometh knowledge and understanding.
— PROVERBS 2:6

Trust in the Lord with all thine heart; and lean not unto thine own understanding. — If any of you lack wisdom let him ask of God, that giveth to all men liberally and upbraideth not; and it shall be given him. — The foolishness of God is wiser than men; and the weakness of God is stronger than men. — God hath chosen the foolish things of the world to confound the wise. That no flesh should glory in his presence. — The entrance of thy words giveth light; it giveth understanding unto the simple. — Thy word have I hid in my heart, that I might not sin against thee. — All bare him witness, and wondered at the gracious words which proceeded out of his mouth. — Never man spake like this man. — Of him are ye in Christ Jesus, who of God is made unto us wisdom, and righteousness, and sanctification, and redemption.

Proverbs 3:5   James 1:5   1 Corinthians 1:25,27,29
Psalm 119:130,11   Luke 4:22.   John 7:46   1 Corinthians 1:30

FEBRUARY 19 EVENING

The year of my redeemed is come.
— ISAIAH 63:4

Ye shall hallow the fiftieth year and proclaim liberty throughout all the land unto all the inhabitants thereof: it shall be a jubilee unto you; and ye shall return every man unto his possession…and unto his family. — Thy dead men shall live, together with my dead body shall they arise. Awake and sing, ye that dwell in dust: for thy dew is as the dew of herbs and the earth shall cast out the dead. — The Lord himself shall descend from heaven with a shout, with the voice of the archangel and with the trump of God: and the dead in Christ shall rise first: then we which are alive and remain shall be caught up together with them in the clouds, to meet the Lord in the air: and so shall we ever be with the Lord. — I will ransom them from the power of the grave; I will redeem them from death: O death, I will be thy plagues; O grave, I will be thy destruction. — Their Redeemer is strong; the Lord of hosts is his name.

Leviticus 25:10   Isaiah 26:19   1 Thessalonians 4:16,17
Hosea 13:14   Jeremiah 50:34

FEBRUARY 20 MORNING

*He shall see of the travail of his soul
and shall be satisfied.*
— ISAIAH 53:11

Jesus...said, It is finished: and he bowed his head, and gave up the ghost. — He hath made him to be sin for us, who knew no sin; that we might be made the righteousness of God in him. — This people have I formed for myself; they shall shew forth my praise. — To the intent that now unto the principalities and powers in heavenly places might be known by the church the manifold wisdom of God, according to the eternal purpose which be purposed in Christ Jesus our Lord. — That in the ages to come he might shew the exceeding riches of his grace in his kindness toward us through Christ Jesus. — After that ye believed, ye were sealed with that Holy Spirit of promise, which is the earnest of our inheritance until the redemption of the purchased possession, unto the praise of his glory. — Ye are a chosen generation, a royal priesthood, a holy nation, a peculiar people; that ye should shew forth the praises of him who hath called you out of darkness into his marvellous light.

John 19:30 2 Corinthians 5:21 Isaiah 43:21
Ephesians 3:10,11, 2:7, 1:13 1 Peter 2:9

FEBRUARY 20 EVENING

The day of temptation in the wilderness.
— HEBREWS 3:8

Let no man say, when he is tempted, I am tempted of God: for God cannot be tempted with evil, neither tempteth he any man: but every man is tempted when he is drawn away of his own lust, and enticed. Then when lust hath conceived, it bringeth forth sin. — They lusted exceedingly in the wilderness, and tempted God in the desert. — Jesus being full of the Holy Ghost was led by the Spirit into the wilderness, being forty days tempted of the devil. And in those days he did eat nothing: and when they were ended, he afterward hungered. And the devil said unto him, If thou be the Son of God, command this stone that it be made bread. — He himself hath suffered being tempted, he is able to succour them that are tempted. — Simon, Simon...Satan hath desired to have you, that he might sift you as wheat: but I have prayed for thee that thy faith fail not.

James 1:13-15 Psalm 106:14 Luke 4:1-3 Hebrews 2:18 Luke 22:31,32

FEBRUARY 21 MORNING

I am the Lord which sanctify you.
— LEVITICUS 20:8

I am the Lord your God, which have separated you from other people. And ye shall be holy unto me: for I the Lord am holy, and have severed you from other people, that ye should be mine. — Sanctified by God the Father. — Sanctify them through thy truth: thy word is truth. — The very God of peace sanctify you wholly; and I pray God your whole spirit and soul and body be preserved blameless unto the coming of our Lord Jesus Christ. — Jesus...that he might sanctify the people with his own blood, suffered without the gate. — Our Saviour Jesus Christ...gave himself for us, that he might redeem us from all iniquity, and purify unto himself a peculiar people, zealous of good works. — Both he that sanctifieth and they who are sanctified are all of one: for which cause he is not ashamed to call them brethren. — For their sakes I sanctify myself, that they also might be sanctified through the truth. — Through sanctification of the Spirit, unto obedience, and sprinkling of the blood of Jesus Christ.

Leviticus 20:24,26 Jude 1   John 17:17 1   Thessalonians 5:23
Hebrews 13:12   Titus 2:13.14   Hebrews 2:11   John 17:19 1   Peter 1:2

FEBRUARY 21 EVENING

Light is sown for the righteous,
and gladness for the upright in heart.
— PSALM 97:11

They that sow in tears shall reap in joy. He that goeth forth and weepeth, bearing precious seed, shall doubtless come again with rejoicing, bringing his sheaves with him. — That which thou sowest, thou sowest not that body that shall be. — Blessed be the God and Father of our Lord Jesus Christ, which according to his abundant mercy hath begotten us again unto a lively hope by the resurrection of Jesus Christ from the dead. Wherein ye greatly rejoice, though now for a season, if need be, ye are in heaviness through manifold temptations: that the trial of your faith, being much more precious than of gold that perisheth, though it be tried with fire, might be found unto praise and honour and glory at the appearing of Jesus Christ.

Psalm 126:5,6 1   Corinthians 15:37 1   Peter 1:3,6,7

FEBRUARY 22 MORNING

What man is he that feareth the Lord?
Him shall he teach in the way that he shall choose.
— PSALM 25:12

The light of the body is the eye: if therefore thine eye be single thy whole body shall be full of light. — Thy word is a lamp unto my feet, and a light unto my path. — Thine ears shall hear a word behind thee, saying, This is the way, walk ye in it, when ye turn to the right hand, and when ye turn to the left. — I will instruct thee and teach thee in the way which thou shalt go: I will guide thee with mine eye. Be ye not as the horse or as the mule, which have no understanding: whose mouth must be held in with bit and bridle, lest they come near unto thee. Many sorrows shall be to the wicked: but he that trusteth in the Lord, mercy shall compass him about. Be glad in the Lord, and rejoice, ye righteous: and shout for joy, all ye that are upright in heart. — O Lord, I know that the way of man is not in himself: it is not in man that walketh to direct his steps.

Matthew 6:22   Psalm 119:105   Isaiah 30:21   Psalm 32:8-11   Jeremiah 10:23

FEBRUARY 22 EVENING

When thou liest down, thou shall not be afraid:
yea, thou shalt lie down, and thy sleep shall be sweet.
— PROVERBS 3:24

There arose a great storm of wind, and the waves beat into the ship, so that it was now full. And he was in the hinder part of the ship, asleep on a pillow. — Be careful for nothing; but in every thing by prayer and supplication with thanksgiving let your requests be made known unto God. And the peace of God, which passeth all understanding, shall keep your hearts and minds through Christ Jesus. — I will both lay me down in peace, and sleep: for thou, Lord, only makest me dwell in safety. — He giveth his beloved sleep. — They stoned Stephen, calling upon God, and saying, Lord Jesus, receive my spirit. And he kneeled down, and cried with a loud voice, Lord, lay not this sin to their charge. And when he had said this, he fell asleep. — Absent from the body...present with the Lord.

Mark. 4:37,38   Philippians 4:6,7   Psalms 4:8, 127:2
Acts 7:59,60   2 Corinthians 5:8

FEBRUARY 23 MORNING

The blood of sprinkling,
that speaketh better things than that of Abel.
— HEBREWS 12:24

Behold the Lamb of God, which taketh away the sin of the world. — The Lamb slain from the foundation of the world. — It is not possible that the blood of bulls and of goats should take away sins. Wherefore when he cometh into the world, he saith, Sacrifice and offering thou wouldest not, but a body hast thou prepared me. By the which will we are sanctified through the offering of the body of Jesus Christ once for all. — Abel...brought of the firstlings of his flock and of the fat thereof...The Lord had respect unto Abel and to his offering. — Christ...hath loved us, and hath given himself for us, an offering and a sacrifice to God for a sweetsmelling savour. — Let us draw near with a true heart in full assurance of faith, having our hearts sprinkled from an evil conscience, and our bodies washed with pure water. — Having...boldness to enter into the holiest by the blood of Jesus.

John 1:29   Revelation 13:8   Hebrews 10:4,5,10
Genesis 4:4   Ephesians 5:2   Hebrews 10:22,19

FEBRUARY 23 EVENING

Who knoweth the power of thine anger?
— PSALM 90:11

From the sixth hour there was darkness over all the land unto the ninth hour. And about the ninth hour Jesus cried with a loud voice, saying, Eli, Eli, lama sabachthani? that is to say, My God, my God, why hast thou forsaken me? — The Lord hath laid on him the iniquity of us all. — There is therefore now no condemnation to them which are in Christ Jesus. — Being justified by faith, we have peace with God through our Lord Jesus Christ. — Christ hath redeemed us from the curse of the law, being made a curse for us. — God sent his only begotten Son into the world, that we might live through him. Herein is love, not that we loved God, but that he loved us, and sent his Son to be the propitiation for our sins. — That he might be just, and the justifier of him which believeth in Jesus.

Matthew 27:45,46   Isaiah 53:6   Romans 8:1, 5:1
Galatians 3:13   John 4:9,10   Romans 3:26

FEBRUARY 24 MORNING

*Thus saith the Lord God,
I will yet for this be enquired of.*
— EZEKIEL 36:37

Ye have not, because ye ask not. — Ask, and it shall be given you; seek, and ye shall find; knock, and it shall be opened unto you: for every one that asketh receiveth; and he that seeketh findeth; and to him that knocketh it shall be opened. — This is the confidence that we have in him, that, if we ask anything according to his will, he heareth us: and if we know that he hear us, whatsoever we ask, we know that we have the petitions that we desired of him. — If any of you lack wisdom, let him ask of God, that giveth to all men liberally, and upbraideth not; and it shall be given him. — Open thy mouth wide, and I will fill it. — Men ought always to pray, and not to faint. — The eyes of the Lord are upon the righteous, and his ears are open unto their cry. The Lord heareth, and delivereth them out of all their troubles. — Ye shall ask in my name; and I say not unto you, that I will pray the Father for you: for the Father himself loveth you, because ye have loved me. Ask, and ye shall receive, that your joy may be full.

James 4:2   Matthew 7:7,8 1   John 5:14,15   James 1:5
Psalm 81:10   Luke 18:1   Psalm 34:15,17   John 16:26,27,24

FEBRUARY 24 EVENING

*Shall we receive good at the hand of God,
and shall we not receive evil?*
— JOB 2:10

I know, O Lord, that thy judgments are right, and that thou in faithfulness hast afflicted me. — O Lord, thou art our father, we are the clay, and thou our potter; and we all are the work of thy hand. — It is the Lord: let him do what seemeth him good. — Righteous art thou, O Lord, when I plead with thee: yet let me talk with thee of thy judgments. — He shall sit as a refiner and purifier of silver. — Whom the Lord loveth he chasteneth, and scourgeth every son whom he receiveth. — It is enough for the disciple that he be as his master, and the servant as his lord. — Though he were a Son, yet learned he obedience by the things which he suffered. — Rejoice, inasmuch as ye are partakers of Christ's sufferings; that, when his glory shall be revealed, ye may be glad also with exceeding joy. — These are they which came out of great tribulation, and have washed their robes, and made them white in the blood of the Lamb.

Psalm 119:75   Isaiah 64:8 1   Samuel 3:18   Jeremiah 12:1   Malachi 3:3
Hebrews 12:6   Matthew 10:25   Hebrews 5:8 1   Peter 4:13   Revelation 7:14

FEBRUARY 25 MORNING

Resist the devil, and he will flee from you.
— JAMES 4:7

When the enemy shall come in like a flood, the Spirit of the Lord shall lift up a standard against him. — Get thee hence, Satan: for it is written, Thou shalt worship the Lord thy God, and him only shalt thou serve. Then the devil leaveth him, and, behold, angels came and ministered unto him. — Be strong in the Lord, and in the power of his might. Put on the whole armour of God, that ye may be able to stand against the wiles of the devil. — And have no fellowship with the unfruitful works of darkness, but rather reprove them. — Lest Satan should get an advantage of us: for we are not ignorant of his devices. — Be sober, be vigilant; because your adversary the devil, as a roaring lion, walketh about, seeking whom he may devour; whom resist stedfast in the faith, knowing that the same afflictions are accomplished in your brethren that are in the world. — This is the victory that overcometh the world, even our faith. — Who shall lay anything to the charge of God's elect? It is God that justifieth.

Isaiah 59:19   Matthew 4:10,11   Ephesians 6:10,11, 5:11
2 Corinthians 2:11 1   Peter 5:8,9 1   John 5:4   Romans 8:33

FEBRUARY 25 EVENING

Oh that I knew where I might find him!
— JOB 23:3

Who is among you that feareth the Lord, that obeyeth the voice of his servant, that walketh in darkness, and hath no light? Let him trust in the name of the Lord, and stay upon his God. — Ye shall seek me, and find me, when ye shall search for me with all your heart. — Seek, and ye shall find; knock, and it shall be opened unto you. For every one that asketh receiveth; and he that seeketh findeth; and to him that knocketh it shall be opened. — Truly our fellowship is with the Father, and with his Son Jesus Christ. — Now in Christ Jesus ye who sometime were far off are made nigh by the blood of Christ. For through him we both have access by one Spirit unto the Father. — If we say that we have fellowship with him, and walk in darkness, we lie, and do not the truth. — Lo, I am with you alway. — I will never leave thee, nor forsake thee. — The Comforter...dwelleth with you, and shall be in you.

Isaiah 50:10   Jeremiah 29:13   Luke 11:9,10 1   John 1:3   Ephesians 2:13,18
1 John 1:6   Matthew 28:20   Hebrews 13:5   John 14:16,17

FEBRUARY 26 MORNING

*Let us search and try our ways,
and turn again to the Lord.*
— LAMENTATIONS 3:40

Examine me, O Lord, and prove me; try my reins and my heart. — Behold, thou desirest truth in the inward parts: and in the hidden part thou shalt make me to know wisdom. — I thought on my ways, and turned my feet unto thy testimonies. I made haste and delayed not to keep thy commandments. — Let a man examine himself, and so let him eat of that bread, and drink of that cup. — If we confess our sins, he is faithful and just to forgive us our sins, and to cleanse us from all unrighteousness. — We have an advocate with the Father, Jesus Christ the righteous: and he is the propitiation for our sins. — Having therefore, brethren, boldness to enter into the holiest by the blood of Jesus, by a new and living way which he hath consecrated for us, through the veil, that is say, his flesh: and having a high priest over the house of God; let us draw near with a true heart, in full assurance of faith, having our hearts sprinkled from an evil conscience, and our bodies washed with pure water.

Psalms 26:2, 51:6, 119:59,60 1 Corinthians 11:28
1 John 1:9, 2:1   Hebrews 10:19-22

FEBRUARY 26 EVENING

*There was a rainbow round about the throne,
in sight like unto an emerald.*
— REVELATION 4:3

This is the token of the covenant which I make between me and you and every living creature that is with you, for perpetual generations: I do set my bow in the cloud...and I will look upon it, that I may remember the everlasting covenant between God and every living creature of all flesh that is upon the earth. — An everlasting covenant, ordered in all things and sure. — That by two immutable things, in which it was impossible for God to lie, we might have a strong consolation, who have fled for refuge to lay hold upon the hope set before us. — We declare unto you glad tidings, how that the promise which was made unto the fathers, God hath fulfilled the same unto their children, in that He hath raised up Jesus again. — Jesus Christ the same yesterday, and today, and for ever.

Genesis 9:12,13,16 2 Samuel 23:5
Hebrews 6:18   Acts 13:32   Hebrews 13:8

FEBRUARY 27 MORNING

Reckon ye yourselves to be dead indeed unto sin,
but alive unto God through Jesus Christ our Lord.
— ROMANS 6:11

He that heareth my word, and believeth on him that sent me, hath everlasting life, and shall not come into condemnation; but is passed from death unto life. — I through the law am dead to the law, that I might live unto God. I am crucified with Christ; nevertheless I live; yet not I, but Christ liveth in me: and the life which I now live in the flesh I live by the faith of the Son of God, who loved me, and gave himself for me. — Because I live, ye shall live also. — I give unto them eternal life: and they shall never perish, neither shall any man pluck them out of my hand. My Father, which gave them me, is greater than all; and no man is able to pluck them out of my Father's hand. I and my Father are one. — If ye then be risen with Christ, seek those things which are above, where Christ sitteth on the right hand of God...For ye are dead, and your life is hid with Christ in God.

John 5:24   Galatians 2:19,20   John 14:19, 10:28-30   Colossians 3:1,3

FEBRUARY 27 EVENING

God...giveth...liberally, and upbraideth not.
— JAMES 1:5

Woman, where are those thine accusers? Hath no man condemned thee? She said, No man, Lord. And Jesus said unto her, Neither do I condemn thee: go, and sin no more. — The grace of God, and the gift by grace, which is by one man, Jesus Christ, hath abounded unto many...The free gift is of many offences unto justification. — God, who is rich in mercy, for his great love wherewith he loved us, even when we were dead in sins, hath quickened us together with Christ, (by grace ye are saved) and hath raised us up together, and made us sit together in heavenly places in Christ Jesus: that in the ages to come he might shew the exceeding riches of his grace in his kindness toward us through Christ Jesus. — He that spared not his own Son, but delivered him up for us all, how shall he not with him also freely give us all things?

John 8:10,11   Romans 5:15,16   Ephesians 2:4-7   Romans 8:32

FEBRUARY 28 MORNING

*God so loved the world,
that he gave his only begotten Son,
that whosoever believeth in him should not perish,
but have everlasting life.*
— JOHN 3:16

God...hath reconciled us to himself by Jesus Christ, and hath given to us the ministry of reconciliation; to wit, that God was in Christ, reconciling the world unto himself, not imputing their trespasses unto them; and hath committed unto us the word of reconciliation. Now then we are ambassadors for Christ, as though God did beseech you by us: we pray you in Christ's stead, be ye reconciled to God. For he hath made him to be sin for us, who knew no sin; that we might be made the righteousness of God him. — God is love. In this was manifested the love of God toward us, because that God sent his only begotten Son into the world that we might live through him. Herein is love, not that we loved God, but that he loved us, and sent his Son to be the propitiation for our sins. Beloved, if God so loved us, we ought also to love one another.

2 Corinthians 5:18-21 1 John 4:8-11

FEBRUARY 28 EVENING

The spirit of man is the candle of the Lord.
— PROVERBS 20:27

He that is without sin among you, let him first cast a stone at her...And they which heard it, being convicted by their own conscience, went out one by one, beginning at the eldest, even unto the last. — Who told thee that thou wast naked? Hast thou eaten of the tree, whereof I commanded thee that thou shouldest not eat? — To him that knoweth to do good, and doeth it not, to him it is sin. — If our heart condemn us, God is greater than our heart, and knoweth all things. Beloved, if our heart condemn us not, then have we confidence toward God. — All things indeed are pure; but it is evil for that man who eateth with offence. Happy is he that condemneth not himself in that thing which he alloweth. — Search me, O God, and know my heart: try me, and know my thoughts: and see if there be any wicked way in me, and lead me in the way everlasting.

John 8:7,9   Genesis 3:11   James 4:17
1 John 3:20,21   Romans 14:20,22   Psalm 139:23,24

FEBRUARY 29 MORNING

*Boast not thyself of tomorrow;
for thou knowest not what a day may bring forth.*
— PROVERBS 27:1

Behold, now is the accepted time; behold, now is the day of salvation. — Yet a little while is the light with you. Walk while ye have the light, lest darkness come upon you: for he that walketh in darkness knoweth not whither he goeth. While ye have light, believe in the light, that ye may be the children of light. — Whatsoever thy hand findeth to do, do it with thy might; for there is no work, nor device, nor knowledge, nor wisdom, in the grave, whither thou goest. — Soul, thou hast much goods laid up for many years; take thine ease, eat, drink, and be merry...Thou fool, this night thy soul shall be required of thee: then whose shall those things be, which thou hast provided? So is he that layeth up treasure for himself, and is not rich toward God. — What is your life? It is even a vapour that appeareth for a little time, and then vanisheth away. — The world passeth away, and the lust thereof: but he that doeth the will of God abideth for ever.

2 Corinthians 6:2   John 12:35,36
Ecclesiastes 9:10   Luke 12:19-21   1 John 2:17

FEBRUARY 29 EVENING

Thou art the same, and thy years shall have no end.
— PSALM 102:27

Before the mountains were brought forth, or ever thou hadst formed the earth and the world, even from everlasting to everlasting, thou art God. — I am the Lord, I change not; therefore ye sons of Jacob are not consumed. — The same yesterday, and today, and forever. — Every good gift and every perfect gift is from above, and cometh down from the Father of lights, with whom is no variableness, neither shadow of turning. — The gifts and calling of God are without repentance. — God is not a man, that he should lie: neither the son of man, that he should repent. — It is of the Lord's mercies that we are not consumed, because his compassions fail not. — This man, because he continueth ever, hath an unchangeable priesthood. Wherefore he is able also to save them to the uttermost that come unto God by him, seeing he ever liveth to make intercession for them. — Fear not; I am the first and the last.

Psalm 90:2   Malachi 3:6   Hebrews 13:8   James 1:17   Romans 11:29
Numbers 23:19   Lamentations 3:22   Hebrews 7:24,25   Revelation 1:17

MARCH 1 MORNING

The fruit of the Spirit is love.
— *GALATIANS 5:22*

God is love: and he that dwelleth in love dwelleth in God, and God in him. — The love of God is shed abroad in our hearts by the Holy Ghost which is given unto us. — Unto you...which believe he is precious. — We love him, because he first loved us. — The love of Christ constraineth us; because we thus judge, that if one died for all, then were all dead: and that he died for all, that they which live should not henceforth live unto themselves, but unto him which died for them, and rose again. — Ye yourselves are taught of God to love one another. — This is my commandment, That ye love one another, as I have loved you. — Above all things have fervent charity among yourselves: for charity shall cover the multitude of sins. — Walk in love, as Christ also hath loved us, and hath given himself for us, an offering and a sacrifice to God for a sweetsmelling savour.

1 John 4:16   Romans 5:5   1 Peter 2:7   1 John 4:19   2 Corinthians 5:14,15
1 Thessalonians 4:9   John 15:12   1 Peter 4:8   Ephesians 5:2

MARCH 1 EVENING

Jehovah-nissi: The Lord my banner.
— Exodus 17:15

If God be for us, who can be against us? — The Lord is on my side; I will not fear: what can man do unto me? — Thou hast given a banner to them that fear thee. The Lord is my light and my salvation; whom shall I fear? — The Lord is the strength of my life; of whom shall I be afraid? Though an host should encamp against me, my heart shall not fear: though war should rise against me, in this will I be confident. — Behold, God himself is with us for our captain. — The Lord of hosts is with us; the God of Jacob is our refuge. — These shall make war with the Lamb, and the Lamb shall overcome them. — Why do the heathen rage, and the people imagine a vain thing? He that sitteth in the heavens shall laugh: the Lord shall have them in derision. — Take counsel together, and it shall come to nought; speak the word, and it shall not stand: for God is with us.

Romans 8:31   Psalm 118:6, 60:4, 27:1,3   2 Chronicles 13:12
Psalm 46:7   Revelation 17:14   Psalm 2:1,4   Isaiah 8:10

MARCH 2 MORNING

*God hath caused me to be fruitful
in the land of my affliction.*
— GENESIS 41:52

Blessed be God, even the Father of our Lord Jesus Christ, the Father of mercies, and the God of all comfort; who comforteth us in all our tribulation, that we may be able to comfort them which are in any trouble, by the comfort wherewith we ourselves are comforted of God. For as the sufferings of Christ abound in us, so our consolation also aboundeth by Christ. — Now for a season, if need be, ye are in heaviness through manifold temptations: that the trial of your faith, being much more precious than of gold that perisheth, though it be tried with fire, might be found unto praise and honour and glory at the appearing of Jesus Christ. — The Lord stood with me, and strengthened me. — Let them that suffer according to the will of God commit the keeping of their souls to him in well doing, as unto a faithful Creator.

2 Corinthians 1:3-5   1 Peter 1:6,7   2 Timothy 4:17   1 Peter 4:19

MARCH 2 EVENING

There remaineth therefore a rest to the people of God.
— HEBREWS 4:9

There the wicked cease from troubling; and there the weary be at rest. There the prisoners rest together; they hear not the voice of the oppressor. — Blessed are the dead which die in the Lord from henceforth; they...rest from their labours; and their works do follow them. — Our friend Lazarus sleepeth... Jesus spake of his death: but they thought that he had spoken of taking of rest in sleep. — We that are in this tabernacle do groan, being burdened. — Ourselves also, which have the firstfruits of the Spirit, even we ourselves groan within ourselves, waiting for the adoption, to wit, the redemption of our body. For we are saved by hope: but hope that is seen is not hope...But if we hope for that we see not, then do we with patience wait for it.

Job 3:17,18   Revelation 14:13   John 11:11,13
2 Corinthians 5:4   Romans 8:23-25

MARCH 3 MORNING

*Trust in the Lord with all thine heart;
and lean not unto thine own understanding.
In all thy ways acknowledge him,
and he shall direct thy paths.*
— PROVERBS 3:5,6

Trust in him at all times; ye people, pour out your heart before him: God is a refuge for us. — I will instruct thee and teach thee in the way which thou shalt go: I will guide thee with mine eye. Be ye not as the horse, or as the mule, which have no understanding: whose mouth must be held in with bit and bridle, lest they come near unto thee. Many sorrows shall be to the wicked: but he that trusteth in the Lord, mercy shall compass him about. — Thine ears shall hear a word behind thee, saying, This is the way, walk ye in it, when ye turn to the right hand, and when ye turn to the left. — If thy presence go not with me, carry us not up hence. For wherein shall it be known here that I and thy people have found grace in thy sight? Is it not in that thou goest with us? So shall we be separated, I and thy people, from all the people that are upon the face of the earth.

Psalms 62:8, 32:8-10 Isaiah 30:21 Exodus 33:15,16

MARCH 3 EVENING

The prize of the high calling of God in Christ Jesus.
— PHILIPPIANS 3:14

Thou shalt have treasure in heaven:...come and follow me. — I am...thy exceeding great reward. — Well done, thou good and faithful servant: thou hast been faithful over a few things, I will make thee ruler over many things: enter thou into the joy of thy lord. — They shall reign for ever and ever. — Ye shall receive a crown of glory that fadeth not away. — The crown of life. — A crown of righteousness. — An incorruptible crown. — Father, I will that they also, whom thou hast given me, be with me where I am; that they may behold my glory, which thou has given me. — So shall we ever be with the Lord. — I reckon that the sufferings of this present time are not worthy to be compared with the glory which shall be revealed in us.

Matthew 19:21 Genesis 15:1 Matthew 25:21 Revelation 22:5 1 Peter 5:4
James 1:12 2 Timothy 4:8 1 Corinthians 9:25
John 17:24 1 Thessalonians 4:17 Romans 8:18

MARCH 4 MORNING

*Set your affection on things above,
not on things on the earth.*
— COLOSSIANS 3:2

Love not the world, neither the things that are in the world. If any man love the world, the love of the Father is not in him. — Lay not up for yourselves treasures upon earth, where moth and rust doth corrupt, and where thieves break through and steal: but lay up for yourselves treasures in heaven, where neither moth nor rust doth corrupt, and where thieves do not break through nor steal: for where your treasure is, there will your heart be also. — We walk by faith, not by sight. — We faint not; but though our outward man perish, yet the inward man is renewed day by day. For our light affliction which is but for a moment, worketh for us a far more exceeding and eternal weight of glory: while we look not at the things which are seen, but at the things which are not seen: for the things which are seen are temporal; but the things which are not seen are eternal. — An inheritance incorruptible, and undefiled, and that fadeth not away, reserved in heaven for you.

1 John 2:15   Matthew 6:19-21 2   Corinthians 5:7, 4:16-18 1   Peter 1:4

MARCH 4 EVENING

He bowed his shoulder to bear.
— GENESIS 49:15

Take, my brethren, the prophets, who have spoken in the name of the Lord, for an example of suffering affliction, and of patience. — Now all these things happened unto them for ensamples: and they are written for our admonition, upon whom the ends of the world are come. — Shall we receive good at the hand of God, and shall we not receive evil? In all this did not Job sin with his lips. — Aaron held his peace. — It is the Lord; let him do what seemeth him good. — Cast thy burden upon the Lord, and he shall sustain thee. — Surely he hath borne our griefs, and carried our sorrows. — Come unto me, all ye that labour and are heavy laden, and I will give you rest. Take my yoke upon you, and learn of me; for I am meek and lowly in heart: and ye shall find rest unto your souls. For my yoke is easy, and my burden is light.

James 5:10 1   Corinthians 10:11   Job 2:10   Leviticus 10:3 1   Samuel 3:18
Psalm 55:22   Isaiah 53:4   Matthew 11:28-30

MARCH 5 MORNING

O Lord, I am oppressed; undertake for me.
— ISAIAH 38:14

Unto thee lift I up mine eyes, O thou that dwellest in the heavens. Behold, as the eyes of servants look unto the hand of their masters, and as the eyes of a maiden unto the hand of her mistress; so our eyes wait upon the Lord our God. — Hear my cry, O God; attend unto my prayer. From the end of the earth will I cry unto thee, when my heart is overwhelmed: lead me to the rock that is higher than I. For thou hast been a shelter for me, and a strong tower from the enemy. I will abide in thy tabernacle for ever: I will trust in the covert of thy wings. — Thou hast been a strength to the poor, a strength to the needy in his distress, a refuge from the storms. — Christ...suffered for us, leaving us an example, that ye should follow his steps: who did no sin, neither was guile found in his mouth: who, when he was reviled, reviled not again; when he suffered, he threatened not; but committed himself to him that judgeth righteously.

Psalms 123:1,2, 61:1-4   Isaiah 25:4 1   Peter 2:21-23

MARCH 5 EVENING

Fight the good fight of faith.
— 1 TIMOTHY 6:12

We were troubled on every side; without were fightings, within were fears. — Fear not: for they that be with us are more than they that be with them. — Strong in the Lord, and in the power of his might. — Thou comest to me with a sword, and with a spear, and with a shield: but I come to thee in the name of the Lord of hosts, the God of the armies of Israel, whom thou hast defied. — God is my strength and power...he teacheth my hands to war; so that a bow of steel is broken by mine arms. — Our sufficiency is of God. — The angel of the Lord encampeth round about them that fear him, and delivereth them. — Behold, the mountain was full of horses and chariots of fire round about Elisha. — The time would fail me to tell of [those] who through faith subdued kingdoms... out of weakness were made strong, waxed valiant in fight, turned to flight the armies of the aliens.

2 Corinthians 7:5 2   Kings 6:16   Ephesians 6:10
1   Samuel 17:45 2   Samuel 22:33,35
2 Corinthians 3:5   Psalm 34:7 2   Kings 6:17   Hebrews 11:32-34

MARCH 6 MORNING

He preserveth the way of his saints.
— PROVERBS 2:8.

The Lord your God...went in the way before you, to search you out a place to pitch your tents in, in fire by night, to shew you by what way ye should go, and in a cloud by day. — As an eagle stirreth up her nest, fluttereth over her young, spreadeth abroad her wings, taketh them, beareth them on her wings: so the Lord alone did lead him. — The steps of a good man are ordered by the Lord: and he delighteth in his way. Though he fall, he shall not be utterly cast down: for the Lord upholdeth him with his hand. — Many are the afflictions of the righteous: but the Lord delivereth him out of them all. — For the Lord knoweth the way of the righteous; but the way of the ungodly shall perish. — We know that all things work together for good to them that love God, to them who are the called according to his purpose. — With us is the Lord our God to help us, and to fight our battles. — The Lord thy God in the midst of thee is mighty; he will save, he will rejoice over thee with joy.

Deuteronomy 1:32,33, 32:11,12   Psalms 37:23,24, 34:19, 1:6
Romans 8:28 2 Chronicles 32:8   Zephaniah 3:17

MARCH 6 EVENING

My God, my God, why hast thou forsaken me?
— MATTHEW 27:46

He was wounded for our transgressions, he was bruised for our iniquities: the chastisement of our peace was upon him;...the Lord hath laid on him the iniquity of us all...For the transgression of my people was he stricken...It pleased the Lord to bruise him; he hath put him to grief. — Jesus our Lord...was delivered for our offences. — Christ hath once suffered for sins, the just for the unjust, that he might bring us to God. — Who his own self bare our sins in his own body on the tree, that we, being dead to sins, should live unto righteousness: by whose stripes ye were healed. — He hath made him to be sin for us, who knew no sin; that we might be made the righteousness of God in him. — Christ hath redeemed us from the curse of the law, being made a curse for us.

Isaiah 53:5,6,8,10   Romans 4:24,25
1 Peter 3:18, 2:24 2 Corinthians 5:21   Galatians 3:13

MARCH 7 MORNING

Thy Maker is thine husband;
the Lord of hosts is his name.
— ISAIAH 54:5

This is a great mystery: but I speak concerning Christ and the church. — Thou shalt no more be termed Forsaken...but thou shalt be called Hephzibah...for the Lord delighteth in thee. And as the bridegroom rejoiceth over the bride, so shall thy God rejoice over thee. — He hath sent me...to comfort all that mourn; to appoint unto them that mourn in Zion, to give unto them beauty for ashes, the oil of joy for mourning, the garment of praise for the spirit of heaviness. — I will greatly rejoice in the Lord, my soul shall be joyful in my God; for he hath clothed me with the garments of salvation, as a bridegroom decketh himself with ornaments, and as a bride adorneth herself with her jewels. — I will betroth thee unto me for ever; yea, I will betroth thee unto me in righteousness, and in judgment, and in lovingkindness and in mercies. — Who shall separate us from the love of Christ?

Ephesians 5:32   Isaiah 62:4,5, 61:1-3,10
Hosea 2:19   Romans 8:35

MARCH 7 EVENING

My times are in thy hand.
— PSALM 31:15

All his saints are in thy hand. — The word of the Lord came unto Elijah, saying, Get thee hence, and turn thee eastward, and hide thyself by the brook Cherith, that is before Jordan. And it shall be, that thou shalt drink of the brook; and I have commanded the ravens to feed thee there. And the word of the Lord can unto him, saying, Arise, get thee to Zarephath, which belongeth to Zidon, and dwell there: behold, I have commanded a widow woman there to sustain thee. — Take no thought for your life, what ye shall eat, or what ye shall drink; nor yet for your body, what ye shall put on. Your heavenly Father knoweth that ye have need of all these things. — Trust in the Lord with all thine heart; and lean not unto thine own understanding. In all thy ways acknowledge him, and he shall direct thy paths. — Casting all your care upon him; for he cares for you.

Deuteronomy 33:3 1   Kings 17:2-4,8,9
Matthew 6:25,32   Proverbs 3:5,6 1   Peter 5:7

MARCH 8 MORNING

Thou hast cast all my sins behind thy back.
— ISAIAH 38:17

Who is a God like unto thee, that pardoneth iniquity, and passeth by the transgression of the remnant of his heritage? He retaineth not his anger forever, because he delighteth in mercy. He will turn again, he will have compassion upon us; he will subdue our iniquities; and thou wilt cast all their sins into the depths of the sea. — For a small moment have I forsaken thee; but with great mercies will I gather thee. In a little wrath I hid my face from thee for a moment; but with everlasting kindness will I have mercy on thee, saith the Lord thy Redeemer. — I will forgive their iniquity, and I will remember their sin no more. — Blessed is he whose transgression is forgiven, whose sin is covered. Blessed is the man unto whom the Lord imputeth not iniquity, and in whose spirit there is no guile. — The blood of Jesus Christ his Son cleanseth us from all sin.

Micah 7:18,19   Isaiah 54:7,8   Jeremiah 31:34   Psalm 32:1,2 1   John 1:7

MARCH 8 EVENING

I know whom I have believed,
and am persuaded that he is able.
— 2 TIMOTHY 1:12

Able to do exceeding abundantly above all that we ask or think. — Able to make all grace abound toward you; that ye, always having all sufficiency in all things, may abound to every good work. — Able to succour them that are tempted. — Able...to save them to the uttermost that come unto God by him, seeing he ever liveth to make intercession for them. — Able to keep you from falling, and to present you faultless before the presence of his glory with exceeding joy. — Able to keep that which I have committed unto him against that day. — Who shall change our vile body, that it may be fashioned like unto his glorious body, according to the working whereby he is able even to subdue all things unto himself. — Believe ye that I am able to do this?...Yea, Lord. According to your faith be it unto you.

Ephesians 3:20 2   Corinthians 9:8   Hebrews 2:18, 7:25
Jude 24 2   Timothy 1:12   Philippians 3:21
Matthew 9:28,29

MARCH 9 MORNING

The living God giveth us richly all things to enjoy.
— 1 TIMOTHY 6:17

Beware that thou forget not the Lord thy God, in not keeping his commandments, and his judgments, and his statutes, which I command thee this day: lest when thou hast eaten and art full, and hast built goodly houses, and dwelt therein;...then thine heart be lifted up, and thou forget the Lord thy God:...for it is he that giveth thee power to get wealth. — Except the Lord build the house, they labour in vain that build it: except the Lord keep the city, the watchman waketh but in vain. It is vain for you to rise up early, to sit up late, to eat the bread of sorrows: for so he giveth his beloved sleep. — They got not the land in possession by their own sword, neither did their own arm save them: but thy right hand, and thine arm, and the light of thy countenance, because thou hadst a favour unto them— There be many that say, Who will shew us any good? Lord, lift thou up the light of thy countenance upon us.

Deuteronomy 8:11,12,14,18   Psalms 127:1,2, 44:3, 4:6

MARCH 9 EVENING

They sang as it were a new song
— REVELATION 14:3

A new and living way, which he hath consecrated for us. — Not by works of righteousness which we have done, but according to his mercy he saved us, by the washing of regeneration, and renewing of the Holy Ghost; which he shed on us abundantly through Jesus Christ our Saviour. — By grace are ye saved through faith; and that not of yourselves: it is the gift of God; not of works, lest any man should boast. — Not unto us, O Lord, not unto us, but unto thy name give glory. — Unto him that loved us, and washed us from our sins in own blood, and hath made us kings and priests unto God and Father; to him be glory and dominion for ever and ever. Amen. — Thou wast slain, and hast redeemed us to God by thy blood out of every kindred, and tongue, and people, and nation. — I beheld, and, lo, a great multitude, which no man could number...cried saying, Salvation to our God which sitteth upon the throne, and unto the Lamb.

Hebrews 10:20   Titus 3:5,6   Ephesians 2:8,9
Psalm 115:1   Revelation 1:5, 5:9, 7:9,10

MARCH 10 MORNING

The Lord will provide.
— GENESIS 22:14

God will provide himself a lamb for a burnt offering. — Behold, the Lord's hand is not shortened, that it cannot save; neither his ear heavy, that it cannot hear. — There shall come out of Sion the Deliverer, and shall turn away ungodliness from Jacob. — Happy is he that hath the God of Jacob for his help, whose hope is in the Lord his God. — Behold, the eye of the Lord is upon them that fear him, upon them that hope in his mercy; to deliver their soul from death. — My God shall supply all your need, according to his riches in glory by Christ Jesus. — He hath said, I will never leave thee, nor forsake thee. So that we may boldly say, The Lord is my helper, and I will not fear what man shall do unto me. — The Lord is my strength and my shield; my heart trusteth in him, and I am helped: therefore my heart greatly rejoiceth: and with my song will I praise him.

Genesis 22:8   Isaiah 59:1   Romans 11:26   Psalm 146:5, 33:18,19
Philippians 4:19   Hebrews 13:5,6   Psalm 28:7

MARCH 10 EVENING

He feedeth among the lilies.
— SONG OF SOLOMON 2:16

Where two or three are gathered together in my name, there am I in the midst of them. — If a man love me, he will keep my words: and my Father will love him, and we will come unto him, and make our abode with him. — If ye keep my commandments, ye shall abide in my love; even as I have kept my Father's commandments, and abide in his love. — Let my beloved come into his garden, and eat his pleasant fruits. — I am come into my garden, my sister, my spouse: I have gathered my myrrh with my spice; I have eaten my honeycomb with my honey. — The fruit of the Spirit is love, joy, peace, longsuffering, gentleness, goodness, faith, meekness, temperance. — Herein is my Father glorified, that ye bear much fruit; so shall ye be my disciples. — Every branch that beareth fruit, he purgeth it, that it may bring forth more fruit. — Being filled with the fruits of righteousness, which are by Jesus Christ, unto the glory and praise of God.

Matthew 18:20   John 14:23, 15:10   Song of Solomon 4:16, 5:1
Galatians 5:22,23   John 15:8,2   Philippians 1:11

MARCH 11 MORNING

The Lord bless thee, and keep thee.
— NUMBERS 6:24

The blessing of the Lord, it maketh rich, and he addeth no sorrow with it. — Thou, Lord, wilt bless the righteous; with favour wilt thou compass him as with a shield. — He will not suffer thy foot to be moved: he that keepeth thee will not slumber. Behold, he that keepeth Israel shall neither slumber nor sleep. The Lord is thy keeper: the Lord is thy shade upon thy right hand. The Lord shall preserve thee from all evil: he shall preserve thy soul. The Lord shall preserve thy going out and thy coming in from this time forth, and even for evermore. — I the Lord do keep it; I will water it every moment: lest any hurt it, I will keep it night and day. — Holy Father, keep through thine own name those whom thou hast given me. While I was with them in the world, I kept them in thy name: those that thou gavest me I have kept. — The Lord shall deliver me from every evil work, and will preserve me unto his heavenly kingdom: to whom be glory for ever and ever. Amen.

Proverbs 10:22   Psalms 5:12, 121:3,5,7,8   Isaiah 27:3
John 17:11,12   2 Timothy 4:18

MARCH 11 EVENING

Jesus wept.
— JOHN 11:35

A man of sorrows, and acquainted with grief. — We have not an high priest which cannot be touched with the feeling of our infirmities. — It became him, for whom are all things, and by whom are all things, in bringing many sons unto glory, to make the captain of their salvation perfect through sufferings. — Though he were a Son, yet learned he obedience by the things which he suffered. — I was not rebellious, neither turned away back. I gave my back to the smiters, and my cheeks to them that plucked off the hair: I hid not my face from shame and spitting. — Behold how he loved. — He took not on him the nature of angels; but he took on him the seed of Abraham. In all things it behooved him to be made like unto his brethren, that he might be a merciful and faithful high priest in things pertaining to God, to make reconciliation for the sins of the people.

Isaiah 53:3   Hebrews 4:15, 2:10, 5:8
Isaiah 50:5,6   John 11:36   Hebrews 2:16,17

MARCH 12 MORNING

The Lord make his face shine upon thee,
and be gracious unto thee.
The Lord lift up his countenance upon thee,
and give thee peace.
— NUMBERS 6:25,26

No man hath seen God at any time; the only begotten Son, which is in the bosom of the Father, he hath declared him. — The brightness of his glory, and the express image of his person. — The god of this world hath blinded the minds of them which believe not, lest the light of the glorious gospel of Christ, who is the image of God, should shine unto them. — Make thy face to shine upon thy servant: save me for thy mercies sake. Let me not be ashamed, O Lord; for I have called upon thee. — Lord, by thy favour thou hast made my mountain to stand strong: thou didst hide thy face, and I was troubled. — Blessed is the people that know the joyful sound: they shall walk, O Lord, in the light of thy countenance. — The Lord will give strength unto his people; the Lord will bless his people with peace. — Be of good cheer; it is I; be not afraid.

John 1:18   Hebrews 1:3   2 Corinthians 4:4
Psalms 31:16,17, 30:7, 89:15, 29:11   Matthew 14:27

MARCH 12 EVENING

Things that are pleasing in his sight.
— 1 JOHN 3:22

Without faith it is impossible to please him. — So then they that are in the flesh cannot please God. — The Lord taketh pleasure in his people. — This is thankworthy, if a man for conscience toward God endure grief, suffering wrongfully. If, when ye do well, and suffer for it, ye take it patiently, this is acceptable with God. — The ornament of a meek and quiet spirit...is in the sight of God of great price. — Whoso offereth praise glorifieth me: and to him that ordereth his conversation aright will I shew the salvation of God. — I will praise the name of God with a song, and will magnify him with thanksgiving. This also shall please the Lord better than an ox or bullock that hath horns and hoofs. — I beseech you...brethren, by the mercies of God, that ye present your bodies a living sacrifice, holy, acceptable unto God, which is your reasonable service.

Hebrews 11:6   Romans 8:8   Psalm 149:4   1 Peter 2:19,20, 3:4
Psalms 50:23, 69:30,31   Romans 12:1

MARCH 13 MORNING

*There is one God,
and one mediator between God and man,
the man Christ Jesus.*
— 1 TIMOTHY 2:5

Forasmuch...as the children are partakers of flesh and blood, he also himself likewise took part of the same. — Look unto me, and be ye saved, all the ends of the earth: for I am God, and there is none else. — We have an advocate with the Father, Jesus Christ the righteous. — In Christ Jesus, ye who sometime were far off, are made nigh by the blood of Christ. For he is our peace. — By his own blood he entered in once into the holy place, having obtained eternal redemption for us. And for this cause he is the mediator of the new testament, that by means of death, for the redemption of the transgressions that were under the first testament, they which are called might receive the promise of eternal inheritance. — He is able also to save them to the uttermost that come unto God by him, seeing he ever liveth to make intercession for them.

Hebrews 2:14   Isaiah 45:22   1 John 2:1   Ephesians 2:13,14   Hebrews 9:12,15, 7:25

MARCH 13 EVENING

O my God, my soul is cast down within me.
— PSALM 42:6

Thou wilt keep him in perfect peace, whose mind is stayed on thee: because he trusteth in thee. Trust ye in the Lord for ever: for in the Lord JEHOVAH is everlasting strength. — Cast thy burden upon the Lord, and he shall sustain thee. — He hath not despised nor abhorred the affliction of the afflicted; neither hath he hid his face from him; but when he cried unto him, he heard. — Is any among you afflicted? let him pray. — Let not your heart be troubled, neither let it be afraid. — Take no thought for your life, what ye shall eat, or what ye shall drink; nor yet for your body, what ye shall put on. Behold the fowls of the air: for they sow not, neither do they reap, nor gather into barns; yet your heavenly Father feedeth them. Are ye not much better than they?— Be not faithless, but believing. — Lo, I am with you alway.

Isaiah 26:3,4   Psalms 55:22, 22:24   James 5:13   John 14:27   Matthew 6:25,26   John 20:27   Matthew 28:20

MARCH 14 MORNING

Adorn the doctrine of God our Saviour in all things.
— TITUS 2:10

Let your conversation be as it becometh the gospel of Christ. — Abstain from all appearance of evil. — If ye be reproached for the name of Christ, happy are ye. But let none of you suffer as a murderer, or as a thief, or as an evildoer, or as a busybody in other men's matters. — Be blameless and harmless, the sons of God, without rebuke, in the midst of a crooked and perverse nation, among whom ye shine as lights in the world. — Let your light so shine before men, that they may see your good works, and glorify your Father which is in heaven. — Let not mercy and truth forsake thee: bind them about thy neck; write them upon the table of thine heart; so shalt thou find favour and good understanding in the sight of God and man. — Brethren, whatsoever things are true, whatsoever things are honest, whatsoever things are just, whatsoever things are pure, whatsoever things are lovely, whatsoever things are of good report; if there be any virtue, and if there be any praise, think on these things.

Philippians 1:27 1 Thessalonians 5:22 1 Peter 4:14,15 Philippians 2:15
Matthew 5:16 Proverbs 3:3,4 Philippians 4:8

MARCH 14 EVENING

The words that I speak unto you,
they are spirit, and they are life.
— JOHN 6:63

Of his own will begat he us with the word of truth. — The letter killeth, but the spirit giveth life. — Christ...loved the church, and gave himself for it; that he might sanctify and cleanse it with the washing of water by the word, that he might present it to himself a glorious church, not having spot, or wrinkle, or any such thing. — Wherewithal shall a young man cleanse his way? By taking heed thereto according to thy word. Thy word hath quickened me. Thy word have I hid in mine heart, that I might not sin against thee. I will not forget thy word. I trust in thy word. The law of thy mouth is better unto me than thousands of gold and silver. I will never forget thy precepts: for with them thou hast quickened me. How sweet are thy words unto my taste! yea, sweeter than honey to my mouth! Through thy precepts I get understanding: therefore I hate every false way.

James 1:18 2 Corinthians 3:6 Ephesians 5:25-27
Psalm 119:9,50,11,16,42,72,93,103,104

MARCH 15 MORNING

Perfect through sufferings.
— HEBREWS 2:10

My soul is exceeding sorrowful, even unto death: tarry here, and watch with me. And he went a little farther, and fell on his face, and prayed, saying, O my Father, if it be possible, let this cup pass from me: nevertheless not as I will, but as thou wilt. — And being in an agony he prayed more earnestly: and his sweat was as it were great drops of blood falling down to the ground. — The sorrows of death compassed me, and the pains of hell gat hold upon me: I found trouble and sorrow. — Reproach hath broken my heart; and I am full of heaviness: and I looked for some to take pity, but there was none; and for comforters, but I found none. — I looked on my right hand, and behold, but there was no man that would know me: refuge failed me; no man cared for my soul. — He is despised and rejected of men; a man of sorrows, and acquainted with grief: and we hid as it were our faces from him; he was despised, and we esteemed him not.

Matthew 26:38,39   Luke 22:44   Psalms 116:3, 69:20, 142:4   Isaiah 53:3

MARCH 15 EVENING

The Lord made heaven and earth,
the sea, and all that in them is.
— EXODUS 20:11

The heavens declare the glory of God; and the firmament sheweth his handywork. — By the word of the Lord were the heavens made; and all the host of them by the breath of his mouth. For he spake, and it was done; he commanded, and it stood fast. — Behold, the nations are as a drop of a bucket, and are counted as the small dust of the balance: behold, he taketh up the isles as a very little thing. — Through faith we understand that the worlds were framed by the word of God, so that things which are seen were not made of things which do appear. — When I consider thy heavens, the work of thy fingers, the moon and the stars, which thou hast ordained; what is man, that thou art mindful of him? And the son of man, that thou visitest him?

Psalms 19:1, 33:6,9   Isaiah 40:15   Hebrews 11:3   Psalm 8:3,4

MARCH 16 MORNING

What is your life?
It is even a vapour, that appeareth for a little time,
and then vanisheth away.
— JAMES 4:14

My days are swifter than a post: they flee away, they see no good. They are passed away as the swift ships: as the eagle that hasteth to the prey. — Thou carriest them away as with a flood; they are as a sleep…in the morning they are like grass which groweth up. In the morning it flourisheth, and groweth up: in the evening it is cut down, and withereth. — Man that is born of a woman is of few days, and full of trouble. He cometh forth like a flower, and is cut down. — The world passeth away, and the lust thereof: but he that doeth the will of God abideth for ever. — They shall perish, but thou shalt endure: yea, all of them shall wax old like a garment; as a vesture shalt thou change them, and they shall be changed: but thou art the same, and thy years shall have no end. — Jesus Christ, the same yesterday, and today, and forever.

Job 9:25,26   Psalm 90:5,6   Job 14:2.1
John 2:17   Psalm 102:26,27   Hebrews 13:8

MARCH 16 EVENING

I will sing with the spirit,
and I will sing with the understanding also.
— 1 CORINTHIANS 14:15

Be filled with the Spirit, speaking to yourselves in psalms and hymns and spiritual Song, singing and making melody in your heart to the Lord. — Let the word of Christ dwell in you richly in all wisdom; teaching and admonishing one another in psalms and hymns and spiritual songs, singing with grace in your hearts to the Lord. — My mouth shall speak the praise of the Lord: and let all flesh bless his holy name for ever and ever. — Praise ye the Lord: for it is good to sing praises unto our God; for it is pleasant; and praise is comely. Sing unto the Lord with thanksgiving; sing praise upon the harp unto our God. — I heard a voice from heaven, as the voice of many waters, and as the voice of a great thunder; and I heard the voice of harpers harping with their harps.

Ephesians 5:18,19   Colossians 3:16   Psalms 145:21, 147:1,7   Revelation 14:2

MARCH 17 MORNING

He shall put his hand upon the head of the burnt offering;
and it shall be accepted for him
to make atonement for him.
— LEVITICUS 1:4

    Ye know that ye were not redeemed with corruptible things, as silver and gold, from your vain conversation received by tradition from your fathers; but with the precious blood of Christ, as of a lamb without blemish and without spot. — Who his own self bare our sins in his own body on the tree. — He hath made us accepted in the Beloved. As lively stones...built up a spiritual house, a holy priesthood, to offer up spiritual sacrifices, acceptable to God by Jesus Christ. — I beseech you therefore, brethren, by the mercies of God, that ye present your bodies a living sacrifice, holy, acceptable unto God, which is your reasonable service. — Now unto him that is able to keep you from falling, and to present you faultless before the presence of his glory with exceeding joy, to the only wise God our Saviour, be glory and majesty, dominion and power, both now and ever.

    1 Peter 1:18,19, 2:24   Ephesians 1:6 1   Peter 2:5   Romans 12:1 Jude 24,25

MARCH 17 EVENING

In all points tempted like as we are, yet without sin.
— HEBREWS 4:15

    When the woman saw that the tree was good for food (the lust of the flesh), and that it was pleasant to the eyes (the lust of the eyes), and a tree to be desired to make one wise (the pride of life), she took of the fruit thereof, and did eat, and gave also unto her husband with her; and he did eat. — When the tempter came to [Jesus], he said, if thou be the Son of God, command that these stones be made bread (the lust of the flesh). But he answered...Man shall not live by bread alone, but by every word that proceedeth out of the mouth of God. The devil...sheweth him all the kingdoms of the world, and the glory of them (the lust of the eyes, and the pride of life). Then saith Jesus unto him, Get thee hence, Satan. — In that he himself hath suffered being tempted, he is able to succour them that are tempted. — Blessed is the man that endureth temptation.

    Genesis 3:6 1   John 2:16   Matthew 4:3,4,8-10
    1 John 2:16   Hebrews 2:18   James 1:12

MARCH 18 MORNING

Mine eyes fail with looking upward.
— ISAIAH 38:14

Have mercy upon me, O Lord; for I am weak: O Lord, heal me; for my bones are vexed. — My soul is also sore vexed: but thou, O Lord, how long? Return, O Lord, deliver my soul: oh save me for thy mercies' sake. — My heart is sore pained within me: and the terrors of death are fallen upon me. Fearfulness and trembling are come upon me, and horror hath overwhelmed me. And I said, Oh that I had wings like a dove! For then would I fly away, and be at rest. — Ye have need of patience. — While they looked stedfastly toward heaven as he went up, behold, two men stood by them in white apparel; which also said, Ye men of Galilee, why stand ye gazing up into heaven? This same Jesus, which is taken up from you into heaven, shall so come in like manner as ye have seen him go into heaven. — Our conversation is in heaven; from whence also we look for the Saviour, the Lord Jesus Christ. — That blessed hope,...the glorious appearing of the great God and our Saviour Jesus Christ.

Psalms 6:2-4, 55:4-6   Hebrews 10:36   Acts 1:10,11   Philippians 3:20   Titus 2:13

MARCH 18 EVENING

His name shall be in their foreheads.
— REVELATION 22:4

I am the good shepherd, and know my sheep. — The foundation of God standeth sure, having this seal, The Lord knoweth them that are his. And, Let every one that nameth the name of Christ depart from iniquity. — The Lord is good, a strong hold in the day of trouble; and he knoweth them that trust in him. — Hurt not the earth, neither the sea, nor the trees, till we have sealed the servants of our God in their foreheads. — After that ye believed, ye were sealed with that holy Spirit of promise, which is the earnest of our inheritance. — Now he which stablisheth us with you in Christ, and hath anointed us, is God; who hath also sealed us, and given the earnest of the Spirit in our hearts. — I will write upon him the name of my God, and the name of the city of my God, which is new Jerusalem, which cometh down out of heaven from my God: and I will write upon him my new name. — This is the name wherewith she shall be called, The Lord our Righteousness.

John 10:14   2 Timothy 2:19   Nahum 1:7   Revelation 7:3   Ephesians 1:13,14   2 Corinthians 1:21,22   Revelation 3:12   Jeremiah 33:16

MARCH 19 MORNING

God, having raised up his Son Jesus,
sent him to bless you,
in the turning away every one of you from his iniquities.
— ACTS 3:26

Blessed be the God and Father of our Lord Jesus Christ, which according to his abundant mercies hath begotten us again unto a lively hope by the resurrection of Jesus Christ from the dead. — Saved by his life. — Our Saviour Jesus Christ...who gave himself for us that he might redeem us from all iniquity, and purify unto himself a peculiar people, zealous of good works. — As he which hath called you is holy, so be ye holy in all manner of conversation; because it is written, Be ye holy for I am holy. — The God and Father of our Lord Jesus Christ...hath blessed us with all spiritual blessings in heavenly places in Christ. — In him dwelleth all the fulness of the Godhead bodily. And ye are complete in him. — Of his fulness have all we received, and grace for grace. — He that spared not his own son, but delivered him up for us all, how shall he not with him also freely give us all things?

1 Peter 1:3   Romans 5:10   Titus 2:13,14 1 Peter 1:15,16   Ephesians 1:3   Colossians 2:9,10   John 1:16   Romans 8:32

MARCH 19 EVENING

Strengthen thou me according unto thy word.
— PSALM 119:28

Remember the word unto thy servant, upon which thou has caused me to hope. — O Lord, I am oppressed; undertake for me. — Heaven and earth shall pass away: but my words shall not pass away. — Ye know in all your hearts and in all your souls, that not one thing hath failed of all the good things which the Lord your God spake concerning you; all are come to pass unto you, and not one thing hath failed thereof. — Fear not: peace be unto thee, be strong, yea, be strong. And when he had spoken unto me, I was strengthened, and said, Let my lord speak; for thou hast strengthened me. — Be strong...and work: for I am with you, saith the Lord of hosts. — Not by might nor by power, but by my spirit, saith the Lord of hosts. — Be strong in the Lord, and in the power of his might.

Psalm 119:49   Isaiah 38:14   Luke 21:33   Joshua 23:14
Daniel 10:19   Haggai 2:4   Zechariah 4:6   Ephesians 6:10

MARCH 20 MORNING

The entrance of thy words giveth light.
— PSALM 119:130

This...is the message which we have heard of him, and declare unto you, that God is light, and in him is no darkness at all. — God, who commanded the light to shine out of darkness, hath shined in our hearts, to give the light of the knowledge of the glory of God in the face of Jesus Christ. — The Word was God. In him was life; and the life was the light of men. — If we walk in the light, as he is in the light, we have fellowship one with another and the blood of Jesus Christ his Son cleanseth us from all sin. — Thy word have I hid in mine heart, that I might not sin against thee. — Ye are clean through the word which I have spoken unto you. — Ye were sometimes darkness, but now are ye light in the Lord: walk as children of light. — Ye are a chosen generation, a royal priesthood, a holy nation, a peculiar people; that ye should shew forth the praises of him who hath called you out of darkness into his marvellous light.

1 John 1:5 2 Corinthians 4:6 John 1:1,4 1 John 1:7
Psalm 119:11 John 15:3 Ephesians 5:8 1 Peter 2:9

MARCH 20 EVENING

Noah was a just man.
— GENESIS 6:9

The just shall live by faith. — Noah builded an altar unto the Lord; and took of every clean beast, and of every clean fowl, and offered burnt offerings on the altar. And the Lord smelled a sweet savour. — The Lamb slain from the foundation of the world. — Being justified by faith, we have peace with God through our Lord Jesus Christ. — By the deeds of the law there shall no flesh be justified in his sight: for by the law is the knowledge of sin. But now the righteousness of God without the law is manifested, being witnessed by the law and the prophets; even the righteousness of God which is by faith of Jesus Christ unto all and upon all them that believe for there is no difference. — We... joy in God, through our Lord Jesus Christ, by whom we have now received the atonement. — Who shall lay any thing to the charge of God's elect? It is God that justifieth. — Whom he did predestinate, them he also called: and whom he called, them he also justified.

Galatians 3:11 Genesis 8:20,21 Revelation 13:8
Romans 5:1, 3:20-22, 5:11, 8:33,30

MARCH 21 MORNING

Be watchful, and strengthen the things which remain, that are ready to die.
— REVELATION 3:2

The end of all things is at hand: be ye therefore sober, and watch unto prayer. — Be sober, be vigilant; because your adversary the devil, as a roaring lion, walketh about, seeking whom he may devour. — Take heed to thyself, and keep thy soul diligently, lest thou forget the things which thine eyes have seen, and lest they depart from thy heart all the days of thy life. — The just shall live by faith: but if any man draw back, my soul shall have no pleasure in him. But we are not of them who draw back unto perdition; but of them that believe to the saving of the soul. — What I say unto you I say unto all, Watch. — Fear thou not; for I am with thee: be not dismayed; for I am thy God: I will strengthen thee; yea, I will help thee; yea, I will uphold thee with the right hand of my righteousness. I the Lord thy God will hold thy right hand.

1 Peter 4:7, 5:8   Deuteronomy 4:9   Hebrews 10:38,39   Mark 13:37   Isaiah 41:10,13

MARCH 21 EVENING

Is his mercy clean gone for ever?
— PSALM 77:8

His mercy endureth for ever. — The Lord is longsuffering, and of great mercy. — Who is a God like unto thee, that pardoneth iniquity?...he retaineth not his anger for ever, because he delighteth in mercy. He will turn again, he will have compassion upon us; he will subdue our iniquities; and thou wilt cast all their sin into the depths of the sea. — Not by works of righteousness which we have done, but according to his mercy he saved us. — Blessed be God, even the Father of our Lord Jesus Christ, the Father of mercies, and the God of all comfort; who comforteth us in all our tribulation, that we may be able to comfort them which are in any trouble, by the comfort wherewith we ourselves are comforted of God. — A merciful and faithful high priest in things pertaining to God to make reconciliation for the sins of the people. For in that himself hath suffered being tempted, he is able to succour them that are tempted.

Psalm 136:23   Numbers 14:18   Micah 7:18,19
Titus 3:5   2 Corinthians 1:3,4   Hebrews 2:17,18

MARCH 22 MORNING

Lot lifted up his eyes, and beheld all the plain of Jordan,
that it was well watered every where,
before the Lord destroyed Sodom and Gomorrah,
even as the garden of the Lord.
Then Lot chose him all the plain of Jordan.
— GENESIS 13:10,11

Just Lot...that righteous man. — Be not deceived; God is not mocked: for whatsoever a man soweth, that shall he also reap. — Remember Lot's wife. — Be ye not unequally yoked together with unbelievers: for what fellowship hath righteousness with unrighteousness? And what communion hath light with darkness? Wherefore come out from among them, and be ye separate, saith the Lord, and touch not the unclean thing. — Be not ye...partakers with them. For ye were sometime darkness, but now are ye light in the Lord: walk as children of light: proving what is acceptable unto the Lord. And have no fellowship with the unfruitful works of darkness, but rather reprove them.

2 Peter 2:7,8   Galatians 6:7   Luke 17:32
2 Corinthians 6:14,17   Ephesians 5:7,8,10,11

MARCH 22 EVENING

If so be the Lord will be with me,
then I shall be able to drive them out, as the Lord said.
— JOSHUA 14:12

He hath said, I will never leave thee, nor forsake thee. So that we may boldly say, The Lord is my helper, and I will not fear what man shall do unto me. — I will go in the strength of the Lord GOD: I will make mention of thy righteousness, even of thine only. — The work of righteousness shall be peace; and the effect of righteousness quietness and assurance for ever. — Stand...having your loins girt about with truth, and having on the breastplate of righteousness. For we wrestle not against flesh and blood, but against principalities, against powers, against the rulers of the darkness of this world, against spiritual wickedness in high places. Wherefore take unto you the whole armour of God, that ye may be able to withstand in the evil day, and having done all, to stand. — The Lord is with thee...Go in this thy might.

Hebrews 13:5,6   Psalm 71:16   Isaiah 32:17
Ephesians 6:14,12,13   Judges 6:12,14

MARCH 23 MORNING

Holy, holy, holy, Lord God Almighty.
— REVELATION 4:8

Thou art holy, O thou that inhabitest the praises of Israel. — Draw not nigh hither; put off thy shoes from off thy feet, for the place whereon thou standest is holy ground...I am the God of thy father, the God of Abraham, the God of Isaac, and the God of Jacob. And Moses hid his face; for he was afraid to look upon God. — To whom then will ye liken me, or shall I be equal? saith the Holy One. — I am the Lord thy God, the Holy One of Israel, thy Saviour. I, even I, am the Lord; and beside me there is no saviour. — As he which hath called you is holy, so be ye holy in all manner of conversation; because it is written, Be ye holy; for I am holy. — Know ye not that your body is the temple of the Holy Ghost which is in you, which ye have of God, and ye are not your own. — Ye are the temple of the living God; as God hath said, I will dwell in them, and walk in them; and I will be their God, and they shall be my people. — Can two walk together, except they be agreed?

Psalm 22:3   Exodus 3:5,6   Isaiah 40:25, 43:3,11 1 Peter 1:15,16
1 Corinthians 6:19 2 Corinthians 6:16   Amos 3:3

MARCH 23 EVENING

They constrained him, saying, Abide with us.
— LUKE 24:29

Behold, I stand at the door, and knock: if any man hear my voice, and open the door, I will come in to him, and will sup with him, and he with me. — Tell me, O thou whom my soul loveth, where thou feedest, where thou makest thy flock to rest at noon: for why should I be as one that torrent aside by the flocks of thy companions? — I found him whom my soul loveth: I held him, and would not let him go. — Let my beloved come into his garden, and eat his pleasant fruits. — I am come into my garden. — I said not unto the seed of Jacob, Seek ye me in vain. — Lo, I am with you alway, even unto the end of the world. — I will never leave thee, nor forsake thee. — Where two or three are gathered together in my name, there am I in the midst of them. — The world seeth me no more; but, ye see me.

Revelation 3:20 Song of Solomon 1:7, 3:4, 4:16, 5:1   Isaiah 45:19
Matthew 28:20   Hebrews 13:5   Matthew 18:20   John 14:19

MARCH 24 MORNING

*Abraham believed in the Lord;
and he counted it to him for righteousness.*
— GENESIS 15:6

He staggered not at the promise of God through unbelief; but was strong in faith, giving glory to God; and being fully persuaded that, what he had promised, he was able also to perform. And therefore it was imputed to him for righteousness. Now it was not written for his sake alone, that it was imputed to him: but for us also, to whom it shall be imputed, if we believe on him that raised up Jesus our Lord from the dead. — The promise, that he should be the heir of the world, was not to Abraham, or to his seed, through the law, but through the righteousness of faith. — The just shall live by faith. — Let us hold fast the profession of our faith without wavering; (for he is faithful that promised). — Our God is in the heavens; he hath done whatsoever he hath pleased. — With God nothing shall be impossible...And blessed is she that believed: for there shall be a performance of those things which were told her from the Lord.

Romans 4:20-24,13, 1:17   Hebrews 10:23   Psalm 115:3   Luke 1:37,45

MARCH 24 EVENING

God hath called you unto his kingdom and glory.
— 1 THESSALONIANS 2:12

My kingdom is not of this world: if my kingdom were of this world, then would my servants fight...but now is my kingdom not from hence. — Expecting till his enemies be made his footstool. — The kingdoms of this world are become the kingdoms of our Lord, and of his Christ; and he shall reign for ever and ever. — Thou hast made us unto our God kings and priests: and we shall reign on the earth. — I saw thrones, and they sat upon them, and judgment was given unto them;...and they lived and reigned with Christ a thousand years. — Then shall the righteous shine forth as the sun in the kingdom of their Father. — Fear not, little flock; for it is your Father's good pleasure to give you the kingdom. — I appoint unto you a kingdom, as my Father hath appointed unto me; that ye may eat and drink at my table in my kingdom, and sit on thrones judging the twelve tribes of Israel. — Thy kingdom come.

John 18:36   Hebrews 10:13   Revelation 11:15, 5:10, 20:4
Matthew 13:43   Luke 12:32, 22:29,30   Matthew 6:10

MARCH 25 MORNING

I will never leave thee, nor forsake thee.
— HEBREWS 13:5

So that we may boldly say, The Lord is my helper, and I will not fear what man shall do unto me. — Behold, I am with thee, and will keep thee in all places whither thou goest, and will bring thee again into this land; for I will not leave thee, until I have done that which I have spoken to thee of. — Be strong and of a good courage, fear not, nor be afraid of them: for the Lord thy God, he it is that doth go with thee; he will not fail thee, nor forsake thee. — Demas hath forsaken me, having loved this present world. At my first answer no man stood with me, but all men forsook me: I pray God that it may not be laid to their charge. Notwithstanding the Lord stood with me, and strengthened me. — When my father and my mother forsake me, then the Lord will take me up. — Lo, I am with you alway, even unto the end of the world. — I am he that liveth, and was dead; and, behold, I am alive for evermore. — I will not leave you comfortless; I will come to you. — My peace I give unto you.

Hebrews 13:6   Genesis 28:15   Deuteronomy 31:6   2 Timothy 4:10,16,17
Psalm 27:10   Matthew 28:20   Revelation 1:18   John 14:18,27

MARCH 25 EVENING

Master, we have toiled all the night,
and have taken nothing;
nevertheless at thy word I will let down the net.
— LUKE 5:5

All power is give unto me in heaven and in earth. Go ye therefore and teach all nations, baptizing them in the name of the Father, and of the Son, and of the Holy Ghost:...and, lo, I am with you alway, even unto the end of the world. — The kingdom of heaven is like unto a net, that was cast into the sea. — Though I preach the gospel, I have nothing to glory of: necessity is laid upon me; yea, woe is unto me, if I preach not gospel! I am made all things to all men, that I might by all means save some. — Let us not be weary in well doing: for in due season we shall reap, if we faint not. — My word...shall not return unto me void, but it shall accomplish that which I please. — So then neither is he that planteth any thing, neither he that watereth; but God that giveth the increase.

Matthew 28:18-20, 13:47   1 Corinthians 9:16,22
Galatians 6:9   Isaiah 55:11   1 Corinthians 3:7

MARCH 26 MORNING

*The kingdom of heaven is as a man
travelling into a far country, who called his own servants,
and delivered unto them his goods...
to every man according to his several ability.*
— MATTHEW 25:14,15

Know ye not, that to whom ye yield yourselves servants to obey, his servants ye are to whom ye obey? — All these worketh that one and the selfsame Spirit, dividing to every man severally as he will. The manifestation of the Spirit is given to every man to profit withal. — As every man hath received the gift, even so minister the same one to another, as good stewards of the manifold grace of God. — It is required in stewards, that a man be found faithful. — Unto whomsoever much is given, of him shall be much required: and to whom men have committed much, of him they will ask the more. — Who is sufficient for these things? — I can do all things through Christ which strengtheneth me.

Romans 6:16 1 Corinthians 12:11,7 1 Peter 4:10 1 Corinthians 4:2 Luke 12:48 2 Corinthians 2:16 Philippians 4:13

MARCH 26 EVENING

Distributing to the necessity of saints.
— ROMANS 12:13

David said, Is there yet any that is left...of the house of Saul, that I may shew him kindness for Jonathan's sake? — Come, ye blessed of my Father, inherit the kingdom prepared for you from the foundation of the world: for I was an hungered, and ye gave me meat: I was thirsty, and ye gave me drink: I was a stranger, and ye took me in: naked, and ye clothed me: I was sick, and ye visited me: I was in prison, and ye came unto me. Inasmuch as ye have done it unto one of the least of these my brethren, ye have done it unto me. — Whosoever shall give to drink one of these little ones a cup of cold water only in the name of a disciple, verily I say unto you, he shall in no wise lose his reward. — To do good and to communicate forget not: for with such sacrifices God is well pleased. — God is not unrighteous to forget your work and labour of love, which ye have shewed toward his name, in that ye have ministered to the saints, and do minister.

2 Samuel 9:1 Matthew 25:34-36,40, 10:42 Hebrews 13:16, 6:10

MARCH 27 MORNING

To him that soweth righteousness shall be a sure reward.
— PROVERBS 11:18

After a long time the lord of those servants cometh, and reckoneth with them. And so he that had received five talents came and brought other five talents, saying, Lord, thou deliveredst unto me five talents: behold, I have gained beside them five talents more. His lord said unto him, Well done, thou good and faithful servant: thou hast been faithful over a few things, I will make thee ruler over many things; enter thou into the joy of thy lord. — We must all appear before the judgment seat of Christ; that every one may receive the things done in his body, according to that he hath done, whether it be good or bad. — I have fought a good fight, I have finished my course, I have kept the faith: henceforth there is laid up for me a crown of righteousness, which the Lord, the righteous judge, shall give me at that day: and not to me only, but unto all them also that love his appearing. — Behold, I come quickly: hold that fast which thou hast, that no man take thy crown.

Matthew 25:19-21 2 Corinthians 5:10 2 Timothy 4:7,8 Revelation 3:11

MARCH 27 EVENING

God is faithful.
— 1 CORINTHIANS 10:13

God is not a man that he should lie; neither the Son of man that he should repent: hath he said, and shall he not do it? Or hath he spoken, and shall he not make it good? — The Lord sware and will not repent. — God, willing more abundantly to shew unto the heirs of promise the immutability of his counsel, confirmed it by an oath: that by two immutable things, in which it was impossible for God to lie, we might have a strong consolation, who have fled for refuge to lay hold upon the hope set before us. — Wherefore let them that suffer according to the will of God commit the keeping of their souls to him in well doing, as unto a faithful Creator. — I know whom I have believed, and am persuaded that he is able to keep that which I have committed unto him against that day— Faithful is he that calleth you, who also will do it. — All the promises of God in him are yea, and in him Amen, unto the glory of God by us.

Numbers 23:19 Hebrews 7:21, 6:17,18 1 Peter 4:19
2 Timothy 1:12 1 Thessalonians 5:24 2 Corinthians 1:20

MARCH 28 MORNING

Be strong and of a good courage.
— *JOSHUA 1:18*

    The Lord is my light and my salvation: whom shall I fear? The Lord is the strength of my life: of whom shall I be afraid? — He giveth power to the faint; and to them that have no might he increaseth strength. Even the youths shall faint and be weary, and the young men shall utterly fall: but they that wait upon the Lord shall renew their strength; they shall mount up with wings as eagles; they shall run, and not be weary; and they shall walk, and not faint. — My flesh and my heart faileth: but God is the strength of my heart, and my portion for ever. — If God be for us, who can be against us? — The Lord is on my side; I will not fear: what can man do unto me? — Through thee will we push down our enemies: through thy name will we tread them under that rise up against us. — We are more than conquerors through him that loved us. — Arise therefore, and be doing, and the Lord be with thee.

    Psalm 27:1   Isaiah 40:29-31   Psalm 73:26   Romans 8:31
    Psalms 118:6, 44:5   Romans 8:37 1   Chronicles 22:16

MARCH 28 EVENING

Our friend sleepeth.
— *JOHN 11:11*

    I would not have you to be ignorant, brethren, concerning them which are asleep, that ye sorrow not, even as others which have no hope. For if we believe that Jesus died and rose again, even so them also which sleep in Jesus will God bring with him. — If the dead rise not, then is not Christ raised: and if Christ be not raised, your faith is vain; ye are yet in your sins. Then they also which are fallen asleep in Christ are perished. But now is Christ risen from the dead, and become the firstfruits of them that slept. — It came to pass, when all the people were clean passed over Jordan, that the Lord spake unto Joshua, saying, Take you hence out of the midst of Jordan, out of the place where the priests' feet stood firm, twelve stones...and these stones shall be for a memorial unto the children of Israel for ever. — This Jesus hath God raised up, whereof we all are witnesses. — Witnesses chosen before of God...who did eat and drink with him after he rose from the dead.

    1 Thessalonians 4:13,14 1   Corinthians 15:16-18,20   Joshua 4:1,3,7   Acts 2:32, 10:41

MARCH 29 MORNING

*Come, ye blessed of my Father, inherit the kingdom
prepared for you from the foundation of the world.*
— *MATTHEW 25:34*

Fear not, little flock; for it is your Father's good pleasure to give you the kingdom. — Hath not God chosen the poor of this world rich in faith, and heirs of the kingdom which he hath promised to them that love him? — Heirs of God, and joint-heirs with Christ; if so be that we suffer with him, that we may be also glorified together. — The Father himself loveth you, because ye have loved me. — God is not ashamed to be called their God: for he hath prepared for them a city. — He that overcometh shall inherit all things; and I will be his God, and he shall be my son. — There is laid up for me a crown of righteousness, which the Lord, the righteous judge, shall give me at that day: and not to me only, but unto all them also that love his appearing. — He which hath begun a good work in you will perform it until the day of Jesus Christ.

Luke 12:32   James 2:5   Romans 8:17   John 16:27   Hebrews 11:16
Revelation 21:71   1 Timothy 4:8   Philippians 1:6

MARCH 29 EVENING

*Riches are not forever;
and doth the crown endure to every generation?*
— *PROVERBS 27:24*

Surely every man walketh in a vain shew: surely they are disquieted in vain: he heapeth up riches, and knoweth not who shall gather them. — Set your affection on things above, not on things on the earth. — Lay not up for yourselves treasures upon earth, where moth and rust doth corrupt, and where thieves break through and steal: but lay up for yourselves treasures in heaven. For where your treasure is, there will your heart be also. — They do it to obtain a corruptible crown, but we an incorruptible. — We look not at the things which are seen but at the things which are not seen. — To him that soweth righteousness shall be a sure reward. — There is laid up for me a crown of righteousness which the Lord, the righteous judge, shall give me at that day, and not to me only but unto all them also that love his appearing. — A crown of glory that fadeth not away.

Psalm 39:6   Colossians 3:2   Matthew 6:19-21   1 Corinthians 9:25
2 Corinthians 4:18   Proverbs 11:18   2 Timothy 4:8   1 Peter 5:4

MARCH 30 MORNING

Isaac went out to meditate in the field at the eventide.
— GENESIS 24:63

Let the words of my mouth, and the meditation of my heart, be acceptable in thy sight, O Lord, my strength, and my redeemer. — When I consider thy heavens, the work of thy fingers, the moon and the stars, which thou hast ordained; what is man, that thou art mindful of him? And the son of man, that thou visitest him? — The works of the Lord are great, sought out of all them that have pleasure therein. — Blessed is the man that walketh not in the counsel of the ungodly, nor standeth in the way of sinners, nor sitteth in the seat of the scornful. But his delight is in the law of the Lord; and in his law doth he meditate day and night. — This book of the law shall not depart out of thy mouth; but thou shalt meditate therein day and night. — My soul shall be satisfied as with marrow and fatness; and my mouth shall praise thee with joyful lips: when I remember thee upon my bed, and meditate on thee in the night watches.

Psalms 19:14, 8:3,4, 111:2, 1:1,2   Joshua 1:8   Psalm 63:5,6

MARCH 30 EVENING

How long wilt thou forget me, O Lord!
For ever?
How long wilt thou hide thy face from me?
— PSALM 13:1

Every good gift, and every perfect gift is from above, and cometh down from the Father of lights, with whom is no variableness, neither shadow of turning. — But Zion said, The Lord hath forsaken me, and my Lord hath forgotten me. Can a woman forget her suckling child, that she should not have compassion on the son of her womb? Yea, they may forget, yet will I not forget thee. — Thou shalt not be forgotten of me. I have blotted out, as a thick cloud, thy transgressions, and, as a cloud, thy sins. — Jesus loved Martha, and her sister, and Lazarus. When he had heard therefore that he was sick, he abode two days still in the same place where he was. — A woman...cried unto him, saying, Have mercy on me, O Lord, thou son of David! But he answered her not a word. — The trial of your faith, being much more precious than of gold that perisheth.

James 1:1   Isaiah 49:14,15   Isaiah 44:21,22
John 11:5,6   Matthew 15:22,23 1   Peter 1:7

MARCH 31 MORNING

*My God shall supply all your need
according to his riches in glory by Christ Jesus.*
— PHILIPPIANS 4:19

Seek ye first the kingdom of God, and his righteousness; and all...things shall be added unto you. — He that spared not his Son, but delivered him up for us all, how shall he not with him freely give us all things? — All things are yours; whether Paul or Apollos, or Cephas, or the world, or life, or death, or things present, or things to come; all are yours; and ye are Christ's; and Christ is God's. — As having nothing, and yet possessing all things. — The Lord is my shepherd; I shall not want. — The Lord God is a sun and shield: the Lord will give grace and glory: no good thing will be withheld from them that walk uprightly. — The living God...giveth us richly all things to enjoy. — God is able to make all grace abound toward you; that ye, always having all sufficiency in all things, may abound to every good work.

Matthew 6:33   Romans 8:32   1 Corinthians 3:21-23   2 Corinthians 6:10
Psalms 23:1, 84:11   1 Timothy 6:17   2 Corinthians 9:8

MARCH 31 EVENING

What communion hath light with darkness?
— 2 CORINTHIANS 6:14

Men loved darkness rather than light, because their deeds were evil. — Ye are all the children of light, and the children of the day: we are not of the night, nor of darkness. — Darkness hath blinded his eyes. — Thy word is a lamp unto my feet, and a light unto my path. — The dark places of the earth are full of the habitations of cruelty. — Love is of God; and every one that loveth is born of God, and knoweth God. He that loveth not knoweth not God; for God is love. — The way of the wicked is as darkness: they know not at what they stumble. The path of the just is as the shining light, that shineth more and more unto the perfect day. — I am come a light into the world, that whosoever believeth on me should not abide in darkness. — Ye were sometime darkness, but now are ye light in the Lord: walk as children of light.

John 3:19   1 Thessalonians 5:5   1 John 2:11   Psalms 119:105, 74:20
1 John 4:7,8   Proverbs 4:19,18   John 12:46   Ephesians 5:8

APRIL 1 MORNING

The fruit of the Spirit is joy.
— GALATIANS 5:22

Joy in the Holy Ghost. — Unspeakable and full of glory. — Sorrowful, yet always rejoicing;...exceeding joyful in all our tribulation. — We glory in tribulations. — Jesus the author and finisher of our faith;...for the joy that was set before him, endured the cross, despising the shame. — These things have I spoken unto you, that my joy might remain in you, and that your joy might be full. — As the sufferings of Christ abound in us, so our consolation also aboundeth by Christ. — Rejoice in the Lord alway: and again I say, Rejoice. — The joy of the Lord is your strength. — In thy presence is fulness of joy: at thy right hand there are pleasures for evermore. — For the Lamb which is in the midst of the throne shall feed them, and shall lead them unto living fountains of waters: and God shall wipe away all tears from their eyes.

Romans 14:17   1 Peter 1:8   2 Corinthians 6:10, 7:4   Romans 5:3   Hebrews 12:2   John 15:11   2 Corinthians 1:5   Philippians 4:4.   Nehemiah 8:10   Psalm 16:11   Revelation 7:17

APRIL 1 EVENING

Jehovah-shalom: (The Lord send peace.)
— JUDGES 6:24

Behold, a son shall be born to thee, who shall be a man of rest, and I will give him rest from all his enemies round about: for his name shall be Solomon, and I will give peace and quietness unto Israel in his days. — Behold, a greater than Solomon is here. — Unto us a child is born, unto us a son is given; and the government shall be upon his shoulder, and his name shall be called Wonderful, Counsellor, the mighty God, the everlasting Father, the Prince of Peace. — My people shall dwell in a peaceable habitation, and in sure dwellings, and in quiet resting places; when it shall hail, coming down on the forest; and the city shall be low in a low place. — He is our peace. — This man shall be the peace when the Assyrian shall come into our land. — These shall make war with the Lamb, and the Lamb shall overcome them: for he is Lord of lords, and King of kings. — Peace I leave with you, my peace I give unto you.

1 Chronicles 22:9   Matthew 12:42   Isaiah 9:6, 32:18,19   Ephesians 2:14   Micah 5:5   Revelation 17:14   John 14:27

APRIL 2 MORNING

If ye do return unto the Lord with all your hearts,
then put away the strange gods and Ashtaroth from among you,
and prepare your hearts unto the Lord, and serve him only.
— 1 SAMUEL 7:3

Little children, keep yourselves from idols. — Come out from among them, and be ye separate, saith the Lord, and touch not the unclean thing; and I will receive you, and will be a Father unto you, and ye shall be my sons and daughters, saith the Lord Almighty. — Ye cannot serve God and Mammon. — Thou shalt worship no other god: for the Lord, whose name is Jealous, is a jealous God. — Serve him with a perfect heart with a willing mind: for the Lord searcheth all hearts, and understandeth all the imaginations of the thoughts. — Behold, thou desireth truth in the inward parts: and in the hidden part thou shalt make me to know wisdom. — Man looketh on the outward appearance, but the Lord looketh on the heart. — Beloved, if our heart condemn us not, then have we confidence toward God.

1 John 5:21 2 Corinthians 6:17,18 Matthew 6:24 Exodus 34:14
1 Chronicles 28:9 Psalm 51:6 1 Samuel 16:7 1 John 3:21

APRIL 2 EVENING

When the Son of man cometh,
shall he find faith on the earth?
— LUKE 18:8

He came unto his own, and his own received him not. — The Spirit speaketh expressly, that in the latter times some shall from the faith. — Preach the word; be instant in season, out of season; reprove, rebuke, exhort with all longsuffering and doctrine. For the time will come when they will not endure sound doctrine; but after their own lusts shall they heap to themselves teachers, having itching ears; and they shall turn away their ears from the truth and shall be turned unto fables. — Of that day and that hour knoweth no man, no, not the angels which are in heaven, neither the Son, but the Father. Take ye heed, watch and pray: for ye know not when the time is. — Blessed are those servants, whom the lord when he cometh shall find watching. — Looking for that blessed hope...the glorious appearing of the great God, and our Saviour Jesus Christ,

John 1:11 1 Timothy 4:1 2 Timothy 4:2-4
Mark 13:32,33 Luke 12:37 Titus 2:13

APRIL 3 MORNING

Beloved, be not ignorant of this one thing,
that one day is with the Lord as a thousand years,
and a thousand years as one day.
The Lord is not slack concerning his promise,
as some men count slackness.
— 2 PETER 3:8,9

My thoughts are not your thoughts, neither are your ways my ways, saith the Lord. For as the heavens are higher than the earth, so are my ways higher than your ways, and my thoughts than your thoughts. For as the rain cometh down, and the snow from heaven, and returneth not thither, but watereth the earth...so shall my word be that goeth forth out of my mouth: it shall not return unto me void, but it shall accomplish that which I please, and it shall prosper in the thing whereto I sent it. — God hath concluded them all in unbelief, that he might have mercy upon all. O the depth of the riches both of the wisdom and knowledge of God! How unsearchable are his judgments, and his ways past finding out!

Isaiah 55:8-11   Romans 11:32,33

APRIL 3 EVENING

Ye were as a firebrand plucked out of the burning.
— AMOS 4:11

The sinners in Zion are afraid; fearfulness hath surprised the hypocrites. Who among us shall dwell with the devouring fire? Who among us shall dwell with everlasting burnings? — We had the sentence of death in ourselves, that we should not trust in ourselves, but in God which raiseth the dead: who delivered us from so great a death, and doth deliver: in whom we trust that he will yet deliver us. — The wages of sin is death; but the gift of God is eternal life through Jesus Christ our Lord. — It is a fearful thing to fall into the hands of the living God. — Knowing therefore the terror of the Lord, we persuade men. — Be instant in season, out of season. — Others save with fear, pulling them out of the fire. — Not by might, nor by power, but by my Spirit, saith the Lord of hosts. — Who will have all men to be saved, and to come unto the knowledge of the truth.

Isaiah 33:14 2   Corinthians 1:9,10   Romans 6:23
Hebrews 10:31 2   Corinthians 5:11 2   Timothy 4:2
Jude 23   Zechariah 4:6 1   Timothy 2:4

APRIL 4 MORNING

Fear not; I am the first and the last.
— REVELATION 1:17

Ye are not come unto the mount that might be touched, and that burned with fire, nor unto blackness, and darkness, and tempest, but ye are come unto mount Sion...to God the Judge of all, and to the spirits of just men made perfect, and to Jesus the mediator of the new covenant. — Jesus the author and finisher of our faith. — We have not a high priest which cannot be touched with the feeling of our infirmities; but was in all points tempted like as we are, yet without sin. Let us therefore come boldly unto the throne of grace, that we may obtain mercy, and find grace to help in time of need. — Thus saith the Lord the King of Israel, and his redeemer the Lord of hosts; I am the first, and I am the last; and beside me there is no God. — The mighty God, The everlasting Father, The Prince of Peace. — Art thou not from everlasting, O Lord my God, mine Holy One? — Who is God, save the Lord? And who is a rock, save our God?

Hebrews 12:18,22-24, 12:2, 4:15,16
Isaiah 44:6, 9:6   Habakkuk 1:12   2 Samuel 22:32

APRIL 4 EVENING

Lead me to the rock that is higher than I.
— PSALM 61:2

Be careful for nothing; but in every thing by prayer and supplication with thanksgiving let your requests be made known unto God. And the peace of God, which passeth all understanding, shall keep your hearts and minds through Christ Jesus. — When my spirit was overwhelmed within me, then thou knewest my path. — He knoweth the way that I take: when he hath tried me, I shall come forth as gold. — Lord, thou hast been our dwelling place in all generations. — Thou hast been a strength to the poor, a strength to the needy in his distress, a refuge from the storm, a shadow from the heaven. — Who is a rock save our God? — They shall never perish, neither shall any man pluck them out of my hand. — Uphold me according unto thy word, that I may live: and let me not be ashamed of my hope. — Which hope we have as an anchor of the soul, both sure and stedfast, and which entereth into that within the veil.

Philippians 4:6,7   Psalm 142:3   Job 23:10   Psalm 90:1   Isaiah 25:4   Psalm 18:31
John 10:28   Psalm 119:116   Hebrews 6:19

APRIL 5 MORNING

I will not let thee go, except thou bless me.
— GENESIS 32:26

Let him take hold of my strength, that he may make peace with me; and he shall make peace with me. — O woman, great is thy faith; be it unto thee even as thou wilt. — According to your faith be it unto you. — Let him ask in faith, nothing wavering. For he that wavereth is like a wave of the sea driven with the wind and tossed. For let not that man think that he shall receive any thing of the Lord. — They drew nigh unto the village, whither they went: and [Jesus] made as though he would have gone further. But they constrained him, saying, Abide with us:...he vanished out of their sight. And they said one to another, Did not our heart burn within us, while he talked with us by the way, and while he opened to us the scriptures? — I pray thee, if I have found grace in thy sight, shew me now thy way, that I may know thee, that I may find grace in thy sight. — My presence shall go with thee, and I will give thee rest.

Isaiah 27:5   Matthew 15:28, 9:29   James 1:6,7
Luke 24:28,29,31,32   Exodus 33:13, 14

APRIL 5 EVENING

Jesus the author and finisher of our faith.
— HEBREWS 12:2

I am Alpha and Omega, the beginning and the ending, saith the Lord, which is, and which was, and which is to come, the Almighty. — Who hath wrought and done it, calling the generations from the beginning? I the Lord, the first, and with the last: I am he. — Sanctified by God the Father, and preserved in Jesus Christ. — The very God of peace sanctify you wholly: and I pray God your whole spirit and soul and body be preserved blameless unto the coming of our Lord Jesus Christ. Faithful is he that calleth you, who also will do it. — He which hath begun a good work in you will perform it until the day of Jesus Christ. — Are ye so foolish? having begun in the Spirit, are ye now made perfect by the flesh?— The Lord will perfect that which concerneth me. — It is God which worketh in you both to will and to do of his good pleasure.

Revelation 1:8   Isaiah 41:4 Jude 1
1 Thessalonians 5:23,24   Philippians 1:6   Galatians 3:3   Psalm 138:8
Philippians 2:13

APRIL 6 MORNING

He ever liveth to make intercession.
— HEBREWS 7:25

Who is he that condemneth? it is Christ that died...who also maketh intercession for us. — Christ is not entered into the holy places made with hands, which are the figures of the true; but into heaven itself, now to appear in the presence of God for us. — If any man sin, we have an advocate with the Father, Jesus Christ the righteous. — There is one God, and one mediator between God and men, the man Christ Jesus. — Seeing...that we have a great high priest, that is passed into the heavens, Jesus the Son of God, let us hold fast our profession. For we have not an high priest which cannot be touched with the feeling of our infirmities; but was in all points tempted like as we are, yet without sin. Let us therefore come boldly unto the throne of grace, that we may obtain mercy, and find grace to help in time of need. — Through him we...have access by one Spirit unto the Father.

Romans 8:34   Hebrews 9:24   1 John 2:1
1 Timothy 2:5   Hebrews 4:14-16   Ephesians 2:18

APRIL 6 EVENING

They that know thy name will put their trust in thee.
— PSALM 9:10

This is his name whereby he shall be called, THE LORD OUR RIGHTEOUSNESS. — I will go in the strength of the Lord God: I will make mention of thy righteousness, even of thine only. — His name shall be called Wonderful, Counsellor. — O Lord, I know that the way of man is not in himself: it is not in man that walketh to direct his steps. — The mighty God, The everlasting Father. — I know whom I have believed, and am persuaded that he is able to keep that which I have committed unto him against that day. — The Prince of Peace. — He is our peace. — Being justified by faith, we have peace with God through our Lord Jesus Christ. — The name of the Lord is a strong tower: the righteous runneth into it, and is safe. — Woe to them that go down to Egypt for help. — As birds flying, so will the Lord of hosts defend Jerusalem; defending also he will deliver it; and passing over he will preserve it.

Jeremiah 23:6   Psalm 71:16   Isaiah 9:6   Jeremiah 10:23   Isaiah 9:6
2 Timothy 1:12   Isaiah 9:6   Ephesians 2:14   Romans 5:1
Proverbs 18:10   Isaiah 31:1,5

APRIL 7 MORNING

As sorrowful, yet always rejoicing;
as poor, yet making many rich;
as having nothing, and yet possessing all things.
— 2 CORINTHIANS 6:10

We...rejoice in hope of the glory of God. And not only so, but we glory in tribulations also. — I am filled with comfort, I am exceeding joyful in all our tribulation. — Believing, ye rejoice with joy unspeakable and full of glory. — In a great trial of affliction the abundance of their joy and their deep poverty abounded unto the riches of their liberality. — Unto me, who am less than the least of all saints, is this grace given, that I should preach among the Gentiles the unsearchable riches of Christ; and to make all men see what is the fellowship of the mystery, which from the beginning of the world hath been hid in God, who created all things by Jesus Christ. — Hath not God chosen the poor of this world rich in faith, and heirs of the kingdom which he hath promised to them that love him? — God is able to make all grace abound toward you; that ye, always having all sufficiency in all things, may abound to every good work.

Romans 5:2,3　2 Corinthians 7:4　1 Peter 1:8
2 Corinthians 8:2　Ephesians 3:8,9　James 2:5　2 Corinthians 9:8

APRIL 7 EVENING

The Lord strengthen him upon the bed of languishing:
thou wilt make all his bed in his sickness.
— PSALM 41:3

In all their affliction he was afflicted, and the angel of his presence saved them: in his love and in his pity he redeemed them; and he bare them, and carried them. — He whom thou lovest is sick. — My grace is sufficient for thee: for my strength is made perfect in weakness. — Most gladly therefore will I rather glory in my infirmities, that the power of Christ may rest upon me. — I can do all things through Christ which strengtheneth me. — We faint not;...though our outward man perish, yet the inward man is renewed day by day. — In him we live, and move, and have our being. — He giveth power to the faint; and to them that have no might he increaseth strength. Even the youths shall faint and be weary, and the young men shall utterly fall: but they that wait upon the Lord shall renew their strength. — The eternal God is thy refuge, and underneath are the everlasting arms.

Isaiah 63:9　John 11:3　2 Corinthians 12:9　Philippians 4:13　2 Corinthians 4:16
Acts 17:28　Isaiah 40:29-31　Deuteronomy 33:27

APRIL 8 MORNING

In everything ye are enriched by him.
— *1 CORINTHIANS 1:5*

When we were yet without strength, in due time Christ died for the ungodly. — He that spared not his own Son, but delivered him up for us all, how shall he not with him also freely give us all things? — In him dwelleth all the fulness of the Godhead bodily. And ye are complete in him, which is the head of all principality and power. — Abide in me, and I in you. As the branch cannot bear fruit of itself, except it abide in the vine; no more can ye, except ye abide in me. I am the vine ye are the branches: he that abideth in me and I in him, the same bringeth forth much fruit: for without me ye can do nothing. — To will is present with me; but how to perform that which is good I find not. — Unto every one of us is given grace according to the measure of the gift of Christ. — If ye abide in me, and my words abide in you, ye shall ask what ye will, and it shall be done unto you. — Let the word of Christ dwell in you richly in all wisdom.

Romans 5:6   Romans 8:32   Colossians 2:9,10   John 15:4,5
Romans 7:18   Ephesians 4:7   John 15:7   Colossians 3:16

APRIL 8 EVENING

They shall see his face.
— *REVELATION 22:4*

I beseech thee shew me thy glory. And he said, Thou canst not see my face: for there shall no man see me, and live. — No man hath seen God at any time; the only begotten Son, which is in the bosom of the Father, he hath declared him. — Every eye shall see him, and they also which pierced him: and all kindreds of the earth shall wail because of him. — I shall see him, but not now: I shall behold him, but not nigh. — I know that my Redeemer liveth, and that he shall stand at the latter day upon the earth: and though after my skin worms destroy this body, yet in my flesh shall I see God. — I will behold thy face in righteousness: I shall be satisfied, when I awake, with thy likeness. — We shall be like him; for we shall see him as he is. — The Lord himself shall descend from heaven... the dead in Christ shall rise first: then we which are alive and remain shall be caught up together with them in the clouds, to meet the Lord in the air: and so shall we ever be with the Lord.

Exodus 33:18,20   John 1:18   Revelation 1:7   Numbers 24:17
Job 19:25,26   Psalm 17:15   1 John 3:2   1 Thessalonians 4:16,17

APRIL 9 MORNING

Fear not; for I have redeemed thee.
— ISAIAH 43:1

Fear not; for thou shalt not be ashamed: neither be thou confounded; for thou shalt not be put to shame: for thou shalt forget the shame of thy youth, and shalt not remember the reproach of thy widowhood any more. — For thy Maker is thine husband; the Lord of hosts is his name; and thy Redeemer the Holy One of Israel. — I have blotted out, as a thick cloud, thy transgressions, and, as a cloud, thy sins: return unto me; for I have redeemed thee. — With the precious blood of Christ, as of a lamb without blemish and without spot. — Their Redeemer is strong; the Lord of hosts is his name: he shall throughly plead their cause. — My Father, which gave them me, is greater than all; and no man is able to pluck them out of my Father's hand. — Grace be to you and peace from God the Father, and from our Lord Jesus Christ, who gave himself for our sins, that he might deliver us from this present evil world, according to the will of God and our Father: to whom be glory for ever and ever. Amen.

Isaiah 54:4,5, 44:22 1 Peter 1:19 Jeremiah 50:34 John 10:29 Galatians 1:3-5

APRIL 9 EVENING

I will mention the lovingkindnesses of the Lord,
and the praises of the Lord,
according to all that the Lord hath bestowed on us.
— ISAIAH 63:7

He brought me up...out of an horrible pit, out of the miry clay, and set my feet upon a rock, and established my goings. — The Son of God...loved me, and gave himself for me. — He that spared not his own Son, but delivered him up for us all, how shall he not with him also freely give us all things? — God commendeth his love toward us, in that, while we were yet sinners, Christ died for us. — Who hath also sealed us, and given the earnest of the Spirit in our hearts. — Which is the earnest of our inheritance until the redemption of the purchased possession, unto the praise of his glory. — God, who is rich in mercy, for his great love wherewith he loved us, even when we were dead in sins, hath quickened us together with Christ, (by grace ye are saved;) and hath raised us up together, and made us sit together in heavenly places in Christ Jesus.

Psalm 40:2 Galatians 2:20 Romans 8:32, 5:8
2 Corinthians 1:22 Ephesians 1:14, 2:4-6

APRIL 10 MORNING

I am black, but comely.
— SONG OF SOLOMON 1:5

Behold, I was shapen in iniquity; and in sin did my mother conceive me. — Thy renown went forth among the heathen for thy beauty: for it was perfect through my comeliness, which I had put upon thee, saith the Lord God. — I am a sinful man, O Lord. — Behold, thou art fair, my love; behold, thou art fair. — I abhor myself, and repent in dust and ashes. — Thou art all fair, my love; there is no spot in thee. — When I would do good, evil is present with me. — Be of good cheer; thy sins be forgiven thee. — I know that in me (that is, in my flesh) dwelleth no good thing— Ye are complete in him. — Perfect in Christ Jesus. — Ye are washed...ye are sanctified...ye are justified in the name of the Lord Jesus, and by the Spirit of our God. — That ye should shew forth the praises of him who hath called you out of darkness into his marvellous light.

Psalm 51:5   Ezekiel 16:14   Luke 5:8 Song of Solomon 4:1   Job 42:6
Song of Solomon 4:7   Romans 7:21   Matthew 9:2   Romans 7:18
Colossians 2:10, 1:28 1   Corinthians 6:11 1   Peter 2:9

APRIL 10 EVENING

All that will live godly in Christ Jesus
shall suffer persecution.
— 2 TIMOTHY 3:12

I am come to set a man at variance against his father, and the daughter against her mother and the daughter-in-law against her mother-in-law. And a man's foes shall be they of his own household. — Whosoever...will be a friend of the world is the enemy of God. — Love not the world, neither the things that are in the world. If any man love the world the love of the Father is not in him. For all that is in the world, the lust of the flesh, and the lust of the eyes, and the pride of life, is not of the Father, but is of the world. — If the world hate you, ye know that it hated me before it hated you. If ye were of the world, the world would love his own: but because ye are not of the world, but I have chosen you out of the world, therefore the world hateth you. The servant is not greater than his lord. — I have given them thy word; and the world hath hated them, because they are not of the world, even as I am not of the world.

Matthew 10:35,36   James 4:4 1   John 2:15,16   John 15:18-20, 17:14

APRIL 11 MORNING

*In the multitude of words there wanteth not sin:
but he that refraineth his lips is wise.*
— PROVERBS 10:19

My beloved brethren, let every man be swift to hear, slow to speak, slow to wrath. — He that is slow to anger is better than the mighty: and he that ruleth his spirit than he that taketh a city. — If any man offend not in word, the same is a perfect man, and able to bridle the whole body. — By thy words thou shalt be justified and by thy words thou shalt be condemned. — Set a watch, O Lord, before my mouth; keep the door of my lips. — Christ...suffered for us, leaving us an example, that ye should follow his steps: who did no sin, neither was guile found in his mouth: who when he was reviled, reviled not again; when he suffered, he threatened not; but committed himself to him that judgeth righteously. — Consider him that endured such contradiction of sinners against himself, lest ye be wearied and faint in your minds. — In their mouth was found no guile: for they are without fault before the throne of God.

James 1:19   Proverbs 16:32   James 3:2   Matthew 12:3
Psalm 141:3   1 Peter 2:21-23   Hebrews 12:3   Revelation 14:5

APRIL 11 EVENING

Teach me thy way, O Lord.
— PSALM 27:11

I will instruct thee and teach thee in the way which thou shalt go: I will guide thee with mine eye. — Good and upright is the Lord: therefore will he teach sinners in the way. The meek will he guide in judgment: and the meek will he teach his way. — I am the door: by me if any man enter in, he shall be saved, and shall go in and out, and find pasture. — Jesus saith unto him, I am the way, the truth, and the life: no man cometh unto the Father, but by me. — Having... boldness to enter into the holiest by the blood of Jesus, by a new and living way, which he hath consecrated for us, through the veil, that is to say, his flesh; and having an high priest over the house of God; let us draw near with a true heart in full assurance of faith. — Then shall we know, if we follow on to know the Lord. — All the paths of the Lord are mercy and truth unto such as keep his covenant and his testimonies.

Psalms 32:8, 25:8,9   John 10:9, 14:6
Hebrews 10:19-22   Hosea 6:3   Psalm 25:10

APRIL 12 MORNING

What the law could not do,
in that it was weak through the flesh,
God sending his own Son in the likeness of sinful flesh,
and for sin, condemned sin in the flesh.
— ROMANS 8:3

The law having a shadow of good things to come, and not the very image of the things, can never with those sacrifices which they offered year by year continually make the comers thereunto perfect. For then would they not have ceased to be offered? — By him all that believe are justified from all things, from which ye could not be justified by the law of Moses. — Forasmuch...as the children are partakers of flesh and blood, he also himself likewise took part of the same; that through death he might destroy him that had the power of death, that is the devil; and deliver them who through fear of death were all their lifetime subject to bondage. For verily he took not on him the nature of angels; but he took on him the seed of Abraham. Wherefore in all things it behoved him to be made like unto his brethren.

Hebrews 10:1,2   Acts 13:39   Hebrews 2:14-17

APRIL 12 EVENING

All have sinned, and come short of the glory of God.
— ROMANS 3:23

There is none righteous, no, not one: there is none that doeth good, no, not one. — There is not a just man upon earth, that doeth good, and sinneth not. — How can he be clean that is born of a woman? — Let us therefore fear, lest a promise being left us of entering into his rest, any of you should seem to come short of it. — I acknowledge my transgressions: and my sin is ever before me. Behold, I was shapen in iniquity; and in sin did my mother conceive me. — The Lord...hath put away thy sin; thou shalt not die. — Whom he justified, them he also glorified. — We all, with open face beholding as in a glass the glory of the Lord, are changed into the same image from glory to glory, even as by the Spirit of the Lord. — If ye continue in the faith grounded and settled, and be not moved away from the hope of the gospel. — Walk worthy of God, who hath called you unto his kingdom and glory.

Romans 3:10,12   Ecclesiastes 7:20   Job 25:4   Hebrews 4:1   Psalm 51:3,5
2 Samuel 12:13   Romans 8:30 2   Corinthians 3:18   Colossians 1:23
1 Thessalonians 2:12

APRIL 13 MORNING

Honour the Lord with thy substance,
and with the firstfruits of all thine increase.
— PROVERBS 3:9

He which soweth sparingly shall reap also sparingly; and he which soweth bountifully shall reap also bountifully. — Upon the first day of the week let every one of you lay by him in store, as God hath prospered him. — God is not unrighteous to forget your work and labour of love, which ye have shewed toward his name, in that ye have ministered to the saints and do minister. — I beseech you...brethren, by the mercies of God, that ye present your bodies a living sacrifice, holy, acceptable unto God, which is your reasonable service. — The love of Christ constraineth us; because we thus judge, that if one died for all, then were all dead: and that he died for all, that they which live should not henceforth live unto themselves, but unto him which died for them, and rose again. — Whether therefore ye eat, or drink, or whatsoever ye do, do all to the glory of God.

2 Corinthians 9:6 1 Corinthians 16:2 Hebrews 6:10
Romans 12:1 2 Corinthians 5:14,15 1 Corinthians 10:31

APRIL 13 EVENING

There shall be no night there.
— REVELATION 21:25

The Lord shall be unto thee an everlasting light, and thy God thy glory. — The city had no need of the sun, neither of the moon, to shine in it: for the glory of God did lighten it, and the Lamb is the light thereof. — They need no candle, neither light of the sun; for the Lord God giveth them light. — Ye are a chosen generation, a royal priesthood, an holy nation, a peculiar people; that ye should shew forth the praises of him who hath called you out of darkness into his marvellous light. — Giving thanks unto the Father, which hath made us meet to be partakers of the inheritance of the saints in light: who hath delivered us from the power of darkness, and hath translated us into the kingdom of his dear Son. — Ye were sometime darkness, but now are ye light in the Lord: walk as children of light. — We are not of the night, nor of darkness. — The path of the just is as the shining light, that shineth more and more unto the perfect day.

Isaiah 60:19 Revelation 21:23, 22:5 1 Peter 2:9 Colossians 1:12,13
Ephesians 5:8 1 Thessalonians 5:5 Proverbs 4:18

APRIL 14 MORNING

My soul shall be satisfied as with marrow and fatness;
and my mouth shall praise thee with joyful lips:
when I remember thee upon my bed,
and meditate on thee in the night watches.
— PSALM 63:5,6

How precious...are thy thoughts unto me, O God! How great is the sum of them! If I should count them, they are more in number than the sand: when I awake, I am still with thee. — How sweet are thy words unto my taste! yea, sweeter than honey to my mouth!— Thy love is better than wine. — Whom have I in heaven but thee? And there is none upon earth that I desire beside thee. — Thou art fairer than the children of men. — As the apple tree among the trees of the wood, so is my beloved among the sons. I sat down under his shadow with great delight, and his fruit was sweet to my taste. He brought me to the banqueting house, and his banner over me was love. — His countenance is as Lebanon, excellent as the cedars. His mouth is most sweet: yea, he is altogether lovely. This is my beloved, and this is my friend.

Psalms 139:17,18, 119:103   Song of Solomon 1:2
Psalms 73:25, 45:2   Song of Solomon 2:3,4, 5:15,16

APRIL 14 EVENING

Restore unto me the joy of thy salvation.
— PSALM 51:12

I have seen his ways, and will heal him: I will lead him also, and restore comforts unto him and to his mourners. — Come now, and let us reason together, saith the Lord: though your sins be as scarlet, they shall be as white as snow; though they be red like crimson, they shall be as wool. — Return, ye backsliding children, and I will heal your backslidings. Behold, we come unto thee; for thou art the Lord our God. — I will hear what God the Lord will speak: for he will speak peace unto his people, and to his saints: but let them not turn again to folly. — Bless the Lord, O my soul, and forget not all his benefits: who forgiveth all thine iniquities; who healeth all thy diseases. — He restoreth my soul. — O Lord, I will praise thee: though thou wast angry with me, thine anger is turned away, and thou comfortedst me. — Hold thou me up, and I shall be safe. — I, even I, am he that blotteth out thy transgressions for mine own sake, and will not remember thy sins.

Isaiah 57:18, 1:18   Jeremiah 3:22   Psalms 85:8, 103:2,3, 23:3
Isaiah 12:1   Psalm 119:117   Isaiah 43:25

APRIL 15 MORNING

Their Redeemer is strong.
— JEREMIAH 50:34

I know your manifold transgressions and your mighty sins. — I have laid help upon one that is mighty. — The Lord...thy Saviour and thy Redeemer, the mighty one of Jacob. — Mighty to save. — Able to keep you from falling. — Where sin abounded, grace did much more abound. — He that believeth on him is not condemned: but he that believeth not is condemned already, because he hath not believed in the name of the only begotten Son of God. — He is able...to save them to the uttermost that come unto God by him. — Is my hand shortened at all, that it cannot redeem? — Who shall separate us from the love of Christ?...I am persuaded, that neither death, nor life, nor angels, nor principalities, nor powers, nor things present, nor things to come, nor height, nor depth, nor any other creature, shall be able to separate us from the love of God, which is in Christ Jesus our Lord.

Amos 5:12   Psalm 89:19   Isaiah 49:26, 63:1 Jude 24   Romans 5:20
John 3:18   Hebrews 7:25   Isaiah 50:2   Romans 8:35,38,39

APRIL 15 EVENING

Seekest thou great things for thyself?
Seek them not.
— JEREMIAH 45:5

Take my yoke upon you, and learn of me; for I am meek and lowly in heart: and ye shall find rest unto your souls. — Let this mind be in you, which was also in Christ Jesus; who, being in the form of God, thought it not robbery to be equal with God: but made himself of no reputation, and took upon him the form of a servant, and was made in the likeness of men: and being found in fashion as a man, he humbled himself, and became obedient unto death, even the death of the cross. — He that taketh not his cross, and followeth after me, is not worthy of me. — Christ...suffered for us, leaving us an example, that ye should follow his steps. — Godliness with contentment is great gain. For we brought nothing into this world, and it is certain we can carry nothing out. And having food and raiment let us be therewith content. — I have learned, in whatsoever state I am, therewith to be content.

Matthew 11:29   Philippians 2:5-8   Matthew 10:38
1 Peter 2:21 1   Timothy 6:6-8   Philippians 4:11

APRIL 16 MORNING

*I said in my haste, I am cut off from before thine eyes:
nevertheless thou heardest the voice of my supplications
when I cried unto thee.*
— PSALM 31:22

I sink in deep mire, where there is no standing: I am come into deep waters, where the floods overflow me. — Waters flowed over mine head; then I said, I am cut off. I called upon thy name, O Lord, out of the low dungeon. Thou hast heard my voice: hide not thine ear at my breathing, at my cry. Thou drewest near in the day that I called upon thee: thou saidst, Fear not. — Will the Lord cast off for ever? And will he be favourable no more? Is his mercy clean gone for ever? Doth his promise fail for evermore? Hath God forgotten to be gracious? hath he in anger shut up his tender mercies? And I said, This is my infirmity: but I will remember the years of the right hand of the most High. I will remember the works of the Lord: surely I will remember thy wonders of old. — I had fainted, unless I had believed to see the goodness of the Lord in the land of the living.

Psalm 69:2   Lamentations 3:54-57   Psalms 77:7-11, 27:13

APRIL 16 EVENING

*He shall call upon me,
and I will answer him:
I will be with him in trouble,
I will deliver him.*
— PSALM 91:15

And Jabez called on the God of Israel, saying, Oh that thou wouldest bless me indeed, and enlarge my coast, and that thine hand might be with me, and that thou wouldest keep me from evil, that it may not grieve me! And God granted him that which he requested. — Ask what I shall give thee. And Solomon said unto God...Give me now wisdom and knowledge, that I may go out and come in before this people. — And God gave Solomon wisdom and understanding exceeding much, and largeness of heart, even as the sand that is on the sea shore. — Asa cried unto the Lord his God, and said, Lord, it is nothing with thee to help, whether with many, or with them that have no power...O Lord, thou art our God; let not man prevail against thee. So the Lord smote the Ethiopians before Asa. — O thou that hearest prayer, unto thee shall all flesh come.

1 Chronicles 4:10   2 Chronicles 1:7,8,10
1 Kings 4:29   2 Chronicles 14:11,12   Psalm 65:2

APRIL 17 MORNING

Whoso offereth praise glorifieth me.
— PSALM 50:23

Let the word of Christ dwell in you richly in all wisdom; teaching and admonishing one another in psalms and hymns and spiritual Song, singing with grace in your hearts to the Lord. And whatsoever ye do in word or deed, do all in the name of the Lord Jesus, giving thanks to God and the Father by him. — Glorify God in your body, and in your spirit, which are God's. — Ye are a royal priesthood...that ye should shew forth the praises of him who hath called you out of darkness into his marvellous light. — Ye...as lively stones, are built up a spiritual house, a holy priesthood, to offer up spiritual sacrifices, acceptable to God by Jesus Christ. — By him...let us offer the sacrifice of praise to God continually, that is, the fruit of our lips, giving thanks to his name. — My soul shall make her boast in the Lord: the humble shall hear thereof, and be glad. O magnify the Lord with me, and let us exalt his name together.

Colossians 3:16,17 1 Corinthians 6:20 1 Peter 2:9,5 Hebrews 13:15 Psalm 34:2,3

APRIL 17 EVENING

Draw me, we will run after thee.
— SONG OF SOLOMON 1:4

I have loved thee with an everlasting love: therefore with lovingkindness have I drawn thee. — I drew them with cords of a man, with bands of love. — I, if I be lifted up from the earth, will draw all men unto me. — Behold the Lamb of God. — As Moses lifted up the serpent in the wilderness, even so must the Son of man be lifted up: that whosoever believeth in him should not perish, but have eternal life. — Whom have I in heaven but thee? And there is none upon earth that I desire beside thee. — We love him, because he first loved us. — My beloved spake, and said unto me, Rise up, my love, my fair one, and come away. For, lo, the winter is past, the rain is over and gone; the flowers appear on the earth; the time of the singing of birds is come, and the voice of the turtle is heard in our land; the fig tree putteth forth her green figs, and the vines with the tender grape give a good smell. Arise, my love, my fair one, and come away.

Jeremiah 31:3 Hosea 11:4 John 12:32, 1:36, 3:14,15 Psalm 73:25 1 John 4:19 Song of Solomon 2:10-13

APRIL 18 MORNING

I will raise them up a Prophet from among their brethren, like unto thee.
— *DEUTERONOMY 18:18*

[Moses] stood between the Lord and you at that time, to shew you the word of the Lord: for ye were afraid. — There is one God, and one mediator between God and men, the man Christ Jesus. — Now the man Moses was very meek, above all the men which were upon the face of the earth. — Take my yoke upon you, and learn of me; for I am meek and lowly in heart: and ye shall find rest unto your souls. — Let this mind be in you, which was also in Christ Jesus: who, being in the form of God, thought it not robbery to be equal with God: but made himself of no reputation, and took upon him the form of a servant, and was made in the likeness of men. — Moses verily was faithful in all his house, as a servant, for a testimony of those things which were to be spoken after; but Christ as a son over his own house; whose house are we, if we hold fast the confidence and the rejoicing of the hope firm unto the end.

Deuteronomy 5:5　1 Timothy 2:5　Numbers 12:3
Matthew 11:29　Philippians 2:5-7　Hebrews 3:5,6

APRIL 18 EVENING

Everlasting consolation.
— *2 THESSALONIANS 2:16*

I will remember my covenant with thee in the days of thy youth, and I will establish unto thee an everlasting covenant. — By one offering he hath perfected for ever them that are sanctified. — He is able to save them to the uttermost that come unto God by him, seeing he ever liveth to make intercession for them. — I know whom I have believed, and am persuaded that he is able to keep that which I have committed unto him against that day. — The gifts and calling of God are without repentance. — Who shall separate us from the love of Christ? — The Lamb which is in the midst of the throne shall feed them, and shall lead them unto living fountains of waters: and God shall wipe away all tears from their eyes. — So shall we ever be with the Lord. Wherefore comfort one another with these words. — This is not your rest. — Here have we no continuing city, but we seek one to come.

Ezekiel 16:60　Hebrews 10:14, 7:25　2 Timothy 1:12　Romans 11:29, 8:35
Revelation 7:17　1 Thessalonians 4:17,18　Micah 2:10　Hebrews 13:14

APRIL 19 MORNING

*Verily, verily, I say unto you,
I am the door of the sheep.
— JOHN 10:7*

The veil of the temple was rent in twain from the top to the bottom. — Christ...hath once suffered for sins, the just for the unjust, that he might bring us to God. — The way into the holiest of all was not yet made manifest, while as the first tabernacle was yet standing. — I am the door: by me if any man enter in, he shall be saved, and shall go in and out, and find pasture. — No man cometh unto the Father, but by me. — Through him we...have access by one Spirit unto the Father. Now therefore ye are no more strangers and foreigners, but fellow citizens with the saints, and of the household of God. — Having...boldness to enter into the holiest by the blood of Jesus, by a new and living way, which he hath consecrated for us, through the veil, that is to say, his flesh. — We have peace with God through our Lord Jesus Christ: by whom also we have access by faith into this grace wherein we stand, and rejoice in hope of the glory of God.

Matthew 27:51 1 Peter 3:18 Hebrews 9:8 John 10:9, 14:6
Ephesians 2:18,19 Hebrews 10:19,20 Romans 5:1,2

APRIL 19 EVENING

*His word was in mine heart
as a burning fire shut up in my bones,
and I was weary with forbearing, and I could not stay.
— JEREMIAH 20:9*

Necessity is laid upon me; yea woe is unto me, if I preach not the gospel! What is my reward then? Verily that, when I preach the gospel, I may make the gospel of Christ without charge, that I abuse not my power in the gospel. — They called them, and commanded them not to speak at all nor teach in the name of Jesus. But Peter and John answered and said unto them...We cannot but speak the things which we have seen and heard. — The love of Christ constraineth us. — I was afraid, and went and hid thy talent in the earth...Thou wicked and slothful servant...thou oughtest...to have put my money to the exchangers, and then at my coming I should have received mine own with usury. — Go...to thy friends, and tell them how great things the Lord hath done for thee.

1 Corinthians 9:16,18 Acts 4:18-20
2 Corinthians 5:14 Matthew 25:25-27 Mark 5:19

APRIL 20 MORNING

*There shall cleave nought
of the cursed thing to thine hand.*
— DEUTERONOMY 13:17

Come out from among them, and be ye separate, saith the Lord, and touch not the unclean thing. — Dearly beloved, I beseech you as strangers and pilgrims, abstain from fleshly lusts, which war against the soul. — Hating even the garment spotted by the flesh. — Beloved, now are we the sons of God... And it doth not yet appear what we shall be: but we know that, when he shall appear, we shall be like him: for we shall see him as he is. And every man that hath this hope in him purifieth himself, even as he is pure. — The grace of God that bringeth salvation hath appeared to all men, teaching us that, denying ungodliness and worldly lusts, we should live soberly, righteously, and godly, in this present world; looking for that blessed hope, and the glorious appearing of the great God and our Saviour Jesus Christ: who gave himself for us, that he might redeem us from all iniquity, and purify unto himself a peculiar people, zealous of good works.

2 Corinthians 6:17 1 Peter 2:11 Jude 23 1 John 3:2,3 Titus 2:11-14

APRIL 20 EVENING

*Who art thou Lord?
I am Jesus.*
— ACTS 26:15

It is I; be not afraid. — When thou passest through the waters, I will be with thee: and through the rivers, they shall not overflow thee: when thou walkest through the fire, thou shalt not be burned; neither shall the flame kindle upon thee. For I am the Lord thy God...thy Saviour. — Though I walk through the valley of the shadow of death, I will fear no evil: for thou art with me; thy rod and thy staff they comfort me. — Emmanuel, God with us. — Thou shalt call his name JESUS: for he shall save his people from their sins. — If any man sin, we have an advocate with the Father, Jesus Christ the righteous. — Who is he that condemneth? It is Christ that died, yea rather, that is risen again, who is even at the right hand of God, who also maketh intercession for us. Who shall separate us from the love of Christ? Shall tribulation, or distress, or persecution, or famine, or nakedness, or peril, or sword?

Matthew 14:27 Isaiah 43:2,3 Psalm 23:4
Matthew 1:23, 21 1 John 2:1 Romans 8:34,35

APRIL 21 MORNING

Stand fast in the Lord.
— *PHILIPPIANS 4:1*

My foot hath held his steps, his way have I kept, and not declined. — The Lord loveth judgment, and forsaketh not his saints; they are preserved for ever. — The Lord shall preserve thee from all evil: he shall preserve thy soul. — The just shall live by faith: but if any man draw back, my soul shall have no pleasure in him. But we are not of them who draw back into perdition; but of them that believe to the saving of the soul. — If they had been of us, they would no doubt have continued with us: but they went out, that they might be made manifest that they were not all of us. — If ye continue in my word then are ye my disciples indeed. — He that shall endure unto the end, the same shall be saved. — Watch ye, stand fast in the faith, quit you like men, be strong. — Hold that fast which thou hast, that no man take thy crown. — He that overcometh, the same shall be clothed in white raiment; and I will not blot out his name out of the book of life.

Job 23:11   Psalms 37:28, 121:7   Hebrews 10:38,39 1   John 2:19   John 8:31
Matthew 24:13 1   Corinthians 16:13   Revelation 3:11, 3:5

APRIL 21 EVENING

Enoch walked with God.
— *GENESIS 5:22*

Can two walk together, except they be agreed? — Having made peace through the blood of his cross...You, that were sometimes alienated and enemies in your mind by wicked works, yet now hath he reconciled in the body of his flesh through death, to present you holy and unblameable and unreproveable in his sight. — In Christ Jesus ye who sometimes were far off are made nigh by the blood of Christ. — If, when we were enemies, we were reconciled to God by the death of his Son, much more, being reconciled, we shall be saved by his life. And not only so, but we also joy in God through our Lord Jesus Christ. — Our fellowship is with the Father, and with his Son Jesus Christ. — The grace of the Lord Jesus Christ, and the love of God, and the communion of the Holy Ghost, be with you all. Amen.

Amos 3:3   Colossians 1:20-22   Ephesians 2:13
Romans 5:10,11 1   John 1:3 2   Corinthians 13:14

APRIL 22 MORNING

*If his offering be a burnt sacrifice of the herd,
let him offer a male without blemish:
he shall offer it of his own voluntary will.
And he shall put his hand
upon the head of the burnt offering;
and it shall be accepted for him
to make atonement for him.
— LEVITICUS 1:3,4*

God will provide himself a lamb for a burnt offering. — Behold the Lamb of God, which taketh away the sin of the world. — We are sanctified through the offering of the body of Jesus Christ once for all. — A ransom for many. — No man taketh it from me, but I lay it down of myself. I have power to lay it down, and I have power to take it again. — I will love them freely. — The Son of God... loved me and gave himself for me. — He hath made him to be sin for us, who knew no sin; that we might be made the righteousness of God in him. — He hath made us accepted in the beloved.

Genesis 22:8   John 1:29   Hebrews 10:10   Matthew 20:28   John 10:18
Hosea 14:4   Galatians 2:20   2 Corinthians 5:21   Ephesians 1:6

APRIL 22 EVENING

*Great is thy mercy toward me:
and thou hast delivered my soul from the lowest hell.
— PSALM 86:13*

Fear him which is able to destroy both soul and body in hell. — Fear not: for I have redeemed thee, I have called thee by thy name; thou art mine. I, even I, am the Lord; and beside me there is no saviour. I, even I, am he that blotteth out thy transgressions for mine own sake, and will not remember thy sins. — They that trust in their wealth, and boast themselves in the multitude of their riches; none of them can by any means redeem his brother, nor give to God a ransom for him: for the redemption of their soul is precious. — I have found a ransom. — God, who is rich in mercy, for his great love wherewith he loved us, even when we were dead in sins, hath quickened us together with Christ. — Neither is there salvation in any other: for there is none other name under heaven given among men, whereby we must be saved.

Matthew 10:28   Isaiah 43:1,11,25   Psalm 49:6-8
Job 33:24   Ephesians 2:4,5   Acts 4:12

APRIL 23 MORNING

The Lord was my stay.
— PSALM 18:18

Truly in vain is salvation hoped for from the hills, and from the multitude of mountains: truly in the Lord our God is the salvation of Israel. — The Lord is my rock, and my fortress, and my deliverer; my God, my strength, in whom I will trust; my buckler, and the horn of my salvation, and my high tower. — Cry out and shout, thou inhabitant of Zion; for great is the Holy One of Israel in the midst of thee. — The angel of the Lord encampeth round about them that fear him, and delivereth them. The righteous cry, and the Lord heareth, and delivereth them out of all their troubles. — The eternal God is thy refuge, and underneath are the everlasting arms. — So that we may boldly say, The Lord is my helper, and I will not fear what man shall do unto me. — For who is God save the Lord? or who is a rock save our God? It is God that girdeth me with strength, and maketh my way perfect. — By the grace of God I am what I am.

Jeremiah 3:23   Psalm 18:2   Isaiah 12:6   Psalm 34:7,17   Deuteronomy 33:27
Hebrews 13:6   Psalm 18:31,32   1 Corinthians 15:10

APRIL 23 EVENING

All we like sheep have gone astray.
— ISAIAH 53:6

If we say that we have no sin, we deceive ourselves, and the truth is not in us. — There is none righteous, no, not one: there is none that understandeth. They are all gone out of the way, they are together become unprofitable. — Ye were as sheep going astray; but are now returned unto the Shepherd and Bishop of your souls. — I have gone astray like a lost sheep; seek thy servant; for I do not forget thy commandments. — He restoreth my soul: he leadeth me in the paths of righteous for his name's sake. — My sheep hear my voice, and I know them, and they follow me: and I give unto them eternal life; and they shall never perish, neither shall any man pluck them out of my hand. — What man of you, having an hundred sheep, if he lose one of them, doth not leave the ninety and nine in the wilderness, and go after that which is lost, until he find it?

1 John 1:8   Romans 3:10-12   1 Peter 2:25
Psalm 119:176, 23:3   John 10:27,28   Luke 15:4

APRIL 24 MORNING

*The Lord visited Sarah as he had said,
and the Lord did unto Sarah as he had spoken.*
— GENESIS 21:1

Trust in him at all times; ye people, pour out your heart before him: God is a refuge for us. — David encouraged himself in the Lord his God. — God will surely visit you, and bring you out of this land unto the land which he sware to Abraham, to Isaac, and to Jacob. — I have seen, I have seen the affliction of my people which is in Egypt, and I have heard their groaning, and am come down to deliver them. He brought them out, after that he had shewed wonders and signs in the land of Egypt, and in the Red sea, and in the wilderness forty years. — There failed not ought of any good thing which the Lord had spoken unto the house of Israel: all came to pass. — He is faithful that promised. — Hath he said, and shall he not do it? or hath he spoken, and shall he not make it good? — Heaven and earth shall pass away, but my words shall not pass away— The grass withereth, the flower fadeth: but the word of our God shall stand for ever.

Psalm 62:8 1 Samuel 30:6 Genesis 50:24 Acts 7:34,36 Joshua 21:45
Hebrews 10:23 Numbers 23:19 Matthew 24:35 Isaiah 40:8

APRIL 24 EVENING

The eyes of all wait upon thee.
— PSALM 145:15

He giveth to all life, and breath, and all things. — The Lord is good to all: and his tender mercies are over all his works. — Behold the fowls of the air: for they sow not, neither do they reap, nor gather into barns; yet your heavenly Father feedeth them. — The same Lord over all is rich unto all that call upon him. — I will lift up mine eyes unto the hills, from whence cometh my help. — Behold, as the eyes of servants look unto the hand of their masters, and as the eyes of a maiden unto the hand of her mistress; so our eyes wait upon the Lord our God. — The Lord is a God of judgment: blessed are all they that wait for him. — And it shall be said in that day, Lo, this is our God; we have waited for him, and he will save us: this is the Lord; we have waited for him, we will be glad and rejoice in his salvation. — If we hope for that we see not, then do we with patience wait for it.

Acts 17:25 Psalm 145:9 Matthew 6:26 Romans 10:12
Psalm 121:1, 123:2 Isaiah 30:18, 25:9 Romans 8:25

APRIL 25 MORNING

Thou shalt call his name JESUS:
for he shall save his people from their sins.
— MATTHEW 1:21

Ye know that he was manifested to take away our sins. — That we, being dead to sins, should live unto righteousness. — He is able also to save them to the uttermost that come unto God by him. — He was wounded for our transgressions, he was bruised for our iniquities: the chastisement of our peace was upon him; and with his stripes we are healed. The Lord hath laid on him the iniquity of us all. — Thus it behoved Christ to suffer...that repentance and remission of sins should be preached in his name among all nations. — He appeared to put away sin by the sacrifice of himself. — Him hath God exalted with his right hand to be a Prince and a Saviour,...to give repentance. — Through this man is preached unto you the forgiveness of sins: and by him all that believe are justified from all things, from which ye could not be justified by the law of Moses. — Your sins are forgiven you for his name's sake.

1 John 3:5　1 Peter 2:24　Hebrews 7:25　Isaiah 53:5,6　Luke 24:46,47　Hebrews 9:26　Acts 5:31, 13:38,39　1 John 2:12

APRIL 25 EVENING

Our Lord Jesus Christ...though he was rich,
yet for your sakes...became poor,
that ye through his poverty might be rich.
— 2 CORINTHIANS 8:9

It pleased the Father that in him should all fulness dwell. — The brightness of his glory, and the express image of his person, and upholding all things by the word of his power, when he had by himself purged our sins, sat down on the right hand of the Majesty on high; being made so much better than the angels, as he hath by inheritance obtained a more excellent name than they. — Who, being in the form of God, thought it not robbery to be equal with God: but made himself of no reputation. — The foxes have holes, and the birds of the air have nests; but the Son of man hath not where to lay his head. — All things are yours; whether Paul, or Apollos, or Cephas, or the world, or life, or death, or things present, or things to come; all are yours; and ye are Christ's; and Christ is God's.

Colossians 1:19　Hebrews 1:3,4　Philippians 2:6,7　Matthew 8:20　1 Corinthians 3:21-23

APRIL 26 MORNING

His left hand is under my head,
and his right hand doth embrace me.
— SONG OF SOLOMON 2:6

Underneath are the everlasting arms. — When [Peter] saw the wind boisterous, he was afraid; and beginning to sink, he cried, saying, Lord, save me. And immediately Jesus stretched forth his hand, and caught him, and said unto him, O thou of little faith, wherefore didst thou doubt? — The steps of a good man are ordered by the Lord: and he delighteth in his way. Though he fall, he shall not be utterly cast down: for the Lord upholdeth him with his hand. — The beloved of the Lord shall dwell in safety by him; and the Lord shall cover him all the day long, and he shall dwell between his shoulders. — Casting all your care upon Him, for he careth for you. — He that toucheth you, toucheth the apple of his eye. — They shall never perish, neither shall any man pluck them out of my hand. My Father, which gave them me, is greater than all.

Deuteronomy 33:27   Matthew 14:30,31   Psalm 37:23,24
Deuteronomy 33:12 1   Peter 5:7   Zechariah 2:8   John 10:28,29

APRIL 26 EVENING

Who is she that looketh forth as the morning,
fair as the moon, clear as the sun,
and terrible as an army with banners?
— SONG OF SOLOMON 6:10

The church of God, which he hath purchased with his own blood. — Christ loved the church, and gave himself for it; that he might sanctify and cleanse it with the washing of water by the word, that he might present it to himself a glorious church, not having spot, or wrinkle, or any such thing; but that it should be holy and without blemish. — There appeared a great wonder in heaven; a woman clothed with the sun. — The marriage of the Lamb is come, and his wife hath made herself ready. And to her was granted that she should be arrayed in fine linen, clean and white: for the fine linen is the righteousness of saints. — The righteousness of God which is by faith of Jesus Christ unto all and upon all them that believe. — The glory which thou gavest me I have given them.

Acts 20:28   Ephesians 5:25-27
Revelation 12:1, 19:7,8   Romans 3:22   John 17:22

APRIL 27 MORNING

Brethren, the time is short.
— *1 CORINTHIANS 7:29*

Man that is born of a woman is of few days, and full of trouble. He cometh forth like a flower, and is cut down: he fleeth also as a shadow, and continueth not. — The world passeth away, and the lust thereof: but he that doeth the will of God abideth for ever. — As in Adam all die, even so in Christ shall all be made alive. Death is swallowed up in victory. — Whether we live, we live unto the Lord; and whether we die, we die unto the Lord: whether we live therefore, or die, we are the Lord's. — To live is Christ, and to die is gain. — Cast not away...your confidence, which hath great recompence of reward. For ye have need of patience, that, after ye have done the will of God, ye might receive the promise. For yet a little while, and he that shall come will come, and will not tarry. — The night is far spent, the day is at hand: let us therefore cast off the works of darkness, and let us put on the armour of light. — The end of all things is at hand: be ye therefore sober, and watch unto prayer.

Job 14:1,2   1 John 2:17   1 Corinthians 15:22,54   Romans 14:8
Philippians 1:21   Hebrews 10:35-37   Romans 13:12   1 Peter 4:7

APRIL 27 EVENING

A new name.
— *REVELATION 2:17*

The disciples were called Christians first in Antioch. — Let every one that nameth the name of Christ depart from iniquity. — They that are Christ's have crucified the flesh with the affections and lusts. — Ye are bought with a price: therefore glorify God in your body, and in your spirit, which are God's. — God forbid that I should glory, save in the cross of our Lord Jesus Christ, by whom the world is crucified unto me, and I unto the world. For in Christ Jesus neither circumcision availeth any thing, nor uncircumcision, but a new creature. — Be ye...followers of God, as dear children; and walk in love, as Christ also hath loved us, and hath given himself for us an offering and a sacrifice to God for a sweetsmelling savour. But fornication, and all uncleanness, or covetousness, let it not be once named among you, as becometh saints. Now are ye light in the Lord: walk as children of light.

Acts 11:26   2 Timothy 2:19   Galatians 5:24
1 Corinthians 6:20   Galatians 6:14,15   Ephesians 5:1-3,8

APRIL 28 MORNING

Behold the Lamb of God.
— JOHN 1:29

It is not possible that the blood of bulls and of goats should take away sins. Wherefore when he cometh into the world, he saith, Sacrifice and offering thou wouldest not, but a body hast thou prepared me: in burnt offerings and sacrifices for sin thou hast had no pleasure. Then said I, Lo, I come (in the volume of the book it is written of me) to do thy will, O God. — He was oppressed, and he was afflicted, yet he opened not his mouth; he is brought as a lamb to the slaughter, and as a sheep before her shearers is dumb, so he openeth not his mouth. — Ye were not redeemed with corruptible things, as silver and gold... but with the precious blood of Christ, as of a lamb without blemish and without spot:...manifest in these last times for you who by him do believe in God...that your faith and hope might be in God. . — Worthy is the Lamb that was slain to receive power, and riches and wisdom, and strength, and honour, and glory, and blessing.

Hebrews 10:4-7   Isaiah 53:7   1 Peter 1:18-21   Revelation 5:12

APRIL 28 EVENING

I will hope continually,
and will yet praise thee more and more.
— PSALM 71:14

1Not as though I had already attained, either were already perfect. — Leaving the principles of the doctrine of Christ, let us go on unto perfection; not laying again the foundation of repentance from dead works, and of faith toward God. — The path of the just is as the shining light, that shineth more and more unto the perfect day. — I love the Lord, because he hath heard my voice and my supplications. Because he hath inclined his ear unto me, therefore will I call upon him as long as I live. — I will bless the Lord all times: his praise shall continually be in my mouth. — Praise waiteth for thee, O God, in Sion. — They rest not day and night, saying, Holy, holy, holy, Lord God Almighty. — Whoso offereth praise glorifieth me. — Rejoice evermore. Pray without ceasing. In everything give thanks: for this is the will of God in Christ Jesus concerning you. — Rejoice in the Lord, always; and again I say, Rejoice.

Philippians 3:12   Hebrews 6:1   Proverbs 4:18   Psalms 116:1,2, 34:1, 65:1
Revelation 4:8   Psalm 50:23   1 Thessalonians 5:16-18   Philippians 4:4

APRIL 29 MORNING

Consider how great things He hath done for you.
— 1 SAMUEL 12:24

Thou shalt remember all the way which the Lord thy God led thee these forty years in the wilderness, to humble thee, and to prove thee, to know what was in thine heart, whether thou wouldest keep his commandments, or no. Thou shalt also consider in thine heart, that, as a man chasteneth his son, so the Lord thy God chasteneth thee. — I know, O Lord, that thy judgments are right, and that thou in faithfulness hast afflicted me. It is good for me that I have been afflicted; that I might learn thy statutes. Before I was afflicted I went astray: but now have I kept thy word. — The Lord hath chastened me sore: but he hath not given me over unto death. — He hath not dealt with us after our sins, nor rewarded us according to our iniquities. For as the heaven is high above the earth, so great is his mercy toward them that fear him. He knoweth our frame; he remembereth that we are dust.

Deuteronomy 8:2,5
Psalms 119:75,71,67, 118:18, 103:10,11,14

APRIL 29 EVENING

*That blessed hope...the glorious appearing
of the great God and our Saviour Jesus Christ.*
— TITUS 2:13

Which hope we have as an anchor of the soul, both sure and stedfast, and which entereth into that within the veil: whither the forerunner is for us entered, even Jesus. — Whom the heaven must receive until the times of restitution of all things. — When he shall come to be glorified in his saints, and to be admired in all them that believe. — The whole creation groaneth and travaileth in pain together until now. And not only they, but ourselves also...groan within ourselves, waiting for the adoption, to wit, the redemption of our body. — Beloved, now are we the sons of God, and it doth not yet appear what we shall be: but we know that, when he shall appear, we shall be like him; for we shall see him as he is. — When Christ, who is our life, shall appear, then shall ye also appear with him in glory. — Surely I come quickly. Amen. Even so, come, Lord Jesus.

Hebrews 6:19,20   Acts 3:21   2 Thessalonians 1:10   Romans 8:22,23
1 John 3:2   Colossians 3:4   Revelation 22:20

APRIL 30 MORNING

Whoso keepeth his word,
in him verily is the love of God perfected.
— 1 JOHN 2:5

The God of peace, that brought again from the dead our Lord Jesus, that great shepherd of the sheep, through the blood of the everlasting covenant, make you perfect in every good work to do his will, working in you that which is well pleasing in his sight, through Jesus Christ; to whom be glory for ever and ever. Amen. — Hereby we do know that we know him, if we keep his commandments. — If a man love me, he will keep my words: and my Father will love him, and we will come unto him, and make our abode with him. — Whosoever abideth in him sinneth not: whosoever sinneth hath not seen him, neither known him. Little children, let no man deceive you: he that doeth righteousness is righteous, even as he is righteous. — Herein is our love made perfect, that we may have boldness in the Day of Judgment: because as he is, so are we in this world.

Hebrews 13:20,21　1 John 2:3　John 14:23　1 John 3:6,7, 4:17

APRIL 30 EVENING

He that is slow to wrath is of great understanding.
— PROVERBS 14:29

The Lord passed by before him, and proclaimed, The Lord, The Lord God, merciful and gracious, longsuffering. — The Lord is not slack concerning his promise, as some men count slackness; but is longsuffering to us-ward, not willing that any should perish, but that all should come to repentance. — Be ye...followers of God, as dear children; and walk in love. — The fruit of the Spirit is love, joy, peace, longsuffering, gentleness, goodness, faith, meekness, temperance: against such there is no law. — This is thankworthy, if a man for conscience toward God endure grief, suffering wrongfully. If, when ye do well, and suffer for it, ye take it patiently, this is acceptable with God. Christ...suffered for us, leaving us an example, that ye should follow his steps: who, when he was reviled, reviled not again; when he suffered, he threatened not; but committed himself to him that judgeth righteously. — Be ye angry, and sin not.

Exodus 34:6　2 Peter 3:9　Ephesians 5:1
Galatians 5:22,23　1 Peter 2:19-21,23　Ephesians 4:26

MAY 1 MORNING

The fruit of the Spirit is peace.
— GALATIANS 5:22

To be spiritually minded is life and peace. — God hath called us to peace. — Peace I leave with you, my peace I give unto you: not as the world giveth, give I unto you. Let not your heart be troubled, neither let it be afraid. — The God of hope fill you with all joy and peace in believing, that ye may abound in hope, through the power of the Holy Ghost. — I know whom I have believed, and am persuaded that he is able to keep that which I have committed unto him against that day. — Thou wilt keep him in perfect peace, whose mind is stayed on thee: because he trusteth in thee. — The work of righteousness shall be peace; and the effect of righteousness quietness and assurance for ever. And my people shall dwell in a peaceable habitation, and in sure dwellings, and in quiet resting places. — Whoso hearkeneth unto me shall dwell safely, and shall be quiet from fear of evil. — Great peace have they which love thy law: and nothing shall offend them.

Romans 8:6 1 Corinthians 7:15 John 14:27 Romans 15:13 2 Timothy 1:12 Isaiah 26:3, 32:17,18 Proverbs 1:33 Psalm 119:165

MAY 1 EVENING

Jehovah-shammah (The Lord is there).
— EZEKIEL 48:35

Behold, the tabernacle of God is with men, and he will dwell with them, and they shall be his people, and God himself shall be with them, and be their God. — I saw no temple:...for the Lord God Almighty and the Lamb are the temple. The city had no need of the sun, neither of the moon, to shine in it: for the glory of God did lighten it, and the Lamb is the light thereof. — I shall be satisfied, when I awake, with thy likeness. — Whom have I in heaven but thee? And there is none upon earth that I desire beside thee. — Judah shall dwell for ever, and Jerusalem from generation to generation. For I will cleanse their blood that I have not cleansed: for the Lord dwelleth in Zion. — Sing and rejoice, O daughter of Zion; for, lo, I come, and I will dwell in the midst of thee, saith the Lord. — There shall be no more curse: but the throne of God and of the Lamb shall be in it; and his servants shall serve him.

Revelation 21:3, 22,23 Psalms 17:15, 73:25 Joel 3:20,21 Zechariah 2:10 Revelation 22:3

MAY 2 MORNING

*Surely the Lord is in this place;
and I knew it not.
— GENESIS 28:16*

Where two or three are gathered together in my name, there am I in the midst of them. — Lo, I am with you alway, even unto the end of the world. — My presence shall go with thee, and I will give thee rest. — Whither shall I go from thy spirit? Or whither shall I flee from thy presence? If I ascend up into heaven, thou art there: if I make my bed in hell, behold, thou art there. — Am I a God at hand, saith the Lord, and not a God afar off? Can any hide himself in secret places that I shall not see him? saith the Lord, Do not I fill heaven and earth? saith the Lord. — Behold, the heaven and heaven of heavens cannot contain thee, how much less this house that I have builded? — Thus saith the high and lofty One that inhabiteth eternity, whose name is Holy: I dwell in the high and holy place, with him also that is of a contrite and humble spirit, to revive the spirit of the humble, and to revive the heart of the contrite ones. — Ye are the temple of living God.

Matthew 18:20, 28:20   Exodus 33:14   Psalm 139:7,8   Jeremiah 23:23,24
1 Kings 8:27   Isaiah 57:15 2   Corinthians 6:16

MAY 2 EVENING

*Keep yourselves from idols.
— 1 JOHN 5:21*

My son, give me thine heart. — Set your affection on things above, not on things on the earth. — Son of man, these men have set up their idols in their heart and put the stumblingblock of their iniquity before their face: should I be enquired of at all by them? — Mortify...your members which are upon the earth; fornication, uncleanness, inordinate affection, evil concupiscence, and covetousness, which is idolatry. — They that will be rich fall into temptation and a snare. For the love of money is the root of all evil: which while some coveted after, they have erred from the faith, and pierced themselves through with many sorrows. But thou, O man of God, flee these things. — If riches increase, set not your heart upon them. — My fruit is better than gold, yea, than fine gold; and my revenue than choice silver. — Where your treasure is, there will your heart be also. — The Lord looketh on the heart.

Proverbs 23:26   Colossians 3:2   Ezekiel 14:3   Colossians 3:5
1 Timothy 6:9-11   Psalm 62:10   Proverbs 8:19   Matthew 6:21 1   Samuel 16:7

MAY 3 MORNING

*Be ye perfect,
even as your Father which is in heaven is perfect.*
— MATTHEW 5:48

I am the Almighty God; walk before me, and be thou perfect. — Ye shall be holy unto me: for I the Lord am holy, and have severed you from other people, that ye should be mine. — Ye are bought with a price: therefore glorify God in your body, and in your spirit, which are God's. — Ye are complete in him, which is the head of all principality and power. — Who gave himself for us, that he might redeem us from all iniquity. — Be diligent that ye may be found of him in peace, without spot, and blameless. — Blessed are the undefiled in the way, who walk in the law of the Lord. — Whoso looketh into the perfect law of liberty, and continueth therein, he being not a forgetful hearer, but a doer of the work, this man shall be blessed in his deed. — Search me, O God, and know my heart: try me, and know my thoughts: and see if there be any wicked way in me, and lead me in the way everlasting.

Genesis 17:1   Leviticus 20:26   1 Corinthians 6:20   Colossians 2:10   Titus 2:14
2 Peter 3:14   Psalm 119:1   James 1:25   Psalm 139:23,24

MAY 3 EVENING

Perfecting holiness in the fear of God.
— 2 CORINTHIANS 7:1

Dearly beloved, let us cleanse ourselves from all filthiness of the flesh and spirit. — Behold, thou desirest truth in the inward parts: and in the hidden part thou shalt make me to know wisdom. — Teaching us that denying ungodliness and worldly lusts, we should live soberly, righteously, and godly, in this present world. — Let your light so shine before men, that they may see your good works, and glorify your Father which is in heaven. — Not as though I had already attained, either were already perfect. — Every man that hath this hope in him purifieth himself, even as he is pure. — Now he that hath wrought us for the selfsame thing is God, who also hath given unto us the earnest of the Spirit. — For the perfecting of the saints, for the work of the ministry, for the edifying of the body of Christ: till we all come in the unity of the faith, and of the knowledge of the Son of God, unto a perfect man, unto the measure of the stature of the fulness of Christ.

2 Corinthians 7:1   Psalm 51:6   Titus 2:12   Matthew 5:16
Philippians 3:12   1 John 3:3   2 Corinthians 5:5   Ephesians 4:12,13

MAY 4 MORNING

Behold,
the Lord's hand is not shortened, that it cannot save;
neither is his ear heavy, that it cannot hear.
— ISAIAH 59:1

In the day when I cried thou answeredst me, and strengthenedst me with strength in my soul. — While I was speaking in prayer, even the man Gabriel, whom I had seen in the vision at the beginning, being caused to fly swiftly, touched me about the time of the evening oblation. — Hide not thy face far from me; put not thy servant away in anger: thou hast been my help, leave me not, neither forsake me, O God of my salvation. — Be not thou far from me, O Lord, O my strength, haste thee to help me. — Ah Lord God! behold, thou hast made the heaven and the earth by thy great power and stretched out arm, and there is nothing too hard for thee. — Who delivered us from so great a death, and doth deliver: in whom we trust that he will yet deliver us. — Shall not God avenge his own elect, which cry day and night unto him though he bear long with them? I tell you that he will avenge them speedily.

Psalm 138:3   Daniel 9:21   Psalms 27:9, 22:19
Jeremiah 32:17   2 Corinthians 1:10   Luke 18:7,8

MAY 4 EVENING

I have glorified thee on the earth.
— JOHN 17:4

My meat is to do the will of him that sent me, and to finish his work. — I must work the works of him that sent me, while it is day: the night cometh, when no man can work. — Wist ye not that I must be about my Father's business? And they understood not the saying which he spake unto them. — This sickness is not unto death, but for the glory of God, that the Son of God might be glorified thereby. Said I not unto thee, that if thou wouldest believe, thou shouldest see the glory of God? — Jesus increased in wisdom and stature, and in favour with God and man. — Thou art my beloved Son; in thee I am well pleased. — All bare him witness, and wondered at the gracious words, which proceeded out of his mouth. — Thou art worthy...for thou wast slain, and hast redeemed us to God by thy blood, out of every kindred, and tongue, and people, and nation; and hast made us unto our God kings and priests: and we shall reign on the earth.

John 4:34, 9:4   Luke 2:49,50   John 11:4,40
Luke 2:52, 3:22, 4:22   Revelation 5:9,10

MAY 5 MORNING

Take no thought, saying, What shall we eat?
Or, What shall we drink?
Or, Wherewithal shall we be clothed?
For your heavenly Father knoweth
that ye have need of all these things.
— MATTHEW 6:31,32

 O fear the Lord, ye his saints: for there is no want to them that fear him. The young lions do lack, and suffer hunger: but they that seek the Lord shall not want any good thing. — No good thing will he withhold from them that walk uprightly. O Lord of hosts, blessed is the man that trusteth in thee. — I would have you without carefulness. — Be careful for nothing; but in everything by prayer and supplication with thanksgiving let your requests be made known unto God. — Are not two sparrows sold for a farthing? And one of them shall not fall on the ground without your Father. The very hairs of your head are all numbered. Fear ye not therefore, ye are of more value than many sparrows. — Why are ye so fearful? How is it that ye have no faith? — Have faith in God.

Psalms 34:9,10, 84:11,12   1 Corinthians 7:32
Philippians 4:6   Matthew 10:29-31   Mark 4:40, 11:22

MAY 5 EVENING

He spread a cloud for a covering;
and fire to give light in the night.
— PSALM 105:39

 Like as a father pitieth his children, so the LORD pitieth them that fear him. For he knoweth our frame; he remembereth that we are dust. — The sun shall not smite thee by day, nor the moon by night. — There shall be a tabernacle for a shadow in the daytime from the heat, and for a place of refuge, and for a covert from storm and from rain. — The LORD is thy keeper: the LORD is thy shade upon thy right hand. The Lord shall preserve thy going out and thy coming in from this time forth, and even for evermore. — The Lord went before them by day in a pillar of a cloud, to lead them the way; and by night in a pillar of fire, to give them light; to go by day and night: he took not away the pillar of the cloud by day, nor the pillar of fire by night, from before the people. — Jesus Christ the same yesterday, and today, and forever.

Psalms 103:13,14, 121:6   Isaiah 4:6   Psalm 121:5,8   Exodus 13:21,22   Hebrews 13:8

MAY 6 MORNING

Mercy and truth are met together;
righteousness and peace have kissed each other.
— PSALM 85:10

A just God and a Saviour. — The Lord is well pleased for his righteousness' sake; he will magnify the law, and make it honourable. — God was in Christ reconciling the world unto himself, not imputing their trespasses unto them. — Whom God hath set forth to be a propitiation through faith in his blood to declare his righteousness for the remission of sins that are past, through the forbearance of God; to declare I say at this time his righteousness: that he might be just and the justifier of him which believeth in Jesus. — He was wounded for our transgressions, he was bruised for our iniquities: the chastisement of our peace was upon him; and with his stripes, we are healed. — Who shall lay any thing to the charge of God's elect? It is God that justifieth. — To him that worketh not, but believeth on him that justifieth the ungodly; his faith is counted for righteousness.

Isaiah 45:21, 42:21 2 Corinthians 5:19
Romans 3:25,26 Isaiah 53:5 Romans 8:33, 4:5

MAY 6 EVENING

How are the dead raised up?
And with what body do they come?
— 1 CORINTHIANS 15:35

Beloved, now are we the sons of God;...it doth not appear what we shall be: but we know that, when he shall appear we shall be like him; for we shall see him as he is. — As we have borne the image of the earthy, we shall also bear the image of heavenly. — The Saviour, the Lord Jesus Christ;...shall change our vile body, that it may be fashioned like unto his glorious body, according to the working whereby he is able even to subdue all things unto himself. — Jesus himself stood in the midst of them, and saith unto them, Peace be unto you. But they were terrified and affrighted, and supposed that they had seen a spirit. — He was seen of Cephas, then of the twelve: after that he was seen of above five hundred brethren at once. — If the Spirit of him that raised up Jesus from the dead dwell in you, he that raised up Christ from the dead shall also quicken your mortal bodies by his Spirit that dwelleth in you.

1 John 3:2 1 Corinthians 15:49 Philippians 3:20,21
Luke 24:36,37 1 Corinthians 15:5,6 Romans 8:11

MAY 7 MORNING

*Ye shall hear of wars and rumours of wars:
see that ye be not troubled.*
— MATTHEW 24:6

God is our refuge and strength, a very present help in trouble. Therefore will not we fear, though the earth be removed, and though the mountains be carried into the midst of the sea; though the waters thereof roar and be troubled, though the mountains shake with the swelling thereof. — Come, my people, enter thou into thy chambers, and shut thy doors about thee: hide thyself as it were for a little moment, until the indignation be overpast. For, behold, the Lord cometh out of his place to punish the inhabitants of the earth for their iniquity. — In the shadow of thy wings will I make my refuge, until these calamities be overpast. — Your life is hid with Christ in God. — He shall not be afraid of evil tidings: his heart is fixed, trusting the Lord. — These things I have spoken unto you, that in me ye might have peace. In the world ye shall have tribulation: but be of good cheer; I have overcome the world.

Psalm 46:1-3   Isaiah 26:20,21   Psalm 57:1
Colossians 3:3   Psalm 112:7   John 16:33

MAY 7 EVENING

They persecute him whom thou hast smitten.
— PSALM 69:26

It is impossible but that offences will come: but woe unto him, through whom they come!— Him, being delivered by the determinate counsel and foreknowledge of God, ye have taken, and by wicked hands have crucified and slain. — They did spit in his face, and buffeted him; and others smote him with the palms of their hands, saying, Prophesy unto us, thou Christ, Who is he that smote thee? — Likewise also the chief priests mocking him, with the scribes and elders, said, He saved others; himself he cannot save. If he be the King of Israel, let him now come down from the cross. — Of a truth against thy holy child Jesus, whom thou hast anointed, both Herod, and Pontius Pilate, with the Gentiles, and the people of Israel, were gathered together, to do whatsoever thy hand and thy counsel determined before to be done. — Surely he hath borne our grief, and carried our sorrows: yet we did esteem him stricken, smitten of God, and afflicted.

Luke 17:1   Acts 2:23   Matthew 26:67,68, 27:41,42   Acts 4:27,28   Isaiah 53:4

MAY 8 MORNING

It pleased the Lord to bruise him; he hath put him to grief.
— ISAIAH 53:10

Now is my soul troubled; and what shall I say? Father, save me from this hour: but for this cause came I unto this hour. Father, glorify thy name. Then came there a voice from heaven, saying, I have both glorified it, and will glorify it again. — Father, if thou be willing, remove this cup from me: nevertheless not my will, but thine, be done. — And there appeared an angel unto him from heaven, strengthening him. — Being found in fashion as a man, he humbled himself, and became obedient unto death, even the death of the cross. — Therefore doth my Father love me, because I lay down my life, that I might take it again. — For I came down from heaven, not to do mine will, but the will of him that sent me. — The cup which my father hath given me, shall I not drink it? — The Father hath not left me alone; for I do always those things that please him. — My beloved Son, in whom I am well pleased. — Mine elect, in whom my soul delighteth.

John 12:27,28   Luke 22:42,43   Philippians 2:8
John 10:17, 6:38, 18:11, 8:29   Matthew 3:17   Isaiah 42:1

MAY 8 EVENING

Ye that are the Lord's remembrancers, keep not silence.
— ISAIAH 62:6

Thou...hast made us unto our God kings and priests. — The sons of Aaron, the priests, shall blow with the trumpets; and they shall be to you for an ordinance for ever throughout your generations. And if ye go to war in your land against the enemy that oppresseth you, then ye shall blow an alarm with the trumpets; and ye shall be remembered before the Lord your God, and ye shall be saved from your enemies. — I said not unto the seed of Jacob, Seek ye me in vain. — Their voice was heard, and their prayer came up to his holy dwelling place, even unto heaven. — The eyes of the Lord are upon the righteous, and his ears are open unto their cry. — Pray one for another: the effectual fervent prayer of a righteous man availeth much. — Come, Lord Jesus. — Make no tarrying, O my God. — Looking for and hasting unto the coming of the day of God.

Revelation 5:9,10   Numbers 10:8,9   Isaiah 45:19   2 Chronicles 30:27
Psalm 34:15   James 5: 16   2 Peter 3:12   Revelation 22:20   Psalm 40:17

MAY 9 MORNING

*Faith is the substance of things hoped for,
the evidence of things not seen.*
— HEBREWS 11:1

If in this life only we have hope in Christ, we are of all men most miserable. — Eye hath not seen, nor ear heard, neither have entered into the heart of man, the things which God hath prepared for them that love him. But God hath revealed them unto us by his Spirit. — After that ye believed ye were sealed with that holy Spirit of promise, which is the earnest of our inheritance until the redemption of the purchased possession. — Jesus saith unto him, Thomas, because thou hast seen me, thou hast believed; blessed are they that have not seen, and yet have believed. — Whom having not seen, ye love; in whom, though now ye see him not, yet believing, ye rejoice with joy unspeakable and full of glory: receiving the end of your faith, even the salvation of your souls. — We walk by faith, not by sight. — Cast not away therefore your confidence, which hath great recompence of reward.

1 Corinthians 15:19, 2:9,10   Ephesians 1:13,14
John 20:29 1   Peter 1:8,9 2   Corinthians 5:7   Hebrews 10:35

MAY 9 EVENING

It is I; be not afraid.
— JOHN 6:20

When I saw him, I fell at his feet as dead. And he laid his right hand upon me, saying unto me, Fear not; I am the first and the last: I am he that liveth, and was dead; and, behold, I am alive for evermore, Amen; and have the keys of hell and of death. — I, even I, am he that blotteth out thy transgressions for mine own sake, and will not remember thy sins. — Woe is me! For I am undone;... mine eyes have seen the King, the Lord of hosts. Then flew one of the seraphims unto me, having a live coal in his hand, which he had taken with the tongs from off the altar: and he laid it upon my mouth, and said, Lo, this hath touched thy lips; and thine iniquity is taken away, and thy sin purged. — I have blotted out, as a thick cloud, thy transgressions, and, as a cloud, thy sins: return unto me; for I have redeemed thee. — If any man sin, we have an advocate with the Father, Jesus Christ the righteous.

Revelation 1:17,18   Isaiah 43:25, 6:5-7, 44:22.1   John 2:1

MAY 10 MORNING

For this purpose the Son of God was manifested,
that he might destroy the works of the devil.
— 1 JOHN 3:8

We wrestle not against flesh and blood, but against principalities, against powers, against the rulers of the darkness of this world, against spiritual wickedness in high places. — Forasmuch...as the children are partakers of flesh and blood, he also himself likewise took part of the same; that through death he might destroy him that had the power of death, that is, the devil. — And having spoiled principalities and powers, he made a shew of them openly, triumphing over them. — I heard a loud voice saying in heaven, Now is come salvation, and strength, and the kingdom of our God, and the power of his Christ: for the accuser of our brethren is cast down, which accused them before our God day and night. And they overcame him by the blood of the Lamb, and by the word of their testimony; and they loved not their lives unto the death. — Thanks be to God, which giveth us the victory through our Lord Jesus Christ.

Ephesians 6:12   Hebrews 2:14   Colossians 2:15
Revelation 12:10,11 1   Corinthians 15:57

MAY 10 EVENING

Vanity of vanities; all is vanity.
— ECCLESIASTES 1:2

We spend our years as a tale that is told. The days of our years are threescore years and ten; and if by reason of strength they be fourscore years, yet is their strength labour and sorrow; for it is soon cut off, and we fly away. — If in this life only we have hope in Christ, we are of all men most miserable. — Here have we no continuing city, but we seek one to come. — I am the Lord, I change not. — Our conversation (citizenship) is in heaven; from whence also we look for the Saviour, the Lord Jesus Christ; who shall change our vile body that it may be fashioned like unto his glorious body, according to the working whereby he is able even to subdue all things unto himself. — The creature was made subject to vanity, not willingly but by reason of him who hath subjected the same in hope. — Jesus Christ the same yesterday, and today, and forever. — Holy, holy, holy, Lord God Almighty, which was, and is, and is to come.

Psalm 90:9,10 1   Corinthians 15:19   Hebrews 13:14   Malachi 3:6
Philippians 3:20,21   Romans 8:20   Hebrews 13:8   Revelation 4:8

MAY 11 MORNING

Awake to righteousness, and sin not.
— 1 CORINTHIANS 15:34

Ye are all the children of light, and the children of the day. Therefore let us not sleep, as do others; but let us watch and be sober. — It is high time to awake out of sleep: for now is our salvation nearer than when we believed. The night is far spent, the day is at hand: let us therefore cast off the works of darkness, and let us put on the armour of light. — Wherefore take unto you the whole armour of God, that ye may be able to withstand in the evil day, and having done all, to stand. — Cast away from you all your transgressions, whereby ye have transgressed: and make you a new heart and a new spirit. — Lay apart all filthiness and superfluity of naughtiness, and receive with meekness the engrafted word, which is able to save your souls. — Little children, abide in him that, when he shall appear, we may have confidence, and not be ashamed before him at his coming. If ye know that he is righteous, ye know that every one that doeth righteousness is born of him.

1 Thessalonians 5:5,6   Romans 13:11,12   Ephesians 6:13
Ezekiel 18:31   James 1:21 1   John 2:28,29

MAY 11 EVENING

My sheep hear my voice.
— JOHN 10:27

Behold, I stand at the door, and knock: If any man hear my voice, and open the door, 1 will come in to him, and will sup with him, and he with me. — I sleep, but my heart waketh: it is the voice of my beloved that knocketh, saying, Open to me, my sister, my love, my dove, my undefiled. I opened to my beloved; but my beloved had withdrawn himself, and was gone: my soul failed when he spake: I sought him, but I could not find him; I called him, but he gave me no answer. — Speak; for thy servant heareth. — When Jesus came to the place, he looked up, and saw him, and said unto him, Zacchaeus, make haste and come down; for to day I must abide at thy house. And he made haste, and came down, and received him joyfully. — I will hear what God the Lord will speak: for he will speak peace unto his people, and to his saints: but let them not turn again to folly.

Revelation 3:20   Song of Solomon 5:2,6
1 Samuel 3:10   Luke 19:5,6   Psalm 85:8

MAY 12 MORNING

Beloved, let us love one another:
for love is of God; and everyone that loveth
is born of God, and knoweth God.
— 1 JOHN 4:7

The love of God is shed abroad in our hearts by the Holy Ghost, which is given unto us. — Ye have not received the spirit of bondage again to fear; but ye have received the Spirit of adoption, whereby we cry, Abba, Father. The Spirit itself beareth witness with our spirit, that we are the children of God. — He that believeth on the Son of God hath the witness in himself. — In this was manifested the love of God toward us, because that God sent his only begotten Son into the world, that we might live through him. — In whom we have redemption through his blood, the forgiveness of sins, according to the riches of his grace. — That in the ages to come he might shew the exceeding riches of his grace in his kindness toward us through Christ Jesus. — Beloved, if God so loved us, we ought also to love one another.

Romans 5:5, 8:15,16 1 John 5:10, 4:9 Ephesians 1:7, 2:7 1 John 4:11

MAY 12 EVENING

Reproach hath broken my heart.
— PSALM 69:20

Is not this the carpenter's son? — Can there any good thing come out of Nazareth? — Say we not well that thou are a Samaritan, and hast a devil? — He casteth out devils through the prince of the devils. — We know that this man is a sinner. — He deceiveth the people. — This man blasphemeth. — Behold a man gluttonous and a winebibber, a friend of publicans and sinners. — It is enough for the disciple that he be as his master, and the servant as his lord. — This is thankworthy, if a man for conscience toward God endure grief, suffering wrongfully. For even hereunto were ye called: because Christ also suffered for us, leaving us an example, that we should follow his steps. Who did no sin, neither was guile found in his mouth: who when he was reviled, reviled not again; when he suffered, he threatened not; but committed himself to him that judgeth righteously. — If ye be reproached for the name of Christ, happy are ye.

Matthew 13:55   John 1:46, 8:48   Matthew 9:34   John 9:24, 7:12
Matthew 9:3, 11:19, 10:25 1   Peter 2:19-23, 4:14

MAY 13 MORNING

Pray everywhere, lifting up holy hands,
without wrath and doubting.
— 1 TIMOTHY 2:8

The true worshippers shall worship the Father in spirit and in truth: for the Father seeketh such to worship him. God is a Spirit: and they that worship him must worship him in spirit and in truth. — Then shalt thou call, and the Lord shall answer; thou shalt cry, and he shall say, Here I am. — When ye stand praying, forgive, if ye have ought against any. — Without faith it is impossible to please him: for he that cometh to God must believe that he is, and that he is a rewarder of them that diligently seek him. — Let him ask in faith, nothing wavering. For he that wavereth is like a wave of the sea, driven with the wind and tossed. For let not that man think that he shall receive anything of the Lord. — If I regard iniquity in my heart, the Lord will not hear me. — My little children, these things write I unto you, that ye sin not. And if any man sin, we have an advocate with the Father, Jesus Christ the righteous: and he is the propitiation for our sins.

John 4:23,24   Isaiah 58:9   Mark 11:25   Hebrews 11:6
James 1:6,7   Psalm 66:18   1 John 2:1,2

MAY 13 EVENING

My heart panteth,
my strength faileth me.
— PSALM 38:10

Hear my cry, O God; attend unto my prayer. From the end of the earth will I cry unto thee, when my heart is overwhelmed: lead me to the rock that is higher than I. — He said unto me, My grace is sufficient for thee: for my strength is made perfect in weakness. Most gladly therefore will I rather glory in my infirmities, that the power of Christ may rest upon me. For when I am weak, then am I strong. — When (Peter) saw the wind boisterous, he was afraid; and beginning to sink, he cried, saying, Lord, save me. And immediately Jesus stretched forth his hand, and caught him, and said unto him, O thou of little faith, wherefore didst thou doubt? — If thou faint in the day of adversity, thy strength is small. — He giveth power to the faint; and to them that have no might he increaseth strength. — The eternal God is thy refuge, and underneath are the everlasting arms. — Strengthened with all might, according to his glorious power.

Psalm 61:1,2   2 Corinthians 12:9,10   Matthew 14:30,31
Proverbs 24:10   Isaiah 40:29   Deuteronomy 33:27   Colossians 1:11

MAY 14 MORNING

The fellowship of His sufferings.
— PHILIPPIANS 3:10

It is enough for the disciple that he be as his master, and the servant as his lord. — He is despised and rejected of men; a man of sorrows, and acquainted with grief; and we hid as it were our faces from him; he was despised, and we esteemed him not. — In the world ye shall have tribulation. — Because ye are not of the world, but I have chosen you out of the world, therefore the world hateth you. — I looked for some to take pity, but there was none. — At my first answer no man stood with me, but all men forsook me. — The foxes have holes, and the birds of the air have nests; but the Son of man hath not where to lay his head. — Here have we no continuing city, but we seek one to come. — Let us run with patience the race that is set before us, looking unto Jesus the author and finisher of our faith; who for the joy that was set before him endured the cross, despising the shame, and is set down at the right hand of the throne of God.

Matthew 10:25   Isaiah 53:3   John 16:33, 15:19   Psalm 69:20
2 Timothy 4:16   Matthew 8:20   Hebrews 13:14, 12:1,2

MAY 14 EVENING

They overcame...by the blood of the Lamb.
— REVELATION 12:11

Who shall lay anything to the charge of God's elect? It is God that justifieth. Who is he that condemneth? It is Christ that died. — It is the blood that maketh an atonement for the soul. — I am the LORD. The blood shall be to you for a token upon the houses where ye are: and when I see the blood, I will pass over you. — There is...no condemnation to them which are in Christ Jesus. — What are these which are arrayed in white robes? And whence came they? These are they which came out of great tribulation, and have washed their robes, and made them white in the blood of the Lamb. — Unto him that loved us, and washed us from our sins in his own blood, and hath made us kings and priests unto God and his Father; to him be glory and dominion for ever and ever. Amen.

Romans 8:33,34   Leviticus 17:11   Exodus 12:12,13
Romans 8:1   Revelation 7:13,14, 1:5,6

MAY 15 MORNING

God shall wipe away all tears:...
there shall be no more death, neither sorrow...
for the former things are passed away.
— REVELATION 21:4

He will swallow up death in victory; and the Lord God will wipe away tears from off all faces; and the rebuke of his people shall he take away from off all the earth: for the Lord hath spoken it. — Thy sun shall no more go down; neither shall thy moon withdraw itself: for the Lord shall be thine everlasting light, and the days of thy mourning shall be ended. — The inhabitant shall not say, I am sick: the people that dwell therein shall be forgiven their iniquity. — The voice of weeping shall be no more heard in her, nor the voice of crying. — Sorrow and sighing shall flee away. — I will ransom them from the power of the grave; I will redeem them from death: O death, I will be thy plagues; O grave, I will be thy destruction. — The last enemy that shall be destroyed is death. Then shall be brought to pass the saying that is written, Death is swallowed up in victory. — The things which are not seen are eternal.

Isaiah 25:8, 60:20, 33:24, 65:19, 35:10   Hosea 13:14 1   Corinthians 15:26,54, 4:18

MAY 15 EVENING

Raised up together in Christ Jesus.
— EPHESIANS 2:6

Fear not;...I am he that liveth. — Father, I will that they also, whom thou hast given me, be with me where I am. — We are members of his body, of his flesh, and of his bones. — He is the head of the body, the church: who is the beginning, the firstborn from the dead. — Ye are complete in him, which is the head. — Forasmuch...as the children are partakers of flesh and blood, he also himself likewise took part of the same; that through death he might destroy him that had the power of death, that is, the devil: and deliver them who through fear of death were all their lifetime subject to bondage. — This corruptible must put on incorruption, and this mortal must put on immortality. So when this corruptible shall have put on incorruption, and this mortal shall have put on immortality, then shall be brought to pass the saying that is written, Death is swallowed up in victory.

Revelation 1:17,18   John 17:24   Ephesians 5:30
Colossians 1:18, 2:10   Hebrews 2:14,15 1   Corinthians 15:53,54

MAY 16 MORNING

A servant of Jesus Christ.
— ROMANS 1:1

Ye call me Master and Lord: and ye say well; for so I am. — If any man serve me, let him follow me; and where I am, there shall also my servant be: if any man serve me, him will my Father honour. — Take my yoke upon you, and learn of me; for I am meek and lowly in heart: and ye shall find rest unto your souls. For my yoke is easy, and my burden is light. — What things were gain to me, those I counted loss for Christ. — Being made free from sin, and become servants to God, ye have your fruit unto holiness, and the end everlasting life. — Henceforth I call you not servants; for the servant knoweth not what his lord doeth: but I have called you friends; for all things that I have heard of my Father I have made known unto you. — Thou art no more a servant, but a son. — Stand fast therefore in the liberty wherewith Christ hath made us free, and be not entangled again with the yoke of bondage. For, brethren, ye have been called unto liberty; only use not liberty for an occasion to the flesh.

John 13:13, 12:26   Matthew 11:29,30   Philippians 3:7
Romans 6:22   John 15:15   Galatians 4:7, 5:1,13

MAY 16 EVENING

I will bless the Lord, who hath given me counsel.
— PSALM 16:7

His name shall be called Wonderful, Counsellor. — Counsel is mine, and sound wisdom: I am understanding, I have strength. — Thy word is a lamp unto my feet, and a light unto my path. — Trust in the Lord with all thine heart; and lean not unto thine own understanding. In all thy ways acknowledge him, and he shall direct thy paths. — O Lord, I know that the way of man is not in himself: it is not in man that walketh to direct his steps. — Thine ears shall hear a word behind thee, saying, This is the way, walk ye in it, when ye turn to the right hand, and when ye turn to the left. — Commit thy works unto the Lord, and thy thoughts shall be established. — He knoweth the way that I take. — Man's goings are of the Lord: how can a man then understand his own way? — Thou shalt guide me with thy counsel, and afterward receive me to glory. — This God is our God for ever and ever: he will be our guide even unto death.

Isaiah 9:6   Proverbs 8:14   Psalm 119:105   Proverbs 3:5,6   Jeremiah 10:23
Isaiah 30:21   Proverbs 16:3   Job 23:10   Proverbs 20:24   Psalms 73:24, 48:14

MAY 17 MORNING

I am the Lord your God; walk in my statutes,
and keep my judgments, and do them.
— EZEKIEL 20:19

As he which hath called you is holy, so be ye holy in all manner of conversation. — He that saith he abideth in him ought himself also so to walk, even as he walked. If ye know that he is righteous, ye know that every one that doeth righteousness is born of him. — Circumcision is nothing, and uncircumcision is nothing, but the keeping of the commandments of God. — Whosoever shall keep the whole law, and yet offend in one point, he is guilty of all. — Not that we are sufficient of ourselves to think anything, as of ourselves; but our sufficiency is of God. — Teach me, O Lord, the way of thy statutes. — Work out your own salvation with fear and trembling. For it is God which worketh in you both to will and to do of his good pleasure. — The God of peace...make you perfect in every good work to do his will, working in you that which is well pleasing in his sight, through Jesus Christ.

1 Peter 1:15   1 John 2:6,29   1 Corinthians 7:19   James 2:10   Corinthians 3:5
Psalm 119:33   Philippians 2:12,13   Hebrews 13:20,21

MAY 17 EVENING

I have exalted one chosen out of the people.
— PSALM 89:19

Verily he took not on him the nature of angels; but he took on him the seed of Abraham. In all things it behoved him to be made like unto his brethren. — Upon the likeness of the throne was the likeness as the appearance of a man above upon it. — The Son of man...which is in heaven. — Behold my hands and my feet, that it is I myself: handle me, and see; for a spirit hath not flesh and bones, as ye see me have. — He made himself of no reputation, and took upon him the form of a servant, and was made in the likeness of men: and being found in fashion as a man, he humbled himself, and became obedient unto death, even the death of the cross. Wherefore God also hath highly exalted him, and given him a name which is above every name: that at the name of Jesus every knee should bow. — Be watchful, and strengthen the things which remain, that are ready to die: for I have not found thy works perfect before God.

Hebrews 2:16,17   Ezekiel 1:26   John 3:13
Luke 24:39   Philippians 2:7-10   Revelation 3:2

MAY 18 MORNING

As the Father hath life in himself;
so hath he given to the Son to have life in himself.
— JOHN 5:26

Our Saviour Jesus Christ...hath abolished death, and hath brought life and immortality to light through the gospel. — I am the resurrection, and the life. — Because I live, ye shall live also. — We are made partakers of Christ. — Partakers of the Holy Ghost. — Partakers of the divine nature. — The first man Adam was made a living soul; the last Adam was made a quickening spirit. — Behold, I shew you a mystery; We shall not all sleep, but we shall be changed, in a moment, in the twinkling of an eye, at the last trump: for the trumpet shall sound, and the dead shall be raised incorruptible, and we shall be changed. — Holy, holy, holy, Lord God Almighty, which was, and is, and is to come. — Who liveth for ever and ever. — The blessed and only Potentate, the King of kings, and Lord of lords; who only hath immortality. — Unto the King eternal, immortal...be honour and glory for ever and ever. Amen.

2 Timothy 1:10   John 11:25, 14:19   Hebrews 3:14, 6:4   2 Peter 1:4
1 Corinthians 15:45,51,52   Revelation 4:8,9   1 Timothy 6:15,16, 1:17

MAY 18 EVENING

Let us not be desirous of vain glory.
— GALATIANS 5:26

Gideon said unto them, I would desire a request of you, that ye would give me every man the earrings of his prey. (For they had golden earrings, because they were Ishmaelites.) And they answered, We will willingly give them. And they spread a garment, and did cast therein every man the earrings of his prey. And Gideon made an ephod thereof, and put it in his city, even in Ophrah: and all Israel went thither a whoring after it: which thing became a snare unto Gideon, and to his house. — Seekest thou great things for thyself? Seek them not. — Lest I should be exalted above measure through the abundance of the revelations, there was given to me a thorn in the flesh. — Let nothing be done, through strife or vain glory; but in lowliness of mind let each esteem other better than themselves. — Charity envieth not; charity vaunteth not itself, is not puffed up, doth not behave itself unseemly, seeketh not her own. — Take my yoke upon you, and learn of me.

Judges 8:24,25,27   Jeremiah 45:5   2 Corinthians 12:7
Philippians 2:3   1 Corinthians 13:4,5   Matthew 11:29

MAY 19 MORNING

Wash me thoroughly from mine iniquity.
— PSALM 51:2

I will cleanse them from all their iniquity, whereby they have sinned against me; and I will pardon all their iniquities, whereby they have sinned, and whereby they have transgressed against me. — Then will I sprinkle clean water upon you, and ye shall be clean: from all your filthiness, and from all your idols, will I cleanse you. — Except a man be born of water and of the Spirit, he cannot enter into the kingdom of God. — If the blood of bulls and of goats, and the ashes of a heifer sprinkling the unclean, sanctifieth to the purifying of the flesh: how much more shall the blood of Christ, who through the eternal Spirit offered himself without spot to God, purge your conscience from dead works to serve the living God? — He saved them for his name's sake, that he might make his mighty power to be known. — Not unto us, O Lord, not unto us, but unto thy name give glory, for thy mercy, and for thy truth's sake.

Jeremiah 33:8   Ezekiel 36:25   John 3:5   Hebrews 9:13,14   Psalms 106:8, 115:1

MAY 19 EVENING

Fellowship in the gospel.
— PHILIPPIANS 1:5

As the body is one, and hath many members, and all the members of that one body, being many, are one body: so also is Christ. For by one Spirit are we all baptized into one body, whether we be Jews or Gentiles, whether we be bond or free; and have been all made to drink into one Spirit. — God is faithful, by whom ye were called unto the fellowship of his Son Jesus Christ our Lord. — That which we have seen and heard declare we unto you, that ye also may have fellowship with us: and truly our fellowship is with the Father, and with his Son Jesus Christ. — If we walk in the light, as he is in the light, we have fellowship one with another, and the blood of Jesus Christ his Son cleanseth us from all sin. — These words spake Jesus. Neither pray I for these alone, but for them also which shall believe on me through their word; that they all may be one; as thou, Father, art in me, and I in thee, that they also may be one in us.

1 Corinthians 12:12,13, 1:9   1 John 1:3,7   John 17:1,20,21

MAY 20 MORNING

Take heed unto thyself.
— 1 TIMOTHY 4:16

Every man that striveth for the mastery is temperate in all things. Now they do it to obtain a corruptible crown; but we an incorruptible. I therefore so run, not as uncertainly; so fight I, not as one that beateth the air: but I keep under my body, and bring it into subjection lest that by any means, when I have preached to others, I myself should be a castaway. — Put on the whole armour of God, that ye may be able to stand against the wiles of the devil. For we wrestle not against the flesh and blood, but against principalities, against powers, against the rulers of the darkness of this world, against spiritual wickedness in high places. — They that are Christ's have crucified the flesh with the affections and lusts. If we live in the Spirit, let us also walk in the spirit. — For as many as are led by the Spirit of God, they are the sons of God. — Meditate upon these things; give thyself wholly to them; that thy profiting may appear to all.

1 Corinthians 9:25-27   Ephesians 6:11,12
Galatians 5:24,25   Romans 8:14 1   Timothy 4:15

MAY 20 EVENING

Jesus saith unto her, Mary.
— JOHN 20:16

Fear not: for I have redeemed thee, I have called thee by name: Thou art mine. — The sheep hear his voice: and he calleth his own sheep by name. And the sheep follow him: for they know his voice. — Behold, I have graven thee upon the palms of my hands; thy walls are continually before me. — The foundation of God standeth sure, having this seal, The Lord knoweth them that are his. — We have a great high priest, that is passed into the heavens, Jesus the Son of God. — Thou shalt take two onyx stones, and grave on them the names of the children of Israel. And Aaron shall bear their names before the Lord upon his two shoulders for a memorial. And thou shalt make the breastplate of judgment. And thou shalt set in it four rows of stones. And the stones shall be with the names of the children of Israel...and they shall be upon Aaron's heart when he goeth in before the Lord.

Isaiah 43:1   John 10:3,4   Isaiah 49:16 2   Timothy 2:19
Hebrews 4:14   Exodus 28:9,12,15,17,21,30

MAY 21 MORNING

My brethren, be strong in the Lord,
and in the power of his might.
— EPHESIANS 6:10

My grace is sufficient for thee: for my strength is made perfect in weakness. Most gladly therefore will I rather glory in my infirmities, that the power of Christ may rest upon me. Therefore I take pleasure in infirmities, in reproaches, in necessities, in persecutions, in distresses for Christ's sake: for when I am weak, then am I strong. — I will go in the strength of the Lord GOD: I will make mention of thy righteousness, even of thine only. — The gospel of Christ...is the power of God unto salvation. — I can do all things through Christ which strengtheneth me. — I also labour, striving according to his working, which worketh in me mightily. — We have this treasure in earthen vessels, that the excellency of the power may be of God, and not of us. — The joy of the Lord is your strength. — Strengthened with all might, according to his glorious power, unto all patience and longsuffering with joyfulness.

2 Corinthians 12:9,10   Psalm 71:16   Romans 1:16   Philippians 4:13
Colossians 1:29   2 Corinthians 4:7   Nehemiah 8:10   Colossians 1:11

MAY 21 EVENING

Jesus Christ our Lord.
— 1 CORINTHIANS 1:9

Jesus: for he shall save his people from their sins. — He humbled himself, and became obedient unto death, even the death of the cross. Wherefore God also hath highly exalted him, and given him a name which is above every name: that at the name of Jesus every knee should bow, of things in heaven, and things in earth, and things under the earth. — Messias...which is called Christ. — The Lord hath anointed me to preach good tidings unto the meek; he hath sent me to bind up the brokenhearted, to proclaim liberty to the captives. — The last Adam was made a quickening spirit. The second man is the Lord from heaven. — My Lord and my God. — Ye call me Master and Lord: and ye say well; for so I am. If I then, your Lord and Master have washed your feet; ye also ought to wash one another's feet. For I have given you an example, that ye should do as I have done to you.

Matthew 1:21   Philippians 2:8-10   John 4:25   Isaiah 61:1
1 Corinthians 15:45,47   John 20:28, 13:13-15

MAY 22 MORNING

*Peace I leave with you, my peace I give unto you:
not as the world giveth, give I unto you.*
— JOHN 14:27

The world passeth away, and the lust thereof. — Surely every man walketh in a vain shew: surely they are disquieted in vain: he heapeth up riches and knoweth not who shall gather them. — What fruit had ye then in those things whereof ye are now ashamed? For the end of those things is death. — Martha, Martha, thou are careful and troubled about many things: but one thing is needful: and Mary hath chosen that good part, which shall not be taken away from her. — I would have you without carefulness. — These things I have spoken unto you that in me ye might have peace. In the world ye shall have tribulation: but be of good cheer: I have overcome the world. — The Lord of peace himself give you peace always by all means. — The Lord bless thee, and keep thee: the Lord make his face shine upon thee, and be gracious unto thee: the Lord lift up his countenance upon thee, and give thee peace.

1 John 2:17   Psalm 39:6   Romans 6:21   Luke 10:41,42 1   Corinthians 7:32   John 16:33 2   Thessalonians 3:16   Numbers 6:24-26

MAY 22 EVENING

The Spirit helpeth our infirmities.
— ROMANS 8:26

The Comforter, which is the Holy Ghost. — What? Know ye not that your body is the temple of the Holy Ghost which is in you, which ye have of God? — It is God which worketh in you. — We know not what we should pray for as we ought: but the Spirit itself maketh intercession for us with groanings which can not be uttered. And he that searcheth the hearts knoweth what is the mind of the Spirit, because he maketh intercession for the saints according to the will of God. — He knoweth our frame; he remembereth that we are dust. — A bruised reed shall he not break, and the smoking flax shall he not quench. — The spirit indeed is willing, but the flesh is weak. — The Lord is my shepherd; I shall not want. He maketh me to lie down in green pastures: he leadeth me beside the still waters.

John 14:26 1   Corinthians 6:19   Philippians 2:13   Romans 8:26,27   Psalm 103:14   Isaiah 42:3   Matthew 26:41   Psalm 23:1,2

MAY 23 MORNING

*Thou shalt put…stones upon the shoulders of the ephod
for stones of memorial unto the children of Israel:
and Aaron shall bear their names before the Lord.
— EXODUS 28:12*

Jesus…because he continueth ever, hath an unchangeable priesthood. Wherefore he is able also to save them to the uttermost that come unto God by him, seeing he ever liveth to make intercession for them. — Him that is able to keep you from falling, and to present you faultless before the presence of his glory. — Seeing…that we have a great high priest, that is passed into the heavens, Jesus the Son of God, let us hold fast our profession. For we have not a high priest which cannot be touched with the feeling of our infirmities; but was in all points tempted like as we are, yet without sin. Let us therefore come boldly unto the throne of grace. — The beloved of the Lord shall dwell in safety by him: and the Lord shall cover him all the day long, and he shall dwell between his shoulders.

Hebrews 7:24,25 Jude 24   Hebrews 4:14-16   Deuteronomy 33:12

MAY 23 EVENING

*On that night could not the king sleep.
— ESTHER 6:1*

Thou holdest mine eyes waking. — Who is like unto the Lord our God…who humbleth himself to behold the things that are in heaven, and in the earth! — He doeth according to his will in the army of heaven, and among the inhabitants of the earth. — Thy way is in the sea, and thy path in the great waters, and thy footsteps are not known. — Surely the wrath of man shall praise thee: the remainder of wrath shalt thou restrain. — The eyes of the Lord run to and fro throughout the whole earth, to shew himself strong in the behalf of them whose heart is perfect toward him. — We know that all things work together for good to them that love God. — Are not two sparrows sold for a farthing? And one of them shall not fall on the ground without your Father. But the very hairs of your head are all numbered.

Psalms 77:4, 113:5,6   Daniel 4:35   Psalms 77:19, 76:10
2 Chronicles 16:9   Romans 8:28   Matthew 10:29,30

MAY 24 MORNING

Grieve not the holy Spirit of God,
whereby ye are sealed unto the day of redemption.
— EPHESIANS 4:30

The love of the Spirit. — The Comforter, which is the Holy Ghost. — In all their affliction he was afflicted, and the angel of his presence saved them: in his love and in his pity he redeemed them; and he bare them, and carried them all the days of old. But they rebelled, and vexed his Holy Spirit: therefore he turned to be their enemy, and he fought against them. — Hereby know we that we dwell in him, and he in us, because he hath given us of his Spirit. — After that ye believed, ye were sealed with that Holy Spirit of promise, which is the earnest of the inheritance until the redemption of the purchased possession. — This I say then, Walk in the Spirit, and ye shall not fulfil the lusts of the flesh. For the flesh lusteth against the spirit, and the spirit against the flesh: and these are contrary the one to the other: so that ye cannot do the things that ye would. — The Spirit helpeth our infirmities.

Romans 15:30   John 14:26   Isaiah 63:9,10 1   John 4:13
Ephesians 1:13,14   Galatians 5:16,17   Romans 8:26

MAY 24 EVENING

I will go and return to my place,
till they acknowledge their offence,
and seek my face.
— HOSEA 5:15

Your iniquities have separated between you and your God, your sins have hid his face from you. — My beloved had withdrawn himself, and was gone:...I sought him, but I could not find him; I called him, but he gave me no answer. — I hid me, and was wroth, and he went on forwardly in the way of his heart. I have seen his ways, and will heal him. — Hast thou not procured this unto thyself, in that thou hast forsaken the Lord thy God when he led thee by the way? — He arose, and came to his father. But when he was yet a great way off, his father saw him, and had compassion, and ran, and fell on his neck, and kissed him. — I will heal their backsliding, I will love them freely: for mine anger is turned away. — If we confess our sins, he is faithful and just to forgive us our sins, and to cleanse us from all unrighteousness.

Isaiah 59:2   Song of Solomon 5:6   Isaiah 57:17,18
Jeremiah 2:17   Luke 15:20   Hosea 14:4 1   John 1:9

MAY 25 MORNING

*How great is thy goodness,
which thou hast laid up for them that fear thee!*
— PSALM 31:19

Since the beginning of the world men have not heard, nor perceived by the ear, neither hath the eye seen, O God, beside thee, what he hath prepared for him that waiteth for him. — Eye hath not seen, nor ear heard, neither have entered into the heart of man, the things which God hath prepared for them that love him. But God hath revealed them unto us by his Spirit. — Thou wilt shew me the path of life: in thy presence is fulness of joy; at thy right hand there are pleasures for evermore. — How excellent is thy loving kindness, O God! Therefore the children of men put their trust under the shadow of thy wings. They shall be abundantly satisfied with the fatness of thy house; and thou shalt make them drink of the river of thy pleasures. For with thee is the fountain of life: in thy light shall we see light. — Godliness is profitable unto all things, having promise of the life that now is, and of that which is to come.

Isaiah 64:4 1 Corinthians 2:9,10 Psalms 16:11, 36:7-9 1 Timothy 4:8

MAY 25 EVENING

The Son of God...hath his eyes like unto a flame of fire.
— REVELATION 2:1

The heart is deceitful above all things, and desperately wicked: who can know it? I the Lord search the heart, I try the reins, even to give every man according to his ways, and according to the fruit of his doings. — Thou hast set our iniquities before thee, our secret sins in the light of thy countenance. — The Lord turned, and looked upon Peter. And Peter went out, and wept bitterly. — Jesus did not commit himself unto them, because he knew all men, and needed not that any should testify of man: for he knew what was in man. — He knoweth our frame; he remembereth that we are dust. — A bruised reed shall he not break, and the smoking flax shall he not quench. — The Lord knoweth them that are his. — I am the good shepherd, and know my sheep. My sheep hear my voice, and I know them, and they follow me: and I give unto them eternal life; and they shall never perish, neither shall any man pluck them out of my hand.

Jeremiah 17:9,10 Psalm 90:8 Luke 22:61,62 John 2:24,25
Psalm 103:14 Isaiah 42:3. 2 Timothy 2:19 John 10:14,27,28

MAY 26 MORNING

Our Lord Jesus, that great shepherd of the sheep.
— HEBREWS 13:20

The chief Shepherd. — I am the good shepherd, and know my sheep, and am known of mine. My sheep hear my voice, and I know them, and they follow me: and I give unto them eternal life; and they shall never perish, neither shall any man pluck them out of my hand. — The Lord is my shepherd; I shall not want. He maketh me to lie down in green pastures: he leadeth me beside the still waters. He restoreth my soul: he leadeth me in the paths of righteousness for his name's sake. — All we like sheep have gone astray; we have turned every one to his own way; and the LORD hath laid on him the iniquity of us all. — I am the good shepherd: the good shepherd giveth his life for the sheep. — I will seek that which was lost, and bring again that which was driven away, and will bind up that which was broken, and will strengthen that which was sick. — Ye were as sheep going astray; but are now returned unto the Shepherd and Bishop of your souls.

1 Peter 5:4   John 10:14,27,28   Psalm 23:1-3
Isaiah 53:6   John 10:11   Ezekiel 34:16 1   Peter 2:25

MAY 26 EVENING

The city had no need of the sun,
neither of the moon, to shine in it:
for the glory of God did lighten it,
and the Lamb is the light thereof.
— REVELATION 21:23

I saw in the way a light from heaven, above the brightness of the sun, shining round about me. And I said, Who art thou, Lord? And he said, I am Jesus whom thou persecutest. — Jesus taketh Peter, James, and John his brother, and bringeth them up into an high mountain apart, and was transfigured before them: and his face did shine as the sun, and his raiment was white as the light. — The sun shall be no more thy light by day; neither for brightness shall the moon give light unto thee: but the Lord shall be unto thee an everlasting light, and thy God thy glory. Thy sun shall no more go down; neither shall thy moon withdraw itself: for the Lord shall be thine everlasting light, and the days of thy mourning shall be ended. — The God of all grace...hath called us unto his eternal glory by Christ Jesus.

Acts 26:13,15   Matthew 17:1,2   Isaiah 60:19,20 1   Peter 5:10

MAY 27 MORNING

The Lord is good,
a strong hold in the day of trouble;
and he knoweth them that trust in him.
— NAHUM 1:7

Praise the Lord of hosts: for the Lord is good; for his mercy endureth for ever. — God is our refuge and strength, a very present help in trouble. — I will say of the Lord, He is my refuge and my fortress: my God; in him will I trust. — Who is like unto thee, O people saved by the Lord, the shield of thy help, and who is the sword of thy excellency! — As for God, his way is perfect; the word of the Lord is tried: he is a buckler to all them that trust in him. For who is God, save the Lord? And who is a rock, save our God? — If any man love God, the same is known of him. — The foundation of God standeth sure, having this seal, The Lord knoweth them that are his. And, Let every one that nameth the name of Christ depart from iniquity. — The Lord knoweth the way of the righteous: but the way of the ungodly shall perish. — Thou hast found grace in my sight, and I know thee by name.

Jeremiah 33:11   Psalms 46:1, 91:2   Deuteronomy 33:29 2   Samuel 22:31,32   I Corinthians 8:3 2   Timothy 2:19   Psalm 1:6   Exodus 33:17

MAY 27 EVENING

I would have you without carefulness.
— 1 CORINTHIANS 7:32

He careth for you. — The eyes of the Lord run to and fro throughout the whole earth, to shew himself strong in the behalf of them whose heart is perfect toward him. — O taste and see that the Lord is good: blessed is the man that trusteth in him. The young lions do lack, and suffer hunger: but they that seek the Lord shall not want any good thing. — Therefore I say unto you, Take no thought for your life, what ye shall eat, or what ye shall drink; nor yet for your body, what ye shall put on. Is not the life more than meat, and the body than raiment? Behold the fowls of the air: for they sow not, neither do they reap, nor gather into barns; yet your heavenly Father feedeth them. Are ye not much better than they? —Be careful for nothing; but in every thing by prayer and supplication with thanksgiving let your requests be made known unto God. And the peace of God, which passeth all understanding, shall keep your hearts and minds through Christ Jesus.

1 Peter 5:7 2   Chronicles 16:9   Psalm 34:8,10   Matthew 6:25,26   Philippians 4:6,7

MAY 28 MORNING

We look for the Saviour.
— PHILIPPIANS 3:20

The grace of God that bringeth salvation hath appeared to men, teaching us that, denying ungodliness and worldly lusts, should live soberly, righteously, and godly, in this present world, looking for that blessed hope, and the glorious appearing of the great God and our Saviour Jesus Christ; who gave himself for us, that he might redeem us from all iniquity, and purify unto himself a peculiar people, zealous of good works. — We, according to his promise, look for new heavens and a new earth, wherein dwelleth righteousness. Wherefore, beloved, seeing that ye look for such things, be diligent that ye may be found of him in peace, without spot, and blameless. — Christ was once offered to bear the sins of many; and unto them that look for him shall he appear the second time without sin unto salvation. — And it shall be said in that day, Lo, this is our God; we have waited for him, and he will save us: this is the LORD; we have waited for him, we will be glad and rejoice in his salvation.

Titus 2:11-14   2 Peter 3:13,14   Hebrews 9:28   Isaiah 25:9

MAY 28 EVENING

So run, that ye may obtain.
— 1 CORINTHIANS 9:24

The slothful man saith, There is a lion without. — Let us lay aside every weight, and the sin which doth so easily beset us, and let us run with patience the race that is set before us, looking unto Jesus the author and finisher of our faith. — Let us cleanse ourselves from all filthiness of the flesh and spirit, perfecting holiness in the fear of God. — I press toward the mark. — I...so run, not as uncertainly; I keep under my body, and bring it into subjection: lest that by any means,...I myself should be a castaway. — The fashion of this world passeth away. — Nevertheless we, according to his promise, look for new heavens and a new earth, wherein dwelleth righteousness. Wherefore, beloved, seeing that ye look for such things, be diligent. — Gird up the loins of your mind, be sober, and hope to the end for the grace that is to be brought unto you at the revelation of Jesus Christ.

Proverbs 22:13   Hebrews 12:1,2   2 Corinthians 7:1   Philippians 3:14
1 Corinthians 9:26,27, 7:31   2 Peter 3:13,14   1 Peter 1:13

MAY 29 MORNING

The life of the flesh is in the blood:
and I have given it to you upon the altar
to make an atonement for your souls:
for it is the blood that maketh an atonement for the soul.
— LEVITICUS 17:11

Behold the Lamb of God, which taketh away the sin of the world. — The blood of the Lamb. — The precious blood of Christ, as of a lamb without blemish and without spot. — Without shedding of blood is no remission. — The blood of Jesus Christ his Son cleanseth us from all sin. — By his own blood he entered in once into the holy place, having obtained eternal redemption for us. — Having therefore, brethren, boldness to enter into the holiest by the blood of Jesus, by a new and living way, which he hath consecrated for us, through the veil, that is to say, his flesh; let us draw near with a true heart in full assurance of faith. — Ye are bought with a price: therefore glorify God in your body, and in your spirit, which are God's.

John 1:29   Revelation 7:14 1   Peter 1:19   Hebrews 9:22
1 John 1:7   Hebrews 9:12, 10:19,20,22 1   Corinthians 6:20

MAY 29 EVENING

Oh that I had wings like a dove!
For then would I fly away, and be at rest.
— PSALM 55:6

It came to pass, when the sun did arise, that God prepared a vehement east wind; and the sun beat upon the head of Jonah, that he fainted, and wished in himself to die, and said, It is better for me to die than to live. — Job spake, and said, Wherefore is light given to him that is in misery, and life unto the bitter in soul; which long for death, but it cometh not; and dig for it more than for hid treasures? — Many are the afflictions of the righteous: but the Lord delivereth him out of them all. — Now is my soul troubled; and what shall I say? Father, save me from this hour. — In all things it behoved him to be made like unto his brethren, that he might be a merciful and faithful high priest in things pertaining to God, to make reconciliation for the sins of the people. For in that he himself hath suffered being tempted, he is able to succour them that are tempted.

Jonah 4:8   Job 3:2,20,21   Psalm 34:19   John 12:27   Hebrews 2:17,18

MAY 30 MORNING

Let us labour to enter into that rest.
— *HEBREWS 4:11*

Enter ye in at the strait gate: for wide is the gate, and broad is the way, that leadeth to destruction:...strait is the gate, and narrow is the way, which leadeth unto life, and few there be that find it. — The kingdom of heaven suffereth violence, and the violent take it by force. — Labour not for the meat which perisheth, but for that meat which endureth unto everlasting life, which the Son of man shall give unto you. — Give diligence to make your calling and election sure:...for so an entrance shall be ministered unto you abundantly into the everlasting kingdom of our Lord and Saviour Jesus Christ. — So run, that ye may obtain. And every man that striveth for the mastery is temperate in all things. Now they do it to obtain a corruptible crown; but we an incorruptible. — For he that is entered into his rest, he also hath ceased from his own works, as God did from his. — The Lord shall be unto thee an everlasting light, and thy God thy glory.

Matthew 7:13,14, 11:12   John 6:27 2 Peter 1:10,11
1 Corinthians 9:24,25   Hebrews 4:10   Isaiah 60:19

MAY 30 EVENING

Thou hearest me always.
— *JOHN 11:42*

Jesus lifted up his eyes, and said, Father, I thank thee that thou hast heard me. — Father, glorify thy name. Then came there a voice from heaven, saying, I have both glorified it, and will glorify it again. — Lo, I come to do thy will, O God. — Not my will, but thine, be done. — As he is, so are we in this world. — This is the confidence that we have in him, that, if we ask anything according to his will, he heareth us. — Whatsoever we ask, we receive of him, because we keep his commandments, and do those things that are pleasing in his sight. — Without faith it is impossible to please him: for he that cometh to God must believe that He is, and that he is a rewarder of them that diligently seek him. — He ever liveth to make intercession for them. — We have an advocate with the Father, Jesus Christ the righteous.

John 11:41, 12:28   Hebrews 10:7   Luke 22:42
1 John 4:17, 5:14, 3:22   Hebrews 11:6, 7:25 1 John 2:1

MAY 31 MORNING

Thy name shall be called Israel:
for as a prince hast thou power with God and with men, and hast prevailed.
— GENESIS 32:28

By his strength he had power with God: yea, he had power over the angel, and prevailed: he wept, and made supplication unto him. — Abraham staggered not at the promise of God through unbelief; but was strong in faith, giving glory to God. — Have faith in God. For verily I say unto you, That whosoever shall say unto this mountain, Be thou removed, and be thou cast into the sea; and shall not doubt in his heart, but shall believe that those things which he saith shall come to pass; he shall have whatsoever he saith. Therefore I say unto you, What things soever ye desire, when ye pray, believe that ye receive them, and ye shall have them. — If thou canst believe, all things are possible to him that believeth. — Blessed is she that believed: for there shall be a performance of those things which were told her from the Lord. — Lord, increase our faith.

Hosea 12:3,4   Romans 4:20   Mark 11:22-24, 9:23   Luke 1:45, 17:5

MAY 31 EVENING

Little children, abide in him.
— 1 JOHN 2:28

He that wavereth is like a wave of the sea driven with the wind and tossed. Let not that man think that he shall receive anything of the Lord. A double minded man is unstable in all his ways. — I marvel that ye are so soon removed from him that called you into the grace of Christ unto another gospel: which is not another. Though we, or an angel from heaven, preach any other gospel unto you than that which we have preached unto you, let him be accursed. — Christ is become of no effect unto you, whosoever of you are justified by the law; ye are fallen from grace. Ye did run well; who did hinder you? — As the branch cannot bear fruit of itself, except it abide in the vine; no more can ye, except ye abide in me. If ye abide in me, and my words abide in you, ye shall ask what ye will, and it shall be done unto you. — For all the promises of God in him are yea, and in him, Amen, unto the glory of God by us.

James 1:6-8   Galatians 1:6-8, 5:4,7   John 15:4,7   2 Corinthians 1:20

JUNE 1 MORNING

The fruit of the Spirit is longsuffering, gentleness.
— *GALATIANS 5:22*

The Lord, the Lord God, merciful and gracious, longsuffering, and abundant in goodness and truth. — Walk worthy of the vocation wherewith ye are called, with all lowliness and meekness, with longsuffering, forbearing one another in love. — Be ye kind one to another, tenderhearted, forgiving one another, even as God for Christ's sake hath forgiven you. — The wisdom that is from above is first pure, then peaceable, gentle, and easy to be intreated, full of mercy and good fruits, without partiality, and without hypocrisy. — Charity suffereth long, and is kind. — In due season we shall reap, if we faint not. — Be patient therefore, brethren, unto the coming of the Lord. Behold, the husbandman waiteth for the precious fruit of the earth, and hath long patience for it, until he receive the early and latter rain. Be ye also patient; stablish your hearts: for the coming of the Lord draweth nigh.

Exodus 34:6   Ephesians 4:1,2, 32   James 3:17
1 Corinthians 13:4   Galatians 6:9   James 5:7,8

JUNE 1 EVENING

Emmanuel...God with us.
— *MATTHEW 1:23*

Will God in very deed dwell with men on the earth? Behold, heaven and the heaven of heavens cannot contain thee. — The Word was made flesh, and dwelt among us, (and we beheld his glory, the glory as of the only begotten of the Father) full of grace and truth. — Great is the mystery of godliness: God was manifest in the flesh. — God hath in these last days spoken unto us by his Son, whom he hath appointed heir of all things, by whom also he made the worlds. — The first day of the week, when the doors were shut where the disciples were assembled...came Jesus and stood in the midst. Then were the disciples glad, when they saw the Lord. After eight days again his disciples were within, and Thomas with them. Then saith [Jesus] to Thomas, Reach hither thy finger, and behold my hands; and reach hither thy hand, and thrust it into my side: and be not faithless, but believing. Thomas...said, My Lord and my God. — Unto us a Son is given: the mighty God.

2 Chronicles 6:18   John 1:14   1 Timothy 3:16
Hebrews 1:2   John 20:19,20,26-28   Isaiah 9:6

JUNE 2 MORNING

*Thus shall ye eat it; with your loins girded,
and ye shall eat it in haste:
it is the Lord's passover.*
— EXODUS 12:11

Arise ye, and depart; for this is not your rest. — Here have we no continuing city, but we seek one to come. — There remaineth therefore a rest for the people of God. — Let your loins be girded about, and your lights burning; and ye yourselves like unto men that wait for their lord, when he will return from the wedding; that when he cometh and knocketh, they may open unto him immediately. Blessed are those servants, whom the lord when he cometh shall find watching. — Gird up the loins of your mind, be sober, and hope to the end for the grace that is to be brought unto you at the revelation of Jesus Christ. — This one thing I do, forgetting those things which are behind...I press toward the mark for the prize of the high calling of God in Christ Jesus. Let us therefore, as many as be perfect, be thus minded.

Micah 2:10   Hebrews 13:14, 4:9   Luke 12:35-37   1 Peter 1:13   Philippians 3:13-15

JUNE 2 EVENING

The Lord is the portion of mine inheritance and of my cup.
— PSALM 16:5

Heirs of God, and joint-heirs with Christ. — All things are yours. — My beloved is mine. — The Son of God...loved me, and gave himself for me. — The Lord spake unto Aaron, Thou shalt have no inheritance in their land, neither shalt thou have any part among them: I am thy part and thy inheritance among the children of Israel. — Whom have I in heaven but thee? And there is none upon earth that I desire beside thee. My flesh and my heart faileth: but God is the strength of my heart, and my portion forever. — Though I walk through the valley of the shadow of death, I will fear no evil: for thou art with me; thy rod and thy staff they comfort me. — I know whom I have believed, and am persuaded that he is able to keep that which I have committed unto him against that day. — O God, thou art my God; early will I seek thee: my soul thirsteth for thee, my flesh longeth for thee in a dry and thirsty land.

Romans 8:17   1 Corinthians 3:21   Song of Solomon 2:16   Galatians 2:20   Numbers 18:20   Psalms 73:25,26, 23:4   2 Timothy 1:12   Psalm 63:1

JUNE 3 MORNING

Watch, for ye know neither the day nor the hour
wherein the Son of man cometh.
— MATTHEW 25:13

Take heed to yourselves, lest at any time your hearts be overcharged with surfeiting, and drunkenness, and cares of this life, and so that day come upon you unawares. For as a snare shall it come on all them that dwell on the face of the whole earth. Watch ye therefore, and pray always, that ye may be accounted worthy to escape all these things that shall come to pass, and to stand before the Son of man. — The day of the Lord so cometh as a thief in the night. For when they shall say, Peace and safety; then sudden destruction cometh upon them, as travail upon a woman with child; and they shall not escape. But ye, brethren, are not in darkness, that that day should overtake you as a thief. Ye are all the children of light, and the children of the day; we are not of the night, nor of darkness. Therefore let us not sleep, as do others; but let us watch and be sober.

Luke 21:34-36 1 Thessalonians 5:2-6

JUNE 3 EVENING

I am the Almighty God;
walk before me, and be thou perfect.
— GENESIS 17:1

Not as though I had already attained, either were already perfect. I count not myself to have apprehended: but this one thing I do, forgetting those things which are behind, and reaching forth unto those things which are before, I press toward the mark for the prize of the high calling of God in Christ Jesus. — Enoch walked with God and he was not; for God took him. — Grow in grace, and in the knowledge of our Lord and Saviour Jesus Christ. — We all, with open face beholding as in a glass the glory of the Lord, are changed into the same image from glory to glory, even as by the Spirit of the Lord. — These words spake Jesus, I pray not that thou shouldest take them out of the world, but that thou shouldest keep them from the evil. I in them, and thou in me, that they may be made perfect in one.

Philippians 3:12-14   Genesis 5:24 2 Peter 3:18
2 Corinthians 3:18   John 17:1,15,23

JUNE 4 MORNING

*The glory of this latter house
shall be greater than of the former,
and in this place will I give peace.*
— HAGGAI 2:9

The house that is to be built for the Lord must be exceeding magnifical, of fame and of glory throughout all countries. — The glory of the Lord...filled the Lord's house. — Destroy this temple, and in three days I will raise it up. He spake of the temple of his body. — That which was made glorious had no glory in this respect by reason of the glory that excelleth. — The Word was made flesh, and dwelt among us, (and we beheld his glory, the glory as of the only begotten of the Father) full of grace and truth. — God...hath in these last days spoken unto us by his Son, whom he hath appointed heir of all things, by whom also he made the worlds. — Glory to God in the highest, and on earth peace, good will toward men. — The Prince of Peace. — He is our peace. — The peace of God, which passeth all understanding, shall keep your hearts and minds through Christ Jesus.

1 Chronicles 22:5   2 Chronicles 7:2   John 2:19,21
2 Corinthians 3:10   John 1:14
Hebrews 1:1,2   Luke 2:14   Isaiah 9:6   Ephesians 2:14   Philippians 4:7

JUNE 4 EVENING

Let us put on the armour of light.
— ROMANS 13:12

Put...on the lord Jesus Christ. — That I may win Christ, and be found in him, not having mine own righteousness, which is of the law, but that which is through the faith of Christ, the righteousness which is of God by faith. — The righteousness of God which is by faith of Jesus Christ unto all and upon all them that believe. — He hath covered me with the robe of righteousness. — I will go in the strength of the Lord God: I will make mention of thy righteousness, even of thine only. — Ye were sometime darkness, but now are ye light in the Lord: walk as children Light. Have no fellowship with the unfruitful works of darkness but rather reprove them. All things that are reproved are made manifest by the light: for whatsoever doth make manifest is light. Awake thou that sleepest, and rise from the dead, and Christ shall give thee light. See then that ye walk circumspectly.

Romans 13:14   Philippians 3:8,9   Romans 3:22
Isaiah 61:10   Psalm 71:16   Ephesians 5:8,11,13-15

JUNE 5 MORNING

*When ye shall have done all those things
which are commanded you, say,
We are unprofitable servants.*
— LUKE 17:10

Where is boasting then? It is excluded. By what law? Of works? Nay: but by the law of faith. — What hast thou that thou didst not receive? Now if thou didst receive it, why dost thou glory, as if thou hadst not received it? — By grace are ye saved through faith; and that not of yourselves; it is the gift of God: not of works, lest any man should boast. For we are his workmanship, created in Christ Jesus unto good works which God hath before ordained that we should walk in them. — By the grace of God I am what I am: and his grace which was bestowed upon me was not in vain; but I laboured more abundantly than they all: yet not I, but the grace of God which was with me. — For of him, and through Him, and to Him, are all things. — All things come of thee and of thine own have we given thee. — Enter not into judgment with thy servant: for in thy sight shall no man living be justified.

Romans 3:27 1 Corinthians 4:7 Ephesians 2:8-10
1 Corinthians 15:10 Romans 11:36 1 Chronicles 29:14 Psalm 143:2

JUNE 5 EVENING

*He knoweth our frame;
he remembereth that we are dust.*
— PSALM 103:14

The Lord God formed man of the dust of the ground, and breathed into his nostrils the breath of life; and man became a living soul. — I will praise thee; for I am fearfully and wonderfully made: marvellous are thy works; and that my soul knoweth right well. My substance was not hid from thee, when I was made in secret. Thine eyes did see my substance, yet being unperfect; and in thy book all my members were written, which in continuance were fashioned, when as yet there was none of them. — Have we not all one father? Hath not one God created us? — In him we live, and move, and have our being. — Like as a father pitieth his children, so the Lord pitieth them that fear him. — He, being full of compassion, forgave their iniquity, and destroyed them not: yea, many a time turned he his anger away, and did not stir up all his wrath. For he remembered that they were but flesh; a wind that passeth away, and cometh not again.

Genesis 2:7 Psalm 139:14-16 Malachi 2:10 Acts
17:28 Psalms 103:13, 78:38, 39

JUNE 6 MORNING

He will rest in his love.
— ZEPHANIAH 3:17

The Lord did not set his love upon you, nor choose you, because ye were more in number than any people; for ye were the fewest of all people: but because the Lord loved you. — We love him, because he first loved us. — You...hath he reconciled in the body of his flesh through death, to present you holy and unblameable and unreproveable in his sight. — Herein is love, not that we loved God, but that he loved us, and sent his Son to be the propitiation for our sins. — God commendeth his love toward us, in that while we were yet sinners, Christ died for us. — Lo, a voice from heaven, saying, This is my beloved Son, in whom I am well pleased. — Therefore doth my Father love me, because I lay down my life, that I might take it again. — His son...who being the brightness of his glory, and the express image of his person, and upholding all things by the word of his power, when he had by himself purged our sins, sat down on the right hand of the Majesty on high.

Deuteronomy 7:7,8 1   John 4:19   Colossians 1:21,22
1 John 4:10   Romans 5:8   Matthew 3:17   John 10:17   Hebrews 1:2,3

JUNE 6 EVENING

A new and living way.
— HEBREWS 10:20

Cain went out from the presence of the Lord. — Your iniquities have separated between you and your God, and your sins have hid his face from you. — Without holiness, no man shall see the Lord. — I am the way, and the truth, and the life: no man cometh unto the Father, but by me. — Our Saviour Jesus Christ...hath abolished death, and hath brought life and immortality to light through the gospel. — The way into the holiest of all was not yet made manifest, while as the first tabernacle was yet standing. — He is our peace, who hath made both one, and hath broken down the middle wall of partition between us. — The veil of the temple was rent in twain from the top to the bottom. — Strait is the gate, and narrow is the way, which leadeth unto life, and few there be that find it. — Thou wilt shew me the path of life: in thy presence is fulness of joy; at thy right hand there are pleasures for evermore.

Genesis 4:16   Isaiah 59:2   Hebrews 12:14   John 14:6 2   Timothy 1:10
Hebrews 9:8   Ephesians 2:14   Matthew 27:51, 7:14   Psalm 16:11

JUNE 7 MORNING

Men ought always to pray, and not to faint.
— LUKE 18:1

Which of you shall have a friend, and shall go unto him at midnight, and say unto him, Friend, lend me three loaves; for a friend of mine in his journey is come to me and I have nothing to set before him? And he from within shall answer and say, Trouble me not: the door is now shut, and my children are with me in bed; I cannot rise and give thee. I say unto you, Though he will not rise and give him, because he is his friend, yet because of his importunity he will rise and give him as many as he needeth. — Praying always with all prayer and supplication in the Spirit and watching thereunto with all perseverance and supplication for all saints. — I will not let thee go, except thou bless me. — As a prince hast thou power with God and with men. — Continue in prayer, and watch in the same with thanksgiving. — [Jesus] went out into a mountain to pray, and continued all night in prayer to God.

Luke 11:5-8   Ephesians 6:18   Genesis 32:26,28   Colossians 4:2   Luke 6:12

JUNE 7 EVENING

Forgive all my sins.
— PSALM 25:18

Come now, and let us reason together, saith the Lord: though your sins be as scarlet, they shall be as white as snow; though they be red like crimson, they shall be as wool. — Be of good cheer; thy sins be forgiven thee. — I, even I, am he that blotteth out thy transgressions for mine own sake, and will not remember thy sins. — The Son of man hath power on earth to forgive sins. — In Whom we have redemption through his blood, the forgiveness of sins, according to the riches of his grace. — Not by works of righteousness which we have done, but according to His mercy he saved us, by the washing of regeneration, and renewing of the Holy Ghost; which he shed on us abundantly through Jesus Christ our Saviour. — Having forgiven you all trespasses, blotting out the handwriting of ordinances that was against us, which was contrary to us, and took it out of the way, nailing it to his cross. — Bless the Lord, O my soul...who forgives all thine iniquities.

Isaiah 1:18   Matthew 9:2   Isaiah 43:25   Matthew 9:6
Ephesians 1:7   Titus 3:5,6   Colossians 2:13,14   Psalm 103:2,3

JUNE 8 MORNING

The Lord made all that he did to prosper in his hand.
— GENESIS 39:3

Blessed is every one that feareth the Lord; that walketh in his ways. For thou shalt eat the labour of thine hands: happy shalt thou be, and it shall be well with thee. — Trust in the Lord, and do good; so shalt thou dwell in the land, and verily thou shalt be fed. Delight thyself also in the Lord; and he shall give thee the desires of thine heart. — Be not afraid, neither be thou dismayed: for the Lord thy God is with thee whithersoever thou goest. — Seek ye first the kingdom of God, and his righteousness; and all these things shall he added unto you. — As long as he sought the Lord, God made him to prosper. — Beware that thou forget not the Lord thy God, in not keeping his commandments, and his judgments, and his statutes, which I command thee this day: and thou say in thine heart, My power and the might of mine hand hath gotten me this wealth. — Is not the Lord your God with you? and hath he not given you rest on every side?

Psalms 128:1,2, 37:3,4   Joshua 1:9   Matthew 6:33
2 Chronicles 26:5   Deuteronomy 8:11,17 1   Chronicles 22:18

JUNE 8 EVENING

Why reason ye these things in your hearts?
— MARK 2:8

Being not weak in faith, [Abraham] considered not his own body now dead, when he was about an hundred years old, neither yet the deadness of Sarah's womb; he staggered not at the promise of God through unbelief; but was strong in faith, giving glory to God. — Is it easier to say to the sick of the palsy, Thy sins be forgiven thee or to say, Arise, and take up thy bed, and walk? —If thou canst believe, all things are possible to him that believeth. — All power is given unto me in heaven and in earth. — Why are ye so fearful? How is it that ye have no faith? — Behold the fowls of the air;...your heavenly Father feedeth them. Are ye not much better than they? — Why reason ye among yourselves, because ye have brought no bread? Do ye not...remember the five loaves of the five thousand? — My God shall supply all your need according to his riches in glory by Christ Jesus.

Romans 4:19,20   Mark 2:9, 9:23   Matthew 28:18
Mark 4:40   Matthew 6:26, 16:8,9   Philippians 4:19

JUNE 9 MORNING

Never man spake like this man.
— JOHN 7:46

Thou art fairer than the children of men: grace is poured into thy lips: therefore God hath blessed thee for ever. — The Lord GOD hath given me the tongue of the learned, that I should know how to speak a word in season to him that is weary. — His mouth is most sweet: yea, he is altogether lovely. This is my beloved, and this is my friend. — All bare him witness, and wondered at the gracious words which proceeded out of his mouth. — He taught them as one having authority, and not as the scribes. — Let the word of Christ dwell in you richly in all wisdom. — The sword of the Spirit...is the word of God. — The word of God is quick, and powerful, and sharper than any two-edged sword. — The weapons of our warfare are not carnal, but mighty through God to the pulling down of strongholds; casting down imaginations, and every high thing that exalteth itself against the knowledge of God, and bringing into captivity every thought to the obedience of Christ.

Psalm 45:2   Isaiah 50:4   Song of Solomon 5:16   Luke 4:22   Matthew 7:29   Colossians 3:16   Ephesians 6:17   Hebrews 4:12   2 Corinthians 10:4,5

JUNE 9 EVENING

The triumphing of the wicked is short.
— JOB 20:5

Thou shalt bruise his heel. — This is your hour, and the power of darkness. — As the children are partakers of flesh and blood he also himself likewise took part of the same; that through death he might destroy him that had the power of death, that is, the devil. — Having spoiled principalities and powers, he made a shew of them openly, triumphing over them in it. — Be sober, be vigilant; because your adversary the devil, as a roaring lion, walketh about seeking whom he may devour: whom resist stedfast in the faith. — Resist the devil, and he will flee from you. — The wicked plotteth against the just, and gnasheth upon him with his teeth. The Lord shall laugh at him: for he seeth that his day is coming. — The God of peace shall bruise Satan under your feet shortly. — The devil... was cast into the lake of fire and brimstone...and shall be tormented day and night for ever and ever.

Genesis 3:15   Luke 22:53   Hebrews 2:14   Colossians 2:15   1 Peter 5:8,9   James 4:7   Psalm 37:12,13   Romans 16:20   Revelation 20:10

JUNE 10 MORNING

*The younger son took his journey into a far country,
and there wasted his substance with riotous living.*
— LUKE 15:13

Such were some of you: but ye are washed, but ye are sanctified, but ye are justified in the name of the Lord Jesus, and by the Spirit of our God. — We... were by nature the children of wrath, even as others. But God, who is rich in mercy, for his great love wherewith he loved us, even when we were dead in sins, hath quickened us together with Christ, (by grace ye are saved;) and hath raised us up together, and made us sit together in heavenly places in Christ Jesus. — Herein is love, not that we loved God, but that he loved us, and sent his Son to be the propitiation for our sins. — God commendeth his love toward us, in that, while we were yet sinners, Christ died for us. If, when we were enemies, we were reconciled to God by the death of his Son, much more, being reconciled, we shall be saved by his life.

1 Corinthians 6:11   Ephesians 2:3-6 1   John 4:10   Romans 5:8,10

JUNE 10 EVENING

As Christ forgave you, so also do ye.
— COLOSSIANS 3:13

There was a certain creditor which had two debtors: the one owed five hundred pence, and the other fifty. And when they had nothing to pay, he frankly forgave them both. — I forgave thee all that debt; shouldest not thou also have had compassion on thy fellow-servant, even as I had pity on thee? — When ye stand praying, forgive, if ye have ought against any: that your Father also which is in heaven may forgive you your trespasses. But if ye do not forgive, neither will your Father which is in heaven forgive your trespasses. — Put on as the elect of God, holy and beloved, bowels of mercies, kindness, humbleness of mind, meekness, longsuffering; forbearing one another, and forgiving one another, if any man have a quarrel against any. — How oft shall my brother sin against me, and I forgive him? Till seven times? Jesus saith unto him, I say not unto thee, Until seven times: but, until seventy times seven. — Charity...is the bond of perfectness.

Luke 7:41,42   Matthew 18:32,33   Mark 11:25,26
Colossians 3:12,13   Matthew 18:21,22   Colossians 3:14

JUNE 11 MORNING

He arose, and came to his father.
But when he was yet a great way off, his father saw him,
and ran, and fell on his neck, and kissed him.
— LUKE 15:20

The Lord is merciful and gracious, slow to anger, and plenteous in mercy. He will not always chide: neither will he keep his anger for ever. He hath not dealt with us after our sins; nor rewarded us according to our iniquities. For as the heaven is high above the earth, so great is his mercy toward them that fear him. As far as the east is from the west, so far hath he removed our transgressions from us. Like as a father pitieth his children, so the Lord pitieth them that fear him. — Ye have received the Spirit of adoption, whereby we cry, Abba, Father. The Spirit itself beareth witness with our spirit, that we are the children of God. — Ye who sometime were far off are made nigh by the blood of Christ. — Now therefore ye are no more strangers and foreigners, but fellow-citizens with the saints, and of the household of God.

Psalm 103:8-13   Romans 8:15,16   Ephesians 2:13, 19

JUNE 11 EVENING

Behold, I make all things new.
— REVELATION 21:5

Except a man be born again, he cannot see the kingdom of God. — If any man be in Christ, he is a new creature; old things are passed away; behold, all things are become new. — A new heart also will I give you, and a new spirit will I put within you: and I will take away the stony heart out of your flesh, and I will give you an heart of flesh. — Purge out therefore the old leaven, that ye may be a new lump. — The new man, which after God is created in righteousness and true holiness. — Thou shalt be called by a new name, which the mouth of the Lord shall name. — Behold, I create new heavens and a new earth: and the former shall not be remembered, nor come into mind. — Seeing...that all these things shall be dissolved, what manner of persons ought ye to be in all holy conversation and godliness?

John 3:3   2 Corinthians 5:17   Ezekiel 36:26   1 Corinthians 5:7
Ephesians 4:24   Isaiah 62:2, 65:17   2 Peter 3:11

JUNE 12 MORNING

Everything that may abide the fire,
ye shall make it go through the fire,
and it shall be clean.
— NUMBERS 31:23

The Lord your God proveth you, to know whether ye love the Lord your God with all your heart, and with all your soul. — He shall sit as a refiner and purifier of silver: and he shall purify the sons of Levi, and purge them as gold and silver, that they may offer unto the Lord an offering in righteousness. — Every man's work shall be made manifest: for the day shall declare it, because it shall be revealed by fire; and the fire shall try every man's work of what sort it is. — I will turn my hand upon thee, and purely purge away thy dross, and take away all thy tin. — I will melt them and try them. — Thou, O God, hast proved us; thou hast tried us, as silver is tried. We went through fire and through water: but thou broughtest us out into a wealthy place. — When thou walkest through the fire, thou shalt not be burned; neither shall the flame kindle upon thee.

Deuteronomy 13:3   Malachi 3:3 1 Corinthians 3:13
Isaiah 1:25   Jeremiah 9:7   Psalm 66:10,12   Isaiah 43:2

JUNE 12 EVENING

We, being dead to sins, should live unto righteousness.
— 1 PETER 2:24

Put off, concerning the former conversation, the old man, which is corrupt according to the deceitful lusts: and be renewed in the spirit of your mind; and…put on the new man, which after God is created in righteousness and true holiness. — Ye are dead and your life is hid with Christ in God. — As Christ was raised up from the dead by the glory of the Father, even so we also should walk in newness of life. Knowing this, that our old man is crucified with him, that the body of sin might be destroyed, that henceforth we should not serve sin. For he that is dead is freed from sin. Likewise reckon ye also yourselves to be dead indeed unto sin, but alive unto God through Jesus Christ our Lord. Let not sin therefore reign in your mortal body, that ye should obey it in the lusts thereof: but yield yourselves unto God, as those that are alive from the dead, and your members as instruments of righteousness unto God.

Ephesians 4:22-24   Colossians 3:3   Romans 6:4,6,7,11-13

JUNE 13 MORNING

Abide in me, and I in you.
— JOHN 15:4

I am crucified with Christ; nevertheless I live; yet not I, but Christ liveth in me: and the life which I now live in the flesh I live by the faith of the Son of God, who loved me, and gave himself for me. — I know that in me (that is, in my flesh) dwelleth no good thing: for to will is present with me; but how to perform that which is good I find not. O wretched man that I am! Who shall deliver me from the body of this death? I thank God through Jesus Christ our Lord. — If Christ be in you, the body is dead because of sin, but the Spirit is life because of righteousness. — If ye continue in the faith grounded and settled, and be not moved away from the hope of the gospel, which ye have heard. — Little children, abide in him; that, when he shall appear, we may have confidence, and not be ashamed before him at his coming. — He that saith he abideth in him ought himself also so to walk, even as he walked.

Galatians 2:20   Romans 7:18,24,25, 8:10   Colossians 1:23 1   John 2:28,6

JUNE 13 EVENING

Dost thou believe on the Son of God?
— JOHN 9:35

Who is he, Lord, that I might believe on him? — The brightness of his glory, and the express image of his person. — The blessed and only Potentate, the King of kings, and Lord of lords; who only hath immortality, dwelling in the light which no man can approach unto; whom no man hath seen, nor can see: to whom be honour and power everlasting. Amen. — I am Alpha and Omega, the beginning and the ending, saith the Lord, which is, and which was, and which is to come, the Almighty. — Lord, I believe. — I know whom I have believed, and am persuaded that he is able to keep that which I have committed unto him against that day. — Behold, I lay in Sion a chief corner stone, elect, precious: and he that believeth on him shall not be confounded. Unto you therefore which believe he is precious.

John 9:36   Hebrews 1:3 1   Timothy 6:15,16
Revelation 1:8   John 9:38 2   Timothy 1:12 1   Peter 2:6,7

JUNE 14 MORNING

As the sufferings of Christ abound in us,
so our consolation also aboundeth by Christ.
— 2 CORINTHIANS 1:5

The fellowship of his sufferings. — Rejoice, inasmuch as ye are partakers of Christ's sufferings; that, when his glory shall be revealed, ye may be glad also with exceeding joy. — For if we be dead with him, we shall also live with him. — If children, then heirs; heirs of God, and joint-heirs with Christ; if so be that we suffer with him, that we may be also glorified together. — God, willing more abundantly to shew unto the heirs of promise the immutability of his counsel, confirmed it by an oath: that by two immutable things, in which it was impossible for God to lie, we might have a strong consolation, who have fled for refuge to lay hold upon the hope set before us. — Our Lord Jesus Christ Himself, and God, even our Father, which hath loved us, and hath given us everlasting consolation and good hope through grace, comfort your hearts, and stablish you in every good word and work.

Philippians 3:10 1 Peter 4:13 2 Timothy 2:11
Romans 8:17 Hebrews 6:17,18 2 Thessalonians 2:16,17

JUNE 14 EVENING

Martha, Martha, thou art careful and troubled
about many things.
— LUKE 10:41

Consider the ravens: for they neither sow nor reap. Consider the lilies how they grow: they toil not, they spin not. Seek not ye what ye shall eat, or what ye shall drink, neither be ye of doubtful mind. Your Father knoweth that ye have need of these things. — Having food and raiment let us be therewith content... They that will be rich fall into temptation and a snare, and into many foolish and hurtful lusts, which drown men in destruction and perdition. For the love of money is the root of all evil: which while some coveted after, they have erred from the faith, and pierced themselves through with many sorrows. — The cares of this world, and the deceitfulness of riches, and the lust of other things entering in, choke the word, and it becometh unfruitful. — Let us lay aside every weight, and the sin which doth so easily beset us, and let us run with patience the race that is set before us.

Luke 12:24,27,29,30 1 Timothy 6:8-10 Mark 4:19 Hebrews 12:1

JUNE 15 MORNING

The secret things belong unto the Lord our God:
but those which are revealed belong unto us.
— DEUTERONOMY 29:29

Lord, my heart is not haughty, nor mine eyes lofty: neither do I exercise myself in great matters, or in things too high for me. Surely I have behaved and quieted myself, as a child that is weaned of his mother: my soul is even as a weaned child. — The secret of the Lord is with them that fear him: and he will shew them his covenant. — There is a God in heaven that revealeth secrets. — Lo, these are parts of his ways: but how little a portion is heard of him? — Henceforth I call you not servants; for the servant knoweth not what his lord doeth: but I have called you friends; for all things that I have heard of my Father I have made known unto you. — If ye love me, keep my commandments. And I will pray the Father, and he shall give you another Comforter that he may abide with you for ever; even the Spirit of truth.

Psalms 131:1,2, 25:14   Daniel 2:28   Job 26:14   John 15:15, 14:15-17

JUNE 15 EVENING

The Spirit...maketh intercession for the saints
according to the will of God.
— ROMANS 8:27

Verily, verily I say unto you, Whatsoever ye shall ask the Father in my name, he will give it you. Hitherto have ye asked nothing in my name: ask, and ye shall receive, that your joy may be full. — Praying always with all prayer and supplication in the Spirit. — This is the confidence that we have in him, that, if we ask any thing according to his will, he heareth us; and if we know that he hear us, whatsoever we ask, we know that we have the petitions that we desired of him. — This is the will of God, even your sanctification. — God hath... called us...unto holiness:...who hath also given unto us his Holy Spirit. — Rejoice evermore. Pray without ceasing. In every thing give thanks: for this is the will of God in Christ Jesus concerning you. Quench not the Spirit.

John 16:23,24   Ephesians 6:18   1 John 5:14,15   1 Thessalonians 4:3,7,8, 5:16-19

JUNE 16 MORNING

*See that ye walk circumspectly, not as fools, but as wise,
redeeming the time, because the days are evil.*
— EPHESIANS 5:15,16

Take diligent heed to do the commandment and the law, to love the Lord your God, and to walk in all his ways, and to keep his commandments, and to cleave unto him, and to serve him with all your heart and with all your soul. — Walk in wisdom toward them that are without, redeeming the time. Let your speech be always with grace, seasoned with salt, that ye may know how ye ought to answer every man. — Abstain from all appearance of evil. — While the bridegroom tarried, they all slumbered and slept. And at midnight there was a cry made, Behold, the bridegroom cometh; go ye out to meet him. — Watch, therefore, for ye know neither the day nor the hour wherein the Son of man cometh. — Brethren, give diligence to make your calling and election sure; for if we do these things, ye shall never fall. — Blessed are those servants, whom the lord when he cometh shall find watching.

Joshua 22:5   Colossians 4:5,6 1   Thessalonians 5:22
Matthew 25:5,6,13 2   Peter 1:10   Luke 12:37

JUNE 16 EVENING

*Hold that fast which thou hast,
that no man take thy crown.*
— REVELATION 3:11

If I may but touch his garment, I shall be whole. — Lord, if thou wilt, thou canst make me clean. I will; be thou clean. — Faith as a grain of mustard seed. — Cast not away...your confidence, which hath great recompence of reward. — Work out your own salvation with fear and trembling. It is God which worketh in you both to will and to do of his good pleasure. — First the blade, then the ear, after that the full corn in the ear. — Then shall we know, if we follow on to know the Lord. — The kingdom of heaven suffereth violence, and the violent take it by force. — So run, that ye may obtain. — I have fought a good fight, I have finished my course, I have kept the faith: henceforth there is laid up for me a crown of righteousness, which the Lord, the righteous judge, shall give me at that day.

Matthew 9:21, 8:2,3, 17:20   Hebrews 10:35   Philippians 2:12,13
Mark 4:28   Hosea 6:3   Matthew 11:12 1   Corinthians 9:24 2   Timothy 4:7,8

JUNE 17 MORNING

In every thing by prayer and supplication
with thanksgiving
let your requests be made known unto God.
— PHILIPPIANS 4:6

    I love the Lord, because he hath heard my voice and my supplications. Because he hath inclined his ear unto me, therefore will I call upon him as long as I live. — When ye pray, use not vain repetitions, as the heathen do: for they think that they shall be heard for their much speaking. — The Spirit...helpeth our infirmities: for we know not what we should pray for as we ought: but the Spirit itself maketh intercession for us with groanings which cannot be uttered. — I will therefore that men pray everywhere, lifting up holy hands, without wrath and doubting. — Praying always with all prayer and supplication in the Spirit, and watching thereunto with all perseverance and supplication for all saints. — If two of you shall agree on earth as touching any thing that they shall ask, it shall be done for them of my Father which is in heaven.

Psalm 16:1,2   Matthew 6:7   Romans 8:26
1 Timothy 2:8   Ephesians 6:18   Matthew 18:19

JUNE 17 EVENING

All thy works shall praise thee, O Lord;
and thy saints shall bless thee.
— PSALM 145:10

    Bless the Lord, O my soul: and all that is within me, bless his holy name. Bless the Lord, O my soul, and forget not all his benefits. — I will bless the Lord at all times: his praise shall continually be in my mouth. — Every day will I bless thee; and I will praise thy name for ever and ever. — Because thy lovingkindness is better than life, my lips shall praise thee. Thus will I bless thee while I live: I will lift up my hands in thy name. My soul shall be satisfied as with marrow and fatness; and my mouth shall praise thee with joyful lips. — My soul doth magnify the Lord, and my spirit hath rejoiced in God my Saviour. — Thou art worthy, O Lord, to receive glory and honour and power: for thou hast created all things and for thy pleasure they are and were created.

Psalms 103:1,2, 34:1, 145:2, 63:3-5   Luke 1:46,47   Revelation 4:11

JUNE 18 MORNING

*Thou shalt put the mercy seat above upon the ark,
and there I will meet with thee.*
— EXODUS 25:21,22

The way into the holiest of all was not yet made manifest. — Jesus, when he had cried again with a loud voice, yielded up the ghost. And, behold, the veil of the temple was rent in twain from the top to the bottom. — Having...brethren, boldness to enter into the holiest by the blood of Jesus, by a new and living way, which he hath consecrated for us, through the veil, that is to say, his flesh;... let us draw near with a true heart in full assurance of faith, having our hearts sprinkled from an evil conscience, and our bodies washed with pure water. — Let us therefore come boldly unto the throne of grace, that we may obtain mercy, and find grace to help in time of need. — Christ Jesus: whom God hath set forth to be a propitiation [mercy seat] through faith in his blood, to declare his righteousness for the remission of sins that are past, through the forbearance of God. — Through him we have access by one Spirit unto the Father.

Hebrews 9:8   Matthew 27:50,51
Hebrews 10:19,20,22, 4:16   Romans 3:24,25   Ephesians 2:18

JUNE 18 EVENING

Faith as a grain of mustard seed.
— MATTHEW 17:20

Barak said unto [Deborah], if thou wilt go with me, then I will go: but if thou wilt not go with me, then I will not go. God subdued on that day Jabin the king of Canaan. — Gideon...feared his father's household, and the men of the city, that he could not do it by day,...did it by night. And Gideon said unto God, If thou wilt save Israel by mine hand as thou hast said...let me prove, I pray thee. And God did so. — Thou hast a little strength, and hast kept my word, and hast not denied my name. — Who hath despised the day of small things? — We are bound to thank God always for you, brethren, as it is meet, because that your faith groweth exceedingly. — Lord, increase our faith. — I will be as the dew unto Israel: he shall grow as the lily, cast forth his roots as Lebanon. His branches shall spread, and his beauty shall be as the olive tree, and his smell as Lebanon.

Judges 4:8,23, 6:27,36,39,40   Revelation 3:8   Zechariah 4:10
2 Thessalonians 1:3   Luke 17:5   Hosea 14:5,6

JUNE 19 MORNING

Holiness, without which no man shall see the Lord.
— HEBREWS 12:14

Except a man be born again, he cannot see the kingdom of God. — There shall in no wise enter into it any thing that defileth. — There is no spot in thee. — Ye shall be holy: for I the Lord your God am holy. — As obedient children, not fashioning yourselves according to the former lusts in your ignorance: but as he which hath called you is holy, so be ye holy in all manner of conversation; because it is written, Be ye holy; for I am holy. And if ye call on the Father, who without respect of persons judgeth according to every man's work, pass the time of your sojourning here in fear. — Put off concerning the former conversation the old man, which is corrupt according to the deceitful lusts; and be renewed in the spirit of your mind, and...put on the new man, which after God is created in righteousness and true holiness. — He hath chosen us in him before the foundation of the world, that we should be holy and without blame before him in love.

John 3:3   Revelation 21:27   Song of Solomon 4:7
Leviticus 19:2   1 Peter 1:14-17   Ephesians 4:22-24, 1:4

JUNE 19 EVENING

Gold tried in the fire.
— REVELATION 3.18

There is no man that hath left house, or brethren, or sisters, or father, or mother, or wife, or children, or lands, for my sake, and the gospel's, but he shall receive an hundredfold now in this time, houses, and brethren, and sisters, and mothers, and children, and lands, with persecutions; and in the world to come eternal life. — Beloved, think it not strange concerning the fiery trial which is to try you, as though some strange thing happened unto you. — Now for a season, if need be, ye are in heaviness through manifold temptations: that the trial of your faith, being much more precious than of gold that perisheth, though it be tried with fire, might be found unto praise and honour and glory at the appearing of Jesus Christ. — The God of all grace, who hath called us unto his eternal glory by Christ Jesus, after that ye have suffered a while, make you perfect, stablish, strengthen, settle you. — In the world ye shall have tribulation: but be of good cheer; I have overcome the world.

Mark 10:29,30   1 Peter 4:12, 1:6,7, 5:10   John 16:33

JUNE 20 MORNING

Take this child away, and nurse it for me,
and I will give thee thy wages.
— EXODUS 2:9

Go ye...into the vineyard, and whatsoever is right I will give you. — Whosoever shall give you a cup of water to drink in my name, because ye belong to Christ, verily I say unto you, he shall not lose his reward. — The liberal soul shall be made fat: and he that watereth shall be watered also himself. — God is not unrighteous to forget your work and labour of love...in that ye have ministered to the saints, and do minister. — Every man shall receive his own reward according to his own labour. — Lord, when saw we thee an hungered, and fed thee? Or thirsty, and gave thee drink? When saw we thee a stranger, and took thee in? Or naked, and clothed thee? And the King shall answer and say unto them...Inasmuch as ye have done it unto one of the least of these my brethren, ye have done it unto me. Come, ye blessed of my Father, inherit the kingdom prepared for you from the foundation of the world.

Matthew 20:4   Mark 9:41   Proverbs 11:25   Hebrews 6:10
1 Corinthians 3:8   Matthew 25:37,38,40,34

JUNE 20 EVENING

Thou compassest my path and my lying down.
— PSALM 139:3

Jacob awaked out of his sleep, and he said, Surely the Lord is in this place; and I knew it not. And he was afraid and said, How dreadful is this place! This is none other but the house of God, and this is the gate of heaven. — The eyes of the Lord run to and fro throughout the whole earth, to shew himself strong in the behalf of them whose heart is perfect toward him. — I will both lay me down in peace, and sleep: for thou, Lord, only, makest me dwell in safety. — Because thou hast made the Lord, which is my refuge, even the most High, thy habitation; there shall no evil befall thee, neither shall any plague come nigh thy dwelling. For He shall give his angels charge over thee, to keep thee in all thy ways. — When thou liest down, thou shalt not be afraid: yea, thou shalt lie down, and thy sleep shall be sweet. — So he giveth his beloved sleep.

Genesis 28:16,17 2 Chronicles 16:9
Psalms 4:8, 91:9-11   Proverbs 3:24   Psalm 127:2

JUNE 21 MORNING

*Christ suffered for us,
leaving us an example that ye should follow his steps.*
— 1 PETER 2:21

Even the Son of man came not to be ministered unto, but to minister. — Whosoever of you will be the chiefest, shall be servant of all. — Jesus of Nazareth...went about doing good. — Bear ye one another's burdens, and so fulfil the law of Christ. — The meekness and gentleness of Christ. — In lowliness of mind let each esteem other better than themselves. — Father, forgive them: for they know not what they do. — Be ye kind one to another, tenderhearted, forgiving one another, even as God for Christ's sake hath forgiven you. — He that saith he abideth in him, ought himself also so to walk, even as he walked. — Looking unto Jesus, the author and finisher of our faith; who for the joy that was set before him endured the cross, despising the shame, and is set down at the right hand of the throne of God.

Mark 10:45, 44   Acts 10:38   Galatians 6:2   2 Corinthians 10:1   Philippians 2:3
Luke 23:34   Ephesians 4:32   1 John 2:6   Hebrews 12:2

JUNE 21 EVENING

*I sought him, but I could not find him:
I called him, but he gave me no answer.*
— SONG OF SOLOMON 5:6

O Lord, what shall I say, when Israel turneth their backs before their enemies! And the Lord said unto Joshua, Get thee up; wherefore liest thou thus upon thy face? Israel hath sinned, for they have even taken of the accursed thing... and they have put it even among their own stuff. — Behold, the Lord's hand is not shortened, that it cannot save; neither his ear heavy, that it cannot hear: but your iniquities have separated between you and your God, and your sins have hid his face from you, that he will not hear. — If I regard iniquity in my heart, the Lord will not hear me. — Beloved, if our heart condemn us not, then have we confidence toward God. And whatsoever we ask, we receive of him, because we keep his commandments, and do those things that are pleasing in his sight.

Joshua 7:8,10,11   Isaiah 59:1,2   Psalm 66:18   1 John 3:21,22

JUNE 22 MORNING

Ye are dead, and your life is hid with Christ in God.
— COLOSSIANS 3:3

How shall we, that are dead to sin, live any longer therein? — I am crucified with Christ, nevertheless I live; yet not I but Christ liveth in me: and the life which I now live in the flesh I live by the faith of the Son of God, who loved me and gave himself for me. — He died for all, that they which live should not live unto themselves, but unto him which died for them and rose again. — If any man be in Christ, he is a new creature; old things are passed away; behold, all things are become new. — We are in him that is true, even in his Son Jesus Christ. — As thou, Father, art in me, and I in thee, that they also may be one in us. — Ye are the body of Christ, and members in particular. — Because I live, ye shall live also. — To him that overcometh will I give to eat of the hidden manna, and wilt give him a white stone, and in the stone a new name written, which no man knoweth saving he that receiveth it.

Romans 6:2   Galatians 2:20   2 Corinthians 5:15, 17   1 John 5:20   John 17:21   1 Corinthians 12:27   John 14:19   Revelation 2:17

JUNE 22 EVENING

Behold how he loved.
— JOHN 11:36

He died for all. — Greater love hath no man than this, that a man lay down his life for his friends. — He...liveth to make intercession for them. — I go to prepare a place for you. — I will come again, and receive you unto myself that where I am, there ye may be also. — Father, I will that they whom thou hast given me, be with me where I am. — Having loved his own which were in the world, he loved them unto the end. — We love him, because he first loved us. — The love of Christ constraineth us; because we thus judge, that if one died for all, then were all dead: and that he died for all, that they which live should not henceforth live unto themselves, but to him which died for them, and rose again. — If ye keep my commandments, ye shall abide in my love; even as I have kept my Father's commandments, and abide in his love.

2 Corinthians 5:15   John 15:13   Hebrews 7:25   John 14:2-3, 17:24, 13:1   1 John 4:19   2 Corinthians 5:14,15   John 15:10

JUNE 23 MORNING

*I will pray the Father,
and he shall give you another Comforter,
even the Spirit of truth.*
— *JOHN 14:16,17*

It is expedient for you that I go away: for if I go not away, the Comforter will not come unto you; but if I depart, I will send him unto you. — The Spirit itself beareth witness with our spirit, that we are the children of God. — Ye have not received the spirit of bondage again to fear; but ye have received the Spirit of adoption, whereby we cry, Abba, Father. — The Spirit...helpeth our infirmities; for we know not what we should pray for as we ought: but the Spirit itself maketh intercession for us with groanings which cannot be uttered. — The God of hope fill you with all joy and peace in believing, that ye may abound in hope, through the power of the Holy Ghost. — Hope maketh not ashamed; because the love of God is shed abroad in our hearts by the Holy Ghost which is given unto us. — Hereby know we that we dwell in him and he in us, because he hath given us of his Spirit.

John 16:7   Romans 8:16,15,26, 15:13, 5:5   1 John 4:13

JUNE 23 EVENING

*Shall I not seek rest for thee,
that it may be well with thee?*
— *RUTH 3:1*

There remaineth...a rest to the people of God. — My people shall dwell in a peaceable habitation, and in sure dwellings, and in quiet resting places. — There the wicked cease from troubling; and there the weary be at rest. — They...rest from their labours. — The forerunner is for us entered, even Jesus, made an high priest for ever after the order of Melchisedec. — Come unto me, all ye that labour and are heavy laden, and I will give you rest. Take my yoke upon you, and learn of me; for I am meek and lowly in heart: and ye shall find rest unto your souls. For my yoke is easy, and my burden is light. — In returning and rest shall ye be saved; in quietness and in confidence shall be your strength. — The Lord is my shepherd; I shall not want. He maketh me to lie down in green pastures: he leadeth me beside the still waters.

Hebrews 4:9   Isaiah 32:18   Job 3:17   Revelation 14:13
Hebrews 6:20   Matthew 11:28-30   Isaiah 30:15   Psalm 23:1,2

JUNE 24 MORNING

*The ark of the covenant of the Lord went before them
to search out a resting place for them.*
— NUMBERS 10:33

My times are in thy hand. — He shall choose our inheritance for us. — Lead me, O Lord, in thy righteousness;...make thy way straight before my face. — Commit thy way unto the Lord; trust also in him; and he shall bring it to pass. — In all thy ways acknowledge him, and he shall direct thy paths. — Thine ears shall hear a word behind thee, saying, This is the way, walk ye in it, when ye turn to the right hand, and when ye turn to the left. — The Lord is my shepherd; I shall not want. He maketh me to lie down in green pastures; he leadeth me beside the still waters. — Like as a father pitieth his children, so the Lord pitieth them that fear him. For he knoweth our frame; he remembereth that we are dust. — Your heavenly Father knoweth that ye have need of all these things. — Casting all your care upon him; for he careth for you.

Psalms 31:15, 47:4, 5:8, 37:5   Proverbs 3:6   Isaiah 30:21
Psalms 23:1,2, 103:13,14   Matthew 6:32 1 Peter 5:7

JUNE 24 EVENING

*Master, where dwellest thou?
He saith unto them, Come and see.*
— JOHN 1:38,39

In my Father's house are many mansions: if it were not so, I would have told you. I go to prepare a place for you. And if I go and prepare a place for you, I will come again, and receive you unto myself; that where I am, there ye may be also. — To him that overcometh will I grant to sit with me in my throne. — Thus saith the high and lofty One that inhabiteth eternity, whose name is Holy; I dwell in the high and holy place, with him also that is of a contrite and humble spirit, to revive the spirit of the humble, and to revive the heart of the contrite ones. — Behold, I stand at the door, and knock: if any man hear my voice, and open the door, I will come in to him, and will sup with him, and he with me. — Lo, I am with you alway, even unto the end of the world. — How excellent is thy lovingkindness, O God! Therefore, the children of men put their trust under the shadow of thy wings.

John 14:2,3   Revelation 3:21   Isaiah 57:15
Revelation 3:20   Matthew 28:20   Psalm 36:7

JUNE 25 MORNING

When he shall appear, we shall be like him;
we shall see him as he is.
— 1 JOHN 3:2

As many as received him, to them gave he power to become the sons of God, even to them that believe on his name. — Whereby are given unto us exceeding great and precious promises; that by these we might be partakers of the divine nature, having escaped the corruption that is in the world through lust. — Since the beginning of the world men have not heard, nor perceived by the ear, neither hath the eye seen, O God, beside thee, that he hath prepared for him that waiteth for him. — Now we see through a glass. darkly; but then face to face: now I know in part; but then shall I know even as also I am known. — Christ...shall change our vile body...that it may be fashioned like unto his glorious body, according to the working whereby he is able even to subdue all things unto himself. — As for me, I will behold thy face in righteousness: I shall be satisfied, when I awake, with thy likeness.

John 1:12   2 Peter 1:4   Isaiah 64:4
1 Corinthians 13:12   Philippians 3:20,21   Psalm 17:15

JUNE 25 EVENING

The man that is my fellow, saith the Lord of hosts.
— ZECHARIAH 13:7

In him dwelleth all the fulness of the Godhead bodily. — I have laid help upon one that is mighty; I have exalted one chosen out of the people. — I have trodden the winepress alone; and of the people there was none with me. — Great is the mystery of godliness: God was manifest in the flesh. — Unto us a child is born, unto us a son is given, and the government shall be upon his shoulder; and his name shall be called Wonderful, Counsellor, The Mighty God, The Everlasting Father, The Prince of Peace. — The brightness of his glory, and the express image of his person, and upholding all things by the word of his power, when he had by himself purged our sins, sat down on the right hand of the majesty on high. — Unto the Son he saith, Thy throne, O God, is for ever and ever. — Let all the angels of God worship him. — Kings of kings, and Lord of lords.

Colossians 2:9   Psalm 89:19   Isaiah 63:3   1 Timothy 3:16
Isaiah 9:6   Hebrews 1:3,8,6   Revelation 19:16

JUNE 26 MORNING

*Oh that thou wouldest bless me indeed,
and that thou wouldest keep me from evil!
And God granted him that which he requested.
— 1 CHRONICLES 4:10*

The blessing of the Lord, it maketh rich, and he addeth no sorrow with it. — When he giveth quietness, who then can make trouble? And when he hideth his face, who then can behold him? — Salvation belongeth unto the Lord: thy blessing is upon thy people. — How great is thy goodness, which thou hast laid up for them that fear thee; which thou hast wrought for them that trust in thee before the sons of men. — I pray not that thou shouldest take them out of the world, but that thou shouldest keep them from the evil. — Ask, and it shall be given you; seek, and ye shall find; knock, and it shall be opened unto you: for every one that asketh receiveth; and he that seeketh findeth; and to him that knocketh it shall be opened. — The Lord redeemeth the soul of his servants and none of them that trust in him shall be desolate.

Proverbs 10:22   Job 34:29   Psalms 3:8, 31:19
John 17:15   Matthew 7:7,8   Psalm 34:22

JUNE 26 EVENING

*It is a night to be much observed unto the Lord
for bringing them out from the land of Egypt.
— EXODUS 12:42*

The Lord Jesus the same night in which he was betrayed took bread: and when he had given thanks, he brake it, and said, Take, eat: this is my body which is broken for you: this do in remembrance of me. After the same manner also he took the cup, when he had supped, saying, This cup is the new testament in my blood: this do ye, as oft as ye drink it, in remembrance of me. — He...kneeled down, and prayed. And being in an agony he prayed more earnestly: and his sweat was as it were great drops of blood falling down to the ground. — It was the preparation of the passover, and about the sixth hour...they took Jesus, and led him away...into a place called...Golgotha: where they crucified him. — Christ our passover is sacrificed for us: therefore let us keep the feast.

1 Corinthians 11:23-25   Luke 22:41,44   John 19:14,16-18 1   Corinthians 5:7,8

JUNE 27 MORNING

Who shall be able to stand?
— REVELATION 6:17

Who may abide the day of his coming? and who shall stand when he appeareth? For he is like a refiner's fire, and like fullers' soap. — I beheld, and, lo, a great multitude, which no man could number, of all nations, and kindreds, and peoples, and tongues, stood before the throne, and before the Lamb, clothed with white robes, and palms in their hands. These are they which came out of great tribulation, and have washed their robes and made them white in the blood of the Lamb. They shall hunger no more, neither thirst any more: neither shall the sun light on them, nor any heat. For the Lamb, which is in the midst of the throne, shall feed them, and shall lead them unto living fountains of waters: and God shall wipe away all tears from their eyes. — There is no condemnation to them which are in Christ Jesus, who walk not after the flesh, but after the Spirit. — Stand fast therefore in the liberty wherewith Christ hath made us free.

Malachi 3:2 Revelation 7:9,14-17 Romans 8:1 Galatians 5:1

JUNE 27 EVENING

Enter not into judgment with thy servant:
for in thy sight shall no man living be justified.
— PSALM 143:2

Come now, and let us reason together, saith the Lord: though your sins be as scarlet, they shall be as white as snow; though they be red like crimson, they shall be as wool. — Let him take hold of my strength that he may make peace with me; and he shall make peace with me. — Acquaint now thyself with him, and be at peace. — Being justified by faith, we have peace with God through our Lord Jesus Christ. — A man is not justified by the works of the law, but by the faith of Jesus Christ. — By the deeds of the law there shall no flesh be justified in his sight. — By him all that believe are justified from all things, from which ye could not be justified by the law of Moses. — Thanks be to God, which giveth us the victory through our Lord Jesus Christ.

Isaiah 1:18, 27:5 Job 22:21 Romans 5:1 Galatians 2:16
Romans 3:20 Acts 13:39 1 Corinthians 15:57

JUNE 28 MORNING

I know that my Redeemer liveth.
— JOB 19:25

If, when we were enemies, we were reconciled to God by the death of his Son, much more, being reconciled, we shall be saved by his life. — This man, because he continueth ever, hath an unchangeable priesthood. Wherefore he is able also to save them to the uttermost that come unto God by him, seeing he ever liveth to make intercession for them. — Because I live, ye shall live also. — If in this life only we have hope in Christ, we are of all men most miserable. But now is Christ risen from the dead, and become the firstfruits of them that slept. — The Redeemer shall come to Zion, and unto them that turn from transgression in Jacob, saith the Lord. — We have redemption through his blood, the forgiveness of sins, according to the riches of his grace. — Ye were not redeemed with corruptible things, as silver and gold, from your vain conversation received by tradition from your fathers; but with the precious blood of Christ, as of a lamb without blemish and without spot.

Romans 5:10   Hebrews 7:24,25   John 14:19   1 Corinthians 15:19,20
Isaiah 59:20   Ephesians 1:7   1 Peter 1:18,19

JUNE 28 EVENING

The Spirit speaketh expressly,
that in the latter times some shall depart from the faith,
giving heed to seducing spirits.
— 1 TIMOTHY 4:1

Take heed therefore how ye hear. — Let the word of Christ dwell in you richly in all wisdom. — Above all, taking the shield of faith, wherewith ye shall be able to quench all the fiery darts of the wicked. — Great peace have they which love thy law: and nothing shall offend them. How sweet are thy words unto my taste! yea, sweeter than honey to my mouth! Through thy precepts I get understanding: therefore I hate every false way. — Thy word is a lamp unto my feet, and a light unto my path. — I have more understanding than all my teachers: for thy testimonies are my meditation. — Satan himself is transformed into an angel of light. — But though we, or an angel from heaven, preach any other gospel unto you than that which we have preached unto you, let him be accursed.

Luke 8:18   Colossians 3:16   Ephesians 6:16
Psalm 119:165,103,104,105,99   2 Corinthians 11:14   Galatians 1:8

JUNE 29 MORNING

His commandments are not grievous.
— 1 JOHN 5:3

This is the will of him that sent me, that every one which seeth the Son, and believeth on him, may have everlasting life. — Whatsoever we ask, we receive of him, because we keep his commandments, and do those things that are pleasing in his sight. — My yoke is easy, and my burden is light. — If ye love me, keep my commandments. — He that hath my commandments, and keepeth them, he it is that loveth me: and he that loveth me shall be loved of my Father, and I will love him, and will manifest myself to him. — Happy is the man that findeth wisdom, and the man that getteth understanding. — Her ways are ways of pleasantness, and all her paths are peace. — Great peace have they which love thy law and nothing shall offend them. — I delight in the law of God after the inward man. — This is his commandment, That we should believe on the name of his Son Jesus Christ, and love one another. — Love worketh no ill to his neighbour: therefore love is the fulfilling of the law.

John 6:40 1 John 3:22   Matthew 11:30   John 14:15,21   Proverbs 3:13,17
Psalm 119:165   Romans 7:22 1   John 3:23   Romans 13:10

JUNE 29 EVENING

Remember not the sins of my youth,
nor my transgressions.
— PSALM 25:7

I have blotted out, as a thick cloud, thy transgressions, and, as a cloud, thy sins. — I, even I, am he that blotteth out thy transgressions for mine own sake, and will not remember thy sins. — Come now, and let us reason together, saith the Lord: though your sins be as scarlet, they shall be as white as snow; though they be red like crimson, they shall be as wool. — I will forgive their iniquity, and I will remember their sin no more. — Thou wilt cast all their sins into the depths of the sea. — Thou hast in love to my soul delivered it from the pit of corruption: for thou hast cast all my sins behind thy back. — Who is a God like unto thee, that pardoneth iniquity?...he retaineth not his anger for ever, because he delighteth in mercy. — Unto him that loved us, and washed us from our sins in his own blood, to him be glory and dominion for ever and ever. Amen.

Isaiah 44:22, 43:25, 1:18   Jeremiah 31:34
Micah 7:19   Isaiah 38:17   Micah 7:18   Revelation 1:5

JUNE 30 MORNING

As many as I love, I rebuke and chasten.
— REVELATION 3:19

My son, despise not thou the chastening of the Lord, nor faint when thou art rebuked of him: for whom the Lord loveth he chasteneth, and scourgeth every son whom he receiveth. — Even as a father the son in whom he delighteth. — He maketh sore, and bindeth up: he woundeth, and his hands make whole. — Humble yourselves therefore under the mighty hand of God, that he may exalt you in due time. — I have chosen thee in the furnace of affliction. — He doth not afflict willingly nor grieve the children of men. — He hath not dealt with us after our sins; nor rewarded us according to our iniquities. For as the heaven is high above the earth, so great is his mercy toward them that fear him. As far as the east is from the west, so far hath he removed our transgressions from us. Like as a father pitieth his children, so the Lord pitieth them that fear him. For he knoweth our frame; he remembereth that we are dust.

Hebrews 12:5,6   Proverbs 3:12   Job 5:18   1 Peter 5:6
Isaiah 48:10   Lamentations 3:33   Psalm 103:10-14

JUNE 30 EVENING

God is in heaven, and thou upon earth:
therefore let thy words be few.
— ECCLESIASTES. 5:2

When ye pray, use not vain repetitions, as the heathen do: for they think that they shall be heard for their much speaking. Be not ye therefore like unto them: for your Father knoweth what things ye have need of, before ye ask him. — They...called on the name of Baal from morning even until noon, saying, O Baal, hear us. — Two men went up into the temple to pray; the one a Pharisee, and the other a publican. The Pharisee stood and prayed thus with himself, God, I thank thee, that I am not as other men are, extortioners, unjust, adulterers, or even as this publican. And the publican, standing afar off, would not lift up so much as his eyes unto heaven, but smote upon his breast, saying, God be merciful to me a sinner. I tell you, this man went down to his house justified rather than the other. — Lord, teach us to pray.

Matthew 6:7,8   1 Kings 18:26   Luke 18:10,11,13,14, 11:1

JULY 1 MORNING

The fruit of the Spirit is goodness.
— GALATIANS 5:22

Be ye...followers of God, as dear children. — Love your enemies, bless them that curse you, do good to them that hate you, and pray for them which despitefully use you, and persecute you; that ye may be the children of your Father which is in heaven: for he maketh his sun to rise on the evil and on the good, and sendeth rain on the just and on the unjust. — Be ye therefore merciful, as your Father also is merciful. — The fruit of the Spirit is in all goodness and righteousness and truth. — After that the kindness and love of God our Saviour toward man appeared, not by works of righteousness which we have done, but according to his mercy he saved us, by the washing of regeneration, and renewing of the Holy Ghost; which he shed on us abundantly through Jesus Christ our Saviour. — The Lord is good to all: and his tender mercies are over all his works. — He that spared not his own Son, but delivered him up for us all, how shall he not with him also freely give us all things?

Ephesians 5:1   Matthew 5:44,45   Luke 6:36
Ephesians 5:9   Titus 3:4-6   Psalm 145:9   Romans 8:32

JULY 1 EVENING

Ebenezer...Hitherto hath the Lord helped us.
— 1 SAMUEL 7:12

I was brought low, and he helped me. — Blessed be the Lord, because he hath heard the voice of my supplications. The Lord is my strength and my shield; my heart trusted in him, and I am helped: therefore my heart greatly rejoiceth; and with my song will I praise him. — It is better to trust in the Lord than to put confidence in man. It is better to trust in the Lord than to put confidence in princes. — Happy is he that hath the God of Jacob for his help, whose hope is in the Lord his God. — He led them forth by the right way, that they might go to a city of habitation. — There failed not ought of any good thing which the Lord hath spoken unto the house of Israel; all came to pass. — When I sent you without purse, and scrip, and shoes, lacked ye any thing? And they said, Nothing. — Because thou hast been my help, therefore in the shadow of thy wings will I rejoice.

Psalms 116:6, 28:6,7, 118:8,9, 146:5, 107:7
Joshua 21:45   Luke 22:35   Psalm 63:7

JULY 2 MORNING

*This is the ordinance of the passover:
There shall no stranger eat thereof.*
— EXODUS 12:43

We have an altar, whereof they have no right to eat which serve the tabernacle. — Except a man be born again, he cannot see the kingdom of God. — At that time ye were without Christ, being aliens from the commonwealth of Israel, and strangers from the covenants of promise. But now, in Christ Jesus, ye who sometime were far off, are made nigh by the blood of Christ. — For he is our peace, who hath made both one...having abolished in his flesh the enmity, even the law of commandments contained in ordinances; for to make in himself of twain one new man, so making peace. — Now therefore ye are no more strangers and foreigners, but fellow-citizens with the saints, and of the household of God. — If any man hear my voice, and open the door, I will come in to him, and will sup with him, and he with me.

Hebrews 13:10   John 3:3   Ephesians 2:12-15,19   Revelation 3:20

JULY 2 EVENING

[Jesus] prayed the third time, saying the same words.
— MATTHEW 26:44

Who in the days of his flesh...offered up prayers and supplications with strong crying and tears unto him that was able to save him from death. — Then shall we know, if we follow on to know the Lord. — Continuing instant in prayer. — Praying always with all prayer and supplication in the Spirit, and watching thereunto with all perseverance and supplication. — By prayer and supplication with thanksgiving let your requests be made known unto God. And the peace of God, which passeth all understanding, shall keep your hearts and minds through Christ Jesus. — Nevertheless not as I will, but as thou wilt. — This is the confidence that we have in him, that, if we ask any thing according to his will, he heareth us. — Delight thyself...in the Lord; and he shall give thee the desires of thine heart. Commit thy way unto the Lord; trust also in him; and he shall bring it to pass.

Hebrews 5:7, 6:3   Romans 12:12   Ephesians 6:18
Philippians 4:6,7   Matthew 26:39 1   John 5:14   Psalm 37:4,5

JULY 3 MORNING

If children, then heirs;
heirs of God,
and joint-heirs with Christ.
— ROMANS 8:17

If ye be Christ's, then are ye Abraham's seed, and heirs according to the promise. — Behold, what manner of love the Father hath bestowed upon us, that we should be called the sons of God. — Thou art no more a servant, but a son; and if a son, then an heir of God through Christ. — Having predestinated us unto the adoption of children by Jesus Christ to himself, according to the good pleasure of his will. — Father, I will that they also, whom thou hast given me, be with me where I am; that they may behold my glory, which thou hast given me. — He that overcometh, and keepeth my works unto the end, to him I will give power over the nations. — To him that overcometh will I grant to sit with me in my throne, even as I also overcame, and am set down with my Father in his throne.

Galatians 3:29 1 John 3:1 Galatians 4:7
Ephesians 1:5 John 17:24 Revelation 2:26, 3:21

JULY 3 EVENING

Things which are despised, hath God chosen.
— 1 CORINTHIANS 1:28

Behold, are not all these which speak Galilaeans? —Jesus...saw two brethren...casting a net into the sea: for they were fishers. And he saith unto them, Follow me. — Now when they saw the boldness of Peter and John, and perceived that they were unlearned and ignorant men, they marvelled; and they took knowledge of them, that they had been with Jesus. — My speech and my preaching was not with enticing words of man's wisdom, but in demonstration of the Spirit and of power: that your faith should not stand in the wisdom of men, but in the power of God. — Ye have not chosen me, but I have chosen you, and ordained you, that ye should go and bring forth fruit. He that abideth in me, and I in him, the same bringeth forth much fruit: for without me ye can do nothing. — We have this treasure in earthen vessels, that the excellency of the power may be of God.

Acts 2:7 Matthew 4:18,19 Acts 4:13
1 Corinthians 2:4,5 John 15:16,5 2 Corinthians 4:7

JULY 4 MORNING

Leaning on Jesus' bosom.
— JOHN 13:23

As one whom his mother comforteth, so will I comfort you. — They brought young children to him, that he should touch them. And he took them up in his arms, put his hands upon them, and blessed them. — Jesus called his disciples unto him, and said, I have compassion on the multitude, because they continue with me now three days and have nothing to eat; and I will not send them away fasting, lest they faint in the way. — A high Priest...touched with the feeling of our infirmities. — In his love and in his pity he redeemed them. — I will not leave you comfortless: I will come to you. — Can a woman forget her sucking child, that she should not have compassion on the son of her womb? Yea, they may forget, yet will I not forget thee. — The Lamb which is in the midst of the throne shall feed them, and shall lead them unto living fountains of waters: and God shall wipe away all tears from their eyes.

Isaiah 66:13   Mark 10:13,16   Matthew 15:32   Hebrews 4:15
Isaiah 63:9   John 14:18   Isaiah 49:15   Revelation 7:17

JULY 4 EVENING

Jesus Christ the righteous:
the propitiation for our sins.
— 1 JOHN 2:1,2

Toward the mercy seat shall the faces of the cherubim be. And thou shalt put the mercy seat above upon the ark; and in the ark thou shalt put the testimony that I shall give thee. I will meet with thee, and I will commune with thee from above the mercy seat. — Surely his salvation is nigh them that fear him; mercy and truth are met together; righteousness and peace have kissed each other. — If thou, Lord, shouldest mark iniquities, O Lord, who shall stand? But there is forgiveness with thee, that thou mayest be feared. Let Israel hope in the Lord: for with the Lord there is mercy, and with him is plenteous redemption. And he shall redeem Israel from all his iniquities. — All have sinned, and come short of the glory of God; being justified freely by his grace through the redemption that is in Christ Jesus: whom God hath set forth to be a propitiation through faith in his blood, to declare his righteousness for the remission of sins.

Exodus 25:20-22   Psalms 85:9,10, 130:3,4,7,8   Romans 3:23-25

JULY 5 MORNING

We have known and believed
the love that God hath to us.
— 1 JOHN 4:16

God, who is rich in mercy, for his great love wherewith he loved us, even when we were dead in sins, hath quickened us together with Christ, (by grace ye are saved;) and hath raised us up together, and made us sit together in heavenly places in Christ Jesus: that in the ages to come he might shew the exceeding riches of his grace in his kindness toward us through Christ Jesus. —God so loved the world, that he gave his only begotten Son, that whosoever believeth in him should not perish, but have everlasting life. — He that spared not his own Son, but delivered him up for us all, how shall he not with him also freely give us all things? — The Lord is good to all: and his tender mercies are over all his works. — We love him, because he first loved us. — Blessed is she that believed: for there shall be a performance of those things which were told her from the Lord.

Ephesians 2:4-7   John 3:16   Romans 8:32   Psalm 145:9   1 John 4:19   Luke 1:45

JULY 5 EVENING

Mind not high things,
but condescend to men of low estate.
— ROMANS 12:16

My brethren, have not the faith of our Lord Jesus Christ, the Lord of glory, with respect of persons. Hath not God chosen the poor of this world rich in faith, and heirs of the kingdom which he hath promised to them that love him? — Let no man seek his own, but every man another's wealth. — Having food and raiment let us be therewith content. But they that will be rich fall into temptation and a snare, and into many foolish and hurtful lusts, which drown men in destruction and perdition. —God hath chosen the foolish things of the world to confound the wise: and God hath chosen the weak things of the world to confound the things which are mighty; and base things of the world, and things which are despised, hath God chosen, yea, and things which are not, to bring to nought things that are: that no flesh should glory in his presence. — Lord, my heart is not haughty, nor mine eyes lofty.

James 2:1,5   1 Corinthians 10:24   1 Timothy 6:8,9
1 Corinthians 1:27-29   Psalm 131:1

JULY 6 MORNING

Let your speech be always with grace.
— COLOSSIANS 4:6

A word fitly spoken is like apples of gold in pictures of silver. As an earring of gold, and an ornament of fine gold, so is a wise reprover upon an obedient ear. — Let no corrupt communication proceed out of your mouth, but that which is good to the use of edifying, that it may minister grace unto the hearers. — A good man out of the good treasure of the heart bringeth forth good things: and an evil man out of the evil treasure bringeth forth evil things. — By thy words thou shalt be justified. — The tongue of the wise is health. — They that feared the Lord spake often one to another: and the Lord hearkened, and heard it, and a book of remembrance was written before him for them that feared the Lord, and that thought upon his name. — If thou take forth the precious from the vile, thou shalt be as my mouth. — Therefore, as ye abound in every thing, in faith, and utterance, and knowledge, and in all diligence...see that ye abound in this grace also.

Proverbs 25:11,12   Ephesians 4:29   Matthew 12:35,37   Proverbs 12:18
Malachi 3:16   Jeremiah 15:19 2   Corinthians 8:7

JULY 6 EVENING

Thy lovingkindness is before mine eyes.
— PSALM 26:3

The Lord is gracious, and full of compassion; slow to anger, and of great mercy. — Your Father which is in heaven:...maketh his sun to rise on the evil and on the good, and sendeth rain on the just and on the unjust. —Be ye...followers of God, as dear children; and walk in love, as Christ also hath loved us, and hath given himself for us an offering and a sacrifice to God for a sweet-smelling savour. — Be ye kind to one another, tenderhearted, forgiving one another, even as God for Christ's sake hath forgiven you. — Seeing ye have purified your souls in obeying the truth through the Spirit unto unfeigned love of the brethren, see that ye love one another with a pure heart fervently. — The love of Christ constraineth us. — Love ye your enemies, and do good, and lend, hoping for nothing again; and your reward shall be great, and ye shall be the children of the Highest: for he is kind unto the unthankful and to the evil. Be ye therefore merciful, as your Father also is merciful.

Psalm 145:8   Matthew 5:45   Ephesians 5:1,2, 4:32
1 Peter 1:22 2   Corinthians 5:14   Luke 6:35,36

JULY 7 MORNING

*Then was Jesus led up of the spirit into the wilderness
to be tempted of the devil.*
— MATTHEW 4:1

In the days of his flesh, when he had offered up prayers and supplications with strong crying and tears unto him that was able to save him from death, and was heard in that he feared; though he were a Son, yet learned he obedience by the things which he suffered; and being made perfect, he became the author of eternal salvation unto all them that obey him. — We have not an high priest which cannot be touched with the feeling of our infirmities: but was in all points tempted like as we are, yet without sin. — There hath no temptation taken you but such as is common to man: but God is faithful, who will not suffer you to be tempted above that ye are able; but will with the temptation also make a way to escape, that ye may be able to bear it. — My grace is sufficient for thee: for my strength is made perfect in weakness.

Hebrews 5:7-9, 4:15 1 Corinthians 10:13 2 Corinthians 12:9

JULY 7 EVENING

The Son of man came to give his life a ransom for many.
— MATTHEW 20:28

If the blood of bulls and of goats, and the ashes of an heifer sprinkling the unclean, sanctifieth to the purifying of the flesh: how much more shall the blood of Christ, who through the eternal Spirit offered himself without spot to God, purge your conscience from dead works to serve the living God? —He is brought as a lamb to the slaughter. — I lay down my life for the sheep. No man taketh it from me, but I lay it down of myself. I have power to lay it down, and I have power to take it again. — The life of the flesh is in the blood: and I have given it to you upon the altar, to make an atonement for your souls: for it is the blood that maketh an atonement for the soul. — Without shedding of blood is no remission. — While we were yet sinners, Christ died for us. Much more then, being now justified by his blood, we shall be saved from wrath through him.

Hebrews 9:13,14   Isaiah 53:7   John 10:15,18
Leviticus 17:11   Hebrews 9:22   Romans 5:8,9

JULY 8 MORNING

*If we confess our sins,
he is faithful and just to forgive us our sins,
and to cleanse us from all unrighteousness.*
— 1 JOHN 1:9

I acknowledge my transgressions: and my sin is ever before me. Against thee, thee only, have I sinned, and done this evil in thy sight. — And he arose, and came to his father. But when he was yet a great way off, his father saw him, and had compassion, and ran, and fell on his neck, and kissed him. — I have blotted out as a thick cloud, thy transgressions, and, as a cloud, thy sins: return unto me; for I have redeemed thee. — Your sins are forgiven you for his name's sake. — God for Christ's sake hath forgiven you. — That he might be just, and the justifier of him which believeth in Jesus. — Then will I sprinkle clean water upon you, and ye shall be clean. — They shall walk with me in white: for they are worthy. —This is he that came by water and blood, even Jesus Christ: not by water only, but by water and blood.

Psalm 51:3,4   Luke 15:20   Isaiah 44:22 1   John 2:12   Ephesians 4:32
Romans 3:26   Ezekiel 36:25   Revelation 3:4 1   John 5:6

JULY 8 EVENING

Shall the throne of iniquity have fellowship with thee?
— PSALM 94:20

Truly our fellowship is with the Father, and with his Son Jesus Christ. — Beloved, now are we the sons of God, and it doth not yet appear what we shall be: but we know that, when he shall appear, we shall be like him; for we shall see him as he is. And every man that hath this hope in him purifieth himself, even as he is pure. — The prince of this world cometh, and hath nothing in me. — An high priest...holy, harmless, undefiled. — We wrestle not against flesh and blood, but against principalities, against powers, against the rulers of the darkness of this world, against spiritual wickedness in high places. — The prince of the power of the air, the spirit that now worketh in the children of disobedience. — Whosoever is born of God sinneth not; but he that is begotten of God keepeth himself, and that wicked one toucheth him not. And we know that we are of God, and the whole world lieth in wickedness.

1 John 1:3, 3:2,3   John 14:30   Hebrews 7:26
Ephesians 6:12, 2:2 1   John 5:18,19

JULY 9 MORNING

I have caused thine iniquity to pass from thee, and I will clothe thee with change of raiment.
— ZECHARIAH 3:4

Blessed is he whose transgression is forgiven, whose sin is covered. — We are all as an unclean thing. — I know that in me (that is, in my flesh,) dwelleth no good thing: for to will is present with me; but how to perform that which is good I find not. — As many of you as have been baptized into Christ have put on Christ. — Ye have put off the old man with his deeds; and have put on the new man, which is renewed in knowledge after the image of him that created him. — Not having mine own righteousness which is of the law, but...the righteousness which is of God by faith. — Bring forth the best robe, and put it on him. — The fine linen is the righteousness of saints. — I will greatly rejoice in the Lord, my soul shall be joyful in my God; for he hath clothed me with the garments of salvation, he hath covered me with the robe of righteousness.

Psalm 32:1   Isaiah 64:6   Romans 7:18   Galatians 3:27   Colossians 3:9,10   Philippians 3:9   Luke 15:22   Revelation 19:8   Isaiah 61:10

JULY 9 EVENING

The day shall declare it.
— 1 CORINTHIANS 3:13

Judge nothing before the time, until the Lord come, who both will bring to light the hidden things of darkness, and will make manifest the counsels of the hearts: and then shall every man have praise of God. — Why dost thou judge thy brother? Or why dost thou set at nought thy brother? For we shall all stand before the judgment seat of Christ. So then every one of us shall give account of himself to God. Let us not therefore judge one another any more. — God shall judge the secrets of men by Jesus Christ. — The Father judgeth no man, but hath committed all judgment unto the Son: and hath given him authority to execute judgment also, because he is the Son of man. — The Great, the Mighty God, the Lord of hosts, is his name, great in counsel, and mighty in work: for thine eyes are open upon all the ways of the sons of men: to give every one according to his ways, and according to the fruit of his doings.

1 Corinthians 4:5   Romans 14:10,12,13, 2:16   John 5:22,27   Jeremiah 32:18,19

JULY 10 MORNING

The disciple is not above his master.
— MATTHEW 10:24

Ye call me Master and Lord: and ye say well; for so I am. — It is enough for the disciple that he be as his master, and the servant as his lord. — If they have persecuted me, they will also persecute you; if they have kept my saying, they will keep yours also. — I have given them thy word; and the world hath hated them, because they are not of the world, even as I am not of the world. — Consider him that endured such contradiction of sinners against himself, lest ye be wearied and faint in your minds. Ye have not yet resisted unto blood, striving against sin. — Let us run with patience the race that is set before us, looking unto Jesus the author and finisher of our faith; who for the joy that was set before him endured the cross, despising the shame, and is set down at the right hand of the throne of God. — Forasmuch...as Christ hath suffered for us in the flesh, arm yourselves likewise with the same mind.

John 13:13   Matthew 10:25   John 15:20, 17:14   Hebrews 12:3,4,1,2   1 Peter 4:1

JULY 10 EVENING

My son, give me thine heart.
— PROVERBS 23:26

O that there were such an heart in them, that they would fear me, and keep all my commandments always, that it might be well with them, and with their children for ever! — Thy heart is not right in the sight of God. — Because the carnal mind is enmity against God: for it is not subject to the law of God, neither indeed can be. So then they that are in the flesh cannot please God. —They... first gave their own selves to the Lord. — In every work that [Hezekiah] began... to seek his God, he did it with all his heart, and prospered. — Keep thy heart with all diligence; for out of it are the issues of life. —Whatsoever ye do, do it heartily, as to the Lord. — As the servants of Christ, doing the will of God from the heart; with good will doing service, as to the Lord, and not to men. — I will run the way of thy commandments, when thou shalt enlarge my heart.

Deuteronomy 5:29   Acts 8:21   Romans 8:7,8
2 Corinthians 8:5   2 Chronicles 31:21
Proverbs 4:23   Colossians 3:23   Ephesians 6:6,7   Psalm 119:32

JULY 11 MORNING

I am with thee to save thee.
— JEREMIAH 15:20

Shall the prey be taken from the mighty, or the lawful captive delivered? But thus saith the Lord, Even the captives of the mighty shall be taken away, and the prey of the terrible shall be delivered: for I will contend with him that contendeth with thee. And all flesh shall know that I the Lord am thy Saviour and thy Redeemer, the mighty One of Jacob. — Fear thou not; for I am with thee: be not dismayed; for I am thy God: I will strengthen thee; yea, I will help thee; yea, I will uphold thee with the right hand of my righteousness. — We have not an high priest which cannot be touched with the feeling of our infirmities; but was in all points tempted like as we are, yet without sin. — In that he himself hath suffered being tempted, he is able to succour them that are tempted. — The steps of a good man are ordered by the Lord: and he delighteth in his way. Though he fall, he shall not be utterly cast down: for the Lord upholdeth him with his hand.

Isaiah 49:24-26, 41:10   Hebrews 4:15, 2:18   Psalm 37:23,24

JULY 11 EVENING

He satisfieth the longing soul,
and filleth the hungry soul with goodness.
— PSALM 107:9

Ye have tasted that the Lord is gracious. — O God, thou art my God; early will I seek thee: my soul thirsteth for thee, my flesh longeth for thee in a dry and thirsty land, where no water is; to see thy power and thy glory. — My soul longeth, yea, even fainteth for the courts of the Lord: my heart and my flesh crieth out for the living God. — Having a desire to depart, and to be with Christ; which is far better. — I shall be satisfied, when I awake, with thy likeness. — They shall hunger no more, neither thirst any more; neither shall the sun light on them, nor any heat. For the Lamb which is in the midst of the throne shall feed them, and shall lead them unto living fountains of waters: and God shall wipe away all tears from their eyes. — They shall be abundantly satisfied with the fatness of thy house; and thou shalt make them drink of the river of thy pleasures. — My people shall be satisfied with my goodness, saith the Lord.

1 Peter 2:3   Psalms 63:1,2, 84:2   Philippians 1:23   Psalm 17:15
Revelation 7:16,17   Psalm 36:8   Jeremiah 31:14

JULY 12 MORNING

My presence shall go with thee, and I will give thee rest.
— EXODUS 33:14

Be strong and of a good courage, fear not, nor be afraid of them: for the Lord thy God, he it is that doth go with thee; he will not fail thee, nor forsake thee. The Lord, he it is that doth go before thee; he will be with thee, he will not fail thee, neither forsake thee: fear not, neither be dismayed. — Have not I commanded thee? Be strong and of a good courage; be not afraid, neither be thou dismayed: for the Lord thy God is with thee whithersoever thou goest. — In all thy ways acknowledge him, and he shall direct thy paths. — He hath said, I will never leave thee, nor forsake thee. So that we may boldly say, The Lord is my helper, and I will not fear what man shall do unto me. — Our sufficiency is of God. — Lead us not into temptation. — O Lord, I know that the way of man is not in himself: it is not in man that walketh to direct his steps. — My times are in thy hand.

Deuteronomy 31:6,8   Joshua 1:9   Proverbs 3:6   Hebrews 13:5,6
2 Corinthians 3:5   Matthew 6:13   Jeremiah 10:23   Psalm 31:15

JULY 12 EVENING

Let us consider one another
to provoke unto love and to good works.
— HEBREWS 10:24

How forcible are right words! — I stir up your pure minds by way of remembrance. — They that feared the Lord spake often one to another: and the Lord hearkened, and heard it, and a book of remembrance was written before him for them that feared the Lord, and that thought upon his name. — If two of you shall agree on earth as touching any thing that they shall ask, it shall be done for them of my Father which is in heaven. — The Lord God said, It is not good that the man should be alone. — Two are better than one; because they have a good reward for their labour. For if they fall, the one will lift up his fellow: but woe to him that is alone when he falleth; for he hath not another to help him up. — Let...no man put a stumblingblock or an occasion to fall in his brother's way. — Bear ye one another's burdens, and so fulfil the law of Christ. Considering thyself, lest thou also be tempted.

Job 6:25   2 Peter 3:1   Malachi 3:16   Matthew 18:19   Genesis 2:18
Ecclesiastes 4:9,10   Romans 14:13   Galatians 6:2,1

JULY 13 MORNING

I am my Beloved's, and His desire is toward me.
— SONG OF SOLOMON 7:10

I know whom I have believed, and am persuaded that he is able to keep that which I have committed unto him against that day. — I am persuaded, hat neither death, nor life, nor angels nor principalities, nor powers, nor things present, nor things to come, nor height, nor depth, nor any other creature, shall be able to separate us from the love of God, which is in Christ Jesus our Lord. — Those that thou gavest me I have kept, and none of then is lost. — The Lord taketh pleasure in his people. — My delights were with the sons of men. — His great love wherewith he loved us. — Greater love hath no man than this, that a man lay down his life for his friends. — Ye are bought with a price: therefore glorify God in your body, and in your spirit, which are God's. — Whether we live, we live unto the Lord; and whether we die, we die unto the Lord: whether we live therefore, or die, we are the Lord's.

2 Timothy 1:12   Romans 8:38,39   John 17:12   Psalm 149:4   Proverbs 8:31
Ephesians 2:4   John 15:13 1   Corinthians 6:20   Romans 14:8

JULY 13 EVENING

Seek ye out of the book of the Lord.
— ISAIAH 34:16

Ye shall lay up these my words in your heart and in your soul, and bind them for a sign upon your hand, that they may be as frontlets between your eyes. — This book of the law shall not depart out of thy mouth; but thou shalt meditate therein day and night, that thou mayest observe to do according to all that is written therein: for then thou shalt make thy way prosperous, and then thou shalt have good success. — The law of his God is in his heart; none of his steps shall slide. — By the word of thy lips I have kept me from the paths of the destroyer. — Thy word have I hid in mine heart, that I might not sin against thee. — We have...a more sure word of prophecy; whereunto ye do well that ye take heed, as unto a light that shineth in a dark place until the day dawn, and the day star arise in your hearts. — That we through patience and comfort of the scriptures might have hope.

Deuteronomy 11:18   Joshua 1:8
Psalms 37:31, 17:4, 119:11 2   Peter 1:19   Romans 15:4

JULY 14 MORNING

Out of the abundance of the heart the mouth speaketh.
— MATTHEW 12:34

Let the word of Christ dwell in you richly in all wisdom. — Keep thy heart with all diligence; for out of it are the issues of life. — Death and life are in the power of the tongue. — The mouth of the righteous speaketh wisdom, and his tongue talketh of judgment. The law of his God is in his heart: none of his steps shall slide. — Let no corrupt communication proceed out of your mouth, but that which is good to the use of edifying, that it may minister grace unto the hearers. — We cannot but speak the things which we have seen and heard. — I believed, therefore have I spoken. — Whosoever...shall confess me before men, him will I confess also before my Father which is in heaven. — With the heart man believeth unto righteousness; and with the mouth confession is made unto salvation.

Colossians 3:16   Proverbs 4:23, 18:21   Psalm 37:30,31   Ephesians 4:29   Acts 4:20   Psalm 116:10   Matthew 10:32   Romans 10:10

JULY 14 EVENING

I trust I shall shortly see thee,
and we shall speak face to face.
— 3 JOHN 14

Oh that thou wouldest rend the heavens, that thou wouldest come down! — As the hart panteth after the water brooks, so panteth my soul after thee, O God. My soul thirsteth for God, for the living God: when shall I come and appear before God? — Make haste, my beloved, and be thou like to a roe or to a young hart upon the mountains of spices. — Our conversation is in heaven; from whence also we look for the Saviour, the Lord Jesus Christ. — Looking for that blessed hope, and the glorious appearing of the great God and our Saviour Jesus Christ. — God our Saviour, and Lord Jesus Christ, which is our hope. — Whom having not seen, ye love. — He which testifieth these things saith, Surely I come quickly; Amen. Even so, come, Lord Jesus. — It shall be said in that day, Lo, this is our God; we have waited for him, and he will save us: this is the Lord; we have waited for him, we will be glad and rejoice in his salvation.

Isaiah 64:1   Psalm 42:1,2   Song of Solomon 8:14   Philippians 3:20   Titus 2:13   1 Timothy 1:1   1 Peter 1:8   Revelation 22:20   Isaiah 25:9

JULY 15 MORNING

Thy will be done in earth, as it is in heaven.
— MATTHEW 6:10

Bless the Lord, ye his angels, that excel in strength, that do his commandments, hearkening unto the voice of his word. Bless ye the Lord, all ye his hosts; ye ministers of his, that do his pleasure. — I came down from heaven not to do mine own will, but the will of him that sent me. — I delight to do thy will, O my God; yea, thy law is within my heart. — O my Father, if this cup may not pass away from me, except I drink it, thy will be done. — Not every one that saith unto me, Lord, Lord, shall enter into the kingdom of heaven; but he that doeth the will of my Father which is in heaven. — Not the hearers of the law are just before God, but the doers of the law shall be justified. — If ye know these things, happy are ye if ye do them. — To him that knoweth to do good, and doeth it not, to him it is sin. — Be not conformed to this world: but ye be transformed by the renewing of your mind.

Psalm 103:20,21   John 6:38   Psalm 40:8   Matthew 26:42, 7:21
Romans 2:13   John 13:17   James 4:17   Romans 12:2

JULY 15 EVENING

The ear trieth words, as the mouth tasteth meat.
— JOB 34:3

Beloved, believe not every spirit, but try the spirits whether they are of God: because many false prophets are gone out into the world. — Judge not according to the appearance, but judge righteous judgment. — I speak as to wise men; judge ye what I say. — Let the word of Christ dwell in you richly in all wisdom. —He that hath an ear, let him hear what the Spirit saith. — He that is spiritual judgeth all things. — Take heed what ye hear. — I know thy works...and how thou hast tried them which say they are apostles, and are not, and hast found them liars. — Prove all things; hold fast that which is good. —He calleth his own sheep by name, and leadeth them out. And when he putteth forth his own sheep, he goeth before them, and the sheep follow him: for they know his voice. And a stranger will they not follow, but will flee from him: for they know not the voice of strangers.

1 John 4:1   John 7:24   1 Corinthians 10:15   Colossians 3:16   Revelation 2:29
1 Corinthians 2:15   Mark 4:24   Revelation 2:2
1 Thessalonians 5:21   John 10:3-5

JULY 16 MORNING

*Ye shall be unto me a kingdom of priests,
and a holy nation.*
— EXODUS 19:6

Thou wast slain, and hast redeemed us to God by thy blood out of every kindred, and tongue, and people, and nation; and hast made us unto our God kings and priests. — Ye are a chosen generation, a royal priesthood, a holy nation, a peculiar people; that ye should shew forth the praises of him who hath called you out of darkness into his marvellous light. — Ye shall be named the Priests of the Lord: men shall call you the Ministers of our God. — Priests of God and of Christ. — Wherefore, holy brethren, partakers of the heavenly calling, consider the Apostle and High Priest of our profession, Christ Jesus. — By him therefore let us offer the sacrifice of praise to God continually, that is, the fruit of our lips giving thanks to his name. — For we are his workmanship, created in Christ Jesus unto good works, which God hath before ordained that we should walk in them. — The temple of God is holy, which temple ye are.

Revelation 5:9,10 1 Peter 2:9 Isaiah 61:6 Revelation 20:6
Hebrews 3:1, 13:15 Ephesians 2:10 1 Corinthians 3:17

JULY 16 EVENING

*We made our prayer unto our God,
and set a watch against them.*
— NEHEMIAH 4:9

Watch and pray, that ye enter not into temptation. — Continue in prayer, and watch in the same with thanksgiving. — Casting all your care upon him; for he careth for you. Be sober, be vigilant; because your adversary the devil, as a roaring lion, walketh about, seeking whom he may devour: whom resist stedfast in the faith. — Why call ye me, Lord, Lord, and do not the things which I say? — Be ye doers of the word, and not hearers only, deceiving your own selves. — Wherefore criest thou unto me? Speak unto the children of Israel, that they go forward. — Be careful for nothing; but in every thing by prayer and supplication with thanksgiving let your requests be made known unto God. And the peace of God, which passeth all understanding, shall keep your hearts and minds through Christ Jesus.

Matthew 26:41 Colossians 4:2 1 Peter 5:7-9
Luke 6:46 James 1:22 Exodus 14:15 Philippians 4:6,7

JULY 17 MORNING

*Thou art a gracious God, and merciful, slow to anger,
and of great kindness, and repentest thee of the evil.*
— *JONAH 4:2*

I beseech thee, let the power of my Lord be great, according as thou hast spoken, saying, The Lord is longsuffering, and of great mercy, forgiving iniquity and transgression, and by no means clearing the guilty; visiting the iniquity of the fathers upon the children unto the third and fourth generation. — O remember not against us former iniquities: let thy tender mercies speedily prevent us. Help us, O God of our salvation, for the glory of thy name: and deliver us, and purge away our sins, for thy name's sake. — Lord, though our iniquities testify against us, do thou it for thy name's sake: for our backslidings are many; we have sinned against thee. — We acknowledge, O Lord, our wickedness, and the iniquity of our fathers: for we have sinned against thee. —If thou, Lord, shouldest mark iniquities, O Lord, who shall stand? But there is forgiveness with thee, that thou mayest be feared.

Numbers 14:17,18   Psalm 79:8,9   Jeremiah 14:7,20   Psalm 130:3,4

JULY 17 EVENING

Sanctification of the Spirit.
— *2 THESSALONIANS 2:13*

Awake, O north wind; and come, thou south; blow upon my garden, that the spices thereof may flow out. —Behold this selfsame thing, that ye sorrowed after a godly sort, what carefulness it wrought in you, yea, what clearing of yourselves, yea, what indignation, yea, what fear, yea, what vehement desire, yea, what zeal, yea, what revenge! — Fruit of the Spirit is in all goodness and righteousness and truth: proving what is acceptable unto the Lord. — The Comforter is the Holy Ghost. — The love of God is shed abroad in our hearts by the Holy Ghost which is given unto us. — The fruit of the Spirit is love, joy, peace. — In a great trial of affliction the abundance of their joy and their deep poverty abounded unto the riches of their liberality. — All these worketh that one and the selfsame Spirit, dividing to every man severally as he will.

Song of Solomon 4:16 2   Corinthians 7:11   Ephesians 5:9,10   John 14:26
Romans 5:5   Galatians 5:22 2   Corinthians 8:2 1   Corinthians 12:11

JULY 18 MORNING

He calleth his own sheep by name, and leadeth them out.
— *JOHN 10:3*

The foundation of God standeth sure, having this seal, The Lord knoweth them that are his; and, Let every one that nameth the name of Christ, depart from iniquity. — Many will say to me in that day, Lord, Lord, have we not prophesied in thy name? And in thy name have cast out devils? And in thy name done many wonderful works? And then will I profess unto them, I never knew you...depart from me, ye that work iniquity. — The Lord knoweth the way of the righteous; but the way of the ungodly shall perish. — Behold, I have graven thee upon the palms of my hands; thy walls are continually before me. — Set me as a seal upon thine heart, as a seal upon thine arm. — The Lord is good, a strong hold in the day of trouble; and he knoweth them that trust in him. — I go to prepare a place for you. And if I go and prepare a place for you, I will come again, and receive you unto myself; that where I am, there ye may be also.

2 Timothy 2:19   Matthew 7:22,23   Psalm 1:6   Isaiah 49:16
Song of Solomon 8:6   Nahum 1:7   John 14:2,3

JULY 18 EVENING

She hath done what she could.
— *MARK 14:8*

This poor widow hath cast in more than they all. — Whosoever shall give you a cup of water to drink in my name, because ye belong to Christ, verily I say unto you, he shall not lose his reward. — If there be first a willing mind, it is accepted according to that a man hath, and not according to that he hath not. — Let us not love in word, neither in tongue; but in deed and in truth. — If a brother or sister be naked, and destitute of daily food, and one of you say unto them, Depart in peace, be ye warmed and filled; notwithstanding ye give them not those things which are needful to the body; what doth it profit? — He which soweth bountifully, shall reap also bountifully. Every man according as he purposeth in his heart, so let him give; not grudgingly, or of necessity: for God loveth a cheerful giver. — When ye shall have done all those things which are commanded you, say, We are unprofitable servants: we have done that which was our duty to do.

Luke 21:3   Mark 9:41   2 Corinthians 8:12
1 John 3:18   James 2:15,16   2 Corinthians 9:6,7   Luke 17:10

JULY 19 MORNING

He that is mighty hath done to me great things;
and holy is his name.
— LUKE 1:49

Who is like unto thee, O Lord, among the gods? Who is like thee, glorious in holiness, fearful in praises, doing wonders? — Among the gods there is none like unto thee, O Lord; neither are there any works like unto thy works. — Who shall not fear thee, O Lord, and glorify thy name? For thou only art holy. — Hallowed be thy name. — Blessed be the Lord God of Israel; for he hath visited and redeemed his people. — Who is this that cometh from Edom, with dyed garments from Bozrah? This that is glorious in his apparel, travelling in the greatness of his strength? I that speak in righteousness, mighty to save. — I have laid help upon one that is mighty; I have exalted one chosen out of the people. — Now unto him that is able to do exceeding abundantly above all that we ask or think, according to the power that worketh in us...be glory.

Exodus 15:11   Psalm 86:8   Revelation 15:4   Matthew 6:9
Luke 1:68   Isaiah 63:1   Psalm 89:19   Ephesians 3:20,21

JULY 19 EVENING

The dew of Hermon.
— PSALM 133:3

Mount Sion, which is Hermon. — There the Lord commanded the blessing, even life for evermore. — I will be as the dew unto Israel: he shall grow as the lily, and cast forth his roots as Lebanon. — My doctrine shall drop as the rain, my speech shall distil as the dew, as the small rain upon the tender herb, and as the showers upon the grass. — As the rain cometh down, and the snow from heaven, and returneth not thither, but watereth the earth, and maketh it bring forth and bud, that it may give seed to the sower, and bread to the eater: so shall my word be that goeth forth out of my mouth: it shall not return unto me void, but it shall accomplish that which I please, and it shall prosper in the thing whereto I sent it. — God giveth not the Spirit by measure unto him. — And of his fulness have all we received, and grace for grace. — It is like the precious ointment upon the head...even Aaron's...that went down to the skirts of his garments.

Deuteronomy 4:48   Psalm 133:3   Hosea 14:5
Deuteronomy 32:2   Isaiah 55:10,11   John 3:34, 1:16   Psalm 133:2

JULY 20 MORNING

They are not of the world, even as I am not of the world.
— JOHN 17:16

He is despised and rejected of men; a man of sorrows, and acquainted with grief. — In the world ye shall have tribulation: but be of good cheer; I have overcome the world. — Such an high priest became us, who is holy, harmless, undefiled, separate from sinners. — That ye may be blameless and harmless, the sons of God, without rebuke, in the midst of a crooked and perverse nation. — Jesus of Nazareth...went about doing good, and healing all that were oppressed of the devil; for God was with him. — As we have therefore opportunity, let us do good unto all men, especially unto them who are of the household of faith. — That was the true Light, which lighteth every man that cometh into the world. — Ye are the light of the world. A city that is set on a hill cannot be hid. Let your light so shine before men, that they may see your good works, and glorify your Father which is in heaven.

Isaiah 53:3   John 16:33   Hebrews 7:26   Philippians 2:15
Acts 10:38   Galatians 6:10   John 1:9   Matthew 5:14,16

JULY 20 EVENING

He that is of a merry heart hath a continual feast.
— PROVERBS 15:15

The joy of the Lord is your strength. — The kingdom of God is not meat and drink; but righteousness, and peace, and joy in the Holy Ghost. — Be filled with the Spirit; speaking to yourselves in psalms and hymns and spiritual Song, singing and making melody in your heart to the Lord; giving thanks always for all things unto God and the Father in the name of our Lord Jesus Christ. — By him...let us offer the sacrifice of praise to God continually, that is, the fruit of our lips giving thanks to his name. —Although the fig tree shall not blossom, neither shall fruit be in the vines; the labour of the olive shall fail, and the fields shall yield no meat; the flock shall be cut off from the fold, and there shall be no herd in the stalls: yet I will rejoice in the Lord, I will joy in the God of my salvation. — Sorrowful, yet alway rejoicing. — We glory in tribulations also.

Nehemiah 8:10   Romans 14:17   Ephesians 5:18-20   Hebrews 13:15
Habakkuk 3:17,18   2 Corinthians 6:10   Romans 5:3

JULY 21 MORNING

What profit is there of circumcision?
— ROMANS 3:1

Much, every way. — Circumcise yourselves to the Lord, and take away the foreskins of your heart. — If...their uncircumcised hearts be humbled, and they then accept of the punishment of their iniquity: then will I remember my covenant with Jacob, and also my covenant with Isaac, and also my covenant with Abraham will I remember. — Jesus Christ was a minister of the circumcision for the truth of God, to confirm the promises made unto the fathers. — In whom also ye are circumcised with the circumcision made without hands, in putting off the body of the sins of the flesh by the circumcision of Christ. — You, being dead in your sins and the uncircumcision of your flesh, hath he quickened together with him, having forgiven you all trespasses. —Put off concerning the former conversation the old man, which is corrupt according to the deceitful lusts; and be renewed in the spirit of your mind; and...put on the new man, which after God is created in righteousness.

Romans 3:2   Jeremiah 4:4   Leviticus 26:41,42
Romans 15:8   Colossians 2:11,13   Ephesians 4:22-24

JULY 21 EVENING

The veil of the temple was rent in twain
from the top to the bottom.
— MATTHEW 27:51

The Lord Jesus the same night in which he was betrayed took bread: and when he had given thanks, he brake it, and said, Take, eat: this is my body, which is broken for you: this do in remembrance of me. — The bread that I will give is my flesh, which I will give for the life of the world. — Except ye eat the flesh of the Son of man, and drink his blood, ye have no life in you. Whoso eateth my flesh, and drinketh my blood, hath eternal life. He that eateth my flesh, and drinketh my blood, dwelleth in me, and I in him. As the living Father hath sent me, and I live by the Father: so he that eateth me, even he shall live by me. Doth this offend you? What and if ye shall see the Son of man ascend up where he was before? It is the spirit that quickeneth; the flesh profiteth nothing. — A new and living way, which he hath consecrated for us, through the veil, that is to say, his flesh; let us draw near.

1 Corinthians 11:23,24   John 6:51,53,54,56,57,61-63   Hebrews 10:20,22

JULY 22 MORNING

*In that he died, he died unto sin once:
but in that he liveth, he liveth unto God.*
— ROMANS 6:10

He was numbered with the transgressors. — Christ was once offered to bear the sins of many. — Who his own self bare our sins in his own body on the tree, that we, being dead to sins, should live unto righteousness: by whose stripes ye were healed. — By one offering he hath perfected for ever them that are sanctified. — This man, because he continueth ever, hath an unchangeable priesthood. Wherefore he is able also to save them to the uttermost that come unto God by him, seeing he ever liveth to make intercession for them. — While we were yet sinners Christ died for us. Much more then, being now justified by his blood, we shall be saved from wrath through him. — Forasmuch...as Christ hath suffered for us in the flesh, arm yourselves likewise with the same mind: for he that hath suffered in the flesh hath ceased from sin; that he no longer should live the rest of his time in the flesh to the lusts of men, but to the will of God.

Isaiah 53:12   Hebrews 9:28   1 Peter 2:24
Hebrews 10:14, 7:24,25   Romans 5:8,9   1 Peter 4:1,2

JULY 22 EVENING

Keep yourselves in the love of God.
— JUDE 21

Abide in me, and I in you. As the branch cannot bear fruit of itself, except it abide in the vine; no more can ye, except ye abide in me. I am the vine, ye are the branches: He that abideth in me, and I in him, the same bringeth forth much fruit: for without me ye can do nothing. — The fruit of the Spirit is love. — Herein is my Father glorified, that ye bear much fruit; so shall ye be my disciples. As the Father hath loved me, so have I loved you: continue ye in my love. If ye keep my commandments, ye shall abide in my love; even as I have kept my Father's commandments, and abide in his love. — Whoso keepeth his word, in him verily is the love of God perfected. — This is my commandment, That ye love one another, as I have loved you. — God commendeth his love toward us, in that, while we were yet sinners, Christ died for us. — God is love; and he that dwelleth in love dwelleth in God, and God in him.

John 15:4,5   Galatians 5:22   John 15:8-10
1 John 2:5   John 15:12   Romans 5:8   1 John 4:16

JULY 23 MORNING

Then cometh the end.
— *1 CORINTHIANS 15:24*

Of that day and that hour knoweth no man, no, not the angels which are in heaven, neither the Son, but the Father. Take ye heed, watch and pray: for ye know not when the time is. And what I say unto you I say unto all, Watch. — The Lord is not slack concerning his promise, as some men count slackness; but is longsuffering to us-ward, not willing that any should perish, but that all should come to repentance. — The coming of the Lord draweth nigh. The judge standeth before the door. — Surely I come quickly. — Seeing...that all these things shall be dissolved, what manner of persons ought ye to be in all holy conversation and godliness? — The end of all things is at hand: be ye therefore sober, and watch unto prayer. — Let your loins be girded about, and your lights burning; and ye yourselves like unto men that wait for their lord, when he will return from the wedding; that when he cometh and knocketh, they may open unto him immediately.

Matthew 13:32,33,37 2 Peter 3:9 James 5:8,9 Revelation 22:20
2 Peter 3:11 1 Peter 4:7 Luke 12:35,36

JULY 23 EVENING

Brethren, pray for us.
— *1 THESSALONIANS 5:25*

Is any sick among you? let him call for the elders of the church; and let them pray over him. And the prayer of faith shall save the sick, and the Lord shall raise him up. Pray one for another, that ye may be healed. The effectual fervent prayer of a righteous man availeth much. Elias was a man subject to like passions as we are, and he prayed earnestly that it might not rain: and it rained not on the earth by the space of three years and six months. And he prayed again, and the heaven gave rain, and the earth brought forth her fruit. — Praying always with all prayer and supplication in the Spirit, and watching thereunto with all perseverance and supplication for all saints. — Without ceasing I make mention of you always in my prayers. — Always labouring fervently for you in prayers, that ye may stand perfect and complete in all the will of God.

James 5:14-18 Ephesians 6:18 Romans 1:9 Colossians 4:12

JULY 24 MORNING

Patient in tribulation.
— ROMANS 12:12

It is the Lord: let him do what seemeth him good. — Whom, though I were righteous, yet would I not answer, but I would make supplication to my judge. — The Lord gave, and the Lord hath taken away; blessed be the name of the Lord. — What? Shall we receive good at the hand of God, and shall we not receive evil? — Jesus wept. — A man of sorrows, and acquainted with grief. Surely he hath borne our griefs, and carried our sorrows. — Whom the Lord loveth he chasteneth, and scourgeth every son whom he receiveth. Now no chastening for the present seemeth to be joyous, but grievous: nevertheless, afterward it yieldeth the peaceable fruit of righteousness unto them which are exercised thereby. — Strengthened with all might, according to his glorious power, unto all patience and longsuffering with joyfulness. — In the world ye shall have tribulation: but be of good cheer; I have overcome the world.

1 Samuel 3:18   Job 9:15, 1:21, 2:10   John 11:35
Isaiah 53:3,4   Hebrews 12:6,11   Colossians 1:11   John 16:33

JULY 24 EVENING

He staggered not at the promise of God through unbelief.
— ROMANS 4:20

Have faith in God. Whosoever shall say unto this mountain, Be thou removed, and be thou cast into the sea; and shall not doubt in his heart, but shall believe that those things which he saith shall come to pass; he shall have whatsoever he saith. Therefore I say unto you, What things soever ye desire, when ye pray, believe that ye receive them, and ye shall have them. — Without faith it is impossible to please him: for he that cometh to God, must believe that he is, and that he is a rewarder of them that diligently seek him. — He that had received the promises offered up his only begotten son, of whom it was said, That in Isaac shall thy seed be called: accounting that God was able to raise him up, even from the dead. — Being fully persuaded that, what he had promised, he was able also to perform. — Is any thing too hard for the Lord? — With God all things are possible. — Lord, increase our faith.

Mark 11:22-24   Hebrews 11:6,17-19   Romans 4:21
Genesis 18:14   Matthew 19:26   Luke 17:5

JULY 25 MORNING

We know that we have passed from death unto life.
— 1 JOHN 3:14

He that heareth my word and believeth on him that sent me hath everlasting life, and shall not come into condemnation; but is passed from death unto life. — He that hath the Son hath life, and he that hath not the Son of God hath not life. — He which stablisheth us with you in Christ and hath anointed us, is God; who hath also sealed us, and given the earnest of the Spirit in our hearts. — Hereby we know that we are of the truth and shall assure our hearts before him. Beloved, if our heart condemn us not, then have we confidence toward God. — We know that we are of God, and the whole world lieth in wickedness. — You hath he quickened, who were dead in trespasses and sin. — Quickened... together with Christ. — Who hath delivered us from the power of darkness, and hath translated us into the kingdom his dear Son.

John 5:24   1 John 5:12   2 Corinthians 1:21,22
1 John 3:19,21, 5:19   Ephesians 2:1,5   Colossians 1:13

JULY 25 EVENING

Thou wilt shew me the path of life.
— PSALM 16:11

Thus saith the Lord; Behold, I set before you the way of life and the way of death. — I will teach you the good and the right way. — I am the way, the truth, and the life: no man cometh unto the Father, but by me. — Follow me. — There is a way which seemeth right unto a man, but the ends thereof are the ways of death. — Wide is the gate, and broad is the way, that leadeth to destruction, and many there be which go in thereat: because strait is the gate, and narrow is the way, that leadeth unto life, and few there be that find it. — An highway shall be there, and a way, and it shall be called The Way of Holiness; the unclean shall not pass over it; but it shall be for those: the wayfaring men, though fools, shall not err therein. — Then shall we know, if we follow on to know the Lord. — In my Father's house are many mansions: if it were not so I would have told you. I go to prepare a place for you.

Jeremiah 21:8   1 Samuel 12:23   John 14:6   Matthew 14:19
Proverbs 4:12   Matthew 7:13,14   Isaiah 35:8   Hosea 6:3   John 14:2

JULY 26 MORNING

*By faith Abraham...called to go out into a place
which he should after receive for an inheritance, obeyed.*
— HEBREWS 11:8

He shall choose our inheritance for us. — He led him about, he instructed him, he kept him as the apple of his eye. As an eagle stirreth up her nest, fluttereth over her young, spreadeth abroad her wings, taketh them, beareth them on her wings: so the Lord alone did lead him, and there was no strange god with him. — I am the Lord thy God which teacheth thee to profit, which leadeth thee by the way that thou shouldest go. — Who teacheth like Him? — We walk by faith, not by sight. — Here have we no continuing city, but we seek one to come. — Dearly beloved, I beseech you as strangers and pilgrims, abstain from fleshly lusts, which war against the soul. — Arise ye and depart; for this is not your rest: because it is polluted, it shall destroy you, even with a sore destruction.

Psalm 47:4   Deuteronomy 32:10-12   Isaiah 48:17   Job 36:22
2 Corinthians 5:7   Hebrews 13:14 1   Peter 2:11   Micah 2:10

JULY 26 EVENING

Give thanks at the remembrance of his holiness.
— PSALM 97:12

The heavens are not clean in his sight. How much more abominable and filthy is man, which drinketh iniquity like water? — Yea, the stars are not pure in his sight. How much less man, that is a worm? — Who is like unto thee, O Lord, among the gods? Who is like thee, glorious in holiness? — Holy, holy, holy, is the Lord of hosts. — As he which hath called you is holy, so be ye holy in all manner of conversation; because it is written, Be ye holy; for I am holy. — Partakers of his holiness. — The temple of God is holy, which temple ye are. — What manner of persons ought ye to be in all holy conversation and godliness... without spot, and blameless? — Let no corrupt communication proceed out of your mouth, but that which is good to the use of edifying. And grieve not the holy Spirit of God, whereby ye are sealed unto the day of redemption.

Job 15:15,16, 25:5,6   Exodus 15:11   Isaiah 6:3 1   Peter 1:15,16
Hebrews 12:10 1   Corinthians 3:17 2   Peter 3:11,14   Ephesians 4:29,30

JULY 27 MORNING

Christ, who is the image of God.
— 2 CORINTHIANS 4:4

The glory of the Lord shall be revealed, and all flesh shall see it together. — No man hath seen God at any time; the only begotten Son, which is in the bosom of the Father, he hath declared him. And the Word was made flesh, and dwelt among us, (and we beheld his glory, the glory as of the only begotten of the Father,) full of grace and truth. — He that hath seen me hath seen the Father. — The brightness of his glory, and the express image of his person. — God was manifest in the flesh. — In whom we have redemption through his blood, even the forgiveness of sins: who is the image of the invisible God, the firstborn of every creature. — Whom he did foreknow, he also did predestinate to be conformed to the image of his Son, that he might be the firstborn among many brethren. — As we have borne the image of the earthy, we shall also bear the image of the heavenly.

Isaiah 40:5   John 1:18,14, 14:9   Hebrews 1:3 1   Timothy 3:16
Colossians 1:14,15   Romans 8:29 1   Corinthians 15:49

JULY 27 EVENING

Thou hast girded me with strength unto the battle.
— PSALM 18:39

When I am weak, then am I strong. — Asa cried unto the Lord his God, and said, Lord, it is nothing with thee to help, whether with many, or with them that have no power: help us, O Lord our God; for we rest on thee, and in thy name we go against this multitude. O Lord, thou art our God; let not man prevail against thee. — Jehoshaphat cried out, and the Lord helped him. — It is better to trust in the Lord than to put confidence in man. It is better to trust in the Lord than to put confidence in princes. — There is no king saved by the multitude of an host: a mighty man is not delivered by much strength. An horse is a vain thing for safety: neither shall he deliver any by his great strength. — We wrestle not against flesh and blood, but against principalities, against powers, against the rulers of the darkness of this world, against spiritual wickedness in high places. Wherefore take unto you the whole armour of God.

2 Corinthians 12:10 2   Chronicles 14:11, 18:31
Psalms 118:8,9, 33:16,17   Ephesians 6:12,13

JULY 28 MORNING

Walk in love.
— EPHESIANS 5:2

A new commandment I give unto you, That ye love one another; as I have loved you, that ye also love one another. — Above all things have fervent charity among yourselves: for charity shall cover the multitude of sins. — Love covereth all sins. — When ye stand praying, forgive, if ye have ought against any: that your Father also which is in heaven may forgive you your trespasses. — Love ye your enemies, and do good, and lend, hoping for nothing again. — Rejoice not when thine enemy falleth, and let not thine heart be glad when he stumbleth. — Not rendering evil for evil, or railing for railing: but contrary-wise blessing; knowing that ye are thereunto called, that ye should inherit a blessing. — If it be possible, as much as lieth in you, live peaceably with all men. — Be ye kind one to another, tender-hearted, forgiving one another, even as God for Christ's sake hath forgiven you. — My little children, let us not love in word, neither in tongue; but in deed and in truth.

John 13:34 1 Peter 4:8 Proverbs 10:12 Mark 11:25 Luke 6:35 Proverbs 24:17 1 Peter 3:9 Romans 12:18 Ephesians 4:32 1 John 3:18

JULY 28 EVENING

Let your requests be made known unto God.
— PHILIPPIANS 4:6

Abba, Father, all things are possible unto thee; take away this cup from me: nevertheless not what I will, but what thou wilt. — There was given to me a thorn in the flesh. For this thing I besought the Lord thrice, that it might depart from me. And he said unto me, My grace is sufficient for thee: for my strength is made perfect in weakness. Most gladly therefore will I rather glory in my infirmities. — I poured out my complaint before him; I shewed before him my trouble. — Hannah...was in bitterness of soul, and prayed unto the Lord, and wept sore. And she vowed a vow, and said, O Lord of hosts, if thou wilt indeed look on the affliction of thine handmaid, and...wilt give unto thine handmaid a man child, then I will give him unto the Lord all the days of his life. The Lord remembered her. — We know not what we should pray for as we ought. — He shall choose our inheritance for us.

Mark 14:36 2 Corinthians 12:7-9 Psalm 142:2 1 Samuel 1:9-11,20 Romans 8:26 Psalm 47:4

JULY 29 MORNING

*Oh that thou wouldest rend the heavens,
that thou wouldest come down.*
— ISAIAH 64:1

Make haste, my beloved, and be thou like to a roe or to a young hart upon the mountains of spices. — We ourselves groan within ourselves, waiting for the adoption, to wit, the redemption of our body. — Bow thy heavens, O Lord, and come down: touch the mountains, and they shall smoke. — This same Jesus, which is taken up from you into heaven, shall so come in like manner as ye have seen him go into heaven. — Unto them that look for him shall he appear the second time without sin unto salvation. — It shall be said in that day, Lo, this is our God; we have waited for him, and he will save us: this is the Lord; we have waited for him, we will be glad and rejoice in his salvation. — He which testifieth these things saith, Surely I come quickly. Amen. Even so, come, Lord Jesus. — That blessed hope...the glorious appearing of the great God and our Saviour Jesus Christ. — Our conversation is in heaven.

Song of Solomon 8:14   Romans 8:23   Psalm 144:5   Acts 1:11   Hebrews 9:28
Isaiah 25:9   Revelation 22:20   Titus 2:13   Philippians 3:20

JULY 29 EVENING

*Thou hast given me the heritage
of those that fear thy name.*
— PSALM 61:5

No weapon that is formed against thee shall prosper; and every tongue that shall rise against thee in judgment thou shalt condemn. This is the heritage of the servants of the Lord, and their righteousness is of me, saith the Lord. — The angel of the Lord encampeth round about them that fear him, and delivereth them. O taste and see that the Lord is good: blessed is the man that trusteth in him. O fear the Lord, ye his saints: for there is no want to them that fear him. The young lions do lack, and suffer hunger: but they that seek the Lord shall not want any good thing. — The lines are fallen unto me in pleasant places; yea, I have a goodly heritage. — Unto you that fear my name shall the Sun of righteousness arise with healing in his wings: and ye shall go forth, and grow up as calves of the stall. — He that spared not his own Son, but delivered him up for us all, how shall he not with him also freely give us all things?

Isaiah 54:17   Psalms 34:7-10, 16:6   Malachi 4:2   Romans 8:32

JULY 30 MORNING

*Seek those things which are above,
where Christ sitteth on the right hand of God.*
— COLOSSIANS 3:1

Get wisdom, get understanding. — The wisdom that is from above. — The depth saith, It is not in me: and the sea saith, It is not with me. — We are buried with him by baptism into death: that like as Christ was raised up from the dead by the glory of the Father, even so we also should walk in newness of life. For if we have been planted together in the likeness of his death, we shall be also in the likeness of his resurrection. — Let us lay aside every weight, and the sin which doth so easily beset us, and let us run with patience the race that is set before us. — God…hath quickened us together with Christ…and hath raised us up together, and made us sit together in heavenly places in Christ Jesus. — They that say such things declare plainly that they seek a country. — Seek ye the Lord, all ye meek of the earth, which have wrought his judgment; seek righteousness, seek meekness.

Proverbs 4:5   James 3:17   Job 28:14   Romans 6:4,5   Hebrews 12:1
Ephesians 2:4-6   Hebrews 11:14   Zephaniah 2:3

JULY 30 EVENING

Nicodemus…he that came to Jesus by night.
— JOHN 7:50

Peter followed him afar off. — Among the chief rulers also many believed on him; but because of the Pharisees they did not confess him, lest they should be put out of the synagogue: for they loved the praise of men more than the praise of God. — The fear of man bringeth a snare: but whoso putteth his trust in the Lord shall be safe. — Him that cometh to me I will in no wise cast out. — A bruised reed shall he not break, and the smoking flax shall he not quench. — Faith as a grain of mustard seed. — God hath not given us the spirit of fear; but of power, and of love, and of a sound mind. Be not thou therefore ashamed of the testimony of our Lord. — Little children, abide in him; that, when he shall appear, we may have confidence, and not be ashamed before him at his coming. — Whosoever…shall confess me before men, him will I confess also before my Father which is in heaven.

Matthew 26:58   John 12:42,43   Proverbs 29:25   John 6:37   Isaiah 42:3
Matthew 17:20   2 Timothy 1:7,8   1 John 2:28   Matthew 10:32

JULY 31 MORNING

Endure hardness, as a good soldier of Jesus Christ.
— 2 TIMOTHY 2:3

I have given him for a witness to the people, a leader and a commander to the people. — It became him, for whom are all things and by whom are all things, in bringing many sons unto glory, to make the captain of their salvation perfect through suffering. — We must through much tribulation enter into the kingdom of God. — We wrestle not against flesh and blood, but against principalities, against powers, against the rulers of the darkness of this world, against spiritual wickedness in high places. Wherefore take unto you the whole armour of God. — We do not war after the flesh: (for the weapons of our warfare are not carnal, but mighty through God to the pulling down of strongholds). — The God of all grace, who hath called us unto his eternal glory by Christ Jesus, after that ye have suffered a while, make you perfect, stablish, strengthen, settle you.

Isaiah 55:4   Hebrews 2:10   Acts 14:22
Ephesians 6:12,13 2 Corinthians 10:3,4 1 Peter 5:10

JULY 31 EVENING

The unity of the Spirit.
— EPHESIANS 4:3

There is one body, and one Spirit. — Through him we both have access by one Spirit unto the Father. Now therefore ye are no more strangers and foreigners, but fellow-citizens with the saints and of the household of God; and are built upon the foundation of the apostles and prophets, Jesus Christ himself being the chief cornerstone; in whom all the building fitly framed together groweth unto an holy temple in the Lord: in whom ye also are builded together for an habitation of God through the Spirit. — Behold, how good and how pleasant it is for brethren to dwell together in unity! It is like the precious ointment upon the head that ran down upon the beard, even Aaron's beard; that went down to the skirts of his garments. — Seeing ye have purified your souls in obeying the truth through the Spirit unto unfeigned love of the brethren, see that ye love one another with a pure heart fervently.

Ephesians 4:4, 2:18-22   Psalm 133:1,2 1 Peter 1:22

AUGUST 1 MORNING

The fruit of the Spirit is...faith.
— GALATIANS 5:22

By grace are ye saved through faith; and that not of yourselves: it is the gift of God. — Without faith it is impossible to please him. — He that believeth on him is not condemned: but he that believeth not is condemned already, because he hath not believed in the name of the only begotten Son of God. — Lord, I believe; help thou mine unbelief. — Whoso keepeth his word, in him verily is the love of God perfected: hereby know we that we are in him. — Faith worketh by love. — Faith without works is dead. — We walk by faith, not by sight. — I am crucified with Christ: nevertheless I live; yet not I, but Christ liveth in me: and the life which I now live in the flesh I live by the faith of the Son of God, who loved me, and gave himself for me. — Whom having not seen, ye love; in whom, though now ye see him not, yet believing, ye rejoice with joy unspeakable and full of glory; receiving the end of your faith, even the salvation of your souls.

Ephesians 2:8   Hebrews 11:6   John 3:18   Mark 9:24   1 John 2:5   Galatians 5:6   James 2:20   2 Corinthians 5:7   Galatians 2:20   1 Peter 1:8,9

AUGUST 1 EVENING

The Lord is very pitiful, and of tender mercy.
— JAMES 5:11

Like as a father pitieth his children, so the Lord pitieth them that fear him. — The Lord is gracious and full of compassion. He will ever be mindful of his covenant. — He that keepeth thee will not slumber. Behold, he that keepeth Israel shall neither slumber nor sleep. — As an eagle stirreth up her nest, fluttereth over her young, spreadeth abroad her wings, taketh them, beareth them on her wings: so the Lord alone did lead him, and there was no strange god with him. — His compassions fail not. They are new every morning: great is thy faithfulness. — Jesus went forth, and saw a great multitude, and was moved with compassion toward them, and he healed their sick. — The same yesterday, and today, and forever. — The very hairs of your head are all numbered. Are not two sparrows sold for a farthing? And one of them shall not fall on the ground without your Father. Fear ye not, therefore.

Psalms 103:13, 111:4,5, 121:3,4   Deuteronomy 32:11,12   Lamentations 3:22,23   Matthew 14:14   Hebrews 13:8   Matthew 10:30,29,31

AUGUST 2 MORNING

The Lamb slain from the foundation of the world.
— REVELATION 13:8

Your lamb shall be without blemish...and the whole assembly of the congregation of Israel shall kill it in the evening. And they shall take of the blood, and strike it on the two side posts and on the upper door post of the houses, wherein they shall eat it...and when I see the blood, I will pass over you. — The blood of sprinkling. — Christ our passover is sacrificed for us. — Being delivered by the determinate counsel and foreknowledge of God. — According to his own purpose and grace, which was given us in Christ Jesus before the world began. — We have redemption through his blood, the forgiveness of sins. — Forasmuch then as Christ hath suffered for us in the flesh, arm yourselves likewise with the same mind: for he that hath suffered in the flesh hath ceased from sin; that he no longer should live the rest of his time in the flesh to the lusts of men, but to the will of God.

Exodus 12:5-7,13   Hebrews 12:24 2   Corinthians 5:7   Acts 2:23
2 Timothy 1:9   Ephesians 1:7 1   Peter 4:1,2

AUGUST 2 EVENING

I have trodden the winepress alone.
— ISAIAH 63:3

Who is like unto thee, O Lord, among the gods? Who is like thee, glorious in holiness, fearful in praises, doing wonders? — He saw that there was no man, and wondered that there was no intercessor: therefore his arm brought salvation unto him; and his righteousness, it sustained him. — Who his own self bare our sins in his own body on the tree. — Being made a curse for us. — O sing unto the Lord a new song; for he hath done marvellous things: his right hand, and his holy arm, hath gotten him the victory. — Having spoiled principalities and powers, he made a shew of them openly, triumphing over them in it. — He shall see of the travail of his soul, and shall be satisfied: by his knowledge shall my righteous servant justify many; for he shall bear their iniquities. — O my soul, thou hast trodden down strength. — We are more than conquerors through him that loved us. — They overcame by the blood of the Lamb, and by the word of their testimony.

Exodus 15:11   Isaiah 59:16 1   Peter 2:24   Galatians 3:13   Psalm 98:1
Colossians 2:15   Isaiah 53:11   Judges 5:21   Romans 8:37   Revelation 12:11

AUGUST 3 MORNING

His mercy is on them that fear Him.
— LUKE 1:50

Oh how great is thy goodness, which thou hast laid up for them that fear thee; which thou hast wrought for them that trust in thee before the sons of men! Thou shalt hide them in the secret of thy presence from the pride of man: thou shalt keep them secretly in a pavilion from the strife of tongues. —If ye call on the Father, who without respect of persons judgeth according to every man's work, pass the time of your sojourning here in fear. — The Lord is nigh unto all them that call upon him in truth. He will fulfil the desire of them that fear him: he also will hear their cry, and will save them. — Because thine heart was tender, and thou hast humbled thyself before the Lord...and hast rent thy clothes, and wept before me; I also have heard thee, saith the Lord. — To this man will I look, even to him that is poor and of a contrite spirit, and trembleth at my word. — The Lord is nigh unto them that are of a broken heart; and saveth such as be of a contrite spirit.

Psalm 31:19,20 1 Peter 1:17 Psalm 145:18,19
2 Kings 22:19 Isaiah 66:2 Psalm 34:18

AUGUST 3 EVENING

Them that honour me I will honour.
— 1 SAMUEL 2:30

Whosoever...shall confess me before men, him will I confess also before my Father which is in heaven. — He that loveth father or mother more than me is not worthy of me: and he that loveth son or daughter more than me is not worthy of me. And he that taketh not his cross, and followeth after me, is not worthy of me. He that findeth his life shall lose it: and he that loseth his life for my sake shall find it. — Blessed is the man that endureth temptation: for when he is tried, he shall receive the crown of life, which the Lord hath promised to them that love him. — Fear none of these things which thou shalt suffer. Be thou faithful unto death, and I will give thee a crown of life. — Our light affliction, which is but for a moment, worketh for us a far more exceeding and eternal weight of glory. — Praise and honour and glory at the appearing of Jesus Christ.

Matthew 10:32,37-39 James 1:12
Revelation 2:10 2 Corinthians 4:17 1 Peter 1:7

AUGUST 4 MORNING

It is finished:
and he bowed his head, and gave up the ghost.
— JOHN 19:30

Jesus the author and finisher of our faith. — I have glorified thee on the earth: I have finished the work which thou gavest me to do. — We are sanctified through the offering of the body of Jesus Christ once for all. And every priest standeth daily ministering an offering oftentimes the same sacrifices, which can never take away sins: but this man, after he had offered one sacrifice for sins for ever, sat down on the right hand of God; from henceforth expecting till his enemies be made his footstool. For by one offering he hath perfected for ever them that are sanctified. — Blotting out the handwriting of ordinances that was against us, which was contrary to us, and took it out of the way, nailing it to his cross. — I lay down my life, that I might take it again. No man taketh it from me, but I lay it down of myself. I have power to lay it down, and I have power to take it again. — Greater love hath no man than this, that a man lay down his life for his friends.

Hebrews 12:2   John 17:4   Hebrews 10:10-14
Colossians 2:14   John 10:17,18, 15:13

AUGUST 4 EVENING

He sent from above, he took me,
he drew me out of many waters.
— PSALM 18:16

He brought me up...out of an horrible pit, out of the miry clay, and set my feet upon a rock, and established my goings. — You hath he quickened, who were dead in trespasses and sins wherein in time past ye walked according to the course of this world. We all had our conversation in times past in the lusts our flesh. — Hear my cry, O God; attend unto my prayer. From the end the earth will I cry unto thee, when my heart is overwhelmed. — Out of the belly of hell cried I, and thou heardest my voice. For thou hadst cast me into the deep, in the midst of the seas; and the floods compassed me about: all thy billows and thy waves passed over me. — We went through fire and through water: thou broughtest us out into a wealthy place. — When thou passest through the waters, I will be with thee; and through the rivers, they shall not overflow thee.

Psalm 40:2   Ephesians 2:1,3   Psalm 61:1,2
Jonah 2:2,3   Psalm 66:12   Isaiah 43:2

AUGUST 5 MORNING

Walk in newness of life.
— ROMANS 6:4

As ye have yielded your members servants to uncleanness and to iniquity unto iniquity; even so now yield your members servants to righteousness unto holiness. — I beseech you...brethren, by the mercies of God, that ye present your bodies a living sacrifice, holy, acceptable unto God, which is your reasonable service. And be not conformed to this world: but be ye transformed by the renewing of your mind. — If any man be in Christ he is a new creature: old things are passed away; behold, all things are become new. — In Christ Jesus neither circumcision availeth anything, nor uncircumcision, but a new creature. And as many as walk according to this rule, peace be on them, and mercy. — This I say therefore, and testify in the Lord, that ye henceforth walk not as other Gentiles walk, in the vanity of their mind. — Ye have not so learned Christ; if so be that ye have heard him, and have been taught by him, as the truth is in Jesus. Put on the new man, which after God is created in righteousness and true holiness.

Romans 6:19, 12:1,2   2 Corinthians 5:17
Galatians 6:15,16   Ephesians 4:17,20,21,24

AUGUST 5 EVENING

Thy will be done.
— MATTHEW 26:42

O Lord, I know that the way of man is not in himself: it is not in man that walketh to direct his steps. — Not as I will, but as thou wilt. — Surely I have behaved and quieted myself, as a child that is weaned of his mother: my soul is even as a weaned child. — We know not what we should pray for as we ought: but the Spirit itself maketh intercession for us with groanings which cannot be uttered. And he that searcheth the hearts knoweth what is the mind of the Spirit, because he maketh intercession for the saints according to the will of God. — Ye know not what ye ask. — He gave them their request; but sent leanness into their soul. — These things were our examples, to the intent we should not lust after evil things, as they also lusted. — I would have you without carefulness. — Thou wilt keep him in perfect peace, whose mind is stayed on thee: because he trusteth in thee.

Jeremiah 10:23   Matthew 26:39   Psalm 131:2   Romans 8:26,27
Matthew 20:22   Psalm 106:15   1 Corinthians 10:6, 7:32   Isaiah 26:3

AUGUST 6 MORNING

Whom the Lord loveth he correcteth.
— PROVERBS 3:12

See now that I, even I, am he, and there is no god with me: I kill, and I make alive; I wound, and I heal: neither is there any that can deliver out of my hand. — I know the thoughts that I think toward you, saith the Lord, thoughts of peace, and not of evil, to give you an expected end. — My thoughts are not your thoughts, neither are your ways my ways, saith the Lord. — I will allure her, and bring her into the wilderness, and speak comfortably unto her. — As a man chasteneth his son, so the Lord thy God chasteneth thee. — Now no chastening for the present, seemeth to be joyous, but grievous: nevertheless afterward it yieldeth the peaceable fruit of righteousness unto them which are exercised thereby. — Humble yourselves therefore under the mighty hand of God, that he may exalt you in due time. — I know, O Lord, that thy judgments are right, and that thou in faithfulness hast afflicted me.

Deuteronomy 32:39   Jeremiah 29:11   Isaiah 55:8   Hosea 2:14
Deuteronomy 8:5   Hebrews 12:11   1 Peter 5:6   Psalm 119:75

AUGUST 6 EVENING

The earth is the Lord's, and the fulness thereof.
— PSALM 24:1

She did not know that I gave her corn, and wine, and oil, and multiplied her silver and gold. Therefore will I return, and take away my corn in the time thereof, and my wine in the season thereof, and I will recover my wool and my flax. — All things come of thee, and of thine own have we given thee. For we are strangers before thee, and sojourners, as were all our fathers: our days on the earth are as a shadow, and there is none abiding. O Lord our God, all this store...cometh of thine hand, and is all thine own. — Of him, and through him, and to him, are all things: to whom be glory for ever. Amen. — The living God...giveth us richly all things to enjoy. — Every creature of God is good, and nothing to be refused, if it be received with thanksgiving: for it is sanctified by the word of God and prayer. — My God shall supply all your need according to his riches in glory by Christ Jesus.

Hosea 2:8,9   1 Chronicles 29:14-16   Romans 11:36
1 Timothy 6:17, 4:4,5   Philippians 4:19

AUGUST 7 MORNING

The Comforter, which is the Holy Ghost,
whom the Father will send in my name.
— JOHN 14:26

If thou knewest the gift of God, and who it is that saith to thee, Give me to drink; thou wouldest have asked of him, and he would have given thee living water. — If ye...being evil, know how to give good gifts unto your children: how much more shall your heavenly Father give the Holy Spirit to them that ask him? — Verily, verily, I say unto you, Whatsoever ye shall ask the Father in my name, he will give it you. Hitherto have ye asked nothing in my name: ask, and ye shall receive, that your joy may be full. — Ye have not, because ye ask not. — When...the Spirit of truth is come, he will guide you into all truth: for he shall not speak of himself; but whatsoever he shall hear, that shall he speak: and he will shew you things to come. He shall glorify me: for he shall receive of mine, and shall shew it unto you. — They rebelled, and vexed his Holy Spirit: therefore he was turned to be their enemy, and He fought against them.

John 4:10   Luke 11:13   John 16:23,24
James 4:2   John 16:13,14   Isaiah 63:10

AUGUST 7 EVENING

What think ye of Christ?
— MATTHEW 22:42

Lift up your heads, O ye gates; even lift them up, ye everlasting doors; and the King of glory shall come in. Who is this King of glory? The Lord of hosts, he is the King of glory. — He hath on his vesture and on his thigh a name written, KING OF KINGS, AND LORD OF LORDS. — Unto you...which believe he is precious: but unto them which be disobedient, the stone which the builders disallowed, the same is made the head of the corner. — Christ crucified, unto the Jews a stumblingblock, and unto the Greeks foolishness; but unto them which are called, both Jews and Greeks, Christ the power of God, and the wisdom of God. — I count all things but loss for the excellency of the knowledge of Christ Jesus my Lord: for whom I have suffered the loss of all things, and do count them but dung, that I may win Christ. — Lord, thou knowest all things: thou knowest that I love thee.

Psalm 24:9,10   Revelation 19:16   1 Peter 2:7
1 Corinthians 1:23,24   Philippians 3:8   John 21:17

AUGUST 8 MORNING

*The path of the just is as the shining light,
that shineth more and more unto the perfect day.*
— PROVERBS 4:18

Not as though I had already attained, either were already perfect: but I follow after, if that I may apprehend that for which also I am apprehended of Christ Jesus. — Then shall we know, if we follow on to know the Lord. —Then shall the righteous shine forth as the sun in the kingdom of their Father. — We all, with open face beholding as in a glass the glory of the Lord, are changed into the same image from glory to glory, even as by the Spirit of the Lord. — When that which is perfect is come, then that which is in part shall be done away. — For now we see through a glass, darkly; but then face to face: now I know in part; but then shall I know even as also I am known. — Beloved, now are we the sons of God; and it doth not yet appear what we shall be: but we know that, when he shall appear, we shall be like him, for we shall see him as he is. And every man that hath this hope in him purifieth himself, even as he is pure.

Philippians 3:12   Hosea 6:3   Matthew 13:43
2 Corinthians 3:18 1   Corinthians 13:10,12 1 John. 3:2,3

AUGUST 8 EVENING

*Whosoever shall call upon the name of the Lord
shall be saved.*
— ROMANS 10:13

Him that cometh to me I will in no wise cast out. — Lord, remember me when thou comest into thy kingdom. And Jesus said unto him, Verily I say unto thee, Today shalt thou be with me in paradise. — What will ye that I shall do unto you? They say unto him, Lord, that our eyes may be opened. So Jesus had compassion on them, and touched their eyes: and immediately their eyes received sight, and they followed him. — If ye...being evil, know how to give good gifts unto your children: how much more shall your heavenly Father give the Holy Spirit to them that ask him? — I will put my Spirit within you. Thus saith the Lord GOD; I will yet for this be enquired of. —This is the confidence that we have in him, that, if we ask any thing according to his will, he heareth us: and if we know that he hear us, whatsoever we ask, we know that we have the petitions that we desired of him.

John 6:37   Luke 23:42,43   Matthew 20:32-34
Luke 11:13   Ezekiel 6:27,37 1   John 5:14,15

AUGUST 9 MORNING

Thou art all fair, my love;
there is no spot in thee.
— SONG OF SOLOMON 4:7

    The whole head is sick, and the whole heart faint. From the sole of the foot even unto the head there is no soundness in it; but wounds, and bruises, and putrifying sores: they have not been closed, neither bound up, neither mollified with ointment. — We are all as an unclean thing, and all our righteousnesses are as filthy rags. — I know that in me (that is, in my flesh,) dwelleth no good thing. — Ye are washed...ye are sanctified...ye are justified in the name of the Lord Jesus, and by the Spirit of our God. — The King's daughter is all glorious within. — Perfect through my comeliness, which I had put upon thee, saith the Lord GOD. — Let the beauty of the Lord our God be upon us. — These are they which...have washed their robes, and made them white in the blood of the Lamb. — A glorious church, not having spot, or wrinkle, or any such thing; but...holy and without blemish. — Ye are complete in him.

Isaiah 1:5,6, 64:6   Romans 7:18 1   Corinthians 6:11   Psalm 45:13   Ezekiel 16:14   Psalm 90:17   Revelation 7:14   Ephesians 5:27   Colossians 2:10

AUGUST 9 EVENING

Broken cisterns, that can hold no water.
— JEREMIAH 2:13

    Eve...bare Cain, and said, I have gotten a man from the Lord. — Go to, let us build us a city and a tower, whose top may reach unto heaven. The Lord scattered them. — Lot chose him all the plain of Jordan; it was well watered every where, even as the garden of the Lord. But the men of Sodom were wicked and sinners before the Lord exceedingly. — I gave my heart to know wisdom, and to know madness and folly: I perceived that this also is vexation of spirit. For in much wisdom is much grief: and he that increaseth knowledge increaseth sorrow. — I made me great works; I builded me houses; I planted me vineyards: I gathered me also silver and gold. Then I looked on all, and, behold, all was vanity and vexation of spirit. — If any man thirst, let him come unto me, and drink. — He satisfieth the longing soul, and filleth the hungry soul with goodness. — Set your affection on things above, not on things on the earth.

Genesis 4:1, 11:4,8, 13:11,10,13   Ecclesiastes 1:17,18, 2:4,8,11   John 7:37   Psalm 107:9   Colossians 3:2

AUGUST 10 MORNING

I pray not that thou shouldest take them out of the world,
but thou shouldest keep them from the evil.
— JOHN 17:15

Blameless and harmless, the sons of God, without rebuke, in the midst of a crooked and perverse nation, among whom ye shine as lights in the world. — Ye are the salt of the earth...the light of the world...Let your light so shine before men, that they may see your good works, and glorify your Father which is heaven. — I also withheld thee from sinning against me. — The Lord is faithful, who shall stablish you, and keep you from evil. — So did not I, because of the fear of God. — Who gave himself for our sins, that he might deliver us from this present evil world, according to the will of God and our Father. — Now unto him that is able to keep you from falling, and to present you faultless before the presence of his glory with exceeding joy, to the only wise God our Saviour, be glory and majesty, dominion and power, both now and ever. Amen.

Philippians 2:15   Matthew 5:13,14,16   Genesis 20:6
2 Thessalonians 3:3   Nehemiah 5:15   Galatians 1:4 Jude 24,25

AUGUST 10 EVENING

Whoso putteth his trust in the Lord
shall be safe (or set on high).
— PROVERBS 29:25

The Lord is exalted; for he dwelleth on high. — The Lord is high above all nations, and his glory above the heavens. He raiseth up the poor out of the dust, and lifteth the needy out of the dunghill; that he may set him with princes. — God, who is rich in mercy, for his great love wherewith He loved us, even when we were dead in sins, hath quickened us together with Christ, (by grace ye are saved;) and hath raised us up together and made us sit together in heavenly places in Christ Jesus. — He that spared not his own Son, but delivered him up for us all, how shall he not with him also freely give us all things? For I am persuaded, that neither death, nor life, nor angels, nor principalities, nor powers, nor things present, nor things to come, nor height, nor depth, nor any other creature, shall be able to separate us from the love of God, which is in Christ Jesus our Lord.

Isaiah 33:5   Psalm 113:4,7,8   Ephesians 2:4-6   Romans 8:32,38,39

AUGUST 11 MORNING

That through death
He might destroy him that had the power of death.
— HEBREWS 2:14

Our Saviour Jesus Christ...hath abolished death, and hath brought life and immortality to light through the gospel. — He will swallow up death in victory; and the Lord GOD shall wipe away the tears from off all faces; and the rebuke of his people shall he take away from off all the earth: for the Lord hath spoken it. — When this corruptible shall have put on incorruption, and this mortal shall have put on immortality, then shall be brought to pass the saying that is written, Death is swallowed up in victory. O death, where is thy sting? O grave, where is thy victory? The sting of death is sin; and the strength of sin is the law. But thanks be to God, which giveth us the victory through our Lord Jesus Christ. — God hath not given us the spirit of fear; but of power, and of love, and of a sound mind. — Yea, though I walk through the valley of the shadow of death, I will fear no evil: for thou art with me; thy rod and thy staff they comfort me.

2 Timothy 1:10   Isaiah 25:8 1 Corinthians 15:54-57 2 Timothy 1:7   Psalm 23:4

AUGUST 11 EVENING

Where is the way that light dwelleth?
— JOB 38:19

God is light, and in him is no darkness at all. — As long as I am in the world, I am the light of the world. — If we say that we have fellowship with him, and walk in darkness, we lie, and do not the truth: but if we walk in the light, as he is in the light, we have fellowship one with another, and the blood of Jesus Christ his Son cleanseth us from all sin. — The Father...hath made us meet to be partakers of the inheritance of the saints in light, who hath delivered us from the power of darkness, and hath translated us into the kingdom of his dear Son; in whom we have redemption through his blood, even the forgiveness of sins. — Ye are all the children of light, and the children of the day: we are not of the night, nor of darkness. — Ye are the light of the world. A city that is set on an hill cannot be hid. Let your light so shine before men, that they may see your good works, and glorify your Father which is in heaven.

1 John 1:5   John 9:5 1 John 1:6,7   Colossians 1:12-14
1 Thessalonians 5:5   Matthew 5:14,16

AUGUST 12 MORNING

The Lord will not cast off for ever:
but though he cause grief, yet will he have compassion.
— *LAMENTATIONS 3:31,32*

Fear thou not...saith the Lord: for I am with thee; I will not make a full end of thee, but correct thee in measure. — For a small moment have I forsaken thee; but with great mercies will I gather thee. In a little wrath I hid my face from thee for a moment; but with everlasting kindness will I have mercy on thee, saith the Lord thy Redeemer. For the mountains shall depart, and the hills be removed; but my kindness shall not depart from thee, neither shall the covenant of my peace be removed, saith the Lord that hath mercy on thee. O thou afflicted, tossed with tempest, and not comforted, behold, I will lay thy stones with fair colours, and lay thy foundations with sapphires. — I will bear the indignation of the Lord, because I have sinned against him, until he plead my cause, and execute judgment for me: he will bring me forth to the light, and I shall behold his righteousness.

Jeremiah 46:28   Isaiah 54:7,8,10,11   Micah 7:9

AUGUST 12 EVENING

God hath chosen the weak things of the world
to confound the things which are mighty.
— *1 CORINTHIANS 1:27*

When the children of Israel cried unto the Lord, the Lord raised them up a deliverer, Ehud...a man left-handed. After him was Shamgar,...which slew of the Philistines six hundred men with an ox goad: and he also delivered Israel. — The Lord looked upon [Gideon], and said, Go in this thy might:...have not I sent thee? And he said unto him, O my Lord, wherewith shall I save Israel? Behold my family is poor in Manasseh, and I am the least in my father's house. — The Lord said unto Gideon, The people that are with thee are too many for me...lest Israel vaunt themselves against me, saying, Mine own hand hath saved me. — Not by might, nor by power, but by my Spirit, saith the Lord of hosts. — My brethren, be strong in the Lord, and in the power of his might.

Judges 3:15,31, 6:14,15, 7:2   Zechariah 4:6   Ephesians 6:10

AUGUST 13 MORNING

He hath prepared for them a city.
— HEBREWS 11:16

If I go and prepare a place for you, I will come again, and receive you unto myself; that where I am, there ye may be also. — An inheritance incorruptible, and undefiled, and that fadeth not away, reserved in heaven for you. — Here have we no continuing city, but we seek one to come. — This same Jesus, which is taken up from you into heaven, shall so come in like manner as ye have seen him go into heaven. — Be patient therefore, brethren, unto the coming of the Lord. — Behold, the husbandman waiteth for the precious fruit of the earth, and hath long patience for it, until he receive the early and latter rain. Be ye also patient; stablish your hearts: for the coming of the Lord draweth nigh. — Yet a little while, and he that shall come will come, and will not tarry. — We which are alive and remain shall be caught up together with them in the clouds, to meet the Lord in the air: and so shall we ever be with the Lord. Wherefore comfort one another with these words.

John 14:3   1 Peter 1:4   Hebrews 13:14   Acts 1:11
James 5:7,8   Hebrews 10:37   1 Thessalonians 4:17,18

AUGUST 13 EVENING

Base things of the world hath God chosen.
— 1 CORINTHIANS 1:28

Be not deceived: neither fornicators, nor idolaters, nor adulterers, nor effeminate, nor abusers of themselves with mankind, nor thieves, nor covetous, nor drunkards, nor revilers, nor extortioners, shall inherit the kingdom of God. And such were some of you: but ye are washed, but ye are sanctified, but ye are justified in the name of the Lord Jesus, and by the Spirit of our God. — You hath he quickened, who were dead in trespasses and sins; wherein in time past ye walked according to the course of this world; among whom also we all had our conversation in times past in the lusts of our flesh, fulfilling the desires of the flesh and of the mind. — According to his mercy he saved us, by the washing of regeneration, and renewing of the Holy Ghost; which he shed on us abundantly through Jesus Christ our Saviour. — My thoughts are not your thoughts, neither are your ways my ways, saith the Lord.

1 Corinthians 6:9-11   Ephesians 2:1-3   Titus 3:5,6   Isaiah 55:8

AUGUST 14 MORNING

The joy of the Lord is your strength.
— NEHEMIAH 8:10

Sing, O heavens; and be joyful, O earth; and break forth with singing, O mountains: for the Lord hath comforted his people and will have mercy upon his afflicted. — Behold, God is my salvation; I will trust, and not be afraid: for the Lord JEHOVAH is my strength and my song; he also is become my salvation. — The Lord is my strength and my shield; my heart trusted in him, and I am helped: therefore my heart greatly rejoiceth; and with my song will I praise him. — My soul shall be joyful in my God; for he hath clothed me with the garments of salvation, he hath covered me with the robe of righteousness, as a bridegroom decketh himself with ornaments, and as a bride adorneth herself with her jewels. — I have therefore whereof I may glory through Jesus Christ those things which pertain to God. — We...joy in God through our Lord Jesus Christ, by whom we have now received the atonement. — I will joy in the God of my salvation.

Isaiah 49:13, 12:2   Psalm 28:7   Isaiah 61:10
Romans 15:17   Romans 5:11   Habakkuk 3:18

AUGUST 14 EVENING

He hath made with me an everlasting covenant,
ordered in all things, and sure.
— 2 SAMUEL 23:5

I know whom I have believed, and am persuaded that he able to keep that which I have committed unto him against that day. — Blessed be the God and Father of our Lord Jesus Christ, who hath blessed us with all spiritual blessings in heavenly places Christ: according as he hath chosen us in him before the foundation of the world, that we should be holy and without blame before him in love: having predestinated us unto the adoption of children by Jesus Christ to himself, according to the good pleasure of his will. — We know that all things work together for good to them that love God, to them who are the called according to his purpose. For whom he did foreknow, he also did predestinate to be conformed to the image of his Son. Moreover whom be did predestinate, them he also called: and whom he called, them he also justified: and whom he justified, them he also glorified.

2 Timothy 1:12   Ephesians 1:3-5   Romans 8:28-30

AUGUST 15 MORNING

*The God of peace make you perfect
in every good work to do his will.*
— HEBREWS 13:20,21

Be perfect, be of good comfort, be of one mind, live in peace; and the God of love and peace shall be with you. — By grace are ye saved through faith; and that not of yourselves: it is the gift of God; not of works, lest any man should boast. — Every good gift and every perfect gift is from above, and cometh down from the Father of lights, with whom is no variableness neither shadow of turning. — Work out your own salvation with fear and trembling. For it is God which worketh in you both to will and to do of his good pleasure. — Be ye transformed by the renewing of your mind, that ye may prove what is that good, and acceptable, and perfect, will of God. — Being filled with the fruits of righteousness, which are by Jesus Christ, unto the glory and praise of God. — Not that we are sufficient of ourselves to think anything as of ourselves; but our sufficiency is of God.

2 Corinthians 13:11   Ephesians 2:8,9   James 1:17   Philippians 2:12,13
Romans 12:2   Philippians 1:11   2 Corinthians 3:5

AUGUST 15 EVENING

*I will allure her,
and bring her into the wilderness,
and speak comfortably unto her.*
— HOSEA 2:14

Come out from among them, and be ye separate, saith the Lord, and touch not the unclean thing; and I will receive you, and will be a Father unto you, and ye shall be my sons and daughters, saith the Lord Almighty. — Having therefore these promises, dearly beloved, let us cleanse ourselves from all filthiness of the flesh and spirit, perfecting holiness in the fear of God. — Jesus...that he might sanctify the people with his own blood, suffered without the gate. Let us go forth therefore unto him without the camp, bearing his reproach. — [Jesus] said... Come ye yourselves apart into a desert place, and rest a while. — The Lord is my shepherd; I shall not want. He maketh me to lie down in green pastures: he leadeth me beside the still waters. He restoreth my soul: he leadeth me in the paths of righteousness for his name's sake.

2 Corinthians 6:17,15, 7:1   Hebrews 13:12,13   Mark 6:31   Psalm 23:1-3

AUGUST 16 MORNING

The house that is to be builded for the Lord
must be exceeding magnifical.
— *1 CHRONICLES 22:5*

Ye...as lively stones, are built up a spiritual house. — Know ye not that ye are the temple of God, and that the Spirit of God dwelleth in you? If any man defile the temple of God, him shall God destroy; for the temple of God is holy, which temple ye are. — Your body is the temple of the Holy Ghost which is in you, which ye have of God, and ye are not your own. For ye are bought with a price: therefore glorify God in your body and in your spirit, which are God's. — What agreement hath the temple of God with idols? For ye are the temple of the living God; as God has said, I will dwell in them, and walk in them; and I will be their God, and they shall be my people. — Ye...are built upon the foundation of the apostles and prophets, Jesus Christ himself being the chief cornerstone; in whom all the building fitly framed together groweth unto a holy temple in the Lord: in whom ye also are builded together for a habitation of God through the Spirit.

1 Peter 2:5 1 Corinthians 3:16,17, 6:19,20
2 Corinthians 6:16 Ephesians 2:19-22

AUGUST 16 EVENING

He is before all things.
— *COLOSSIANS 1:17*

The Amen; the beginning of the creation of God. — The beginning, the firstborn from the dead; that in all things he might have the pre-eminence. — The Lord possessed me in the beginning of his way, before his works of old. I was set up from everlasting, from the beginning, or ever the earth was. When he prepared the heavens, I was there: when he set a compass upon the face of the depth: when he established the clouds above: when he strengthened the fountains of the deep; when he gave to the sea his decree, that the waters should not pass his commandment. I was daily his delight rejoicing always before him. — Yea, before the day was I am he. — The Lamb slain from the foundation of the world. — The author and finisher of our faith; who for the joy that was set before him, endured the cross, despising the shame, and is set down at the right hand of the throne of God.

Revelation 3:14 Colossians 1:18 Proverbs 8:22,23,27,30
Isaiah 43:13 Revelation 13:8 Hebrews 12:2

AUGUST 17 MORNING

Pray one for another, that ye may be healed.
— JAMES 5:16

Abraham answered and said, Behold now, I have taken upon me to speak unto the Lord, which am but dust and ashes: peradventure there shall lack five of the fifty righteous: wilt thou destroy all city for lack of five? And he said, If I find there forty and five, I will not destroy it. —Father, forgive them; for they know not what they do. — Pray for them which despitefully use you, and persecute you. — I pray for them: I pray not for the world, but for them which thou hast given me; for they are thine. Neither pray I for these alone, but for them also which shall believe on me through their word. — Bear ye one another's burdens, and so fulfil the law of Christ. — The effectual fervent prayer of a righteous man availeth much. Elias was a man subject to like passions as we are, and he prayed earnestly that it might not rain: and it rained not on the earth by the space of three years and six months.

Genesis 18:27,28   Luke 23:34   Matthew 5:44
John 17:9,20   Galatians 6:2   James 5:16,17

AUGUST 17 EVENING

As for man, his days are as grass:
as a flower of the field, so he flourisheth.
For the wind passeth over it, and it is gone;
and the place thereof shall know it no more.
— PSALM 103:15,16

So teach us to number our days, that we may apply our hearts to wisdom. — What shall it profit a man, if he shall gain the whole world, and lose his own soul? —Surely the people is grass. The grass withereth, the flower fadeth: but the word of our God shall stand for ever. — The world passeth away, and the lust thereof: but he that doeth the will of God abideth for ever. —Behold, now is the accepted time; behold, now is the day of salvation. — Use this world, as not abusing it: for the fashion of this world passeth away. — Let us consider one another to provoke unto love and to good works: not forsaking the assembling of ourselves together, as the manner of some is; but exhorting one another; and so much the more, as ye see the day approaching.

Psalm 90:12   Mark 8:36   Isaiah 40:7,8 1   John 2:17
2 Corinthians 6:2 1   Corinthians 7:31   Hebrews 10:24,25

AUGUST 18 MORNING

What God is there in heaven or in earth,
that can do according to thy works,
and according to thy might?
— DEUTERONOMY 3:24

Who in the heaven can be compared unto the Lord? Who among the sons of the mighty can be likened unto the Lord? O Lord God of hosts, who is a strong Lord like unto thee? Or to thy faithfulness round about thee? —Among the gods there is none like unto thee, O Lord; neither are there any works like unto thy works. — For thy word's sake, and according to thine own heart hast thou done all these great things, to make thy servant know them. Wherefore thou art great, O Lord God: for there is none like thee, neither is there any God beside thee, according to all that we have heard with our ears. — Eye hath not seen, nor ear heard, neither have entered into the heart of man, the things which God hath prepared for them that love him. But God hath revealed them unto us by his Spirit. — The secret things belong unto the Lord our God: but those thing which are revealed belong unto us and to our children.

Psalms 89:6,8, 86:8 2 Samuel 7:21,22 1 Corinthians 2:9,10 Deuteronomy 29:29

AUGUST 18 EVENING

He that glorieth, let him glory in the Lord.
— 1 CORINTHIANS 1:31

Let not the wise man glory in his wisdom, neither let the mighty man glory in his might, let not the rich man glory in his riches: but let him that glorieth glory in this, that he understandeth and knoweth me, that I am the Lord. — I count all things but loss for the excellency of the knowledge of Christ Jesus my Lord: for whom I have suffered the loss of all things, and do count them but dung, that I may win Christ. — I am not ashamed of the gospel of Christ: for it is the power of God unto salvation to every one that believeth. — I have whereof I may glory through Jesus Christ in those things which pertain to God. — Whom have I in heaven but thee? And there is none upon earth that I desire beside thee. — My heart rejoiceth in the Lord....I rejoice in thy salvation. — Not unto us, O Lord, not unto us, but unto thy name give glory, for thy mercy, and for thy truth's sake.

Jeremiah 9:23,24 Philippians 3:8 Romans 1:16, 15:17 Psalm 73:25 1 Samuel 2:1 Psalm 115:1

AUGUST 19 MORNING

As he which hath called you is holy,
so be ye holy in all manner of conversation.
— 1 PETER 1:15

Ye know how we exhorted...and charged every one of you, that ye would walk worthy of God, who hath called you unto his kingdom and glory. — Ye should shew forth the praises of him who hath called you out of darkness into his marvellous light. — Ye were sometime darkness, but now are ye light in the Lord: walk as children of light: (for the fruit of the Spirit is in all goodness and righteousness and truth;) proving what is acceptable unto the Lord. And have no fellowship with the unfruitful works of darkness, but rather reprove them. — Being filled with the fruits of righteousness, which are by Jesus Christ, unto the glory and praise of God. — Let your light so shine before men, that they may see your good works, and glorify your Father which is in heaven. — Whether therefore ye eat, or drink, or whatsoever ye do, do all to the glory of God.

1 Thessalonians 2:11,12   1 Peter 2:9   Ephesians 5:8-11
Philippians 1:11   Matthew 5:16   1 Corinthians 10:31

AUGUST 19 EVENING

Ask me of things to come concerning my sons,
and concerning the work of my hands command ye me.
— ISAIAH 45:11

A new heart...will I give you, and a new spirit will I put within you: and I will take away the stony heart out of your flesh, and I will give you an heart of flesh. And I will put my Spirit within you, and cause you to walk in my statutes. Thus saith the Lord God; I will yet for this be enquired of by the house of Israel, to do it for them. — If two of you shall agree on earth as touching anything that they shall ask, it shall be done for them of my Father which is in heaven. For where two or three are gathered together in my name, there am I in the midst of them. —Have faith in God. Verily I say unto you, That whosoever shall say unto this mountain, Be thou removed, and be thou cast into the sea; and shall not doubt in his heart, but shall believe that those things which he saith shall come to pass; he shall have whatsoever he saith.

Ezekiel 36:26,27,37   Matthew 18:19,20   Mark 11:22,23

AUGUST 20 MORNING

God is not a man, that he should lie;
neither the son of man, that he should repent.
— NUMBERS 23:19

The Father of lights, with whom is no variableness, neither shadow of turning. — Jesus Christ, the same yesterday, and today, and for ever. — His truth shall be thy shield and buckler. — God, willing more abundantly to shew unto the heirs of promise the immutability of his counsel, confirmed it by an oath; that by two immutable things, in which it was impossible for God to lie, we might have a strong consolation, who have fled for refuge to lay hold upon the hope set before us. — The faithful God, which keepeth covenant and mercy with them that love him and keep his commandments to a thousand generations. — All the paths of the Lord are mercy and truth unto such as keep his covenant and his testimonies. — Happy is he that hath the God of Jacob for his help, whose hope is in the Lord his God…which keepeth truth for ever.

James 1:17   Hebrews 13:8   Psalm 91:4   Hebrews 6:17,18
Deuteronomy 7:9   Psalms 25:10, 146:5,6

AUGUST 20 EVENING

If thou faint in the day of adversity, thy strength is small.
— PROVERBS 24:10

He giveth power to the faint; and to them that have no might he increaseth strength. — My grace is sufficient for thee: for my strength is made perfect in weakness. — He shall call upon me, and I will answer him: I will be with him in trouble; I will deliver him. — The eternal God is thy refuge, and underneath are the everlasting arms: and he shall thrust out the enemy from before thee. — I looked for some to take pity, but there was none; and for comforters, but I found none. — Every high priest taken from among men is ordained for men in things pertaining to God…who can have compassion on the ignorant, and on them that are out of the way: so also Christ…though he were a Son, yet learned he obedience by the things which he suffered; and being made perfect, he became the author of eternal salvation unto all them that obey him. — Surely he hath borne our griefs, and carried our sorrows.

Isaiah 40:29   2 Corinthians 12:9   Psalm 91:15   Deuteronomy 33:27
Psalm 69:20   Hebrews 5:1,2,5,8,9   Isaiah 53:4

AUGUST 21 MORNING

Thou art my portion, O Lord.
— PSALM 119:57

All things are yours;...and ye are Christ's; and Christ is God's. — Our Saviour Jesus Christ...gave himself for us. — God gave him to be the head over all things to the church. — Christ loved the church, and gave himself for it; that he might present it to himself a glorious church, not having spot, or wrinkle, or any such thing; but that it should be holy and without blemish. — My soul shall make her boast in the Lord. — I will greatly rejoice in the Lord, my soul shall be joyful in my God; for he hath clothed me with the garments of salvation, he hath covered me with the robe of righteousness. — Whom have I in heaven but thee? And there is none upon earth that I desire beside thee. My flesh and my heart faileth: but God is the strength of my heart, and my portion for ever. — O my soul, thou hast said unto the Lord, Thou art my Lord. The Lord is the portion of mine inheritance and of my cup: thou maintainest my lot. The lines are fallen unto me in pleasant places; yea, I have a goodly heritage.

1 Corinthians 3:21,23   Titus 2:13,14   Ephesians 1:22, 5:25,27
Psalm 34:2   Isaiah 61:10   Psalms 73:25,26, 16:2,5,6

AUGUST 21 EVENING

*There is a way which seemeth right unto a man,
but the end thereof are the ways of death.*
— PROVERBS 14:12

He that trusteth in his own heart is a fool. — Thy word is a lamp unto my feet, and a light unto my path. — Concerning the works of men, by the word of thy lips I have kept me from the paths of the destroyer. — If there arise among you a prophet, or a dreamer of dreams, saying, Let us go after other gods, which thou hast not known, and let us serve them; thou shalt not hearken unto the words of that prophet: for the Lord your God proveth you, to know whether ye love the Lord your God with all your heart and with all your soul. Ye shall walk after the Lord your God, and fear him, and keep his commandments, and obey his voice, and ye shall serve him, and cleave unto him. — I will instruct thee and teach thee in the way which thou shalt go; I will guide thee with mine eye.

Proverbs 28:26   Psalms 119:105, 17:4   Deuteronomy 13:1-4   Psalm 32:8

AUGUST 22 MORNING

*None of us liveth to himself,
and no man dieth to himself.*
— ROMANS 14:7

Whether we live, we live unto the Lord; and whether we die, we die unto the Lord: whether we live therefore, or die, we are the Lord's. — Let no man seek his own: but every man another's wealth. — Ye are bought with a price: therefore glorify God in your body, and in your spirit, which are God's. — Christ shall be magnified in my body, whether it be by life, or by death. For to me to live is Christ, and to die is gain. But if I live in the flesh, this is the fruit of my labour: yet what I shall choose I wot not. For I am in a strait betwixt two, having a desire to depart, and to be with Christ; which is far better. — I through the law am dead to the law, that I might live unto God. I am crucified with Christ: nevertheless I live; yet not I, but Christ liveth in me: and the life which I now live in the flesh I live by the faith of the Son of God, who loved me, and gave himself for me.

Romans 14:8 1 Corinthians 10:24, 6:20   Philippians 1:20-23   Galatians 2:19,20

AUGUST 22 EVENING

*God gave Solomon...largeness of heart,
even as the sand that is on the sea shore.*
— 1 KINGS 4:29

Behold, a greater than Solomon is here. — The Prince of Peace. — Scarcely for a righteous man will one die: yet peradventure for a good man some would even dare to die. But God commendeth his love toward us, in that, while we were yet sinners, Christ died for us. — Who, being in the form of God, thought it not robbery to be equal with God: but made himself of no reputation, and took upon him the form of a servant, and was made in the likeness of men: and being found in fashion as a man, he humbled himself, and became obedient unto death, even the death of the cross. — The love of Christ passeth knowledge. — Christ the power of God, and the wisdom of God. — In whom are hid all the treasures of wisdom and knowledge. — The unsearchable riches of Christ. — Of him are ye in Christ Jesus, who of God is made unto us wisdom, and righteousness, and sanctification, and redemption.

Matthew 12:42   Isaiah 9:6   Romans 5:7,8   Philippians 2:6-8
Ephesians 3:19 1 Corinthians 1:24   Colossians 2:3   Ephesians 3:8
1 Corinthians 1:33

AUGUST 23 MORNING

I have loved thee with an everlasting love:
therefore with lovingkindness have I drawn thee.
— JEREMIAH 31:3

We are bound to give thanks alway to God for you, brethren beloved of the Lord, because God hath from the beginning chosen you to salvation through sanctification of the Spirit and belief of the truth: whereunto he called you by our gospel, to the obtaining of the glory of our Lord Jesus Christ. — God... hath saved us, and called us with a holy calling, not according to our works, but according to his own purpose and grace, which was given us in Christ Jesus before the world began. — Thine eyes did see my substance, yet being unperfect; and in thy book all my members were written, which in continuance were fashioned, when as yet there was none of them. — God so loved the world, that he gave his only begotten Son, that whosoever believeth in him should not perish, but have everlasting life. — Herein is love, not that we loved God, but that he loved us, and sent his Son to be the propitiation for our sins.

2 Thessalonians 2:13,14   2 Timothy 1:9   Psalm 139:16   John 3:16   1 John 4:10

AUGUST 23 EVENING

I have made, and I will bear.
— ISAIAH 46:4

Thus saith the Lord that created thee, O Jacob, and he that formed thee, O Israel, Fear not: for I have redeemed thee, I have called thee by thy name; thou art mine. When thou passest through the waters, I will be with thee; and through the rivers, they shall not overflow thee. — Even to your old age I am he; and even to hoar hairs will I carry you. — As an eagle stirreth up her nest, fluttereth over her young, spreadeth abroad her wings, taketh them, beareth them on her wings: so the Lord alone did lead him. — He bare them, and carried them all the days of old. — Jesus Christ the same yesterday, and today, and forever. — For I am persuaded, that neither...height, nor depth, nor any other creature, shall be able to separate us from the love of God, which is in Christ Jesus our Lord. — Can a woman forget her sucking child, that she should not have compassion on the son of her womb? Yea, they may forget, yet will I not forget thee.

Isaiah 43:1,2, 46:4   Deuteronomy 32:11,12
Isaiah 63:9   Hebrews 13:8   Romans 8:38,39   Isaiah 49:15

AUGUST 24 MORNING

I know their sorrows.
— EXODUS 3:7

A man of sorrows and acquainted with grief. — Touched with the feeling of our infirmities. — Himself took our infirmities, and bare our sicknesses. — Jesus being wearied with his journey, sat thus on the well. — When Jesus...saw her weeping, and the Jews also weeping which came with her, he groaned in the spirit, and was troubled. Jesus wept. — For in that he himself hath suffered being tempted, he is able to succour them that are tempted. — He hath looked down from the height of his sanctuary; from heaven did the Lord behold the earth; to hear the groaning of the prisoner; to loose those that are appointed to death. — He knoweth the way that I take: when he hath tried me, I shall come forth as gold. — When my spirit was overwhelmed within me, then thou knewest my path. — He that toucheth you toucheth the apple of his eye. — In all their affliction he was afflicted; and the angel of his presence saved them.

Isaiah 53:3   Hebrews 4:15   Matthew 8:17   John 4:6, 11:33,35   Hebrews 2:18
Psalm 102:19,20   Job 23:10   Psalm 142:3   Zechariah 2:8   Isaiah 63:9

AUGUST 24 EVENING

I must work the works of him that sent me, while it is day.
—JOHN 9:4

The soul of the sluggard desireth, and hath nothing: but the soul of the diligent shall be made fat. — He that watereth shall be watered. — My meat is to do the will of him that sent me, and to finish his work. Say not ye, There are yet four months, and then cometh harvest: behold, I say unto you, Lift up your eyes, and look on the fields; for they are white already to harvest. And he that reapeth receiveth wages, and gathereth fruit unto life eternal: that both he that soweth and he that reapeth may rejoice together. — The kingdom of heaven is like unto a man that is an householder, which went out early in the morning to hire labourers into his vineyard. And when he had agreed with the labourers for a penny a day, he sent them into his vineyard. — Preach the word; be instant in season, out of season. — Occupy till I come. — I laboured more abundantly than they all: yet not I, but the grace of God which was with me.

Proverbs 13:4, 11:25   John 4:34-36   Matthew 20:1,2
2 Timothy 4:2   Luke 19:13 1 Corinthians 15:10

AUGUST 25 MORNING

Look unto the rock whence ye are hewn,
and to the hole of the pit whence ye are digged.
— ISAIAH 51:1

Behold, I was shapen in iniquity. — None eye pitied thee but thou wast cast out in the open field, to the loathing of thy person, in the day that thou wast born. And when I passed by thee, and saw thee polluted in thine own blood, I said unto thee, Live. — He brought me up...out of a horrible pit, out of the miry clay, and set my feet upon a rock, and established my goings. And he hath put a new song in my mouth, even praise unto our God. — When we were yet without strength, in due time Christ died for the ungodly. For scarcely for a righteous man will one die: yet peradventure for a good man some would even dare to die. But God commendeth his love toward us, in that, while we were yet sinners, Christ died for us. — God, who is rich in mercy, for his great love wherewith he loved us, even when we were dead in sins, hath quickened us together with Christ.

Psalm 51:5   Ezekiel 16:5,6   Psalm 40:2,3   Romans 5:6-8   Ephesians 2:4,5

AUGUST 25 EVENING

I will greatly rejoice in the Lord,
my soul shall be joyful in my God.
— ISAIAH 61:10

I will bless the Lord at all times: his praise shall continually be in my mouth. My soul shall make her boast in the Lord: the humble shall hear thereof, and be glad. O magnify the Lord with me, and let us exalt his name together. — The Lord will give grace and glory: no good thing will he withhold from them that walk uprightly. O Lord of hosts, blessed is the man that trusteth in thee. — Bless the Lord, O my soul: and all that is within me, bless his holy name. — Is any merry? Let him sing psalms. — Be filled with the Spirit; speaking to yourselves in psalms and hymns and spiritual Song, singing and making melody in your heart to the Lord; giving thanks always for all things. — Singing with grace in your hearts to the Lord. — At midnight Paul and Silas prayed, and sang praises unto God: and the prisoners heard them. — Rejoice in the Lord alway: and again, I say, Rejoice.

Psalms 34:1-3, 84:11,12, 103:1   James 5:13   Ephesians 5:18-20
Colossians 3:16   Acts 16:25   Philippians 4:4

AUGUST 26 MORNING

Thou shalt make a plate of pure gold,
and grave upon it, like the engravings of a signet:
HOLINESS TO THE LORD.
— *EXODUS 28:36*

Holiness, without which no man can see the Lord. — God is a Spirit: and they that worship him must worship him in spirit and in truth. — But we are all as an unclean thing, and all our righteousnesses are as filthy rags. — I will be sanctified in them that come nigh me, and before all the people I will be glorified. — This is the law of the house: Upon the top of the mountain the whole limit thereof round about shall be most holy. — Holiness becometh thine house, O Lord, for ever. — For their sakes I sanctify myself, that they also might be sanctified through the truth. — Seeing...that we have a great high priest, that is passed into the heavens, Jesus the Son of God, let us...come boldly unto the throne of grace that we may obtain mercy, and find grace to help in time of need.

Hebrews 12:14   John 4:24   Isaiah 64:6   Leviticus 10:3
Ezekiel 43:12   Psalm 93:5   John 17:19   Hebrews 4:14,16

AUGUST 26 EVENING

My cup runneth over.
— *PSALM 23:5*

O taste and see that the Lord is good: blessed is the man that trusteth in him. O fear the Lord, ye his saints: for there is no want to them that fear him. The young lions do lack, and suffer hunger: but they that seek the Lord shall not want any good thing. — His compassions fail not. They are new every morning: great is thy faithfulness. —The Lord is the portion of mine inheritance and of my cup: thou maintainest my lot. The lines are fallen unto me in pleasant places; yea, I have a goodly heritage. — Whether...the world, or life, or death, or things present, or things to come; all are yours. — Blessed be the God and Father of our Lord Jesus Christ, who hath blessed us with all spiritual blessings in heavenly places in Christ. — I have learned, in whatsoever state I am, therewith to be content. — Godliness with contentment is great gain. — My God shall supply all your need according to his riches in glory by Christ Jesus.

Psalm 34:8-10   Lamentations 3:22,23   Psalm 16:5,6   1 Corinthians 3:22
Ephesians 1:3   Philippians 4:11   1 Timothy 6:6   Philippians 4:19

AUGUST 27 MORNING

Thy word is a lamp unto my feet,
and a light unto my path.
— PSALM 119:105

By the word of thy lips I have kept me from the paths of the destroyer. Hold up my goings in thy paths, that my footsteps slip not. — When thou goest, it shall lead thee; when thou sleepest, it shall keep thee; and when thou awakest, it shall talk with thee. For the commandment is a lamp; and the law is light. — Thine ears shall hear a word behind thee, saying, This is the way, walk ye in it, when ye turn to the right hand, and when ye turn to the left. — I am the light of the world: he that followeth me shall not walk in darkness, but shall have the light of life. — We have also a sure word of prophecy; whereunto ye do well that ye take heed, as unto a light that shineth in a dark place. — Now we see through a glass, darkly; but then face to face: now I know in part; but then shall I know even as also I am known. — They need no candle, neither light of the sun; for the Lord God giveth them light: and they shall reign for ever and ever.

Psalm 17:4,5 Proverbs 6:22,23 Isaiah 30:21
John 8:12 2 Peter 1:19 1 Corinthians 13:12 Revelation 22:5

AUGUST 27 EVENING

What meanest thou, O sleeper?
Arise.
— JONAH 1:6

This is not your rest:...it is polluted, it shall destroy you. — Set your affection on things above, not on things on the earth. — If riches increase, set not your heart upon them. — Set your heart and your soul to seek your God: arise therefore. — Why sleep ye? Rise and pray, lest ye enter into temptation. — Take heed to yourselves, lest at any time your hearts be overcharged with surfeiting, and drunkenness, and cares of this life, and so that day come upon you unawares. — While the bridegroom tarried, they all slumbered and slept. — Yet a little while, and he that shall come will come, and will not tarry. — Now it is high time to awake out of sleep: for now is our salvation nearer than when we believed. — Watch ye therefore: for ye know not when the master of the house cometh, at even, or at midnight, or at the cockcrowing, or in the morning: lest coming suddenly he finds you sleeping.

Micah 2:10 Colossians 3:2 Psalm 62:10
1 Chronicles 22:19 Luke 22:46, 21:34
Matthew 25:5 Hebrews 10:37 Romans 13:11 Mark 13:35,36

AUGUST 28 MORNING

*The accuser of our brethren is cast down,
which accused them before our God day and night.*
— REVELATION 12:10

They overcame him by the blood of the Lamb, and by the word of their testimony. — Who shall lay any thing to the charge of God's elect? It is God that justifieth. Who is he that condemneth? It is Christ that died, yea, rather, that is risen again, who is even at the right hand of God, who also maketh intercession for us. — Having spoiled principalities and powers, he made a shew of them openly. — That through death he might destroy him that had the power of death, that is, the devil; and deliver them who through fear of death were all their lifetime subject to bondage. — In all these things we are more than conquerors, through him that loved us. — Put on the whole armour of God, that ye may be able to stand against the wiles of the devil. And take the sword of the Spirit, which is the word of God. — Thanks be to God, which giveth us the victory through our Lord Jesus Christ.

Revelation 12:11   Romans 8:33,34   Colossians 2:15   Hebrews 2:14,15
Romans 8:37   Ephesians 6:11,17 1   Corinthians 15:57

AUGUST 28 EVENING

The tree of life.
— GENESIS 2:9

God hath given to us eternal life, and this life is in his Son. — He gave his only begotten Son, that whosoever believeth in him should not perish, but have everlasting life. — As the Father raiseth up the dead, and quickeneth them; even so the Son quickeneth whom he will. As the Father hath life in himself; so hath he given to the Son to have life in himself. — To him that overcometh will I give to eat of the tree of life, which is in the midst of the paradise of God. — In the midst of the street of it, and on either side of the river, was there the tree of life, which bare twelve manner of fruits, and yielded her fruit every month: and the leaves of the tree were for the healing of the nations. — Happy is the man that findeth wisdom. Length of days is in her right hand. She is a tree of life to them that lay hold upon her: and happy is every one that retaineth her. — Christ Jesus...is made unto us wisdom.

1 John 5:11   John 3:16, 5:21,26   Revelation 2:7, 22:2
Proverbs 3:13,16,18 1   Corinthians 1:30

AUGUST 29 MORNING

Whoso trusteth in the Lord, happy is he.
— PROVERBS 16:20

[Abraham] staggered not at the promise of God through unbelief; but was strong in faith, giving glory to God; and being fully persuaded that, what he had promised, he was able also to perform. — The children of Judah prevailed, because they relied upon the Lord God of their fathers. — God is our refuge and strength, a very present help in trouble. Therefore will not we fear, though the earth be removed, and though the mountains be carried into the midst of the sea. — It is better to trust in the Lord than to put confidence in man. It is better to trust in the Lord than to put confidence in princes. — The steps of a good man are ordered by the Lord: and he delighteth in his way. Though he fall, he shall not be utterly cast down: for the Lord upholdeth him with his hand. — O taste and see that the Lord is good: blessed is the man that trusteth in him. O fear the Lord, ye his saints: for there is no want to them that fear him.

Romans 4:20,21 2 Chronicles 13:18 Psalms 46:1,2, 118:8,9, 37:23,24, 34:8,9

AUGUST 29 EVENING

I will both lay me down in peace, and sleep:
for thou, Lord, only makest me dwell in safety.
— PSALM 4:8

Thou shalt not be afraid for the terror by night. He shall cover thee with his feathers, and under his wings shalt thou trust. — Even as a hen gathereth her chickens under her wings. — He will not suffer thy foot to be moved: he that keepeth thee will not slumber. Behold, he that keepeth Israel shall neither slumber nor sleep. The Lord is thy keeper: the Lord is thy shade upon thy right hand. — I will abide in thy tabernacle for ever: I will trust in the cover of thy wings. — The darkness hideth not from thee; but the night shineth as the day: the darkness and the light are both alike to thee. — He that spared not his own Son, but delivered him up for us all, how shall he not with him also freely give us all things? —Ye are Christ's; and Christ is God's. — I will trust, and not be afraid.

Psalm 91:5,4 Matthew 23:37 Psalms 121:3-5, 61:4, 139:12
Romans 8:32 1 Corinthians 3:23 Isaiah 12:2

AUGUST 30 MORNING

*The king held out...the golden sceptre.
So Esther drew near, and touched the top of the sceptre.*
— ESTHER 5:2

It shall come to pass, when he crieth unto me, that I will hear; for I am gracious. — We have known and believed the love that God hath to us. God is love; and he that dwelleth in love dwelleth in God, and God in him. Herein is our love made perfect, that we may have boldness in the day of judgment: because as he is, so are we in this world. There is no fear in love; but perfect love casteth out fear: because fear hath torment. He that feareth is not made perfect in love. We love him, because he first loved us. — Let us draw near with a true heart, in full assurance of faith, having our hearts sprinkled from an evil conscience, and our bodies washed with pure water. — For through him we...have access by one Spirit unto the Father. — We have boldness and access with confidence by the faith of him. — Let us therefore come boldly unto the throne of grace, that we may obtain mercy, and find grace to help in time of need.

Exodus 22:27 1 John 4:16-19 Hebrews 10:22 Ephesians 2:18, 3:12 Hebrews 4:16

AUGUST 30 EVENING

*They said...it is manna:
for they wist not what it was.*
— EXODUS 16:15

Without controversy great is the mystery of godliness: God was manifest in the flesh. — The bread of God is he which cometh down from heaven, and giveth life unto the world. — Your fathers did eat manna in the wilderness, and are dead. If any man eat of this bread, he shall live for ever: and the bread that I will give is my flesh, which I will give for the life of the world. My flesh is meat indeed, and my blood is drink indeed. — The children of Israel...gathered, some more, some less. He that gathered much had nothing over, and he that gathered little had no lack. They gathered it every morning, every man according to his eating. — Take no thought, saying, What shall we eat: or, What shall we drink? Your heavenly Father knoweth that ye have need of all these things. But seek ye first the kingdom of God and his righteousness; and all these things shall be added unto you.

1 Timothy 3:16 John 6:33,49,51,55 Luke 16:17,18,21 Exodus 16:17,18,21 Matthew 6:31-33

AUGUST 31 MORNING

The free gift is of many offences unto justification.
— ROMANS 5:16

Though your sins be as scarlet, they shall be as white as snow; though they be red like crimson, they shall be as wool. — I, even I, am he that blotteth out thy transgressions for mine own sake, and will not remember thy sins. Put me in remembrance: let us plead together: declare thou, that thou mayest be justified. — I have blotted out, as a thick cloud, thy transgressions, and, as a cloud, thy sins: return unto me; for I have redeemed thee. — God so loved the world, that he gave his only begotten Son, that whosoever believeth in him should not perish, but have everlasting life. — Not as the offence, so also is the free gift. For if through the offence of one many be dead, much more the grace of God, and the gift by grace, which is by one man, Jesus Christ, hath abounded unto many. — And such were some of you: but ye are washed, but ye are sanctified, but ye are justified in the name of the Lord Jesus, and by the Spirit of our God.

Isaiah 1:18, 43:25,26, 44:22   John 3:16   Romans 5:15 1   Corinthians 6:11

AUGUST 31 EVENING

Occupy till I come.
— LUKE 19:13

The Son of man is as a man taking a far journey, who left his house, and gave authority to his servants, and to every man his work, and commanded the porter to watch. — Unto one he gave five talents, to another two, and to another one; to every man according to his several ability; and straightway took his journey. — I must work the works of him that sent me, while it is day: the night cometh, when no man can work. — Wist ye not that I must be about my Father's business? — Leaving us an example, that ye should follow his steps. — Preach the word; be instant in season, out of season; reprove, rebuke, exhort with all longsuffering and doctrine. — Every man's work shall be made manifest: for the day shall declare it. — Therefore, my beloved brethren, be ye stedfast, unmoveable, always abounding in the work of the Lord, forasmuch as ye know that your labour is not in vain in the Lord.

Mark 13:34   Matthew 25:15   John 9:4   Luke 2:49
1 Peter 2:21 2   Timothy 4:2 1   Corinthians 3:13, 15:58

SEPTEMBER 1 MORNING

The fruit of the spirit is meekness.
— *GALATIANS 5:22,23*

The meek...shall increase their joy in the Lord, and the poor among men shall rejoice in the Holy One of Israel. — Except ye be converted, and become as little children, ye shall not enter into the kingdom of heaven. Whosoever therefore shall humble himself as this little child, the same is greatest in the kingdom of heaven. — The ornament of a meek and quiet spirit...is in the sight of God of great price. — Charity vaunteth not itself, is not puffed up. — Follow after meekness. — Take my yoke upon you and learn of me, for I am meek and lowly in heart. — He was oppressed, and he was afflicted, yet he opened not his mouth: he is brought as lamb to the slaughter, and as a sheep before her shearers is dumb so he openeth not his mouth. — Christ also suffered for us, leaving us an example, that ye should follow his steps: who did no sin neither was guile found in his mouth: who, when he was reviled, reviled not again...but committed himself to him that judgeth righteously.

Isaiah 29:19   Matthew 18:3,4 1   Peter 3:4 1   Corinthians 13:4
1 Timothy 6:11   Matthew 11:29   Isaiah 53:7 1   Peter 2:21-23

SEPTEMBER 1 EVENING

If any man will come after me, let him deny himself,
and take up his cross daily, and follow me.
— *LUKE 9:23*

By honour and dishonour, by evil report and good report. — All that will live godly in Christ Jesus shall suffer persecution. — The offence of the cross. — If I yet pleased men, I should not be the servant of Christ. — If ye be reproached for the name of Christ, happy are ye: but let none of you suffer as a murderer, or as a thief, or as an evildoer, or as a busybody in other men's matters. Yet if any man suffer as a Christian, let him not be ashamed; but let him glorify God on this behalf. — Unto you it is given in the behalf of Christ, not only to believe on him, but also to suffer for his sake. — If one died for all, then were all dead: and that he died for all, that they which live should not henceforth live unto themselves, but unto him which died for them, and rose again. — If we suffer, we shall also reign with him.

2 Corinthians 6:8 2   Timothy 3:12   Galatians 5:11, 1:10 1   Peter 4:14-16
Philippians 1:29 2   Corinthians 5:14,15 2   Timothy 2:12

SEPTEMBER 2 MORNING

Wait on the Lord:
be of good courage,
and he shall strengthen thine heart.
— PSALM 27:14

Hast thou not known? Hast thou not heard, that the everlasting God, the Lord, the Creator of the ends of the earth, fainteth not, neither is weary? He giveth power to the faint; and to them that have no might he increaseth strength. — Fear thou not; for I am with thee: be not dismayed; for I am thy God: I will strengthen thee; yea, I will help thee; yea, I will uphold thee with the right hand of my righteousness. — Thou hast been a strength to the poor, a strength to the needy in distress, a refuge from the storm, a shadow from the heat, when the blast of the terrible ones is as a storm against the wall. — The trying of your faith worketh patience. But let patience have her perfect work, that ye may be perfect and entire, wanting nothing. — Cast not away therefore your confidence, which hath great recompence of reward. For ye have need of patience, that, after ye have done the will of God, ye might receive the promise.

Isaiah 40:28,29, 41:10, 25:4   James 1:3,4   Hebrews 10:35,36

SEPTEMBER 2 EVENING

He maketh me to lie down in green pastures.
— PSALM 23:2

The wicked are like the troubled sea, when it cannot rest. There is no peace, saith my God, to the wicked. — Come unto me, all ye that labour and are heavy laden, and I will give you rest. — Rest in the Lord. — He that is entered into his rest, he also hath ceased from his own works. — Be not carried about with divers and strange doctrines. For it is a good thing that the heart be established with grace. — That...we be no more children, tossed to and fro, and carried about with every wind of doctrine, by the sleight of men, and cunning craftiness, whereby they lie in wait to deceive; but speaking the truth in love, may grow up into him in all things, which is the head, even Christ. — I sat down under his shadow with great delight, and his fruit was sweet to my taste. He brought me to the banqueting house, and his banner over me was love.

Isaiah 57:20,21   Matthew 11:28   Psalm 37:7   Hebrews 4:10, 13:9
Ephesians 4:14,15   Song of Solomon 2:3,4

SEPTEMBER 3 MORNING

Neither shall there be leaven seen with thee
in all thy quarters.
— EXODUS 13:7

The fear of the Lord is to hate evil. — Abhor that which is evil. — Abstain from all appearance of evil. — Looking diligently lest any man fail of the grace of God; lest any root of bitterness springing up trouble you, and thereby many be defiled. — If I regard iniquity in my heart, the Lord will not hear me. — Know ye not that a little leaven leaveneth the whole lump? Purge out therefore the old leaven, that ye may be a new lump, as ye are unleavened. For even Christ our passover is sacrificed for us: therefore let us keep the feast, not with old leaven, neither with the leaven of malice and wickedness; but with the unleavened bread of sincerity and truth. — Let a man examine himself, and so let him eat of that bread, and drink of that cup. — Let every one that nameth the name of Christ depart from iniquity. — Such an high priest became us, who is holy, harmless, undefiled, separate from sinners. — In him is no sin.

Proverbs 8:13   Romans 12:9 1   Thessalonians 5:22   Hebrews 12:15   Psalm 66:18   1 Corinthians 5:6-8 1   Corinthians 11:28 2   Timothy 2:19   Hebrews 7:26 1   John 3:5

SEPTEMBER 3 EVENING

The serpent said unto the woman,
Ye shall not surely die:...
your eyes shall be opened, and ye shall be as gods,
knowing good and evil.
— GENESIS 3:4,5

I fear, lest by any means, as the serpent beguiled Eve through his subtlety, so your minds should be corrupted from the simplicity that is in Christ. — My brethren, be strong in the Lord, and in the power of his might. Put on the whole armour of God, that ye may be able to stand against the wiles of the devil. Take unto you the whole armour of God, that ye may be able to withstand in the evil day, and having done all, to stand. Stand therefore, having your loins girt about with truth, and having on the breastplate of righteousness; and your feet shod with the preparation of the gospel of peace; above all, taking the shield of faith, wherewith ye shall be able to quench all the fiery darts of the wicked. And take the helmet of salvation, and the sword of the Spirit, which is the word of God. — Lest Satan should get an advantage of us; for we are not ignorant of his devices.

2 Corinthians 11:3   Ephesians 6:10,11,13-17 2   Corinthians 2:11

SEPTEMBER 4 MORNING

Sit still, my daughter.
— RUTH 3:18

Take heed, and be quiet; fear not, neither be fainthearted. — Be still, and know that I am God. — Said I not unto thee, that, if thou wouldest believe, thou shouldest see the glory of God?— The loftiness of man shall be bowed down, and the haughtiness of men shall be made low: and the Lord alone shall be exalted in that day. — Mary...sat at Jesus' feet, and heard his word. — Mary hath chosen that good part, which shall not be taken away from her. — In returning and rest shall ye be saved; in quietness and in confidence shall be your strength. — Commune with your own heart upon your bed, and be still. — Rest in the Lord, and wait patiently for him: fret not thyself because of him who prospereth in his way, because of the man who bringeth wicked devices to pass. — He shall not be afraid of evil tidings: his heart is fixed, trusting in the Lord. His heart is established. — He that believeth shall not make haste.

Isaiah 7:4   Psalm 46:10   John 11:40   Isaiah 2:17   Luke 10:39, 42
Isaiah 30:15   Psalm 4:4, 37:7, 112:7,8   Isaiah 28:16

SEPTEMBER 4 EVENING

What I do thou knowest not now;
but thou shalt know hereafter.
— JOHN 13:7

Thou shalt remember all the way which the Lord thy God led thee these forty years in the wilderness, to humble thee, and to prove thee, to know what was in thine heart, whether thou wouldest keep his commandments, or no. — When I passed by thee, and looked upon thee, behold, thy time was the time of love; yea, I sware unto thee, and entered into a covenant with thee, saith the Lord God, and thou becamest mine. — Whom the Lord loveth he chasteneth. — Beloved, think it not strange concerning the fiery trial which is to try you, as though some strange thing happened unto you: but rejoice, inasmuch as ye are partakers of Christ's sufferings; that, when his glory shall be revealed, ye may be glad also with exceeding joy. — Our light affliction, which is but for a moment, worketh for us a far more exceeding and eternal weight of glory; while we look not at the things which are seen, but at the things which are not seen.

Deuteronomy 8:2   Ezekiel 16:8   Hebrews 12:6
1 Peter 4:12,13 2   Corinthians 4:17,18

SEPTEMBER 5 MORNING

As the body is one, and hath many members...
so also is Christ.
— *1 CORINTHIANS 12:12*

He is the head of the body, the church. — The head over things to the church, which is his body, the fullness of him that filleth all in all. — We are members of his body, of his flesh, and of his bones. — A body hast thou prepared me. — Thine eyes did see my substance, yet being unperfect; and in thy book all my members were written, which in continuance were fashioned, when as yet there was none of them. — Thine they were, and thou gavest them me. — He hath chosen us in him before the foundation of the world. — Whom he did foreknow, he also did predestinate to be conformed to the image of his Son. — Grow up into him in all things, which is the head, even Christ: from whom the whole body fitly joined together, and compacted by that which every joint supplieth...maketh increase of the body unto the edifying of itself in love.

Colossians 1:18   Ephesians 1:22,23, 5:30   Hebrews 10:5   Psalm 139:16
John 17:6   Ephesians 1:4   Romans 8:29   Ephesians 4:15,16

SEPTEMBER 5 EVENING

The fountain of living waters.
— *JEREMIAH 2:13*

How excellent is thy lovingkindness, O God! Therefore the children of men put their trust under the shadow of thy wings. They shall be abundantly satisfied with the fatness of thy house and thou shalt make them drink of the river of thy pleasures. For with thee is the fountain of life. — Thus saith the Lord God, Behold, my servants shall eat, but ye shall be hungry: behold, my servants shall drink, but ye shall be thirsty. — Whosoever drinketh of the water that I shall give him shall never thirst; but the water that I shall give him shall be him a well of water springing up into everlasting life. — This spake he of the Spirit, which they that believe on him should receive. — Ho, every one that thirsteth, come ye to the waters. — The Spirit and the bride say, Come. And let him that heareth say, Come. And let him that is athirst come. And whosoever will, let him take the water of life freely.

Psalm 36:7-9   Isaiah 65:13   John 4:14, 7:39   Isaiah 55:1   Revelation 22:17

SEPTEMBER 6 MORNING

*Let us lift up our heart with our hands
unto God in the heavens.*
— LAMENTATIONS 3:41

Who is like unto the Lord our God, who dwelleth on high, who humbleth himself to behold the things that are in heaven, and in the earth!— Unto thee, O Lord, do I lift up my soul. — I stretch forth my hands unto thee: my soul thirsteth after thee, as a thirsty land. Hide not thy face from me, lest I be like unto them that go down into the pit. Cause me to hear thy lovingkindness in the morning; for in thee do I trust: cause me to know the way wherein I should walk; for I lift up my soul unto thee. — Because thy lovingkindness is better than life, my lips shall praise thee. Thus will I bless thee while I live: I will lift up my hands in thy name. — Rejoice the soul of thy servant: for unto thee, O Lord, do I lift up my soul. For thou, Lord, art good, and ready to forgive; and plenteous in mercy unto all them that call upon thee. — Whatsoever ye shall ask in my name, that will I do.

Psalms 113:5,6, 25:1, 143:6-8, 63:3,4, 86:4,5   John 14:13

SEPTEMBER 6 EVENING

Watchman, what of the night?
— ISAIAH 21:11

It is high time to awake out of sleep: for now is our salvation nearer than when we believed. The night is far spent, the day is at hand: let us therefore cast off the works of darkness, and let us put on the armour of light. — Learn a parable of the fig tree; When his branch is yet tender, and putteth forth leaves, ye know that summer is nigh: so likewise ye, when ye shall see all these things, know that it is near, even at the doors. Heaven and earth shall pass away, but my words shall not pass away. — I wait for the Lord, my soul doth wait, and in his word do I hope. My soul waiteth for the Lord more than they that watch for the morning: I say, more than they that watch for the morning. — He which testifieth these things saith, Surely I come quickly. Amen. Even so, come, Lord Jesus. — Watch...for ye know neither the day nor the hour wherein the Son of man cometh.

Romans 13:11,12   Matthew 24:32,33,35   Psalm 130:5,6
Revelation 22:20   Matthew 25:13

SEPTEMBER 7 MORNING

Rejoicing in hope.
— ROMANS 12:12

The hope which is laid up for you in heaven. — If in this life only we have hope in Christ, we are of all men most miserable. — We must through much tribulation enter into the kingdom of God. — Whosoever doth not bear his cross, and come after me cannot be my disciple. — No man should be moved by these afflictions, for yourselves know that we are appointed thereunto. — Rejoice in the Lord alway: and again I say, Rejoice. — The God of hope fill you with all joy and peace in believing, that ye may abound in hope, through the power of the Holy Ghost. — Blessed be the God and Father of our Lord Jesus Christ, which according to his abundant mercy hath begotten us again unto lively hope by the resurrection of Jesus Christ from the dead. — Whom having not seen, ye love; in whom though now ye see him not, yet believing, ye rejoice with joy unspeakable and full of glory. — By whom also we have access by faith into this grace wherein we stand, and rejoice in hope of the glory of God.

Colossians 1:5 1 Corinthians 15:19 Acts 14:22 Luke 14:27
1 Thessalonians 3:3 Philippians 4:4 Romans 15:13 1 Peter 1:3,8 Romans 5:2

SEPTEMBER 7 EVENING

I am poor and needy;
yet the Lord thinketh upon me.
— PSALM 40:17

I know the thoughts that I think toward you, saith the Lord, thoughts of peace, and not of evil. — My thoughts are not your thoughts, neither are your ways my ways, saith the Lord. For as the heavens are higher than the earth, so are my ways higher than your ways, and my thoughts than your thoughts. — How precious...are thy thoughts unto me, O God! How great is the sum of them! If I should count them, they are more in number than the sand: when I awake, I am still with thee. — Lord, how great are thy works! and thy thoughts are very deep. — Many, O Lord my God, are thy wonderful works which thou hast done, and thy thoughts which are to us-ward. — Not many mighty, not many noble, are called. — Hath not God chosen the poor of this world rich in faith, and heirs of the kingdom? — Having nothing, and yet possessing all things. — The unsearchable riches of Christ.

Jeremiah 29:11 Isaiah 55:8,9 Psalms 139:17,18. 92:5, 40:5
1 Corinthians 1:26 James 2:5 2 Corinthians 6:10 Ephesians 3:8

SEPTEMBER 8 MORNING

*Thou art weighed in the balances,
and art found wanting.*
— DANIEL 5:27

The Lord is a God of knowledge, and by him, actions are weighed. — That which is highly esteemed among men is abomination in the sight of God. — The Lord seeth not as man seeth; for man looketh on the outward appearance, but the Lord looketh on the heart. — Be not deceived, God is not mocked: for whatsoever a man soweth, that shall he also reap. For he that soweth to his flesh shall of the flesh reap corruption; but he that soweth to the Spirit shall of the spirit reap life everlasting. — What is a man profited if he shall gain the whole world, and lose his own soul? or what shall a man give in exchange for his soul?— What things were gain to me, those I counted loss for Christ. — Behold, thou desirest truth in the inward parts. — Thou hast proved mine heart; thou hast visited me in the night; thou hast tried me, and shalt find nothing.

1 Samuel 2:3   Luke 16:15   1 Samuel 16:7   Galatians 6:7,8
Matthew 16:26   Philippians 3:7   Psalms 51:6, 17:3

SEPTEMBER 8 EVENING

Christ the firstfruits.
— 1 CORINTHIANS 15:23

Except a corn of wheat fall into the ground and die, it abideth alone: but if it die, it bringeth forth much fruit. — If the firstfruit be holy the lump is also holy: and if the root be holy, so are the branches. — Now is Christ risen from the dead, and become the firstfruits of them that slept. — If we have been planted together in the likeness of his death we shall be also in the likeness of his resurrection. — The Lord Jesus Christ...shall change our vile body, that it may be fashioned like unto his glorious body, according to the working whereby he is able even to subdue all things unto himself. — The firstborn from the dead. — If the Spirit of him that raised up Jesus from the dead dwell in you, he that raised up Christ from the dead shall also quicken our mortal bodies by his Spirit that dwelleth in you. — I am the resurrection, and the life: he that believeth in me, though he were dead, yet shall he live.

John 12:24   Romans 11:16   1 Corinthians 15:20   Romans 6:5
Philippians 3:20,21   Colossians 1:18   Romans 8:11   John 11:25

SEPTEMBER 9 MORNING

He hath filled the hungry with good things;
and the rich he hath sent empty away.
— LUKE 1:53

Thou sayest, I am rich, and increased with goods and have need of nothing: and knowest not that thou art wretched, and miserable, and poor, and blind, and naked. I counsel thee to buy of me gold tried in the fire, that thou mayest be rich. As many as I love, I rebuke and chasten: be zealous therefore and repent. — Blessed are they which do hunger and thirst after righteousness: for they shall be filled. — When the poor and needy seek water, and there is none, and their tongue faileth for thirst, I the Lord will hear them, I the God of Israel will not forsake them. — I am the Lord thy God...open thy mouth wide and I will fill it. — Wherefore do ye spend money for that which is not bread? And your labour for that which satisfieth not? Hearken diligently unto me, and eat ye that which is good, and let your soul delight itself in fatness. — I am the bread of life: he that cometh to me shall never hunger; and he that believeth on me shall never thirst.

Revelation 3:17-19   Matthew 5:6   Isaiah 41:17   Psalm 81:10   Isaiah 55:2   John 6:35

SEPTEMBER 9 EVENING

My feet were almost gone;
my steps had well nigh slipped.
— PSALM 73:2

When I said, My foot slippeth; thy mercy, O Lord, held me up. — The Lord said, Simon, Simon, behold Satan hath desired to have you, that he may sift you as wheat: but I have prayed for thee, that thy faith fail not. — A just man falleth seven times, and riseth up again. — Although he fall, he shall not be utterly cast down: for the Lord upholdeth him with his hand. — Rejoice not against me, O my enemy: when I fall, I shall arise: when I sit in darkness, the Lord shall be a light unto me. — He shall deliver thee in six troubles: yea, in seven there shall no evil touch thee. — If any man sin, we have an advocate with the Father, Jesus Christ the righteous. — Wherefore he is able also to save them to the uttermost that come unto God by him, seeing he ever liveth to make intercession for them.

Psalm 94:18   Luke 22:31,32   Proverbs 24:16   Psalm 37:24   Micah 7:8   Job 5:19   1 John 2:1   Hebrews 7:25

SEPTEMBER 10 MORNING

I will give them one heart, and one way,
that they may fear me forever,
for the good of them, and of their children after them.
— JEREMIAH 32:39

A new heart...will I give you and a new spirit will I put within you. — Good and upright is the Lord: therefore will he teach sinners in the way. The meek will he guide in judgment: and the meek will he teach his way. All the paths of the Lord are mercy and truth unto such as keep his covenant and his testimonies. — That they all may be one; as thou, Father, art in me, and I in thee, that they also may be one in us: that the world may believe that thou hast sent me. — I...beseech you that ye walk worthy of the vocation wherewith ye are called, with all lowliness and meekness...endeavouring to keep the unity of the Spirit in the bond of peace. There is one body, and one Spirit, even as ye are called in one hope of your calling; one Lord, one faith, one baptism, one God and Father of all, who is above all, and through all, and in you all.

Ezekiel 36:26   Psalm 25:8-10   John 17:21   Ephesians 4:1-6

SEPTEMBER 10 EVENING

They that wait upon the Lord shall renew their strength.
— ISAIAH 40:31

When I am weak, then am I strong. — God shall be my strength. — He said unto me, My grace is sufficient for thee: for my strength is made perfect in weakness. Most gladly therefore will I rather glory in my infirmities, that the power of Christ may rest upon me. — Let him take hold of my strength. — Cast thy burden upon the Lord, and he shall sustain thee. — The arms of his hands were made strong by the hands of the mighty God of Jacob. — I will not let thee go, except thou bless me. — Thou comest to me with a sword, and with a spear, and with a shield: but I come to thee in the name of the Lord of hosts, the God of the armies of Israel, whom thou hast defied. — Plead my cause, O Lord, with them that strive with me: fight against them that fight against me. Take hold of shield and buckler, and stand up for mine help.

2 Corinthians 12:10   Isaiah 49:5 2   Corinthians 12:9   Isaiah 27:5
Psalm 55:22   Genesis 49:24, 32:26 1   Samuel 17:45   Psalm 35:1,2

SEPTEMBER 11 MORNING

Be not conformed to this world:
but be ye transformed by the renewing of your mind.
— ROMANS 12:2

Thou shalt not follow a multitude to do evil. — Know ye not that the friendship of the world is enmity with God? Whosoever therefore will be a friend of the world is the enemy of God. — What fellowship hath righteousness with unrighteousness? And what communion hath light with darkness? And what concord hath Christ with Belial? or what part hath he that believeth with an infidel? And what agreement hath the temple of God with idols?— Love not the world, neither the things that are in the world. If any man love the world, the love of the Father is not in him. The world passeth away, and the lust thereof, but he that doeth the will of God abideth for ever. — In time past ye walked according to the course of this world, according to the prince of the power of the air, the spirit that now worketh in the children of disobedience. — Ye have not so learned Christ; if so be that ye have heard him...as the truth is in Jesus.

Exodus 23:2   James 4:4   2 Corinthians 6:14-16
1 John 2:15,17   Ephesians 2:2, 4:20,21

SEPTEMBER 11 EVENING

Man goeth forth unto his work
and to his labour until the evening.
— PSALM 104:23

In the sweat of thy face shalt thou eat bread, till thou return unto the ground. — We commanded you, that if any would not work, neither should he eat. — Study to be quiet, and to do your own business, and to work with your own hands. — Whatsoever thy hand findeth to do, do it with thy might; for there is no work, nor device, nor knowledge, nor wisdom, in the grave, whither thou goest. — The night cometh when no man can work. — Let us not be weary in well doing: for in due season we shall reap, if we faint not. — Always abounding in the work of the Lord forasmuch as ye know that your labour is not in vain in the Lord. — There remaineth...a rest to the people of God. — Unto us, which have borne the burden and heat of the day. — This is the rest wherewith ye may cause the weary to rest; and this is the refreshing.

Genesis 3:19   2 Thessalonians 3:10   1 Thessalonians 4:11   Ecclesiastes 9:10   John 9:4
Galatians 6:9   1 Corinthians 15:58   Hebrews 4:9   Matthew 20:12   Isaiah 28:12

SEPTEMBER 12 MORNING

I have seen his ways, and will heal him.
— ISAIAH 57:18

I am the Lord that healeth thee. — O Lord, thou hast searched me, and known me. Thou knowest my downsitting and mine uprising, thou understandest my thought afar off. Thou compassest my path and my lying down, and art acquainted with all my ways. — Thou hast set our iniquities before thee, our secret sins in the light of thy countenance. — All things are naked and opened unto the eyes of him with whom we have to do. — Come now, and let us reason together, saith the Lord: though your sins be as scarlet, they shall be as white as snow; though they be red like crimson, they shall be as wool. — He is gracious unto him, and saith, Deliver him from going down to the pit: I have found a ransom. — He was wounded for our transgressions, he was bruised for our iniquities: the chastisement of our peace was upon him: and with his stripes we are healed. — He hath sent me to bind up the brokenhearted. — Thy faith hath made thee whole; go in peace, and be whole of thy plague.

Exodus 15:26 Psalms 139:1-3, 90:8 Hebrews 4:13
Isaiah 1:18 Job 33:24 Isaiah 53:5, 61:1 Mark 5:34

SEPTEMBER 12 EVENING

The Lord taketh my part.
— PSALM 118:7

The Lord hear thee in the day of trouble; the name of the God of Jacob defend thee; send thee help from the sanctuary, and strengthen thee out of Zion. We will rejoice in thy salvation, and in the name of our God we will set up our banners. Some trust in chariots, and some in horses: but we will remember the name of the Lord our God. They are brought down and fallen: but we are risen, and stand upright. — When the enemy shall come in like a flood, the Spirit of the Lord shall lift up a standard against him. — There hath no temptation taken you but such as is common to man: but God is faithful, who will not suffer you to be tempted above that ye are able: but will with the temptation also make a way to escape, that ye may be able to bear it. — If God be for us, who can be against us? — The Lord is on my side; I will not fear. — Our God whom we serve is able to deliver us, and he will deliver us.

Psalm 20:1,2,5,7,8 Isaiah 59:19 1 Corinthians 10:13
Romans 8:31 Psalm 118:6 Daniel 3:17

SEPTEMBER 13 MORNING

If any man thirst, let him come unto me, and drink.
— JOHN 7:37

My soul longeth, yea, even fainteth for the courts of the Lord: my heart and my flesh crieth out for the living God. — O God, thou art my God; early will I seek thee: my soul thirsteth for thee, my flesh longeth for thee in a dry and thirsty land where no water is; to see thy power and thy glory, so as I have seen thee in the sanctuary. — Ho, every one that thirsteth, come ye to the waters, and he that hath no money; come ye, buy, and eat; yea, come, buy wine and milk without money and without price. — The Spirit and the bride say, Come. And let him that heareth say, Come. And let him that is athirst come. And whosoever will, let him take the water of life freely. — Whosoever drinketh of the water that I shall give him shall never thirst; but the water that I shall give him shall be in him a well of water springing up into everlasting life. — My blood is drink indeed. — Eat, O friends; drink, yea, drink abundantly, O beloved.

Psalms 84:2, 63:1,2   Isaiah 55:1   Revelation 22:17
John 4:14, 6:55   Song of Solomon 5:1

SEPTEMBER 13 EVENING

Ye are the salt of the earth.
— MATTHEW 5:13

That which is not corruptible. — Being born again, not of corruptible seed, but of incorruptible, by the word of God, which liveth and abideth for ever. — He that believeth in me, though he were dead, yet shall he live. — The children of God, being the children of the resurrection. — The uncorruptible God. — If any man have not the Spirit of Christ, he is none of his. And if Christ be in you, the body is dead because of sin; but the Spirit is life because of righteousness. But if the Spirit of him that raised up Jesus from the dead dwell in you, he that raised up Christ from the dead shall also quicken your mortal bodies by his Spirit that dwelleth in you. — It is sown in corruption; it is raised in incorruption. — Have salt in yourselves, and have peace one with another. — Let no corrupt communication proceed out of your mouth, but that which is good to the use of edifying, that it may minister grace unto the hearers.

1 Peter 3:4, 1:23   John 11:25   Luke 20:36   Romans 1:23, 8:9-11
1 Corinthians 15:42   Mark 9:50   Ephesians 4:29

SEPTEMBER 14 MORNING

I, even I, am he that comforteth you.
— ISAIAH 51:12

Blessed be God, even the Father of our Lord Jesus Christ, the father of mercies, and the God of all comfort; who comforteth us in all our tribulation, that we may be able to comfort them which are in any trouble, by the comfort wherewith we ourselves are comforted of God. — Like as a father pitieth his children, so the Lord pitieth them that fear him. For he knoweth our frame; he remembereth that we are dust. — As one whom his mother comforteth, so will I comfort you. — Casting all your care upon him, for he careth for you. — Thou, O Lord, art a God full of compassion, and gracious, longsuffering, and plenteous in mercy and truth. — Another Comforter...even the Spirit of truth. — The Spirit...helpeth our infirmities. — God shall wipe away all tears from their eyes; and there shall be no more death, neither sorrow, nor crying, neither shall there be any more pain: for the former things are passed away.

2 Corinthians 1:3,4   Psalm 103:13,14   Isaiah 66:13   1 Peter 5:7
Psalm 86:15   John 14:16,17   Romans 8:26   Revelation 21:4

SEPTEMBER 14 EVENING

Ye were called unto the fellowship of his Son.
— 1 CORINTHIANS 1:9

He received from God the Father honour and glory, when there came such a voice to him from the excellent glory, This is my beloved Son, in whom I am well pleased. — Behold, what manner of love the Father hath bestowed upon us, that we should be called the sons of God. — Be ye...followers of God, as dear children. — If children, then heirs; heirs of God, and joint-heirs with Christ. — The brightness of his glory, and the express image of his person. — Let your light so shine before men, that they may see your good works, and glorify your Father which is in heaven. — Jesus the author and finisher of our faith; who for the joy that was set before him endured the cross, despising the shame. — These things I speak in the world, that they might have my joy fulfilled in themselves. — As the sufferings of Christ abound in us, so our consolation also aboundeth by Christ.

2 Peter 1:17   1 John 3:1   Ephesians 5:1   Romans 8:17   Hebrews 1:3
Matthew 5:16   Hebrews 12:2   John 17:13   2 Corinthians 1:5

SEPTEMBER 15 MORNING

Sin shall not have dominion over you:
for ye are not under the law, but under grace.
— ROMANS 6:14

What then? Shall we sin, because we are not under the law, but under grace? God forbid. — My brethren, ye...are become dead to the law by the body of Christ; that ye should be married to another, even to him who is raised from the dead, that we should bring forth fruit unto God. — Being not without law to God, but under the law to Christ. — The sting of death is sin; and the strength of sin is the law. But thanks be to God, which giveth us the victory through our Lord Jesus Christ. — The law of the Spirit of life in Christ Jesus hath made me free from the law of sin and death. — Whosoever committeth sin is the servant of sin. — If the Son...shall make you free, ye shall be free indeed. — Stand fast therefore in the liberty wherewith Christ hath made us free, and be not entangled again with the yoke of bondage.

Romans 6:15, 7:4 1 Corinthians 9:21, 15:56,57
Romans 8:2 John 8:34,36 Galatians 5:1

SEPTEMBER 15 EVENING

A double minded man is unstable in all his ways.
— JAMES 1:8

No man, having put his hand to the plough and looking back, is fit for the kingdom of God. — He that cometh to God must believe that he is, and that he is a rewarder of them that diligently seek him. — Let him ask in faith, nothing wavering. For he that wavereth is like a wave of the sea driven with the wind and tossed. For let not that man think that he shall receive anything of the Lord. — What things soever ye desire, when ye pray, believe that ye receive them, and ye shall have them. — Be no more children, tossed to and fro, and carried about with every wind of doctrine, by the sleight of men, and cunning craftiness, whereby they lie in wait to deceive: but speaking the truth in love,...grow up into him in all things which is the head, even Christ. — Abide in me. — Be ye steadfast, unmoveable, always abounding in the work of the Lord, forasmuch as ye know that your labour is not in vain in the Lord.

Luke 9:62 Hebrews 11:6 James 1:6,7 Mark 11:24
Ephesians 4:14,15 John 15:4 1 Corinthians 15:58

SEPTEMBER 16 MORNING

The Lord pondereth the hearts.
— PROVERBS 21:2

The Lord knoweth the way of the righteous: but the way of the ungodly shall perish. — The Lord will shew who are his, and who is holy. — Thy Father which seeth in secret himself shall reward thee openly. — Search me, O God, and know my heart: try me, and know my thoughts: and see if there be any wicked way in me, and lead me in the way everlasting. — There is no fear in love; but perfect love casteth out fear. — Lord, all my desire is before thee; and my groaning is not hid from thee. — When my spirit was overwhelmed within me, then thou knewest my path. — He that searcheth the hearts knoweth what is the mind of the Spirit, because he maketh intercession for the saints according to the will of God. — The foundation of God standeth sure, having this seal, The Lord knoweth them that are his. And, Let every one that nameth the name of Christ depart from iniquity.

Psalm 1:6   Numbers 16:5   Matthew 6:4   Psalm 139:23,24
1 John 4:18   Psalms 38:9, 142:3   Romans 8:27 2 Timothy 2:19

SEPTEMBER 16 EVENING

Weeping may endure for a night,
but joy cometh in the morning.
— PSALM 30:5

No man should be moved by these afflictions: for yourselves know that we are appointed thereunto. For verily, when we were with you, we told you before that we should suffer tribulation. — In me ye...have peace. In the world ye shall have tribulation: but be of good cheer; I have overcome the world. — I shall be satisfied, when I awake, with thy likeness. — The night is far spent, the day is at hand. — He shall be as the light of the morning, when the sun riseth, even a morning without clouds; as the tender grass springing out of the earth by clear shining after rain. — He will swallow up death in victory; and the Lord GOD will wipe away tears from off all faces. — There shall be no more death, neither sorrow, nor crying, neither shall there be any more pain: for the former things are passed away. — We which are alive and remain shall be caught up together with them in the clouds, to meet the Lord in the air. Wherefore comfort one another with these words.

1 Thessalonians 3:3,4   John 16:33   Psalm 17:15   Romans 13:12
2 Samuel 23:4   Isaiah 25:8   Revelation 21:4 1 Thessalonians 4:17,18

SEPTEMBER 17 MORNING

A bruised reed shall he not break.
— MATTHEW 12:20

The sacrifices of God are a broken spirit: a broken and a contrite heart, O God, thou wilt not despise. — He healeth the broken in heart, and bindeth up their wounds. — Thus saith the high and lofty One that inhabiteth eternity, whose name is Holy; I dwell in the high and holy place, with him also that is of a contrite and humble spirit, to revive the spirit of the humble, and to revive the heart of the contrite ones. For I will not contend for ever, neither will I be always wroth: for the spirit should fail before me, and the souls which I have made. — I will seek that which was lost, and bring again that which was driven away, and will bind up that which was broken, and will strengthen that which was sick. — Wherefore lift up the hands which hang down, and the feeble knees; and make straight paths for your feet, lest that which is lame be turned out of the way; but let it rather be healed. — Behold, your God...will come and save you.

Psalms 51:17, 147:3   Isaiah 57:15,16   Ezekiel 34:16   Hebrews 12:12,13   Isaiah 35:4

SEPTEMBER 17 EVENING

O taste and see that the Lord is good:
blessed is the man that trusteth in him.
— PSALM 34:8

When the ruler of the feast had tasted the water that was made wine, and knew not whence it was: he saith...Every man at the beginning doth set forth good wine; and when men have well drunk, then that which is worse: but thou hast kept the good wine until now. — The ear trieth words, as the mouth tasteth meat. — I believed, and therefore have I spoken. — I know whom I have believed. — I sat down under his shadow with great delight, and his fruit was sweet to my taste. — The goodness of God. — He that spared not his own Son, but delivered him up for us all, how shall he not with him also freely give us all things? — As newborn babes, desire the sincere milk of the word, that ye may grow thereby: if so be ye have tasted that the Lord is gracious. — Let all those that put their trust in thee rejoice: let them ever shout for joy.

John 2:9,10.   Job 34:3   2 Corinthians 4:13   2 Timothy 1:12   Song of Solomon 2:3   Romans 2:4, 8:32   1 Peter 2:2,3   Psalm 5:11

SEPTEMBER 18 MORNING

Open thou mine eyes,
that I may behold wondrous things out of thy law.
— PSALM 119:18

Then opened he their understanding, that they might understand the scriptures. — It is given unto you to know the mysteries of the kingdom of heaven, but to them it is not given. — I thank thee, O Father, Lord of heaven and earth, because thou hast hid these things from the wise and prudent, and hast revealed them unto babes. Even so, Father: for so it seemed good in thy sight. — We have received, not the spirit of the world, but the spirit which is of God; that we might know the things that are freely given to us of God. — How precious also are thy thoughts unto me, O God! how great is the sum of them! If I should count them, they are more in number than the sand. — O the depth of the riches both of the wisdom and knowledge of God! How unsearchable are his judgments, and his ways past finding out! For who hath known the mind of the Lord? Or who hath been his counsellor? For of him, and through him, and to him are all things: to whom be glory for ever. Amen.

Luke 24:45   Matthew 13:11, 11:25,26 1   Corinthians 2:12
Psalm 139:17,18   Romans 11:33,34,36

SEPTEMBER 18 EVENING

En-hakkore. (Or, The well of him that cried.)
— JUDGES 15:19

If thou knewest the gift of God, and who it is that saith unto thee, Give me to drink; thou wouldest have asked of him, and he would have given thee living water. — If any man thirst, let him come unto me and drink. This spake he of the Spirit, which they that believe on him should receive. — Prove me now herewith, saith the Lord of hosts, if I will not open you the windows of heaven, and pour you out a blessing, that there shall not be room enough to receive it. — If ye...being evil, know how to give good gifts unto your children: how much more shall your heavenly Father give the Holy Spirit to them that ask him?— Ask, and it shall be given you; seek, and ye shall find. — Because ye are sons, God hath sent forth the Spirit of his Son into your hearts, crying, Abba, Father. — Ye have not received the spirit of bondage again to fear; but ye have received the Spirit of adoption, whereby we cry, Abba, Father.

John 4:10, 7:37,39   Malachi 3:10   Luke 11:13,9   Galatians 4:6   Romans 8:15

SEPTEMBER 19 MORNING

The God of all grace.
— *1 PETER 5:10*

I will proclaim the name of the Lord before thee; and will be gracious to whom I will be gracious. — He is gracious unto him, and saith, Deliver him from going down to the pit: I have found a ransom. — Being justified freely by his grace, through the redemption that is in Christ. — Jesus: whom God hath set forth to be a propitiation through faith in his blood, to declare his righteousness for the remission of sins that are past, through the forbearance of God. — Grace and truth came by Jesus Christ. — By grace are ye saved through faith; and that not of yourselves: it is the gift of God. — Grace, mercy, and peace, from God our Father and Jesus Christ our Lord. — Unto every one of us is given grace according to the measure of the gift of Christ. — As every man hath received the gift, even so minister the same one to another, as good stewards of the manifold grace of God. — He giveth more grace. — Grow in grace, and in the knowledge of our Lord and Saviour Jesus Christ. To him be glory both now and for ever.

Exodus 33:19   Job 33:24   Romans 3:24,25   John 1:17   Ephesians 2:8
1 Timothy 1:2   Ephesians 4:7 1   Peter 4:10   James 4:6 2   Peter 3:18

SEPTEMBER 19 EVENING

I will lift up mine eyes unto the hills,
from whence cometh my help.
My help cometh from the Lord.
— *PSALM 121:1,2*

As the mountains are round about Jerusalem, so the Lord is round about his people from henceforth even for ever. — Unto thee lift I up mine eyes, O thou that dwellest in the heavens. Behold, as the eyes of servants look unto the hand of their masters, and as the eyes of a maiden unto the hand of her mistress; so our eyes wait upon the Lord our God, until that he have mercy upon us. — Because thou hast been my help, therefore in the shadow of thy wings will I rejoice. — O our God, wilt thou not judge them? for we have no might against this great company that cometh against us; neither know we what to do: but our eyes are upon thee. — Mine eyes are ever toward the Lord; for he shall pluck my feet out of the net. — Our help is in the name of the Lord, who made heaven and earth.

Psalms 125:2, 123:1,2, 63:7 2   Chronicles 20:12   Psalms 25:15, 124:8

SEPTEMBER 20 MORNING

Happy is the man that findeth wisdom,
and the man that getteth understanding.
— PROVERBS 3:13

Whoso findeth me findeth life, and shall obtain favour of the Lord. — Thus saith the Lord, Let not the wise man glory in his wisdom, neither let the mighty man glory in his might:...but let him that glorieth glory in this, that he understandeth and knoweth me, that I am the Lord. — The fear of the Lord is the beginning of wisdom. — What things were gain to me, those I counted loss for Christ. Yea doubtless, and I count all things but loss for the excellency of the knowledge of Christ Jesus my Lord: for whom I have suffered the loss of all things, and do count them but dung, that I may win Christ. — In whom are hid all the treasures of wisdom and knowledge. — Counsel is mine, and sound wisdom: I am understanding; I have strength. — Christ Jesus...is made unto us wisdom, and righteousness, and sanctification, and redemption. — He that winneth souls is wise.

Proverbs 8:35   Jeremiah 9:23,24   Proverbs 9:10   Philippians 3:7,8
Colossians 2:3   Proverbs 8:14 1 Corinthians 1:30   Proverbs 11:30

SEPTEMBER 20 EVENING

Poor, yet making many rich.
— 2 CORINTHIANS 6:10

Ye know the grace of our Lord Jesus Christ, that, though he was rich, yet for your sakes he became poor, that ye through his poverty might be rich. — Of his fulness have all we received, and grace for grace. — My God shall supply all your need according to his riches in glory by Christ Jesus. — God is able to make all grace abound toward you; that ye, always having all sufficiency in all things, may abound to every good work. — Hath not God chosen the poor of this world rich in faith, and heirs of the kingdom which he hath promised to them that love him? — Not many wise men after the flesh, not many mighty, not many noble, are called: but God hath chosen the foolish things of the world to confound the wise; and God hath chosen the weak things of the world to confound the things which are mighty. — We have this treasure in earthen vessels, that the excellency of the power may be of God, and not of us.

2 Corinthians 8:9   John 1:16   Philippians 4:19 2 Corinthians 9:8
James 2:5 1 Corinthians 1:26,27 2 Corinthians 4:7

SEPTEMBER 21 MORNING

*We know that all things work together for good
to them that love God.*
— ROMANS 8:28

Surely the wrath of man shall praise thee: the remainder of wrath shalt thou restrain. — Ye thought evil against me: but God meant it unto good. — All things are yours; whether...the world, or life, or death, or things present, or things to come; all are yours; and ye are Christ's; and Christ is God's. — All things are for your sakes, that the abundant grace might through the thanksgiving of many redound to the glory of God. For which cause we faint not; but though our outward man perish, yet the inward man is renewed day by day. For our light affliction, which is but for a moment, worketh for us a far more exceeding and eternal weight of glory. — My brethren, count it all joy when ye fall into divers temptations; knowing this, that the trying of your faith worketh patience. But let patience have her perfect work, that ye may be perfect and entire, wanting nothing.

Psalm 76:10   Genesis 50:20   1 Corinthians 3:21-23
2 Corinthians 4:15-17   James 1:2-4

SEPTEMBER 21 EVENING

The communion of the Holy Ghost be with you all.
— 2 CORINTHIANS 13:14

I will pray the Father, and he shall give you another Comforter, that he may abide with you for ever; even the Spirit of truth; whom the world cannot receive, because it seeth him not, neither knoweth him: but ye know him; for he dwelleth with you, and shall be in you. — He shall not speak of himself. He shall glorify me: for he shall receive of mine, and shall shew it unto you. — The love of God is shed abroad in our hearts by the Holy Ghost which is given unto us. — He that is joined unto the Lord is one spirit. — Know ye not that your body is the temple of the Holy Ghost which is in you, which ye have of God, and ye are not your own? — Grieve not the holy Spirit of God, whereby ye are sealed unto the day of redemption. — The Spirit also helpeth our infirmities: for we know not what we would pray for as we ought: but the Spirit itself maketh intercession for us with groanings which cannot be uttered.

John 14:16,17, 16:13,14   Romans 5:5
1 Corinthians 6:17,19   Ephesians 4:30   Romans 8:26

SEPTEMBER 22 MORNING

My meditation of him shall be sweet:
I will be glad in the Lord.
— PSALM 104:34

As the apple tree among the trees of the wood, so is my beloved among the sons. I sat down under his shadow with great delight, and his fruit was sweet to my taste. — For who in the heaven can be compared unto the Lord? Who among the sons of the mighty can be likened unto the Lord? — My beloved is white and ruddy, the chiefest among ten thousand. — One pearl of great price. — The prince of the kings of the earth. — His head is as the most fine gold, his locks are bushy, and black as a raven. — The head over all things. — He is the head of the body, the church. — His cheeks are as a bed of spices, as sweet flowers. — He could not be hid. — His lips like lilies, dropping sweet smelling myrrh. — Never man spake like this man. — His countenance is as Lebanon, excellent as the cedars. — Make thy face to shine upon thy servant. — Lord, lift thou up the light thy countenance upon us.

Song of Solomon 2:3   Psalm 89:6   Song of Solomon 5:10   Matthew 13:46
Revelation 1:5   Song of Solomon 5:11   Ephesians 1:22   Colossians 1:18
Song of Solomon 5:13   Mark 7:24   Song of Solomon 5:13   John 7:46
Song of Solomon 5:15   Psalms 31:16, 4:6

SEPTEMBER 22 EVENING

O my Father, if it be possible, let this cup pass from me:
nevertheless not as I will, but as thou wilt.
— MATTHEW 26:39

Now is my soul troubled; and what shall I say? Father, save me from this hour: but for this cause came I unto this hour. — I came down from heaven, not to do mine own will, but the will of him that sent me. — He...became obedient unto death, even the death of the cross. — In the days of his flesh, when he had offered up prayers and supplications with strong crying and tears unto him that was able to save him from death, and was heard in that he feared; though he were a Son, yet learned he obedience by the things which he suffered. — Thinkest thou that I cannot now pray to my Father, and he shall presently give me more than twelve legions of angels? — Thus it is written, and thus it behooved Christ to suffer, and to rise from the dead the third day: and that repentance and remission of sins should be preached in his name among all nations, beginning at Jerusalem.

John 12:27   John 6:38   Philippians 2:8   Hebrews
5:7,8   Matthew 26:53   Luke 24:46,47

SEPTEMBER 23 MORNING

Our God hath not forsaken us.
— EZRA 9:9

Beloved, think it not strange concerning the fiery trial which is to try you, as though some strange thing happened unto you. — If ye endure chastening, God dealeth with you as with sons; for what son is he whom the father chasteneth not? But if ye be without chastisement, whereof all are partakers, then are ye bastards, and not sons. — The Lord your God proveth you, to know whether ye love the Lord your God with all your heart and with all your soul. — The Lord will not forsake his people for his great name's sake: because it hath pleased the Lord to make you his people. — Can a woman forget her sucking child, that she should not have compassion on the son of her womb? Yea, they may forget, yet will I not forget thee. — Happy is he that hath the God of Jacob for his help, whose hope is in the Lord his God. — Shall not God avenge his own elect, which cry day and night unto him, though he bear long with them? I tell you that he will avenge them speedily.

1 Peter 4:12   Hebrews 12:7,8   Deuteronomy 13:3
1 Samuel 12:22   Isaiah 49:15   Psalm 146:5   Luke 18:7,8

SEPTEMBER 23 EVENING

He that overcometh shall inherit all things.
— REVELATION 21:7

If in this life only we have hope in Christ, we are of all men most miserable. — Now they desire a better country, that is, an heavenly: wherefore God is not ashamed to be called their God; for he hath prepared for them a city. — An inheritance incorruptible, and undefiled, and that fadeth not away, reserved in heaven for you. — All things are yours;...the world, or life, or death, or things present, or things to come; all are yours. — Eye hath not seen, nor ear heard, neither have entered into the heart of man, the things which God hath prepared for them that love him. But God hath revealed them unto us by his Spirit. — Look to yourselves, that we lose not those things which we have wrought, but that we receive a full reward. — Let us lay aside every weight, and the sin which doth so easily beset us, and let us run with patience the race that is set before us.

1 Corinthians 15:19   Hebrews 11:16 1   Peter 1:4
1 Corinthians 3:21,22, 2:9,10 2 John 8   Hebrews 12:1

SEPTEMBER 24 MORNING

It is good for me to draw near to God.
— PSALM 73:28

Lord, I have loved the habitation of thy house, and the place where thine honour dwelleth. — A day in thy courts is better than a thousand. I had rather be a door-keeper in the house of my God, than to dwell in the tents of wickedness. — Blessed is the man whom thou choosest, and causest to approach unto thee, that he may dwell in thy courts: we shall be satisfied with the goodness of thy house, even of thy holy temple. — The Lord is good unto them that wait for him, to the soul that seeketh him. — Therefore will the Lord wait that he may be gracious unto you, and therefore will he be exalted that he may have mercy upon you: for the Lord is a God of judgment: blessed are all they that wait for him. — Having therefore, brethren, boldness to enter into the holiest by the blood of Jesus, by a new and living way, which he hath consecrated for us:...let us draw near with a true heart in full assurance of faith, having our hearts sprinkled from an evil conscience.

Psalms 26:8, 84:10, 65:4   Lamentations 3:25   Isaiah 30:18   Hebrews 10:19,20,22

SEPTEMBER 24 EVENING

Ye know the grace of our Lord Jesus Christ.
— 2 CORINTHIANS 8:9

The Word was made flesh, and dwelt among us, (and we beheld his glory, the glory as of the only begotten of the Father,) full of grace and truth. — Thou are fairer than the children of men: grace is poured into thy lips. — All bare him witness, and wondered at the gracious words which proceeded out of his mouth. — Ye have tasted that the Lord is gracious. — He that believeth on the Son of God hath the witness in himself. — We speak that we do know, and testify that we have seen. — O taste and see that the Lord is good: blessed is the man that trusteth in him. — I sat down under his shadow with great delight, and his fruit was sweet to my taste. — He said unto me, My grace is sufficient for thee: for my strength is made perfect in weakness. — Unto every one of us is given grace according to the measure of the gift of Christ. — As every man hath received the gift, even so minister the same one to another, as good stewards of the manifold grace of God.

John 1:14   Psalm 45:2   Luke 4:22 1   Peter 2:3
1   John 5:10   John 3:11   Psalm 34:8
Song of Solomon 2:3 2   Corinthians 12:9   Ephesians 4:7 1   Peter 4:10

SEPTEMBER 25 MORNING

*Let patience have her perfect work,
that ye may be perfect and entire, wanting nothing.*
— JAMES 1:4

Now for a season, if need be, ye are in heaviness through manifold temptations: that the trial of your faith, being much more precious than of gold that perisheth, though it be tried with fire, might be found unto praise and honour and glory at the appearing of Jesus Christ. — We glory in tribulations:...knowing that tribulation worketh patience; and patience, experience; and experience, hope. — It is good that a man should both hope and quietly wait for the salvation of the Lord. — Ye have in heaven a better and an enduring substance. Cast not away therefore your confidence, which hath great recompence of reward. For ye have need of patience, that, after ye have done the will of God, ye might receive the promise. — Our Lord Jesus Christ himself, and God, even our Father, which hath loved us, and hath given us everlasting consolation and good hope through grace, comfort your hearts.

1 Peter 1:6,7   Romans 5:3,4   Lamentations 3:26
Hebrews 10:34-36 2 Thessalonians 2:16,17

SEPTEMBER 25 EVENING

God shall judge the secrets of men by Jesus Christ.
— ROMANS 2:16

Judge nothing before the time, until the Lord come, who both will bring to light the hidden things of darkness, and will make manifest the counsels of the hearts: and then shall every man have praise of God. — The Father judgeth no man, but hath committed all judgment unto the Son: because he is the Son of man. — The Son of God...hath his eyes like unto a flame of fire. — They say, How doth God know? And is there knowledge in the most High? — These things thou hast done, and I kept silence; thou thoughtest that I was altogether such an one as thyself: but I will reprove thee, and set them in order before thine eyes. — There is nothing covered, that shall not be revealed; neither hid, that shall not be known. — Lord, all my desire is before thee; and my groaning is not hid from thee. — Examine me, O Lord, and prove me; try my reins and my heart.

1 Corinthians 4:5   John 5:22,27   Revelation 2:18
Psalms 73:11, 50:21   Luke 12:2   Psalms 38:9, 26:2

SEPTEMBER 26 MORNING

A God of truth and without iniquity, just and right is he.
— DEUTERONOMY 32:4

Him that judgeth righteously. — We must all appear before the judgment seat of Christ; that every one may receive the things done in his body, according to that he hath done, whether it be good or bad. — Every one of us shall give account of himself to God. — The soul that sinneth it shall die. — Awake, O sword, against my shepherd, and against the man that is my fellow, saith the Lord of hosts: smite the shepherd. — The Lord hath laid on him the iniquity of us all. — Mercy and truth are met together: righteousness and peace have kissed each other. — Mercy rejoiceth against judgment. — The wages of sin is death; but the gift of God is eternal life through Jesus Christ our Lord. — A just God and a Saviour; there is none beside me. — Just, and the justifier of him which believeth in Jesus. — Justified freely by his grace through the redemption that is in Christ Jesus.

1 Peter 2:23 2 Corinthians 5:10 Romans 14:12 Ezekiel 18:4 Zechariah 13:7 Isaiah 53:6 Psalm 85:10 James 2:13 Romans 6:23 Isaiah 45:21 Romans 3:26,24

SEPTEMBER 26 EVENING

Death is swallowed up in victory.
— 1 CORINTHIANS 15:54

Thanks be to God, which giveth us the victory through our Lord Jesus Christ. — Forasmuch...as the children are partakers of flesh and blood, he also himself likewise took part of the same; that through death he might destroy him that had the power of death, that is, the devil; and deliver them who through fear of death were all their lifetime subject to bondage. — If we be dead with Christ, we believe that we shall also live with him: knowing that Christ being raised from the dead dieth no more; death hath no more dominion over him. For in that he died, he died unto sin once: but in that he liveth, he liveth unto God. — Likewise reckon ye also yourselves to be dead indeed unto sin, but alive unto God through Jesus Christ our Lord. — In all these things we are more than conquerors through him that loved us.

1 Corinthians 15:57 Hebrews 2:14,15 Romans 6:8-10, 6:11, 8:37

SEPTEMBER 27 MORNING

*Humble yourselves under the mighty hand of God,
that he may exalt you in due time.*
— 1 PETER 5:6

Every one that is proud in heart is an abomination to the Lord: though hand join in hand, he shall not be unpunished. — O Lord, thou art our father; we are the clay, and thou our potter; and we all are the work of thy hand. Be not wroth very sore, O Lord, neither remember iniquity for ever: behold, see we beseech thee, we are all thy people. — Thou hast chastised me, and I was chastised, as a bullock unaccustomed to the yoke: turn thou me, and I shall be turned; for thou art the Lord my God. Surely after that I was turned, I repented; and after that I was instructed, I smote upon my thigh: I was ashamed, yea, even confounded, because I did bear the reproach of my youth. — It is good for a man that he bear the yoke in his youth. — Affliction cometh not forth of the dust, neither doth trouble spring out of the ground; yet man is born unto trouble, as the sparks fly upward.

Proverbs 16:5   Isaiah 64:8,9   Jeremiah 31:18,19   Lamentations 3:27   Job 5:6,7

SEPTEMBER 27 EVENING

Yea, hath God said?
— GENESIS 3:1

When the tempter came to Jesus, he said, If thou be the Son of God. — Jesus said unto him, It is written...it is written...it is written. — Then the devil leaveth him. — I may not return with thee. For it was said to me by the word of the Lord, Thou shalt eat no bread nor drink water there. He said unto him, I am a prophet also as thou art; and an angel spake unto me by the word of the Lord, saying, Bring him back with thee into thine house, that he may eat bread and drink water. But he lied unto him. So he went back with him. The man of God... was disobedient unto the word of the Lord: therefore the Lord hath delivered him unto the lion, which hath torn him, and slain him, according to the word of the Lord. — Though we, or an angel from heaven, preach any other gospel unto you than that which we have preached unto you, let him be accursed. — Thy word have I hid in mine heart, that I might not sin against thee.

Matthew 4:3,4,7,10,11   1 Kings 13:16-19,26   Galatians 1:8   Psalm 119:11

SEPTEMBER 28 MORNING

They shall put my name upon the children of Israel;
and I will bless them.
— NUMBERS 6:27

O Lord our God, other lords beside thee have had dominion over us: but by thee only will we make mention of thy name. — We are thine: thou never barest rule over them; they were not called by thy name. — All people of the earth shall see that thou art called by the name of the Lord; and they shall be afraid of thee. — The Lord will not forsake his people for his great name's sake: because it hath pleased the Lord to make you his people. — O Lord, hear; O Lord, forgive; O Lord, hearken and do; defer not, for thine own sake, O my God: for thy city and thy people are called by thy name. — Help us, O God of our salvation, for the glory of thy name: and deliver us, and purge away our sins, for thy name's sake. Wherefore should the heathen say, Where is their God?— The name of the Lord is a strong tower; the righteous runneth into it, and is safe.

Isaiah 26:13, 63:19   Deuteronomy 28:10   1 Samuel 12:22
Daniel 9:19   Psalm 79:9,10   Proverbs 18:10

SEPTEMBER 28 EVENING

The heavens declare the glory of God;
and the firmament sheweth his handywork.
— PSALM 19:1

The invisible things of him from the creation of the world are clearly seen, being understood by the things that are made, even his eternal power and Godhead. — He left not himself without witness. — Day unto day uttereth speech, and night unto night sheweth knowledge. There is no speech nor language, where their voice is not heard. — When I consider thy heavens, the work of thy fingers, the moon and the stars, which thou hast ordained; what is man, that thou art mindful of him? And the son of man, that thou visitest him? — There is one glory of the sun, and another glory of the moon, and another glory of the stars: for one star differeth from another star in glory. So also is the resurrection of the dead. — They that be wise shall shine as the brightness of the firmament; and they that turn many to righteousness as the stars for ever and ever.

Romans 1:20   Acts 14:17   Psalms 19:2,3, 8:3,4
1 Corinthians 15:41,42   Daniel 12:3

SEPTEMBER 29 MORNING

*Hereby perceive we the love of God,
because he laid down his life for us.*
— 1 JOHN 3:16a

The love of Christ, which passeth knowledge. — Greater love hath no man than this, that a man lay down his life for his friends. Ye know the grace of our Lord Jesus Christ, that, though he was rich, yet for your sakes he became poor, that ye through his poverty might be rich. — Beloved, if God so loved us, we ought also to love one another. — Be ye kind one to another, tenderhearted, forgiving one another, even as God for Christ's sake hath forgiven you. — Forbearing one another, and forgiving one another, if any man have a quarrel against any: even as Christ forgave you, so also do ye. — For even the Son of man came not to be ministered unto, but to minister, and to give his life a ransom for many. — Christ...suffered for us, leaving us an example, that ye should follow his steps. — Ye also ought to wash one another's feet. For I have given you an example, that ye should do as I have done to you. — We ought to lay down our lives for the brethren.

Ephesians 3:19   John 15:13 2   Corinthians 8:9 1   John 4:11   Ephesians 4:32   Colossians 3:13   Mark 10:45 1   Peter 2:21   John 13:14,15 1   John 3:16b

SEPTEMBER 29 EVENING

*What things soever the Father doeth,
these also doeth the Son likewise.*
—JOHN 5:19

The Lord giveth wisdom: out of his mouth cometh knowledge and understanding. — I will give you a mouth and wisdom, which all your adversaries shall not be able to gainsay nor resist. — Wait on the Lord: be of good courage, and he shall strengthen thine heart. — My grace is sufficient for thee: for my strength is made perfect in weakness. — Them that are sanctified by God the Father. — He that sanctifieth and they who are sanctified are all of one: for which cause he is not ashamed to call them brethren. — Do not I fill heaven and earth, saith the Lord? — The fulness of him that filleth all in all. — I, even I, am the Lord; and beside me there is no saviour. — This is indeed the Christ, the Saviour of the world. — Grace, mercy, and peace, from God the Father and the Lord Jesus Christ our Saviour.

Proverbs 2:6   Luke 21:15   Psalm 27:14 2   Corinthians 12:9 Jude 1   Hebrews 2:11   Jeremiah 23:24   Ephesians 1:23   Isaiah 43:11   John 4:42   Titus 1:4

SEPTEMBER 30 MORNING

He knoweth the way that I take:
when he hath tried me, I shall come forth as gold.
— JOB 23:10

He knoweth our frame. — He doth not afflict willingly nor grieve the children of men. — The foundation of God standeth sure, having this seal, The Lord knoweth them that are his. And, Let every one that nameth the name of Christ depart from iniquity. But in a great house there are not only vessels of gold and of silver, but also of wood and of earth; and some to honour, and some to dishonour. If a man therefore purge himself from these, he shall be a vessel unto honour, sanctified, and meet for the master's use, and prepared unto every good work. — He shall sit as a refiner and purifier of silver: and he shall purify the sons of Levi, and purge them as gold and silver, that they may offer unto the Lord an offering in righteousness. — I...will refine them as silver is refined... they shall call on my name, and I will hear them: I will say, It is my people: and they shall say, the Lord is my God.

Psalm 103:14   Lamentations 3:33 2   Timothy 2:19-21   Malachi 3:3   Zechariah 13:9

SEPTEMBER 30 EVENING

Shew me thy ways, O Lord; teach me thy paths.
— PSALM 25:4

Moses said unto the Lord, I pray thee, if I have found grace in thy sight, shew me now thy way, that I may know thee. And he said, My presence shall go with thee, and I will give thee rest. — He made known his ways unto Moses, his acts unto the children of Israel. — The meek will he guide in judgment; and the meek will he teach his way. What man is he that feareth the Lord? Him shall teach in the way that he shall choose. — Trust in the Lord with all thine heart; and lean not unto thine own understanding. In all thy ways acknowledge him, and he shall direct thy paths. — Thou wilt shew me the path of life: in thy presence is fulness of joy; at thy right hand there are pleasures for evermore. — I will instruct thee and teach thee in the way which thou shalt go: I will guide thee with mine eye. — The path of the just is as the shining light, that shineth more and more unto the perfect day.

Exodus 33:12-14   Psalms 103:7, 25:9,12   Proverbs 3:5,6   Psalms 16:11, 32:8   Proverbs 4:18

OCTOBER 1 MORNING

The fruit of the Spirit is temperance.
— GALATIANS 5:22

Every man that striveth for the mastery is temperate in all things. Now they do it to obtain a corruptible crown; but we an incorruptible. I therefore so run, not as uncertainly; so fight I, not as one that beateth the air: but I keep under my body, and bring it into subjection: lest that by any means, when I have preached to others, I myself should be a castaway. — Be not drunk with wine, wherein is excess: but be filled with the Spirit. — If any man will come after me let him deny himself, and take up his cross, and follow me. — Let us not sleep, as do others: but let us watch and be sober. For they that sleep in the night; and they that be drunken are drunken in the night. But let us, who are of the day, be sober. — Denying ungodliness and worldly lusts, we should live soberly, righteously, and godly, in this present world: looking for that blessed hope, and the glorious appearing of the great God and our Saviour Jesus Christ.

1 Corinthians 9:25-27   Ephesians 5:18   Matthew 16:24
1 Thessalonians 5:6-8   Titus 2:12,13

OCTOBER 1 EVENING

*Grow up into him in all things,
which is the head, even Christ.*
— EPHESIANS 4:15

First the blade, then the ear, after that the full corn in the ear. — Till we all come to the unity of the faith, and of the knowledge of the Son of God, unto a perfect man, unto the measure of the stature of the fulness of Christ. — They measuring themselves by themselves, and comparing themselves among themselves, are not wise. But he that glorieth, let him glory in the Lord. For not he that commendeth himself is approved, but whom the Lord commendeth. — The body is of Christ. Let no man beguile you of your reward in a voluntary humility and worshipping of angels, intruding into those things which he hath not seen, vainly puffed up by his fleshly mind, and not holding the Head from which all the body by joints and bands, having nourishment ministered and knit together, increaseth with the increase of God. — Grow in grace, and in the knowledge of our Lord and Saviour Jesus Christ.

Mark 4:28   Ephesians 4:13   2 Corinthians 10:12,17,18
Colossians 2:17-19   2 Peter 3:18

OCTOBER 2 MORNING

The goat shall bear upon him all their iniquities
unto a land not inhabited:
and he shall let go the goat in the wilderness.
— LEVITICUS 16:22

As far as the east is from the west, so far hath he removed our transgressions from us. — In those days, and in that time, saith the Lord, the iniquity of Israel shall be sought for, and there shall be none; and the sins of Judah, and they shall not be found: for I will pardon them whom I reserve. — Thou wilt cast all their sins into the depths of the sea. — Who is a God like unto thee, that pardoneth iniquity? — All we like sheep have gone astray; we have turned every one to his own way; and the Lord hath laid on him the iniquity of us all. — He shall bear their iniquities. Therefore will I divide him a portion with the great, and he shall divide the spoil with the strong, because he hath poured out his soul unto death; and he was numbered with the transgressors; and he bare the sin of many, and made intercession for the transgressors. — The Lamb of God, which taketh away the sin of the world.

Psalm 103:12   Jeremiah 50:20   Micah 7:19,18   Isaiah 53:6,11,12   John 1:29

OCTOBER 2 EVENING

Who maketh thee to differ from another?
And what hast thou that thou didst not receive?
— 1 CORINTHIANS 4:7

By the grace of God I am what I am. — Of his own will begat he us with the word of truth. — It is not of him that willeth, nor of him that runneth, but of God that sheweth mercy. — Where is boasting then? It is excluded. — Christ Jesus...is made unto us wisdom, and righteousness, and sanctification, and redemption:...He that glorieth let him glory in the Lord. — You hath he quickened, who were dead in trespasses and sins; wherein in time past ye walked according to the course of this world, according to the prince of the power of the air, the spirit that now worketh in the children of disobedience: among whom also we all had our conversation in times past in the lusts of our flesh, fulfilling the desires of the flesh and of the mind; and were by nature the children of wrath, even as others. — Ye are washed...ye are sanctified...ye are justified in the name of the Lord Jesus, and by the Spirit of our God.

1 Corinthians 15:10   James 1:18   Romans 9:16, 3:27
1 Corinthians 1:30,31   Ephesians 2:1-3 1   Corinthians 6:11

OCTOBER 3 MORNING

Unto him that loved us,
and washed us from our sins in his own blood.
— REVELATION 1:5

Many waters cannot quench love, neither can the floods drown it. Love is strong as death. — Greater love hath no man than this, that a man lay down his life for his friends. — Who his own self bare our sins in his own body on the tree, that we, being dead to sins, should live unto righteousness: by whose stripes ye were healed. — In whom we have redemption through his blood, the forgiveness of sins, according to the riches of his grace. — Ye are washed...ye are sanctified...ye are justified in the name of the Lord Jesus, and by the Spirit of our God. — Ye are a chosen generation, a royal priesthood, a holy nation, a peculiar people; that ye should shew forth the praises of him who hath called you out of darkness into his marvellous light. — I beseech you...brethren, by the mercies of God, that ye present your bodies a living sacrifice, holy, acceptable unto God, which is your reasonable service.

Song of Solomon 8:7,6   John 15:13 1   Peter 2:24   Ephesians 1:7
1 Corinthians 6:11 1   Peter 2:9   Romans 12:1

OCTOBER 3 EVENING

There are differences of administrations,
but the same Lord.
— 1 CORINTHIANS 12:5

Over the king's treasures was Azmaveth the son of Adiel: and over the storehouses...Jehonathan: and over them that did the work of the field for tillage of the ground was Ezri: and over the vineyards was Shimei. These were the rulers of the substance which was king David's. — God hath set some in the church, first apostles, secondarily prophets, thirdly teachers, after that miracles, then gifts of healings, helps, governments, diversities of tongues. All these worketh that one and the selfsame Spirit, dividing to every man severally as he will. — As every man hath received the gift, even so minister the same one to another, as good stewards of the manifold grace of God. If any man speak, let him speak as the oracles of God; if any man minister, let him do it as of the ability which God giveth: that God in all things may be glorified through Jesus Christ, to whom be praise and dominion for ever and ever.

1 Chronicles 27:25-27,31 1   Corinthians 12:28,11 1   Peter 4:10,11

OCTOBER 4 MORNING

*Moses wist not that the skin of his face shone
while he talked with him.*
— EXODUS 34:29

Not unto us, O Lord, not unto us, but unto thy name give glory. — Lord, when saw we thee a hungered, and fed thee? Or thirsty, and gave thee drink? — In lowliness of mind, let each esteem other better than themselves. — Be clothed with humility. — [Jesus] was transfigured before them: and his face did shine as the sun, and his raiment was white as the light. — All that sat in the council, looking stedfastly on Stephen, saw his face as it had been the face of an angel. — The glory which thou gavest me, I have given them. — We all, with open face beholding as in a glass the glory of the Lord, are changed into the same image from glory to glory, even as by the Spirit of the Lord. — Ye are the light of the world. A city that is set on a hill cannot be hid. Neither do men light a candle, and put it under a bushel, but on a candlestick; and it giveth light unto all that are in the house.

Psalm 115:1   Matthew 25:37   Philippians 2:3   1 Peter 5:5   Matthew 17:2
Acts 6:15   John 17:22   2 Corinthians 3:18   Matthew 5:14,15

OCTOBER 4 EVENING

*There are diversities of operations,
but it is the same God which worketh all in all.*
— 1 CORINTHIANS 12:6

There fell some of Manasseh to David. And they helped David against the band of the rovers: for they were all mighty men of valour. — The manifestation of the spirit is given to every man to profit withal. — Of the children of Issachar, which were men that had understanding of the times, to know what Israel ought to do. — To one is given by the Spirit...the word of wisdom, to another the word of knowledge by the same Spirit. — Of Zebulun, such as went forth to battle, expert in war, with all instruments of war, fifty thousand, which could keep rank: they were not of double heart. — A double minded man is unstable in all his ways. — There should be no schism in the body; but...the members should have the same care one for another. And whether one member suffer, all the members suffer with it; or one member be honoured, all the members rejoice with it. — One Lord, one faith, one baptism.

1 Chronicles 12:19,21   1 Corinthians 12:7
1 Chronicles 12:32   1 Corinthians 12:8
1 Chronicles 12:33   James 1:8   1 Corinthians 12:25,26   Ephesians 4:5

OCTOBER 5 MORNING

Call upon me in the day of trouble:
I will deliver thee, and thou shalt glorify me.
— PSALM 50:15

Why art thou cast down, O my soul? and why art thou disquieted within me? hope thou in God: for I shall yet praise him, who is the health of my countenance, and my God. — Lord, thou hast heard the desire of the humble: thou wilt prepare their heart, thou wilt cause thine ear to hear. — For thou, Lord, art good, and ready to forgive; and plenteous in mercy unto all them that call upon thee. — Jacob said unto his household...Let us arise and go up to Bethel; and I will make there an altar unto God, who answered me in the day of my distress, and was with me in the way which I went. — Bless the Lord, O my soul, and forget not all his benefits. — I love the Lord, because he hath heard my voice and my supplications. Because he hath inclined his ear unto me, therefore will I call upon him as long as I live. The sorrows of death compassed me, and the pains of hell gat hold upon me: I found trouble and sorrow. Then called I on the name of the Lord.

Psalms 42:11, 10:17, 86:5   Genesis 35:2,3   Psalms 103:2, 116:1-4

OCTOBER 5 EVENING

Yet a little while and he that shall come will come,
and will not tarry.
— HEBREWS 10:37

Write the vision, and make it plain upon tables, that he may run that readeth it. For the vision is yet for an appointed time, but at the end it shall speak, and not lie: though it tarry, wait for it because it will surely come, it will not tarry. — Beloved, be not ignorant of this one thing, that one day is with the Lord as a thousand years, and a thousand years as one day. The Lord is not slack concerning his promise, as some men count slackness; but is longsuffering to us-ward, not willing that any should perish, but that all should come to repentance. — Thou, O Lord, art a God full of compassion, and gracious, longsuffering and plenteous in mercy and truth. — Oh that thou wouldest rend the heavens, that thou wouldest come down. For since the beginning of the world men have not heard, nor perceived by the ear, neither hath the eye seen, O God, beside thee, what he hath prepared for him that waiteth for him.

Habakkuk 2:2,3 2 Peter 3:8,9   Psalm 86:15   Isaiah 64:1,4

OCTOBER 6 MORNING

The Lord God omnipotent reigneth.
— REVELATION 19:6

I know that thou canst do every thing. — The things which are impossible with men are possible with God. — He doeth according to his will in the army of heaven, and among the inhabitants of the earth: and none can stay his hand, or say unto him, What doest thou? — There is none that can deliver out of my hand: I will work, and who shall let it?— Abba, Father, all things are possible unto thee. — Believe ye that I am able to do this? They said unto him, Yea, Lord. Then touched he their eyes, saying, According to your faith be it unto you. — Lord, if thou wilt, thou canst make me clean. And Jesus put forth his hand and touched him, saying, I will; be thou clean. — The mighty God. — All power is given unto me in heaven and in earth. — Some trust in chariots, and some in horses: but we will remember the name of the Lord our God. — Be strong and courageous, be not afraid nor dismayed…there be more with us than with him.

Job 42:2   Luke 18:27   Daniel 4:35   Isaiah 43:13   Mark 14:36   Matthew 9:28,29, 8:2,3   Isaiah 9:6   Matthew 28:18   Psalm 20:7   2 Chronicles 32:7

OCTOBER 6 EVENING

What is the thing that the Lord hath said unto thee?
— 1 SAMUEL 3:17

He hath shewed thee, O man, what is good; and what doth the Lord require of thee, but to do justly, and to love mercy, and to walk humbly with thy God?— To keep the commandments of the Lord, and his statutes, which I command thee this day for thy good. — As many as are of the works of the law are under the curse: for it is written, Cursed is every one that continueth not in all things which are written in the book of the law to do them. But that no man is justified by the law in the sight of God, it is evident: for The just shall live by faith. Wherefore then serveth the law? It was added because of transgressions, till the seed should come to whom the promise was made. — God, who at sundry times and in divers manners spake in time past unto the fathers by the prophets, hath in these last days spoken unto us by his Son. — Speak, Lord; for thy servant heareth.

Micah 6:8   Deuteronomy 10:13   Galatians 3:10,11,19   Hebrews 1:1,2   1 Samuel 3:9

OCTOBER 7 MORNING

The meek will he teach his way.
— PSALM 25:9

Blessed are the meek. — I returned, and saw under the sun, that the race is not to the swift, nor the battle to the strong, neither yet bread to the wise, nor yet riches to men of understanding, nor yet favour to men of skill. — A man's heart deviseth his way: but the Lord directeth his steps. — Unto thee lift I up mine eyes, O Thou that dwellest in the heavens. Behold, as the eyes of servants look unto the hand of their masters, and as the eyes of a maiden unto the hand of her mistress; so our eyes wait upon the Lord our God. — Cause me to know the way wherein I should walk; for I lift up my soul unto thee. — O our God, wilt thou not judge them? for we have no might against this great company that cometh against us; neither know we what to do: but our eyes are upon thee. — If any of you lack wisdom, let him ask of God, that giveth to all men liberally, and upbraideth not; and it shall be given him. — When he, the Spirit of truth, is come, he will guide you into all truth.

Matthew 5:5   Ecclesiastes 9:11   Proverbs 16:9   Psalms 123:1,2, 143:8
2 Chronicles 20:12   James 1:5   John 16:13

OCTOBER 7 EVENING

O Lord God...with thy blessing
let the house of thy servant be blessed for ever.
— 2 SAMUEL 7:29

Thou blessest, O Lord, and it shall be blessed for ever. — The blessing of the Lord, it maketh rich, and he addeth no sorrow with it. — Remember the words of the Lord Jesus, how he said, It more blessed to give than to receive. — When thou makest a feast call the poor, the maimed, the lame, the blind: and thou shalt be blessed; for they cannot recompense thee: for thou shalt be recompensed at the resurrection of the just. — Come, ye blessed my Father, inherit the kingdom prepared for you from the foundation of the world: for I was an hungred, and ye gave me meat: I was thirsty, and ye gave me drink: I was a stranger, and took me in: naked, and ye clothed me: I was sick, and ye visited me: I was in prison, and ye came unto me. — Blessed is he that considereth the poor: the Lord will deliver him in time of trouble. — The Lord God is a sun and shield.

1 Chronicles 17:27   Proverbs 10:22   Acts 20:35
Luke 14:13,14   Matthew 25:34-36   Psalm 41:1, 84:11

OCTOBER 8 MORNING

I will not fear what man shall do unto me.
— *HEBREWS 13:6*

Who shall separate us from the love of Christ? shall tribulation, or distress, or persecution, or famine, or nakedness, or peril, or sword? Nay, in all these things we are more than conquerors through him that loved us. — Be not afraid of them that kill the body, and after that have no more that they can do. But I will forewarn you whom ye shall fear: Fear him, which after he hath killed hath power to cast into hell: yea, I say unto you, Fear him. — Blessed are they which are persecuted for righteousness' sake: for theirs is the kingdom of heaven. Blessed are ye, when men shall revile you and persecute you, and shall say all manner of evil against you falsely, for my sake. Rejoice, and be exceeding glad: for great is your reward in heaven. — None of these things move me, neither count I my life dear unto myself, so that I might finish my course with joy. — I will speak of thy testimonies...before kings, and will not be ashamed.

Romans 8:35,37   Luke 12:4,5   Matthew 5:10-12   Acts 20:24   Psalm 119:46

OCTOBER 8 EVENING

He set my feet upon a rock.
— *PSALM 40:2*

That Rock was Christ. — Simon Peter...said, Thou art the Christ the Son of the living God. Upon this rock I will build my church; and the gates of hell shall not prevail against it. — Neither is there salvation in any other: for there is none other name under heaven given among men, whereby we must be saved. — Full assurance of faith. Faith without wavering. — Faith, nothing wavering... He that wavereth is like a wave of the sea driven with the wind and tossed. — Who shall separate us from the love of Christ? Shall tribulation, or distress, or persecution, or famine, or nakedness, or peril, or sword? Nay, in all these things we are more than conquerors through him that loved us. For I am persuaded, that neither death, nor life, nor angels, nor principalities, nor powers, nor things present, nor things to come, nor height, nor depth, nor any other creature, shall be able to separate us from the love of God, which is in Christ Jesus our Lord.

1 Corinthians 10:4   Matthew 16:16,18   Acts 4:12
Hebrews 10:22,23   James 1:6   Romans 8:35,37,39

OCTOBER 9 MORNING

Thou art a God ready to pardon, gracious and merciful.
— NEHEMIAH 9:17

The Lord is not slack concerning his promise, as some men count slackness; but is longsuffering to us-ward, not willing that any should perish, but that all should come to repentance. — The longsuffering of our Lord is salvation. — For this cause I obtained mercy, that in me first Jesus Christ might shew forth all longsuffering for a pattern to them which should hereafter believe on him to life everlasting. — Whatsoever things were written aforetime were written for our learning, that we through patience and comfort of the scriptures might have hope. — Despisest thou the riches of his goodness and forbearance and longsuffering; not knowing that the goodness of God leadeth thee to repentance? — Rend your heart, and not your garments, and turn unto the Lord your God: for he is gracious and merciful, slow to anger, and of great kindness, and repenteth him of the evil.

2 Peter 3:9,15 1 Timothy 1:16 Romans 15:4, 2:4 Joel 2:13

OCTOBER 9 EVENING

The words of the Lord are pure words.
— PSALM 12:6

Thy word is very pure: therefore thy servant loveth it. — The statutes of the Lord are right, rejoicing the heart: the commandment of the Lord is pure, enlightening the eyes. — Every word of God is pure: he is a shield unto them that put their trust in him. Add thou not unto his words, lest he reprove thee, and thou be found a liar. — Thy word have I hid in mine heart, that I might not sin against thee. I will meditate in thy precepts, and have respect unto thy ways. — Brethren, whatsoever things are true, whatsoever things are honest, whatsoever things are just, whatsoever things are pure, whatsoever things are lovely, whatsoever things are of good report, if there be any virtue, and if there be any praise, think on these things. — As newborn babes, desire the sincere milk of the word that ye may grow thereby. — We are not as many, which corrupt the word of God: but as of sincerity, but as of God, in the sight of God speak we in Christ. — Nor handling the word of God deceitfully.

Psalms 119:140, 19:8 Proverbs 30:5,6 Psalm 119:11,15
Philippians 4:8 1 Peter 2:2 2 Corinthians 2:17, 4:2

OCTOBER 10 MORNING

The whole family in heaven and earth.
— *EPHESIANS 3:15*

One God and Father of all, who is above all, and through all, and in you all. — Ye are all the children of God by faith in Christ Jesus. — That in the dispensation of the fulness of times, he might gather together in one all things in Christ, both which are in heaven, and which are on earth; even in him. — He is not ashamed to call them brethren. — Behold my mother and my brethren! Whosoever shall do the will of my Father which is in heaven, the same is my brother, and sister, and mother. — Go to my brethren, and say unto them, I ascend unto my Father, and your Father. — I saw under the altar the souls of them that were slain for the word of God, and for the testimony which they held:...and white robes were given unto every one of them; and it was said unto them, that they should rest for a little season, until their fellow-servants also and their brethren, that should be killed as they were, should be fulfilled. — That they without us should not be made perfect.

Ephesians 4:6   Galatians 3:26   Ephesians 1:10   Hebrews 2:11
Matthew 12:49,50   John 20:17   Revelation 6:9-11   Hebrews 11:40

OCTOBER 10 EVENING

After this manner...pray ye:
Our Father which art in heaven.
— *MATTHEW 6:9*

Jesus lifted up his eyes to heaven, and said, Father. — My Father, and your Father. — Ye are all the children of God by faith in Christ Jesus. — Ye have not received the spirit of bondage again to fear; but ye have received the Spirit of adoption, whereby we cry, Abba, Father. The Spirit itself beareth witness with our spirit, that we are the children of God. — Because ye are sons, God hath sent forth the Spirit of his Son into your hearts, crying, Abba, Father. Wherefore thou art no more a servant, but a son. — Verily, verily, I say unto you, Whatsoever ye shall ask the Father in my name, he will give it you. Hitherto have ye asked nothing in my name: ask, and ye shall receive, that your joy may be full. — I will receive you, and will be a Father unto you, and ye shall be my sons and daughters, saith the Lord Almighty.

John 17:1, 20:17   Galatians 3:26   Romans 8:15,16
Galatians 4:6,7   John 16:23,24   2 Corinthians 6:17,18

OCTOBER 11 MORNING

Be not far from me; for trouble is near.
— *PSALM 22:11*

How long wilt thou forget me, O Lord? for ever? How long wilt thou hide thy face from me? How long shall I take counsel in my soul, having sorrow in my heart daily? — Hide not thy face far from me; put not thy servant away in anger: thou hast been my help; leave me not, neither forsake me, O God of my salvation. — He shall call upon me, and I will answer him: I will be with him in trouble; I will deliver him, and honour him. — The Lord is nigh unto all them that call upon him, to all that call upon him in truth. He will fulfil the desire of them that fear him: he also will hear their cry, and will save them. — I will not leave you comfortless: I will come to you. — Lo, I am with you alway, even unto the end of the world. — God is our refuge and strength, a very present help in trouble. — Truly my soul waiteth upon God: from him cometh my salvation. — My soul, wait thou only upon God; for my expectation is from him.

Psalms 13:1,2, 27:9, 91:15, 145:18,19   John 14:18
Matthew 28:20   Psalms 46:1, 62:1,5

OCTOBER 11 EVENING

Hallowed be thy name.
— *MATTHEW 6:9*

Thou shalt worship no other god: for the Lord, whose name is Jealous, is a jealous God. — Who is like unto thee, O Lord, among the gods? Who is like thee, glorious in holiness, fearful in praises, doing wonders?— Holy, holy, holy, Lord God Almighty. — Worship the Lord in the beauty of holiness. — I saw... the Lord sitting upon a throne, high and lifted up, and his train filled the temple. Above it stood the seraphims. And one cried unto another, and said, Holy, holy, holy, is the Lord of hosts; the whole earth is full of his glory. Then said I, Woe is me! For I am undone. — I have heard of thee by the hearing of the ear: but now mine eye seeth thee. Wherefore I abhor myself. — The blood of Jesus Christ his Son cleanseth us from all sin. — That we might be partakers of his holiness. — Having therefore, brethren, boldness to enter into the holiest by the blood of Jesus, let us draw near with a true heart.

Exodus 34:14, 15:11   Revelation 4:8 1 Chronicles 16:29
Isaiah 6:1-3,5   Job 42:5,6 1 John 1:7   Hebrews 12:10, 10:19,22

OCTOBER 12 MORNING

God was in Christ, reconciling the world unto himself,
not imputing their trespasses unto them.
— 2 CORINTHIANS 5:19

It pleased the Father, that in him should all fulness dwell; and, having made peace through the blood of his cross, by him to reconcile all things unto himself. — Mercy and truth are met together; righteousness and peace have kissed each other. — I know the thoughts that I think toward you, saith the Lord, thoughts of peace, and not of evil. — Come now, and let us reason together, saith the Lord: though your sins be as scarlet, they shall be as white as snow; though they be red like crimson, they shall be as wool. — Who is a God like unto thee, that pardoneth iniquity? — Acquaint now thyself with him, and be at peace. — Work out your own salvation with fear and trembling. For it is God which worketh in you both to will and to do of his good pleasure. — Lord, thou wilt ordain peace for us: for thou also hast wrought all our works in us.

Colossians 1:19,20   Psalm 85:10   Jeremiah 29:11   Isaiah 1:18
Micah 7:18   Job 22:21   Philippians 2:12,13   Isaiah 26:12

OCTOBER 12 EVENING

Thy kingdom come.
— MATTHEW 6:10

In the days of these kings shall the God of heaven set up a kingdom, which shall never be destroyed: and the kingdom shall not be left to other people, but it shall break in pieces and consume all these kingdoms, and it shall stand for ever. — A stone...cut out without hands. — Not by might, nor by power, but by my Spirit, saith the Lord of hosts. — The kingdom of God cometh not with observation: neither shall they say, Lo here! or, lo there! for, behold, the kingdom of God is within you. — Unto you it is given to know the mystery of the kingdom of God. So is the kingdom of God, as if a man should cast seed into the ground; and should sleep, and rise night and day, and the seed should spring and grow up, he knoweth not how. But when the fruit is brought forth, immediately he putteth in the sickle, because the harvest is come. — Be ye...ready: for in such an hour as ye think not, the Son of man cometh. — The Spirit and the bride say, Come. And let him that heareth say, Come.

Daniel 2:44,34   Zechariah 4:6   Luke 17:20,21
Mark 4:11,26,27,29   Matthew 24:44   Revelation 22:17

OCTOBER 13 MORNING

*From the first day that thou didst
set thine heart to understand,
and to chasten thyself before thy God,
thy words were heard.*
— DANIEL 10:12

Thus saith the high and lofty One that inhabiteth eternity, whose name is Holy; I dwell in the high and holy place, with him also that is of a contrite and humble spirit, to revive the spirit of the humble, and to revive the heart of the contrite ones. — The sacrifices of God are a broken spirit: a broken and a contrite heart, O God, thou wilt not despise. — Though the Lord be high, yet hath he respect unto the lowly: but the proud he knoweth afar off. — Humble yourselves therefore under the mighty hand of God, that he may exalt you in due time. — God resisteth the proud, but giveth grace unto the humble. — Submit yourselves therefore to God. — Thou, Lord, art good, and ready to forgive; and plenteous in mercy unto all them that call upon thee. Give ear, O Lord, unto my prayer; and attend to the voice of my supplications. In the day of my trouble I will call upon thee: for thou wilt answer me.

Isaiah 57:15   Psalms 51:17, 138:6 1   Peter 5:6   James 4:6,7   Psalm 86:5-7

OCTOBER 13 EVENING

Thy will be done in earth, as it is in heaven.
— MATTHEW 6:10

Understanding what the will of the Lord is. — It is not the will of your Father which is in heaven, that one of these little ones should perish. — This is the will of God, even your sanctification. — That he no longer should live the rest of his time in the flesh to the lusts of men, but to the will of God. — Of his own will begat he us with the word of truth: wherefore lay apart all filthiness. — Be ye holy; for I am holy. — [Jesus] said, Whosoever shall do the will of God, the same is my brother, and my sister, and mother. — Whosoever heareth these sayings of mine, and doeth them, I will liken him unto a wise man, which built his house upon a rock: and the rain descended, and the floods came, and the winds blew, and beat upon that house; and it fell not: for it was founded upon a rock. — The world passeth away, and the lust thereof: but he that doeth the will of God abideth for ever.

Ephesians 5:17   Matthew 18:14 1   Thessalonians 4:3 1   Peter 4:2
James 1:18,21 1   Peter 1:16   Mark 3:34,35   Matthew 7:24,25 1   John 2:17

OCTOBER 14 MORNING

Christ both died, and rose, and revived,
that he might be Lord both of the dead and living.
— ROMANS 14:9

It pleased the Lord to bruise him; he hath put him to grief: when thou shalt make his soul an offering for sin, he shall see his seed, he shall prolong his days, and the pleasure of the Lord shall prosper in his hand. He shall see of the travail of his soul, and shall be satisfied: by his knowledge shall my righteous servant justify many; for he shall bear their iniquities. — Ought not Christ to have suffered these things, and to enter into his glory?— We thus judge, that if one died for all, then were all dead: and that be died for all, that they which live should not henceforth live unto themselves, but unto him which died for them, and rose again. — Let all the house of Israel know assuredly, that God hath made that same Jesus, whom ye have crucified, both Lord and Christ. — Who verily was foreordained before the foundation of the world, but was manifest in these last times for you, who by him do believe in God.

Isaiah 53:10,11   Luke 24:26 2   Corinthians 5:14,15   Acts 2:36 1   Peter 1:20,21

OCTOBER 14 EVENING

Give us this day our daily bread.
— MATTHEW 6:11

I have been young, and now am old; yet have I not seen the righteous forsaken, nor his seed begging bread. — His bread shall be given him; his waters shall be sure. — The ravens brought him bread and flesh in the morning, and bread and flesh in the evening; and he drank of the brook. — My God shall supply all your need according to his riches in glory by Christ Jesus. — Be content with such things as ye have: for he hath said, I will never leave thee, nor forsake thee. — He humbled thee, and suffered thee to hunger, and fed thee with manna...that he might make thee know that man doth not live by bread only, but by every word that proceedeth out of the mouth of the Lord doth man live. — Jesus said unto them, Verily, verily, I say unto you, Moses gave you not that bread from heaven; but my Father giveth you the true bread from heaven. For the bread of God is he which cometh down from heaven, and giveth life unto the world. Then said they unto him, Lord, evermore give us this bread.

Psalm 37:25   Isaiah 33:16 1   Kings 17:6   Philippians 4:19
Hebrews 13:5   Deuteronomy 8:3   John 6:32-34

OCTOBER 15 MORNING

God is my defence.
— PSALM 59:9

The Lord is my rock, and my fortress, and my deliverer; the God of my rock; in him will I trust: he is my shield, and the horn of my salvation, my high tower, and my refuge, my saviour. — The Lord is my strength and my shield; my heart trusted in him, and I am helped: therefore my heart greatly rejoiceth; and with my song will I praise him. — When the enemy shall come in like a flood, the Spirit of the Lord shall lift up a standard against him. — We may boldly say, The Lord is my helper, and I will not fear what man shall do unto me. — The Lord is my light and my salvation; whom shall I fear? the Lord is the strength of my life; of whom shall I be afraid? — As the mountains are round about Jerusalem, so the Lord is round about his people from henceforth even for ever. — Because thou hast been my help, therefore in the shadow of thy wings will I rejoice. — For thy name's sake lead me, and guide me.

2 Samuel 22:2,3   Psalm 28:7   Isaiah 59:19
Hebrews 13:6   Psalms 27:1, 125:2, 63:7, 31:3

OCTOBER 15 EVENING

Forgive us our debts, as we forgive our debtors.
— MATTHEW 6:12

Lord, how oft shall my brother sin against me, and I forgive him? till seven times? Jesus saith unto him, I say not unto thee, Until seven times: but, Until seventy times seven. — O thou wicked servant, I forgave thee all that debt, because thou desiredst me: shouldest not thou also have had compassion on thy fellow-servant, even as I had pity on thee? And his lord was wroth, and delivered him to the tormentors, till he should pay all that was due unto him. So likewise shall my heavenly Father do also unto you, if ye from your hearts forgive not every one his brother their trespasses. — Be ye kind one to another, tenderhearted, forgiving one another, even as God for Christ's sake hath forgiven you. — You...hath he quickened...having forgiven you all trespasses; blotting out the handwriting of ordinances that was against us, which was contrary to us, and took it out of the way, nailing it to his cross. — Even as Christ forgave you, so also do ye.

Matthew 18:21,22,32-35   Ephesians 4:32   Colossians 2:13,14, 3:13

OCTOBER 16 MORNING

*Not slothful in business;
fervent in spirit; serving the Lord.
— ROMANS 12:11*

Whatsoever thy hand findeth to do, do it with thy might; for there is no work, nor device, nor knowledge, nor wisdom, in the grave, whither thou goest. — Whatsoever ye do, do it heartily, as to the Lord, and not unto men; knowing that of the Lord ye shall receive the reward of the inheritance: for ye serve the Lord Christ. — Whatsoever good thing any man doeth, the same shall he receive of the Lord. — I must work the works of him that sent me, while it is day: the night cometh, when no man can work. — Wist ye not that I must be about my Father's business? — The zeal of thine house hath eaten me up. — Brethren, give diligence to make your calling and election sure: for if ye do these things, ye shall never fall. — We desire that every one of you do shew the same diligence to the full assurance of hope unto the end; that ye be not slothful, but followers of them who through faith and patience inherit the promises. — So run, that ye may obtain.

Ecclesiastes 9:10   Colossians 3:23,24   Ephesians 6:8   John 9:4
Luke 2:49   John 2:17 2   Peter 1:10   Hebrews 6:11,12 1   Corinthians 9:24

OCTOBER 16 EVENING

*Lead us not into temptation, but deliver us from evil.
— MATTHEW 6:13*

He that trusteth in his own heart is a fool: but whoso walketh wisely, he shall be delivered. — Let no man say when he is tempted, I am tempted of God: for God cannot be tempted with evil, neither tempteth he any man: but every man is tempted, when he is drawn away of his own lust, and enticed. — Wherefore come out from among them, and be ye separate, saith the Lord, and touch not the unclean thing; and I will receive you. — Lot lifted up his eyes, and beheld all the plain of Jordan, that it was well watered every where...even as the garden of the Lord. Then Lot chose him all the plain of Jordan; but the men of Sodom were wicked and sinners before the Lord exceedingly. — [The Lord] delivered just Lot, vexed with the filthy conversation of the wicked. The Lord knoweth how to deliver the godly out of temptations. — Yea, he shall be holden up: for God is able to make him stand.

Proverbs 28:26   James 1:13,14 2   Corinthians 6:17
Genesis 13:10,11,13 2   Peter 2:7,9   Romans 14:4

OCTOBER 17 MORNING

*In thy name shall they rejoice all the day;
and in thy righteousness shall they be exalted.*
— PSALM 89:16

In the Lord have I righteousness and strength: even to him shall men come; and all that are incensed against him shall be ashamed. In the Lord shall all the seed of Israel be justified, and shall glory. — Be glad in the Lord, and rejoice, ye righteous: and shout for joy, all ye that are upright in heart. — The righteousness of God without the law is manifested, being witnessed by the law and the prophets; even the righteousness of God which is by faith of Jesus Christ unto all and upon all them that believe. To declare...at this time his righteousness: that he might be just, and the justifier of him which believeth in Jesus. — Rejoice in the Lord alway: and again I say, Rejoice. — Whom having not seen, ye love; in whom, though now ye see him not, yet believing, ye rejoice with joy unspeakable and full of glory.

Isaiah 45:24,25   Psalm 32:11   Romans 3:21,22,26   Philippians 4:4   1 Peter 1:8

OCTOBER 17 EVENING

*Thine is the kingdom, and the power,
and the glory, for ever.*
— MATTHEW 6:13

The Lord reigneth, he is clothed with majesty: thy throne is established of old: thou art from everlasting. — The Lord is...great in power. — If God be for us, who can be against us? — Our God whom we serve is able to deliver us, and he will deliver us. — My Father, which gave them me, is greater than all; and no man is able to pluck them out of my Father's hand. — Greater is he that is in you, than he that is in the world. — Not unto us, O Lord, not unto us, but unto thy name give glory. — Thine, O Lord, is the greatness, and the power, and the glory, and the victory, and the majesty: for all that is in the heaven and in the earth is thine; thine is the kingdom, O Lord, and thou art exalted as head above all. Now therefore, our God, we thank thee and praise thy glorious name. But who am I, and what is my people, that we should be able to offer so willingly after this sort? for all things come of thee, and of thine own have we given thee.

Psalm 93:1,2   Nahum 1:3   Romans 8:31   Daniel 3:17   John 10:29
1 John 4:4   Psalm 115:1   1 Chronicles 29:11,13,14

OCTOBER 18 MORNING

*One of the soldiers with a spear pierced his side,
and forthwith came there out blood and water.*
— *JOHN 19:34*

Behold the blood of the covenant, which the Lord hath made with you. — The life of the flesh is in the blood: and I have given it to you upon the altar to make an atonement for your souls. — It is not possible that the blood of bulls and of goats should take away sins. — Jesus said unto them, This is my blood of the new testament, which is shed for many. — By his own blood he entered in once into the holy place, having obtained eternal redemption for us. — Peace through the blood of his cross. — Ye know that ye were not redeemed with corruptible things, as silver and gold...but with the precious blood of Christ, as of a lamb without blemish and without spot...manifest in these last times for you. — Then will I sprinkle clean water upon you and ye shall be clean:...from all your idols, will I cleanse you. — Let us draw near with a true heart in full assurance of faith, having our hearts sprinkled from an evil conscience.

Exodus 24:8   Leviticus 17:11   Hebrews 10:4   Mark 14:24   Hebrews 9:12
Colossians 1:20 1   Peter 1:18-20   Ezekiel 36:25   Hebrews 10:22

OCTOBER 18 EVENING

Amen.
— *MATTHEW 6:13*

Amen: the Lord God...say so too. — He who blesseth himself in the earth shall bless himself in the God of truth (Hebrews The Amen) and he that sweareth in the earth shall swear by the God of truth (The Amen) . — When God made promise to Abraham, because he could swear by no greater, he sware by himself. For men verily swear by the greater: and an oath for confirmation is to them an end of all strife. Wherein God, willing more abundantly to shew unto the heirs of promise the immutability of his counsel, confirmed it by an oath: that by two immutable things, in which it was impossible for God to lie, we might have a strong consolation, who have fled for refuge to lay hold upon the hope set before us. — These things saith the Amen, the faithful and true witness. — For all the promises of God in him are yea, and in him Amen, unto the glory of God by us. — Blessed be the Lord God, the God of Israel, who only doeth wondrous things. And blessed be his glorious name for ever. Amen, and Amen.

1 Kings 1:36   Isaiah 65:16   Hebrews 6:13,16-18
Revelation 3:14 2   Corinthians 1:20   Psalm 72:18,19

OCTOBER 19 MORNING

The Lord shall be thy confidence,
and shall keep thy foot from being taken.
— PROVERBS 3:26

Surely the wrath of man shall praise thee: the remainder of wrath shalt thou restrain. — The king's heart is in the hand of the Lord, as the rivers of water: he turneth it whithersoever he will. — When a man's ways please the Lord, he maketh even his enemies to be at peace with him. — I wait for the Lord, my soul doth wait, and in his word do I hope. My soul waiteth for the Lord more than they that wait for the morning: I say, more than they that watch for the morning. — I sought the Lord, and he heard me, and delivered me from all my fears. — The eternal God is thy refuge, and underneath are the everlasting arms: and he shall thrust out the enemy from before thee; and shall say, Destroy them. — Blessed is the man that trusteth in the Lord, and whose hope the Lord is. — What shall we then say to these things? If God be for us, who can be against us?

Psalm 76:10   Proverbs 21:1, 16:7   Psalms 130:5,6, 34:4
Deuteronomy 33:27   Jeremiah 17:7   Romans 8:31

OCTOBER 19 EVENING

Consolation in Christ...
comfort of love...
fellowship of the Spirit.
— PHILIPPIANS 2:1

Man that is born of a woman is of few days, and full of trouble. He cometh forth like a flower, and is cut down; he fleeth also as a shadow, and continueth not. — My flesh and my heart faileth: but God is the strength of my heart, and my portion for ever. — The Father...shall give you another Comforter, that he may abide with you for ever: the Holy Ghost, whom the Father will send in my name. — Blessed be God, even the Father of our Lord Jesus Christ, the Father of mercies, and the God of all comfort; who comforteth us in all our tribulation, that we may be able to comfort them which are in any trouble, by the comfort wherewith we ourselves are comforted of God. — If we believe that Jesus died and rose again, even so them which sleep in Jesus will God bring with him. And so shall we ever be with the Lord. Wherefore comfort one another with these words.

Job 14:1,2   Psalm 73:26   John 14:16,26
2 Corinthians 1:3,4 1 Thessalonians 4:14,17,18

OCTOBER 20 MORNING

I delight in the law of God after the inward man.
— ROMANS 7:22

O how love I thy law! it is my meditation all the day. — Thy words were found, and I did eat them; and thy word was unto me the joy and rejoicing of mine heart. — I sat down under his shadow with great delight, and his fruit was sweet to my taste. — I have esteemed the words of his mouth more than my necessary food. — I delight to do thy will, O my God: yea, thy law is within my heart. — My meat is to do the will of him that sent me, and to finish his work. — The statutes of the Lord are right, rejoicing the heart: the commandment of the Lord is pure enlightening the eyes. More to be desired are they than gold, yea, than much fine gold: sweeter also than honey and the honeycomb. — Be ye doers of the word, and not hearers only, deceiving your own selves. For if any be a hearer of the word, and not a doer, he is like unto a man beholding his natural face in a glass.

Psalm 119:97   Jeremiah 15:16   Song of Solomon 2:3   Job 23:12
Psalm 40:8   John 4:34   Psalm 19:8,10   James 1:22,23

OCTOBER 20 EVENING

The Lord thy God accept thee.
— 2 SAMUEL 24:23

Wherewith shall I come before the Lord, and bow myself before the high God? Shall I come before him with burnt offerings, with calves of a year old? Will the Lord be pleased with thousands of rams, or with ten thousands of rivers of oil? Shall I give my firstborn for my transgression, the fruit of my body for the sin of my soul? He hath shewed thee, O man, what is good; and what doth the Lord require of thee, but to do justly, and to love mercy, and to walk humbly with thy God? — We are all as an unclean thing, and all our righteousnesses are as filthy rags. — There is none righteous, no, not one. For all have sinned, and come short of the glory of God; being justified freely by his grace through the redemption that is in Christ Jesus: whom God hath set forth to be a propitiation through faith in his blood. To declare...at this time his righteousness: that he might be just, and the justifier of him which believeth in Jesus. — Accepted in the Beloved. — Ye are complete in him.

Micah 6:6-8   Isaiah 64:6   Romans 3:10,23-26   Ephesians 1:6   Colossians 2:10

OCTOBER 21 MORNING

Of his fulness have all we received, and grace for grace.
— *JOHN 1:16*

This is my beloved Son, in whom I am well pleased. — Behold, what manner of love the Father hath bestowed upon us, that we should be called the sons of God. — His Son, whom he hath appointed heir of all things. — If children, then heirs; heirs of God, and joint-heirs with Christ; if so be that we suffer with him, that we may be also glorified together. — I and my Father are one. The Father is in me, and I in him. — My Father, and your Father; and...my God, and your God. — I in them, and thou in me, that they may be made perfect in one. — The Church, which is his body, the fulness of him that filleth all in all. — Having... these promises, dearly beloved, let us cleanse ourselves from all filthiness of the flesh and spirit, perfecting holiness in the fear of God.

Matthew 17:5 1 John 3:1 Hebrews 1:2 Romans 8:17
John 10:30,38, 20:17, 17:23 Ephesians 1:22,23 2 Corinthians 7:1

OCTOBER 21 EVENING

The servant is not greater than his lord;
neither he that is sent greater than he that sent him.
If ye know these things, happy are ye if ye do them.
— *JOHN 13:16,17*

There was...a strife among them, which of them should be accounted the greatest. And he said unto them, The kings of the Gentiles exercise lordship over them; and they that exercise authority upon them are called benefactors. But ye shall not be so: but he that is greatest among you, let him be as the younger; and he that is chief, as he that doth serve. For whether is greater, he that sitteth at meat, or he that serveth? Is not he that sitteth at meat? But I am among you as he that serveth. — Even the Son man came not to be ministered unto, but to minister, and to give his life a ransom for many. — Jesus riseth from supper, and laid aside his garments, and took a towel, and girded himself. After that he poureth water into a basin, and began to wash the disciples' feet, and to wipe them with the towel wherewith he was girded.

Luke 22:24-27 Matthew 20:28 John 13:3-5

OCTOBER 22 MORNING

O God, my heart is fixed.
— PSALM 108:1

The Lord is my light and my salvation; whom shall I fear? the Lord is the strength of my life; of whom shall I be afraid? — Thou wilt keep him in perfect peace, whose mind is stayed on thee: because he trusteth in thee. — He shall not be afraid of evil tidings: his heart is fixed, trusting in the Lord. His heart is established, he shall not be afraid, until he see his desire upon his enemies. — What time I am afraid, I will trust in thee. — In the time of trouble he shall hide me in his pavilion: in the secret of his tabernacle shall he hide me; he shall set me up upon a rock. And now shall mine head be lifted up above mine enemies round about me: therefore will I offer in his tabernacle sacrifices of joy: I will sing, yea, I will sing praises unto the Lord. — The God of all grace, who hath called us unto his eternal glory by Christ Jesus, after that ye have suffered awhile, make you perfect, stablish, strengthen, settle you. To him be glory and dominion for ever and ever.

Psalm 27:1   Isaiah 26:3   Psalms 112:7,8, 56:3, 27:5,6 1   Peter 5:10,11

OCTOBER 22 EVENING

The Lord hath prepared his throne in the heavens;
and his kingdom ruleth over all.
— PSALM 103:19

The lot is cast into the lap; but the whole disposing thereof is of the Lord. — Shall there be evil in a city, and the Lord hath not done it? — I am the Lord, and there is none else; there is no God beside me: I girded thee, though thou hast not known me: that they may know from the rising of the sun, and from the west, that there is none beside me. I am the Lord, and there is none else. I form the light, and create darkness: I make peace, and create evil: I the Lord do all these things. — He doeth according to his will in the army of heaven, and among the inhabitants of the earth: and none can stay his hand, or say unto him, What doest thou? — If God be for us, who can be against us? — He must reign, till he hath put all enemies under his feet. — Fear not, little flock; for it is your Father's good pleasure to give you the kingdom.

Proverbs 16:33   Amos 3:6   Isaiah 45:5-7   Daniel 4:35
Romans 8:31 1   Corinthians 15:25   Luke 12:32

OCTOBER 23 MORNING

A man's life consisteth not in the abundance of the things which he possesseth.
— LUKE 12:15

A little that a righteous man hath is better than the riches of many wicked. — Better is little with the fear of the Lord than great treasure and trouble therewith. — Godliness with contentment is great gain. Having food and raiment let us be therewith content. — Give me neither poverty nor riches; feed me with food convenient for me: lest I be full, and deny thee, and say, Who is the Lord? or lest I be poor, and steal, and take the name of my God in vain. — Give us this day our daily bread. — Take no thought for your life, what ye shall eat, or what ye shall drink; nor yet for your body, what ye shall put on. Is not the life more than meat, and the body than raiment? — When I sent you without purse, and scrip, and shoes, lacked ye any thing? And they said, Nothing. — Let your conversation be without covetousness: and be content with such things as ye have: for he hath said, I will never leave thee, nor forsake thee.

Psalm 37:16   Proverbs 15:16 1   Timothy 6:6,8   Proverbs 30:8,9
Matthew 6:11,25   Luke 22:35   Hebrews 13:5

OCTOBER 23 EVENING

It is the spirit that quickeneth.
— JOHN 6:63

The first man Adam was made a living soul; the last Adam was made a quickening spirit. — That which is born of the flesh is flesh and that which is born of the Spirit is spirit. — Not by works of righteousness which we have done, but according to his mercy he saved us, by the washing of regeneration, and renewing of the Holy Ghost. — If any man have not the Spirit of Christ, he is none of his. And if Christ be in you, the body is dead because of sin; but the Spirit is life because of righteousness. But if the Spirit of him that raised up Jesus from the dead dwell in you, he that raised up Christ from the dead shall also quicken your mortal bodies by his Spirit that dwelleth in you. — I live; yet not I, but Christ liveth in me: and the life which I now live in the flesh I live by the faith of the Son of God. — Reckon ye…yourselves to be dead indeed unto sin, but alive unto God through Jesus Christ our Lord.

1 Corinthians 15:45   John 3:6   Titus 3:5
Romans 8:9-11   Galatians 2:20   Romans 6:11

OCTOBER 24 MORNING

I am cast out of thy sight;
yet I will look again toward thy holy temple.
— JONAH 2:4

Zion said, The Lord hath forsaken me, and my Lord hath forgotten me. Can a woman forget her sucking child, that she should not have compassion on the son of her womb? yea, they may forget, yet will I not forget thee. — I forgat prosperity. And I said, My strength and my hope is perished from the Lord. — Awake, why sleepest thou, O Lord? arise, cast us not off for ever. — Why sayest thou, O Jacob, and speakest, O Israel, My way is hid from the Lord, and my judgment is passed over from my God? — In a little wrath I hid my face from thee for a moment; but with everlasting kindness will I have mercy on thee, saith the Lord thy Redeemer. — Why art thou cast down, O my soul? and why art thou disquieted within me? hope in God: for I shall yet praise him, who is the health of my countenance. — We are troubled on every side, yet not distressed; we are perplexed, but not in despair; persecuted, but not forsaken; cast down, but not destroyed.

Isaiah 49:14,15   Lamentations 3:17,18   Psalm 44:23
Isaiah 40:27, 54:8   Psalm 43:5   2 Corinthians 4:8,9

OCTOBER 24 EVENING

When the poor and needy seek water,
and there is none,
and their tongue faileth for thirst,
I the Lord will hear them.
— ISAIAH 41:17

There be many that say, Who will shew us any good? — What hath man of all his labour, and of the vexation of his heart, wherein he hath laboured under the sun? For all his days are sorrows, and his travail grief; yea, his heart taketh not rest in the night. All is vanity and vexation of spirit. — They have forsaken me the fountain of living waters, and hewed them out cisterns, broken cisterns, that can hold no water. — Him that cometh to me I will in no wise cast out. — I will pour water upon him that is thirsty. — Blessed are they which do hunger and thirst after righteousness: for they shall be filled. — O God, thou art my God; early will I seek thee: my soul thirsteth for thee, my flesh longeth for thee in a dry and thirsty land, where no water is.

Psalm 4:6   Ecclesiastes 2:22,23,17   Jeremiah 2:13
John 6:37   Isaiah 44:3   Matthew 5:6   Psalm 63:1

OCTOBER 25 MORNING

Lo, I am with you alway, even unto the end of the world.
— MATTHEW 28:20

If two of you shall agree on earth as touching any thing that they shall ask, it shall be done for them of my Father which is in heaven. For where two or three are gathered together in my name, there am I in the midst of them. — He that hath my commandments, and keepeth them, he it is that loveth me: and he that loveth me shall be loved of my Father, and I will love him, and will manifest myself to him. — Lord, how is it that thou wilt manifest thyself unto us, and not unto the world?...If a man love me, he will keep my words: and my Father will love him, and we will come unto him, and make our abode with him. — Unto him that is able to keep you from falling, and to present you faultless before the presence of his glory with exceeding joy, to the only wise God our Saviour, be glory and majesty, dominion and power, both now and ever. Amen.

Matthew 18:19,20   John 14:21,22,23 Jude 24,25

OCTOBER 25 EVENING

The end of all things is at hand.
— 1 PETER 4:7

I saw a great white throne, and him that sat on it, from whose face the earth and the heaven fled away. — The heavens and the earth, which are now...are kept in store, reserved unto fire against the day of judgment. — God is our refuge and strength, a very present help in trouble. Therefore will not we fear, though the earth be removed, and though the mountains be carried into the midst of the sea; though the waters thereof roar and be troubled, though the mountains shake with the swelling thereof. — Ye shall hear of wars and rumours of wars: see that ye be not troubled. — We have a building of God, an house not made with hands, eternal in the heavens. — We...look for new heavens and a new earth, wherein dwelleth righteousness. Wherefore, beloved, seeing that ye look for such things, be diligent that ye may be found of him in peace, without spot, and blameless.

Revelation 20:11 2   Peter 3:7   Psalm 46:1-3
Matthew 24:6 2   Corinthians 5:1 2   Peter 3:13,14

OCTOBER 26 MORNING

The Lord reigneth.
— PSALM 99:1

Fear ye not me? saith the Lord: will ye not tremble at my presence, which have placed the sand for the bound of the sea by a perpetual decree, that it cannot pass it: and though the waves thereof toss themselves, yet can they not prevail; though they roar, yet can they not pass over it?— Promotion cometh neither from the east, nor from the west, nor from the south. But God is the judge: he putteth down one, and setteth up another. — He changeth the times and the seasons: he removeth kings, and setteth up kings: he giveth wisdom unto the wise, and knowledge to them that know understanding. — Ye shall hear of wars and rumours of wars: see that ye be not troubled. — If God be for us, who can be against us? — Are not two sparrows sold for a farthing? and one of them shall not fall on the ground without your Father. The very hairs of your head are all numbered. Fear ye not therefore, ye are of more value than many sparrows.

Jeremiah 5:22   Psalm 75:6,7   Daniel 2:21
Matthew 24:6   Romans 8:31   Matthew 10:29-31

OCTOBER 26 EVENING

Take heed to your spirit.
— MALACHI 2:15

Master, we saw one casting out devils in thy name; and we forbad him, because he followeth not with us. And Jesus said unto him, Forbid him not: for he that is not against us is for us. Lord, wilt thou that we command fire to come down from heaven, and consume them, even as Elias did? But he...rebuked them, and said, Ye know not what manner of spirit ye are of. — Eldad and Medad do prophesy in the camp. And Joshua the son of Nun...answered and said, My lord Moses, forbid them. And Moses said unto him, Enviest thou for my sake? would God that all the Lord's people were prophets, and that the Lord would put his spirit upon them! — The fruit of the Spirit is love, joy, peace, longsuffering, gentleness, goodness, faith, meekness, temperance. — And they that are Christ's have crucified the flesh with the affections and lusts. If we live in the Spirit, let us also walk in the Spirit. Let us not be desirous of vain glory, provoking one another, envying one another.

Luke 9:49,50,54,55   Numbers 11:27-29   Galatians 5:22-26

OCTOBER 27 MORNING

Himself took our infirmities, and bare our sicknesses.
— MATTHEW 8:17

Then shall the priest command to take for him that is to be cleansed two birds alive and clean, and cedar wood, and scarlet, and hyssop: and the priest shall command that one of the birds be killed in an earthen vessel over running water: as for the living bird, he shall take it, and the cedar wood, and the scarlet, and the hyssop, and shall dip them and the living bird in the blood of the bird that was killed over the running water: and he shall sprinkle upon him that is to be cleansed from the leprosy seven times, and shall pronounce him clean, and shall let the living bird loose into the open field. — Behold a man full of leprosy: who seeing Jesus fell on his face, and besought him, saying, Lord, if thou wilt, thou canst make me clean. — And Jesus, moved with compassion, put forth his hand, and touched him, and saith unto him, I will; be thou clean. And as soon as he had spoken, immediately the leprosy departed from him, and he was cleansed.

Leviticus 14:4-7   Luke 5:12   Mark 1:41,42

OCTOBER 27 EVENING

He whom thou blessest is blessed.
— NUMBERS 22:6

Blessed are the poor in spirit: for theirs is the kingdom of heaven. Blessed are they that mourn: for they shall be comforted. Blessed are the meek: for they shall inherit the earth. Blessed are they which do hunger and thirst after righteousness: for they shall be filled. Blessed are the merciful: for they shall obtain mercy. Blessed are the pure in heart: for they shall see God. Blessed are the peacemakers: for they shall be called the children of God. Blessed are they which are persecuted for righteousness' sake: for theirs is the kingdom of heaven. Blessed are ye, when men shall revile you, and persecute you, and shall say all manner of evil against you falsely, for my sake. Rejoice, and be exceeding glad: for great is your reward in heaven. — Blessed are they that hear the word of God, and keep it. — Blessed are they that do his commandments, that they may have right to the tree of life, and may enter in through the gates into the city.

Matthew 5:3-12   Luke 11:28   Revelation 22:14

OCTOBER 28 MORNING

He saw that there was no man,
and wondered that there was no intercessor:
therefore his arm brought salvation unto him.
— ISAIAH 59:16

Sacrifice and offering thou didst not desire: mine ears hast thou opened: burnt offering and sin offering hast thou not required. Then said I, Lo, I come: in the volume of the book it is written of me, I delight to do thy will, O my God: yea, thy law is within my heart. — I lay down my life, that I might take it again. No man taketh it from me, but I lay it down of myself. I have power to lay it down, and I have power to take it again. — There is no God else beside me: a just God and a Saviour; there is none beside me. Look unto me, and be ye saved, all the ends of the earth: for I am God, and there is none else. — There is none other name under heaven given among men, whereby we must be saved. — Ye know the grace of our Lord Jesus Christ, that, though he was rich, yet for your sakes he became poor, that ye through his poverty might be rich.

Psalm 40:6-8   John 10:17,18   Isaiah 45:21,22   Acts 4:12   2 Corinthians 8:9

OCTOBER 28 EVENING

The Enemy.
— LUKE 10:19

Be sober, be vigilant; because your adversary the devil, as a roaring lion, walketh about, seeking whom he may devour. — Resist the devil, and he will flee from you. — Put on the whole armour of God, that ye may be able to stand against the wiles of the devil. For we wrestle not against flesh and blood, but against principalities, against powers, against the rulers of the darkness of this world, against spiritual wickedness in high places. Wherefore take unto you the whole armour of God, that ye may be able to withstand in the evil day, and having done all, to stand. Stand therefore having your loins girt about with truth, and having on the breastplate of righteousness; and your feet shod with the preparation of the gospel of peace; above all, taking the shield of faith, wherewith ye shall be able to quench all the fiery darts of the wicked. — Rejoice not against me, O mine enemy: when I fall, I shall arise; when I sit in darkness, the Lord shall be a light unto me.

1 Peter 5:8   James 4:7   Ephesians 6:11-16   Micah 7:8

OCTOBER 29 MORNING

He is altogether lovely.
— SONG OF SOLOMON 5:16

My meditation of him shall be sweet. — My beloved is...the chiefest among ten thousand. — A chief corner stone, elect, precious: and he that believeth on him shall not be confounded. — Thou art fairer than the children of men: grace is poured into thy lips. — God...hath highly exalted him, and given him a name which is above every name. — It pleased the Father that in him should all fulness dwell. — Whom having not seen, ye love; in whom, though now ye see him not, yet believing, ye rejoice with joy unspeakable and full of glory. — I count all things but loss, for the excellency of the knowledge of Christ Jesus my Lord: for whom I have suffered the loss of all things, and do count them but dung, that I may win Christ, and be found in him, not having mine own righteousness which is of the law, but that which is through the faith of Christ, the righteousness which is of God by faith.

Psalm 104:34   Song of Solomon 5:10 1 Peter 2:6   Psalm 45:2
Philippians 2:9   Colossians 1:19 1 Peter 1:8   Philippians 3:8,9

OCTOBER 29 EVENING

David encouraged himself in the Lord his God.
— 1 SAMUEL 30:6

Lord, to whom shall we go? thou hast the words of eternal life. — I know whom I have believed, and am persuaded that he is able to keep that which I have committed unto him against that day. — In my distress I called upon the Lord, and cried unto my God: he heard my voice out of his temple, and my cry came before him, even into his ears. They prevented me in the day of my calamity: but the Lord was my stay. He brought me forth also into a large place; he delivered me, because he delighted in me. — I will bless the Lord at all times: his praise shall continually be in my mouth. My soul shall make her boast in the Lord: the humble shall hear thereof, and be glad. O magnify the Lord with me, and let us exalt his name together. I sought the Lord, and he heard me, and delivered me from all my fears. O taste and see that the Lord is good: blessed is the man that trusteth in him.

John 6:68 2 Timothy 1:12   Psalms 18:6,18,19, 34:1-4,8

OCTOBER 30 MORNING

It is good that a man should both hope
and quietly wait for the salvation of the Lord.
— LAMENTATIONS 3:26

Hath God forgotten to be gracious? hath he in anger shut up his tender mercies?— I said in my haste, I am cut off from before thine eyes: nevertheless thou heardest the voice of my supplications when I cried unto thee. — Shall not God avenge his own elect, which cry day and night unto him, though he bear long with them? I tell you that he will avenge them speedily. — Wait on the Lord, and he shall save thee. — Rest in the Lord, and wait patiently for him: fret not thyself because of him who prospereth in his way, because of the man who bringeth wicked devices to pass. — Ye shall not need to fight in this battle: set yourselves, stand ye still, and see the salvation of the Lord. — Let us not be weary in well doing:...in due season we shall reap, if we faint not. — Behold, the husbandman waiteth for the precious fruit of the earth, and hath long patience for it, until he receive the early and latter rain.

Psalms 77:9, 31:22   Luke 18:7,8   Proverbs 20:22
Psalm 37:7 2 Chronicles 20:17   Galatians 6:9   James 5:7

OCTOBER 30 EVENING

Take us the foxes, the little foxes, that spoil the vines:
for our vines have tender grapes.
— SONG OF SOLOMON 2:15

Who can understand his errors? cleanse thou me from secret faults. — Looking diligently lest any man fail of the grace of God; lest any root of bitterness springing up trouble you, and thereby many be defiled. — Ye did run well; who did hinder you that ye should not obey the truth? — He which hath begun a good work in you will perform it until the day of Jesus Christ: only let your conversation be as it becometh the gospel of Christ. — The tongue is a little member, and boasteth great things. Behold, how great a matter a little fire kindleth! And the tongue is a fire, a world of iniquity: so is the tongue among our members, that it defileth the whole body, and setteth on fire the course of nature; and it is set on fire of hell. The tongue can no man tame; it is an unruly evil, full of deadly poison. — Let your speech be alway with grace, seasoned with salt.

Psalm 19:12   Hebrews 12:15   Galatians 5:7
Philippians 1:6,27   James 3:5,6   Colossians 4:6

OCTOBER 31 MORNING

Not by might, nor by power,
but by my Spirit, saith the Lord of hosts.
— ZECHARIAH 4:6

Who hath directed the Spirit of the Lord, or being his counsellor hath taught him? — God hath chosen the foolish things of the world to confound the wise; and God hath chosen the weak things of the world to confound the things which are mighty; and base things of the world, and things which are despised, hath God chosen, yea, and things which are not, to bring to nought things that are: that no flesh should glory in his presence. — The wind bloweth where it listeth, and thou hearest the sound thereof, but canst not tell whence it cometh, and whither it goeth: so is every one that is born of the Spirit. — Born not of blood, nor of the will of the flesh, nor of the will of man, but of God. — My Spirit remaineth among you: fear ye not. — The battle is not yours, but God's. — The Lord saveth not with sword and spear: for the battle is the Lord's.

Isaiah 40:13 1 Corinthians 1:27-29 John 3:8, 1:13
Haggai 2:5 2 Chronicles 20:15 1 Samuel 17:47

OCTOBER 31 EVENING

Do as thou hast said.
— 2 SAMUEL 7:25

Stablish thy word unto thy servant, who is devoted to thy fear. So shall I have wherewith to answer him that reproacheth me: for I trust in thy word. Remember the word unto thy servant, upon which thou hast caused me to hope. Thy statutes have been my Song in the house of my pilgrimage. The law of thy mouth is better unto me than thousands of gold and silver. For ever, O Lord, thy word is settled in heaven. Thy faithfulness is unto all generations. — God, willing more abundantly to shew unto the heirs of promise the immutability of his counsel, confirmed it by an oath; that by two immutable things, in which it was impossible for God to lie, we might have a strong consolation, who have fled for refuge to lay hold upon the hope set before us: which hope we have as an anchor of the soul, both sure and stedfast, and which entereth into that within the veil; whither the forerunner is for us entered, even Jesus. — Exceeding great and precious promises.

Psalm 119:38,42,49,54,72,89,90 Hebrews 6:17-20 2 Peter 1:4

NOVEMBER 1 MORNING

Blessed is the man that heareth me,
watching daily at my gates,
waiting at the posts of my doors.
— PROVERBS 8:34

Behold, as the eyes of servants look unto the hand of their masters, and as the eyes of a maiden unto the hand of her mistress; so our eyes wait upon the Lord our God, until that he have mercy upon us. — A continual burnt offering throughout your generations at the door of the tabernacle of the congregation before the Lord: where I will meet you, to speak there unto thee. — In all places where I record my name I will come unto thee, and I will bless thee. — Where two or three are gathered together in my name, there am I in the midst of them. — The hour cometh, and now is, when the true worshippers shall worship the Father in spirit and in truth: for the Father seeketh such to worship him. God is a Spirit: and they that worship him must worship him in spirit and in truth. — Praying always with all prayer and supplication in the Spirit. — Pray without ceasing.

Psalm 123:2   Exodus 29:42, 20:24   Matthew 18:20
John 4:23,24   Ephesians 6:18 1   Thessalonians 5:17

NOVEMBER 1 EVENING

His name shall be called Counsellor.
— ISAIAH 9:6

The Spirit of the Lord shall rest upon him, the spirit of wisdom and understanding, the spirit of counsel and might, the spirit of knowledge, and of the fear of the Lord. And shall make him of quick understanding in the fear of the Lord. — Doth not wisdom cry? And understanding put forth her voice? Unto you, O men, I call; and my voice is to the sons of man. O ye simple, understand wisdom: and ye fools, be ye of an understanding heart. Hear; for I will speak of excellent things; and the opening of my lips shall be right things. Counsel is mine, and sound wisdom: I am understanding; I have strength. — The Lord of hosts...is wonderful in counsel, and excellent in working. — If any of you lack wisdom, let him ask of God, that giveth to all men liberally, and upbraideth not; and it shall be given him. — Trust in the Lord with all thine heart; and lean not unto thine own understanding. In all thy ways acknowledge him, and he shall direct thy paths.

Isaiah 11:2,3   Proverbs 8:1,4-6,14   Isaiah 28:29   James 1:5   Proverbs 3:5,6

NOVEMBER 2 MORNING

Ever follow that which is good.
— 1 THESSALONIANS 5:15

For even hereunto were ye called: because Christ also suffered for us, leaving us an example, that ye should follow his steps: who did no sin, neither was guile found in his mouth: who, when he was reviled, reviled not again;... but committed himself to him that judgeth righteously. — Consider him that endured such contradiction of sinners against himself, lest ye be wearied and faint in your minds. — Let us lay aside every weight, and the sin which doth so easily beset us, and let us run with patience the race that is set before us, looking unto Jesus the author and finisher of our faith; who for the joy that was set before him endured the cross, despising the shame, and is set down at the right hand of the throne of God. — Finally, brethren, whatsoever things are true, whatsoever things are honest, whatsoever things are just, whatsoever things are pure, whatsoever things are lovely, whatsoever things are of good report: if there be any virtue, and if there be any praise, think on these things.

1 Peter 2:21-23   Hebrews 12:3,1,2   Philippians 4:8

NOVEMBER 2 EVENING

The mighty God.
— ISAIAH 9:6

Thou art fairer than the children of men: grace is poured into thy lips: therefore God hath blessed thee for ever. Gird thy sword upon thy thigh, O most Mighty, with thy glory and thy majesty. And in thy majesty ride prosperously... Thy throne, O God, is for ever and ever: the sceptre of thy kingdom is a right sceptre. — Thou spakest in vision to thy Holy One, and saidst, I have laid help upon one that is mighty. — The man that is my fellow, saith the Lord of hosts. — Behold, God, is my salvation; I will trust, and not be afraid: for the Lord JEHOVAH is my strength and my song; he also is become my salvation. — Thanks be unto God, which always causes us to triumph in Christ. — Now unto him that is able to keep you from falling, and to present you faultless before the presence of his glory with exceeding joy, to the only wise God our Saviour, be glory and majesty, dominion and power, both now and ever.

Psalms 45:2-4,6, 89:19   Zechariah 13:7   Isaiah 12:2   2 Corinthians 2:14 Jude 24,25

NOVEMBER 3 MORNING

The ways of the Lord are right,
and the just shall walk in them:
but the transgressors shall fall therein.
— HOSEA 14:9

Unto you...which believe he is precious: but unto them which be disobedient...a stone of stumbling, and a rock of offence. — The way of the Lord is strength to the upright: but destruction shall be to the workers of iniquity. — He that hath ears to hear, let him hear. — Whoso is wise, and will observe these things, even they shall understand the lovingkindness of the Lord. — The light of the body is the eye: if therefore thine eye be single, thy whole body shall be full of light. — If any man will do his will, he shall know of the doctrine, whether it be of God. — Whosoever hath, to him shall be given, and he shall have more abundance. — He that is of God heareth God's words: ye therefore hear them not, because ye are not of God. — Ye will not come unto me, that ye might have life. — My sheep hear my voice, and I know them, and they follow me.

1 Peter 2:7,8   Proverbs 10:29   Matthew 11:15   Psalm 107:43   Matthew 6:22
John 7:17   Matthew 13:12   John 8:47, 5:40, 10:27

NOVEMBER 3 EVENING

The everlasting Father.
— ISAIAH 9:6

Hear, O Israel: The Lord our God is one Lord. — I and my Father are one, the Father is in me, and I in him. — Had ye had known me, ye should have known my Father also. — Philip saith unto him, Lord, shew us the Father, and it sufficeth us. Jesus saith unto him, Have I been so long time with you, and yet hast thou not known me, Philip? He that hath seen me hath seen the Father. — Behold I and the children which God hath given me. — He shall see of the travail of his soul, and shall be satisfied. — I am Alpha and Omega, the beginning and the ending, saith the Lord, which is, and which was, and which is to come, the Almighty. — Before Abraham was, I am. — God said unto Moses, I AM THAT I AM: and he said, Thus shalt thou say unto the children of Israel, I AM hath sent me unto you. — Unto the Son he saith, Thy throne, O God, is for ever and ever. — He is before all things, and by him all things consist. — In him dwelleth all the fulness of the Godhead bodily.

Deuteronomy 6:4   John 10:30,38, 8:19, 14:8,9   Hebrews 2:13   Isaiah 53:11
Revelation 1:8   John 8:58   Exodus 3:14   Hebrews 1:8   Colossians 1:17, 2:9

NOVEMBER 4 MORNING

Now for a season, if need be,
ye are in heaviness through manifold temptations.
— 1 PETER 1:6

Beloved, think it not strange concerning the fiery trial which is to try you, as though some strange thing happened unto you: but rejoice, inasmuch as ye are partakers of Christ's sufferings; that, when his glory shall be revealed, ye may be glad also with exceeding joy. — The exhortation...speaketh unto you as unto children, My son, despise not thou the chastening of the Lord, nor faint when thou art rebuked of him. — Now no chastening for the present seemeth to be joyous but grievous: nevertheless, afterward it yieldeth the peaceable fruit of righteousness unto them which are exercised thereby. — We have not a high priest which cannot be touched with the feeling of our infirmities; but was in all points tempted like as we are, yet without sin. — For in that he himself hath suffered being tempted, he is able to succour them that are tempted. — God is faithful, who will not suffer you to be tempted above that ye are able.

1 Peter 4:12,13   Hebrews 12:5, 12:11, 4:15, 2:18 1   Corinthians 10:13

NOVEMBER 4 EVENING

The Prince of Peace.
— ISAIAH 9:6

He shall judge thy people with righteousness, and thy poor with judgment. The mountains shall bring peace to the people, and the little hills, by righteousness. He shall come down like rain upon the mown grass; as showers that water the earth. In his days shall the righteous flourish; and abundance of peace so long as the moon endureth. — Glory to God...on earth peace, good will toward men. — Through the tender mercy of our God;...the dayspring from on high hath visited us. To give light to them that sit in darkness and in the shadow of death, to guide our feet into the way of peace;— peace by Jesus Christ: (he is Lord of all). — These things I have spoken unto you, that in me ye might have peace. In the world ye shall have tribulation: but be of good cheer; I have overcome the world. — Peace I leave with you, my peace I give unto you: not as the world giveth give I unto you. — The peace of God, which passeth all understanding, shall keep your hearts and minds through Christ Jesus.

Psalm 72:2-7 Luke. 2:14, 1:78,79   Acts 10:36   John 16:33, 14:27   Philippians 4:7

NOVEMBER 5 MORNING

*Take thou also unto thee principal spices,
and thou shalt make it an oil of holy ointment.*
— EXODUS 30:23,25

Upon man's flesh shall it not be poured, neither shall ye make any other like it, after the composition of it: it is holy, and it shall be holy unto you. — One Spirit. — Diversities of gifts, but the same Spirit. — Thy God hath anointed thee with the oil of gladness above thy fellows. — God anointed Jesus of Nazareth with the Holy Ghost and with power. — God giveth not the Spirit by measure unto him. — Of his fulness have all we received. — As the same anointing teacheth you of all things, and is truth, and is no lie, and even as it hath taught you, ye shall abide in him. — He which...hath anointed us, is God; who hath also sealed us, and given the earnest of the Spirit in our hearts. — The fruit of the Spirit is love, joy, peace, longsuffering, gentleness, goodness, faith, meekness, temperance: against such there is no law.

Exodus 30:32   Ephesians 4:4 1   Corinthians 12:4   Psalm 45:7   Acts 10:38   John 3:34, 1:16 1   John 2:27 2   Corinthians 1:21,22   Galatians 5:22,23

NOVEMBER 5 EVENING

The fashion of this world passeth away.
— 1 CORINTHIANS 7:31

All the days of Methuselah were nine hundred sixty and nine years: and he died. — Let the brother of low degree rejoice in that he is exalted: but the rich, in that he is made low: because as the flower of the grass he shall pass away. For the sun is no sooner risen with a burning heat, but it withereth the grass, and the flower thereof falleth, and the grace of the fashion of it perisheth: so also shall the rich man fade away in his ways. — For what is your life? It is even a vapour of that appeareth for a little time, and then vanisheth away. — The world passeth away, and the lust thereof: but he that doeth the will of God abideth for ever. — Lord, make me to know mine end, and the measure of my days, what it is; that I may know how frail I am. — When they shall say, Peace and safety; then sudden destruction cometh upon them, as travail upon a woman with child; and they shall not escape. But ye, brethren, are not in darkness, that that day should overtake you as a thief.

Genesis 5:27   James 1:9-11, 4:14 1   John 2:17   Psalm 39:4 1   Thessalonians 5:3,4

NOVEMBER 6 MORNING

When Christ, who is our life, shall appear,
then shall ye also appear with him in glory.
— COLOSSIANS 3:4

I am the resurrection, and the life: he that believeth in me, though he were dead, yet shall he live. — God hath given to us eternal life, and this life is in his Son. He that hath the Son hath life; and he that hath not the Son of God hath not life. — The Lord himself shall descend from heaven with a shout, with the voice of the archangel, and with the trump of God: and the dead in Christ shall rise first: then we which are alive and remain shall be caught up together with them in the clouds, to meet the Lord in the air: and so shall we ever be with the Lord. Wherefore comfort one another with these words. — When he shall appear, we shall be like him; for we shall see him as he is. — It is sown in dishonour; it is raised in glory; it is sown in weakness; it is raised in power. — If I go and prepare a place for you, I will come again, and receive you unto myself; that where I am, there ye may be also.

John 11:25 1   John 5:11,12 1   Thessalonians 4:16-18
1 John 3:2 1   Corinthians 15:43   John 14:3

NOVEMBER 6 EVENING

Lead me in thy truth, and teach me.
— PSALM 25:5

When...the Spirit of truth is come, he will guide you into all truth. — Ye have an unction from the Holy One, and ye know all things. — To the law and to the testimony: if they speak not according to this word, it is because there is no light in them. — All scripture is given by inspiration of God, and is profitable for doctrine, for reproof, for correction, for instruction in righteousness; That the man of God may be perfect, throughly furnished unto all good works. — The holy Scriptures...are able to make thee wise unto salvation through faith which is in Christ Jesus. — I will instruct thee and teach thee in the way which thou shalt go: I will guide thee with mine eye. — The light of the body is the eye: if therefore thine eye be single, thy whole body shall be full of light. — If any man will do his will, he shall know of the doctrine, whether it be of God. — The wayfaring men, though fools, shall not err therein.

John 16:13 1   John 2:20   Isaiah 8:20 2   Timothy 3:16,17,15
Psalm 32:8   Matthew 6:22   John 7:17   Isaiah 35:8

NOVEMBER 7 MORNING

*Oh that men would praise the Lord for his goodness,
and for his wonderful works to the children of men!*
— PSALM 107:8

    O taste and see that the Lord is good: blessed is the man that trusteth in him. — How great is thy goodness, which thou hast laid up for them that fear thee! — This people have I formed for myself; they shall shew forth my praise. — Having predestinated us unto the adoption of children by Jesus Christ to himself, according to the good pleasure of his will, to the praise of the glory of his grace, wherein he hath made us accepted in the beloved. That we should be to the praise of his glory, who first trusted in Christ. — How great is his goodness, and how great is his beauty! — The Lord is good to all: and his tender mercies are over all his works. All thy works shall praise thee, O Lord; and thy saints shall bless thee. They shall speak of the glory of thy kingdom, and talk of thy power; to make known to the sons of men his mighty acts, and the glorious majesty of his kingdom.

    Psalms 34:8, 31:19   Isaiah 43:21   Ephesians 1:5,6,12
Zechariah 9:17   Psalm 145:9-12

NOVEMBER 7 EVENING

Behold, we count them happy which endure.
— JAMES 5:11

    We glory in tribulations:...knowing that tribulation worketh patience; and patience, experience; and experience, hope: And hope maketh not ashamed; because the love of God is shed abroad in our hearts by the Holy Ghost which is given unto us. — No chastening for the present seemeth to be joyous, but grievous: nevertheless afterward it yieldeth the peaceable fruit of righteousness unto them which are exercised thereby. — My brethren, count it all joy when ye fall into divers temptations; knowing this, that the trying of your faith worketh patience. But let patience have her perfect work, that ye may be perfect and entire, wanting nothing. Blessed is the man that endureth temptation: for when he is tried, he shall receive the crown of life, which the Lord hath promised to them that love him. — Most gladly therefore will I rather glory in my infirmities, that the power of Christ may rest upon me. For when I am weak, then am I strong.

    Romans 5:3-5   Hebrews 12:11   James 1:2-4,12 2 Corinthians 12:9,10

NOVEMBER 8 MORNING

Let us, who are of the day, be sober,
putting on the breastplate of faith and love;
and for an helmet, the hope of salvation.
— 1 THESSALONIANS 5:8

Gird up the loins of your mind, be sober, and hope to the end for the grace that is to be brought unto you at the revelation of Jesus Christ. — Stand therefore, having your loins girt about with truth, and having on the breastplate of righteousness; above all, taking the shield of faith, wherewith ye shall be able to quench all the fiery darts of the wicked. And take the helmet of salvation, and the sword of the Spirit, which is the word of God. — He will swallow up death in victory; and the Lord GOD will wipe away tears from off all faces; and the rebuke of his people shall he take away from off all the earth: for the Lord hath spoken it. And it shall be said in that day, Lo, this is our God; we have waited for him, and he will save us: this is the Lord;...we will be glad and rejoice in his salvation. — Faith is the substance of things hoped for, the evidence of things not seen.

1 Peter 1:13   Ephesians 6:14,16,17   Isaiah 25:8,9   Hebrews 11:1

NOVEMBER 8 EVENING

The children of Israel pitched before them
like two little flocks of kids;
but the Syrians filled the country.
— 1 KINGS 20:27

Thus saith the Lord, because the Syrians have said, the Lord is a God of the hills, but he is not God of the valleys; therefore will I deliver all this great multitude into thine hand, and ye shall know that I am the Lord. And they pitched one over against the other seven days; and so it was, that in the seventh day the battle was joined: and the children of Israel slew of the Syrians an hundred thousand footmen in one day. — Ye are of God, little children, and have overcome them; because greater is he that is in you, than he that is in the world. — Fear thou not; for I am with thee: be not dismayed; for I am thy God: I will strengthen thee; yea, I will help thee; yea, I will uphold thee with the right hand of my righteousness. — They shall fight against thee; but they shall not prevail against thee; for I am with thee, saith the Lord, to deliver thee.

1 Kings 20:28,29 1   John 4:4   Isaiah 41:10   Jeremiah 1:19

NOVEMBER 9 MORNING

I have laid help upon one that is mighty;
I have exalted one chosen out of the people.
— PSALM 89:19

I, even I, am the Lord; and beside me there is no saviour. — There is one God, and one mediator between God and men, the man Christ Jesus. — There is none other name under heaven given among men, whereby we must be saved. — The mighty God. — Who made himself of no reputation, and took upon him the form of a servant, and was made in the likeness of men: and being found in fashion as a man, he humbled himself and became obedient unto death, even the death of the cross. Wherefore God also hath highly exalted him, and given him a name which is above every name. — We see Jesus, who was made a little lower than the angels for the suffering of death, crowned with glory and honour; that he by the grace of God should taste death for every man. — Forasmuch... as the children are partakers of flesh and blood, he also himself likewise took part of the same.

Isaiah 43:11   1 Timothy 2:5   Acts 4:12
Isaiah 9:6   Philippians 2:7-9   Hebrews 2:9,14

NOVEMBER 9 EVENING

Gather my saints together unto me,
those that have made a covenant with me by sacrifice.
— PSALM 50:5

Christ was once offered to bear the sins of many; and unto them that look for him shall he appear the second time, without sin, unto salvation. — He is the mediator of the new testament, that by means of death...they which are called might receive the promise of eternal inheritance. — Father, I will that they also, whom thou hast given me, be with me where I am. — Then he shall send his angels, and shall gather together his elect from the four winds, from the uttermost part of the earth, to the uttermost part of heaven. — If any of thine be driven out unto the outmost parts of heaven, from thence will the Lord thy God gather thee, and from thence will he fetch thee. — The dead in Christ shall rise first: then we which are alive and remain shall be caught up together with them in the clouds, to meet be Lord in the air: and so shall we ever be with the Lord.

Hebrews 9:28,15   John 17:24   Mark 13:27
Deuteronomy 30:4   1 Thessalonians 4:16,17

NOVEMBER 10 MORNING

Fruitful in every good work,
and increasing in the knowledge of God.
— COLOSSIANS 1:10

I beseech you...brethren, by the mercies of God, that ye present your bodies a living sacrifice, holy, acceptable unto God, which is your reasonable service. And be not conformed to this world: but be ye transformed by the renewing of your mind, that ye may prove what is that good, and acceptable, and perfect, will of God. — As ye have yielded your members servants to uncleanness and to iniquity unto iniquity; even so now yield your members servants to righteousness unto holiness. — In Christ Jesus neither circumcision availeth any thing, nor uncircumcision, but a new creature. And as many as walk according to this rule, peace be on them, and mercy. — Herein is my Father glorified, that ye bear much fruit; so shall ye be my disciples. — I have chosen you, and ordained you, that ye should go and bring forth fruit, and that your fruit should remain: that whatsoever ye shall ask of the Father in my name, he may give it you.

Romans 12:1,2, 6:19   Galatians 6:15,16   John 15:8,16

NOVEMBER 10 EVENING

I sought him, but I found him not.
— SONG OF SOLOMON 3:1

Return unto the Lord thy God; for thou hast fallen by thine iniquity. — Take with you words, and turn to the Lord: say unto him, Take away all iniquity, and receive us graciously. — Let no man say when he is tempted, I am tempted of God. But every man is tempted, when he is drawn away of his own lust, and enticed. Do not err, my beloved brethren. Every good gift and every perfect gift is from above, and cometh down from the Father of lights, with whom is no variableness, neither shadow of turning. — Wait on the Lord; be of good courage, and he shall strengthen thine heart: wait, I say, on the Lord. — It is good that a man should both hope and quietly wait for the salvation of the Lord. — Shall not God avenge his own elect, which cry day and night unto him, though he bear long with them? — Truly my soul waiteth upon God: from him cometh my salvation. My soul, wait thou only upon God; for my expectation is from him.

Hosea 14:1,2   James 1:13-17   Psalm 27:14
Lamentations 3:26   Luke 18:7   Psalm 62:1,5

NOVEMBER 11 MORNING

He led them on safely.
— PSALM 78:53

I lead in the way of righteousness, in the midst of the paths of judgment. — Behold, I send an Angel before thee, to keep thee in the way, and to bring thee into the place which I have prepared. — In all their affliction he was afflicted, and the angel of his presence saved them: in his love and in his pity he redeemed them; and he bare them, and carried them all the days of old. — They got not the land in possession by their own sword, neither did their own arm save them: but thy right hand, and thine arm, and the light of thy countenance, because thou hadst a favour unto them. — So didst thou lead thy people, to make thyself a glorious name. — Lead me, O Lord, in thy righteousness because of mine enemies; make thy way straight before my face. — O send out thy light and thy truth: let them lead me; let them bring me unto thy holy hill, and to thy tabernacles. Then will I go unto the altar of God, unto God my exceeding joy: yea, upon the harp will I praise thee, O God my God.

Proverbs 8:20   Exodus 23:20   Isaiah 63:9
Psalm 44:3   Isaiah 63:14   Psalms 5:8, 43:3,4

NOVEMBER 11 EVENING

Ye are washed...ye are sanctified...ye are justified.
— 1 CORINTHIANS 6:11

The blood of Jesus Christ his Son cleanseth us from all sin. — The chastisement of our peace was upon him; and with his stripes we are healed. — Christ...loved the church, and gave himself for it; that he might sanctify and cleanse it with the washing of water by the word, that he might present it to himself a glorious church, not having spot, or wrinkle, or any such thing; but that it should be holy and without blemish. — To her was granted that she should be arrayed in fine linen, clean and white: for the fine linen is the righteousness of saints. — Let us draw near with a true heart in full assurance of faith, having our hearts sprinkled from an evil conscience, and our bodies washed with pure water. — Who shall lay any thing to the charge of God's elect? It is God that justifieth. — Blessed is he whose transgression is forgiven. Blessed is the man unto whom the Lord imputeth not iniquity, and in whose spirit there is no guile.

1 John 1:7   Isaiah 53:5   Ephesians 5:25-27   Revelation 19:8
Hebrews 10:22   Romans 8:33   Psalm 32:1,2

NOVEMBER 12 MORNING

Godly sorrow worketh repentance not to be repented of.
— 2 CORINTHIANS 7:10

Peter remembered the word of Jesus, which said unto him, Before the cock crow, thou shalt deny me thrice. And he went out, and wept bitterly. — If we confess our sins, he is faithful and just to forgive us our sins, and to cleanse us from all unrighteousness. — The blood of Jesus Christ his Son cleanseth us from all sin. — Mine iniquities have taken hold upon me, so that I am not able to look up; they are more than the hairs of my head: therefore my heart faileth me. Be pleased, O Lord, to deliver me: O Lord, make haste to help me. — Turn thou to thy God: keep mercy and judgment, and wait on thy God continually. — The sacrifices of God are a broken spirit: a broken and a contrite heart, O God, thou wilt not despise. — He healeth the broken in heart, and bindeth up their wounds. — He hath shewed thee, O man, what is good: and what doth the Lord require of thee, but to do justly, and to love mercy, and to walk humbly with thy God?

Matthew 26:75 1 John 1:9,7 Psalm 40:12,13
Hosea 12:6 Psalms 51:17, 147:3 Micah 6:8

NOVEMBER 12 EVENING

Is it well with thee?
And she answered, it is well.
— 2 KINGS 4:26

We having the same spirit of faith. — As chastened, and not killed; as sorrowful, yet alway rejoicing; as poor, yet making many rich; as having nothing, and yet possessing all things. — We are troubled on every side, yet not distressed; we are perplexed, but not in despair; persecuted, but not forsaken; cast down, but not destroyed; always bearing about in the body the dying of the Lord Jesus, that the life also of Jesus might be made manifest in our body. For which cause we faint not, but though our outward man perish, yet the inward man is renewed day by day. For our light affliction, which is but for a moment, worketh for us a far more exceeding and eternal weight of glory; while we look not at the things which are seen, but at the things which are not seen. — Beloved, I wish above all things that thou mayest prosper and be in health, even as thy soul prospereth.

2 Corinthians 4:13, 6:9,10, 4:8-10,16-18 3 John 2

NOVEMBER 13 MORNING

*Christ loved the church, and gave himself for it;
that he might sanctify and cleanse it
with the washing of water by the word.*
— EPHESIANS 5:25,26

Walk in love, as Christ also hath loved us, and hath given himself for us an offering and a sacrifice to God for a sweetsmelling savour. — Being born again, not of corruptible seed, but of incorruptible, by the word of God, which liveth and abideth for ever. — Sanctify them through thy truth: thy word is truth. — Except a man be born of water and of the Spirit, he cannot enter into the kingdom of God. — Not by works of righteousness which we have done, but according to his mercy he saved us, by the washing of regeneration, and renewing of the Holy Ghost. — Thy word hath quickened me. — The law of the Lord is perfect, converting the soul: the testimony of the Lord is sure, making wise the simple. The statutes of the Lord are right, rejoicing the heart: the commandment of the Lord is pure, enlightening the eyes.

Ephesians 5:2 1 Peter 1:23   John 17:17, 3:5   Titus 3:5   Psalm 119:50, 19:7,8

NOVEMBER 13 EVENING

*Through him we both have access
by one Spirit unto the Father.*
— EPHESIANS 2:18

I in them, and thou in me, that they may be made perfect in one. — Whatsoever ye shall ask in my name, that will I do, that the Father may be glorified in the Son. If ye shall ask any thing in my name, I will do it. And I will pray the Father, and he shall give you another Comforter, that he may abide with you for ever; even the Spirit of truth; whom the world cannot receive, because it seeth him not, neither knoweth him: but ye know him; for he dwelleth with you, and shall be in you. — There is one body, and one Spirit, even as ye are called in one hope of your calling; one Lord, one faith, one baptism, one God and Father of all, who is above all, and through all, and in you all. — When ye pray, say, Our Father which art in heaven. — Having therefore, brethren, boldness to enter into the holiest by the blood of Jesus, by a new and living way...let us draw near.

John 17:23, 14:13,14,16,17   Ephesians 4:4-6   Luke 11:2   Hebrews 10:19,20,22

NOVEMBER 14 MORNING

Thou art my help and my deliverer;
make no tarrying, O my God.
— PSALM 40:17

The steps of a good man are ordered by the Lord: and he delighteth in his way. Though he fall, he shall not be utterly cast down: for the Lord upholdeth him with his hand. — In the fear of the Lord is strong confidence: and his children shall have a place of refuge. — Who art thou, that thou shouldest be afraid of a man that shall die, and of the son of man which shall be made as grass; and forgettest the Lord thy maker? — I am with thee to deliver thee. — Be strong and of a good courage, fear not, nor be afraid of them: for the Lord thy God, he it is that doth go with thee; he will not fail thee, nor forsake thee. — I will sing of thy power; yea, I will sing aloud of thy mercy in the morning: for thou hast been my defence and refuge in the day of my trouble. — Thou art my hiding place; thou shalt preserve me from trouble; thou shalt compass me about with Song of deliverance.

Psalm 37:23,24   Proverbs 14:26   Isaiah 51:12,13
Jeremiah 1:8   Deuteronomy 31:6   Psalms 59:16, 32:7

NOVEMBER 14 EVENING

How wilt thou do in the swellings of Jordan?
— JEREMIAH 12:5

For Jordan overfloweth all his banks all the time of harvest. — The priests that bare the ark of the covenant of the Lord stood firm on dry ground in the midst of Jordan, and all the Israelites passed over on dry ground, until all the people were passed clean over Jordan— We see Jesus, who was made a little lower than the angels, for the suffering of death, crowned with glory and honour; that he by the grace of God should taste death for every man. — Though I walk through the valley of the shadow of death, I will fear no evil: for thou art with me; thy rod and thy staff they comfort me. — When thou passest through the waters, I will be with thee; and through the rivers, they shall not overflow thee. — Fear not; I am the first and the last: I am he that liveth, and was dead; and, behold, I am alive for evermore, Amen; and have the keys of hell and of death.

Joshua 3:15,17   Hebrews 2:9   Psalm 23:4   Isaiah 43:2   Revelation 1:17,18

NOVEMBER 15 MORNING

*God is faithful, by whom ye were called unto the
fellowship of his Son Jesus Christ our Lord.*
— 1 CORINTHIANS 1:9

Let us hold fast the profession of our faith without wavering; for he is faithful that promised. — God hath said, I will dwell in them, and walk in them; and I will be their God, and they shall be my people. — Truly our fellowship is with the Father, and with his Son Jesus Christ. — Rejoice, inasmuch as ye are partakers of Christ's sufferings; that, when his glory shall be revealed, ye may be glad also with exceeding joy. — That ye, being rooted and grounded in love, may be able to comprehend with all saints what is the breadth, and length, and depth, and height; and to know the love of Christ, which passeth knowledge, that ye might be filled with all the fulness of God. — Whosoever shall confess that Jesus is the Son of God, God dwelleth in him, and he in God. — And he that keepeth his commandments dwelleth in him, and he in him.

Hebrews 10:23 2 Corinthians 6:16 1 John 1:3
1 Peter 4:13 Ephesians 3:17-19 1 John 4:15, 3:24

NOVEMBER 15 EVENING

We are his workmanship.
— EPHESIANS 2:10

They brought great stones, costly stones, and hewed stones, to lay the foundation of the house. — The house, when it was in building, was built of stone made ready before it was brought thither: so that there was neither hammer nor axe nor any tool of iron heard in the house, while it was in building. — Ye also, as lively stones, are built up a spiritual house. — Built upon the foundation of the apostles and prophets, Jesus Christ himself being the chief corner stone; in whom all the building fitly framed together groweth unto an holy temple in the Lord: in whom ye also are builded together for an habitation of God through the Spirit. — Which in time past were not a people, but are now the people of God. — Ye are God's building. — Therefore if any man be in Christ, he is a new creature: old things are passed away; behold, all things are become new. — Now he that hath wrought us for the selfsame thing is God, who also hath given unto us the earnest of the Spirit.

1 Kings 5:17, 6:7 1 Peter 2:5 Ephesians 2:20-22
1 Peter 2:10 1 Corinthians 3:9 2 Corinthians 5:17,5

NOVEMBER 16 MORNING

Sanctify them through thy truth:
thy word is truth.
— JOHN 17:17

Now ye are clean through the word which I have spoken unto you. — Let the word of Christ dwell in you richly in all wisdom. — Wherewithal shall a young man cleanse his way? by taking heed thereto according to thy word. With my whole heart have I sought thee: O let me not wander from thy commandments. — When wisdom entereth into thine heart, and knowledge is pleasant unto thy soul: discretion shall preserve thee, understanding shall keep thee. — My foot hath held his steps, his way have I kept, and not declined. Neither have I gone back from the commandment of his lips; I have esteemed the words of his mouth more than my necessary food. — I have more understanding than all my teachers: for thy testimonies are my meditation. — If ye continue in my word, then are ye my disciples indeed; and ye shall know the truth, and the truth shall make you free.

John 15:3   Colossians 3:16   Psalm 119:9,10
Proverbs 2:10,11   Job 23:11,12   Psalm 119:99   John 8:31,32

NOVEMBER 16 EVENING

Fellow citizens with the saints.
— EPHESIANS 2:19

Ye are come unto mount Sion, and unto the city of the living God, the heavenly Jerusalem, and to an innumerable company of angels, to the general assembly and church of the firstborn, which are written in heaven, and to God the Judge of all, and to the spirits of just men made perfect. — These all died in faith, not having received the promises, but having seen them afar off, and were persuaded of them, and embraced them, and confessed that they were strangers and pilgrims on the earth. — Our conversation (Gr. citizenship) is in heaven; from whence also we look for the Saviour, the Lord Jesus Christ: who shall change our vile body, that it may be fashioned like unto his glorious body, according to the working whereby he is able even to subdue all things unto himself. — The Father...hath delivered us from the power of darkness, and hath translated us into the kingdom of his dear Son. — As strangers and pilgrims, abstain from fleshly lusts, which war against the soul.

Hebrews 12:22,23, 11:13   Philippians 3:20,21   Colossians 1:12,13 1   Peter 2:11

NOVEMBER 17 MORNING

Thy thoughts are very deep.
— PSALM 92:5

We...do not cease to pray for you, and to desire that ye might be filled with the knowledge of his will in all wisdom and spiritual understanding. — That ye, being rooted and grounded in love, may be able to comprehend with all saints what is the breadth, and length, and depth, and height; and to know the love of Christ, which passeth knowledge, that ye might be filled with all the fulness of God. — O the depth of the riches both of the wisdom and knowledge of God! how unsearchable are his judgments, and his ways past finding out!— My thoughts are not your thoughts, neither are your ways my ways, saith the Lord. For as the heavens are higher than the earth, so are my ways higher than your ways, and my thoughts than your thoughts. — Many, O Lord my God, are thy wonderful works which thou hast done, and thy thoughts which are to usward: they cannot be reckoned up in order unto thee: if I would declare and speak of them, they are more than can be numbered.

Colossians 1:9   Ephesians 3:17-19   Romans 11:33   Isaiah 55:8,9   Psalm 40:5

NOVEMBER 17 EVENING

Whatsoever a man soweth,
that shall he also reap.
— GALATIANS 6:7

They that plow iniquity, and sow wickedness, reap the same. — They have sown the wind, and they shall reap the whirlwind. — He that soweth to his flesh shall of the flesh reap corruption. — To him that soweth righteousness shall be a sure reward. — He that soweth to the Spirit shall of the Spirit reap life everlasting. And let us not be weary in well doing: for in due season we shall reap, if we faint not. As we have therefore opportunity, let us do good unto all men, especially unto them who are of the household of faith. — There is that scattereth, and yet increaseth; and there is that withholdeth more than is meet, but it tendeth to poverty. — The liberal soul shall be made fat: and he that watereth shall be watered also himself. — He which soweth sparingly shall reap also sparingly; and he which soweth bountifully shall reap also bountifully.

Job 4:8   Hosea 8:7   Galatians 6:8   Proverbs 11:18
Galatians 6:8-10   Proverbs 11:24,25   2 Corinthians 9:6

NOVEMBER 18 MORNING

He stayeth his rough wind in the day of the east wind.
— ISAIAH 27:8

Let us fall now into the hand of the Lord; for his mercies are great. — I am with thee, saith the Lord, to save thee:...I will correct thee in measure, and will not leave thee altogether unpunished. — He will not always chide: neither will he keep his anger for ever. He hath not dealt with us after our sins; nor rewarded us according to our iniquities. For he knoweth our frame; he remembereth that we are dust. — I will spare them, as a man spareth his own son that serveth him. — God is faithful, who will not suffer you to be tempted above that ye are able; but will with the temptation also make a way to escape, that ye may be able to bear it. — Satan hath desired to have you, that he may sift you as wheat: but I have prayed for thee, that thy faith fail not. — Thou hast been a strength to the poor, a strength to the needy in his distress, a refuge from the storm, a shadow from the heat, when the blast of the terrible ones is as a storm against the wall.

2 Samuel 24:14   Jeremiah 30:11   Psalm 103:9,10,14
Malachi 3:17 1   Corinthians 10:13   Luke 22:31,32   Isaiah 25:4

NOVEMBER 18 EVENING

I believed not the words,
until I came, and mine eyes had seen it;
and, behold, the half was not told me.
— 1 KINGS 10:7

The queen of the south shall rise up in the judgment with this generation, and shall condemn it: for she came from the uttermost parts of the earth to hear the wisdom of Solomon; and, behold, a greater than Solomon is here. — We beheld his glory, the glory as of the only begotten of the Father, full of grace and truth. — My speech and my preaching was...in demonstration of the Spirit and of power: that your faith should not stand in the wisdom of men, but in the power of God. But as it is written, Eye hath not seen, nor ear heard, neither have entered into the heart of man, the things which God hath prepared for them that love him. But God hath revealed them unto us by his Spirit: for the Spirit searcheth all things, yea, the deep things of God. — Thine eyes shall see the King in his beauty. — We shall see him as he is. — In my flesh I shall see God. — I shall be satisfied.

Matthew 12:42   John 1:14 1   Corinthians 2:4,5,9,10
Isaiah 33:17 1   John 3:2   Job 19:26   Psalm 17:15

NOVEMBER 19 MORNING

By their fruits ye shall know them.
— MATTHEW 7:20

Little children, let no man deceive you: he that doeth righteousness is righteous, even as he is righteous. — Doth a fountain send forth at the same place sweet water and bitter? Can the fig tree, my brethren, bear olive berries? either a vine, figs? so can no fountain both yield salt water and fresh. Who is a wise man and endued with knowledge among you? let him shew out of a good conversation his works with meekness of wisdom. — Having your conversation honest among the Gentiles: that, whereas they speak against you as evildoers, they may by your good works, which they shall behold, glorify God in the day of visitation. — Either make the tree good, and his fruit good; or else make the tree corrupt, and his fruit corrupt: for the tree is known by his fruit. — A good man out of the good treasure of the heart bringeth forth good things: and an evil man out of the evil treasure bringeth forth evil things. — What could have been done more to my vineyard, that I have not done in it?

1 John 3:7   James 3:11-13 1   Peter 2:12   Matthew 12:33,35   Isaiah 5:4

NOVEMBER 19 EVENING

I will make the place of my feet glorious.
— ISAIAH 60:13

Thus saith the Lord, The heaven is my throne, and the earth is my footstool. — Will God in very deed dwell with men on the earth! Behold, heaven and the heaven of heavens cannot contain thee; how much less this house which I have built! — Thus saith the Lord of hosts, Yet once, it is a little while, and I will shake the heavens, and the earth, and the sea, and the dry land; and I will shake all nations, and the desire of all nations shall come: and I will fill this house with glory, saith the Lord of hosts. The glory of this latter house shall be greater than of the former, saith the Lord of hosts. — I saw a new heaven and a new earth: for the first heaven and the first earth were passed away; and there was no more sea. And I heard a great voice out of heaven, saying, Behold, the tabernacle of God is with men, and he will dwell with them, and they shall be his people, and God himself shall be with them, and be their God.

Isaiah 66:1 2   Chronicles 6:18   Haggai 2:6,7,9   Revelation 21:1,3

NOVEMBER 20 MORNING

When I sit in darkness, the Lord shall be a light unto me.
— MICAH 7:8

When thou passest through the waters, I will be with thee; and through the rivers, they shall not overflow thee: when thou walkest through the fire, thou shalt not be burned; neither shall the flame kindle upon thee. For I am the Lord thy God, the Holy One of Israel, thy Saviour. — I will bring the blind by a way that they knew not; I will lead them in paths that they have not known: I will make darkness light before them, and crooked things straight. These things will I do unto them, and not forsake them. — Yea, though I walk through the valley of the shadow of death, I will fear no evil: for thou art with me; thy rod and thy staff they comfort me. — What time I am afraid, I will trust in thee. In God I will praise his word, in God I have put my trust; I will not fear what flesh can do unto me. — The Lord is my light and my salvation; whom shall I fear? the Lord is the strength of my life; of whom shall I be afraid?

Isaiah 43:2,3, 42:16   Psalms 23:4, 56:3,4, 27:1

NOVEMBER 20 EVENING

One God, and one mediator between God and men,
the man Christ Jesus.
— 1 TIMOTHY 2:5

Hear, O Israel: The Lord our God is one Lord. — A mediator is not a mediator of one, but God is one. — We have sinned with our fathers, we have committed iniquity, we have done wickedly. Our fathers understood not thy wonders in Egypt; they remembered not the multitude of thy mercies... Therefore he said that he would destroy them, had not Moses his chosen stood before him in the breach, to turn away his wrath, lest he should destroy them. — Wherefore, holy brethren, partakers of the heavenly calling, consider the Apostle and High Priest of our profession, Christ Jesus; who was faithful to him that appointed him, as also Moses was faithful in all his house. — He is the mediator of a better covenant, which was established upon better promises. I will be merciful to their unrighteousness, and their sins and their iniquities will I remember no more.

Deuteronomy 6:4   Galatians 3:20   Psalm 106:6,7,23   Hebrews 3:1-3, 8:6,12

NOVEMBER 21 MORNING

Him that cometh to me I will in no wise cast out.
— JOHN 6:37

It shall come to pass, when he crieth unto me, that I will hear; for I am gracious. — I will not cast them away, neither will I abhor them, to destroy them utterly, and to break my covenant with them: for I am the Lord their God. — I will remember my covenant with thee in the days of thy youth, and I will establish unto thee an everlasting covenant. — Come now, and let us reason together, saith the Lord: though your sins be as scarlet, they shall be as white as snow; though they be red like crimson, they shall be as wool. — Let the wicked forsake his way, and the unrighteous man his thoughts: and let him return unto the Lord, and he will have mercy upon him; and to our God, for he will abundantly pardon. — Lord, remember me when thou comest into thy kingdom. And Jesus said unto him, Verily I say unto thee, To day shalt thou be with me in paradise. — A bruised reed shall he not break, and the smoking flax shall he not quench.

Exodus 22:27   Leviticus 26:44   Ezekiel 16:60
Isaiah 1:18, 55:7   Luke 23:42,43   Isaiah 42:3

NOVEMBER 21 EVENING

His dear Son.
— COLOSSIANS 1:13

Lo a voice from heaven, saying, This is my beloved Son, in whom I am well pleased. — Behold my servant, whom I uphold; mine elect, in whom my soul delighteth. — The only begotten Son, which is in the bosom of the Father. — In this was manifested the love of God toward us, because that God sent his only begotten Son into the world, that we might live through him. Herein is love, not that we loved God, but that he loved us, and sent his son to be the propitiation for our sins. And we have known and believed the love that God hath to us. God is love. — The glory which thou gavest me I have given them; that they may be one, even as we are one: I in them, and thou in me, that they may be made perfect in one; and that the world may know that thou hast sent me, and hast loved them, as thou hast loved me. — Behold, what manner of love the Father hath bestowed upon us, that we should be called the sons of God.

Matthew 3:17   Isaiah 42:1   John 1:18
1 John 4:9,10,16   John 17:22-24 1   John 3:1

NOVEMBER 22 MORNING

Praying in the Holy Ghost.
— JUDE 20

God is a Spirit: and they that worship him must worship him in spirit and in truth. — We...have access by one Spirit unto the Father. — O my Father, if it be possible, let this cup pass from me: nevertheless not as I will, but as thou wilt. — The Spirit...helpeth our infirmities: for we know not what we should pray for as we ought: but the Spirit itself maketh intercession for us with groanings which cannot be uttered. And he that searcheth the hearts knoweth what is the mind of the Spirit, because he maketh intercession for the saints according to the will of God. — This is the confidence that we have in him, that, if we ask any thing according to his will, he heareth us. — When he, the Spirit of truth, is come, he will guide you into all truth. — Praying always with all prayer and supplication in the Spirit, and watching thereunto with all perseverance and supplication.

John 4:24   Ephesians 2:18   Matthew 26:39
Romans 8:26,27 1   John 5:14   John 16:13   Ephesians 6:18

NOVEMBER 22 EVENING

There is a hope of a tree, if it be cut down,
that it will sprout again,
and that the tender branch thereof will not cease.
— JOB 14:7

A bruised reed shall he not break. — He restoreth my soul. — Godly sorrow worketh repentance to salvation not to be repented of: but the sorrow of the world worketh death. — No chastening for the present seemeth to be joyous, but grievous: nevertheless, afterward it yieldeth the peaceful fruit of righteousness unto them which are exercised thereby. — Before I was afflicted I went astray: but now have I kept thy word. — After all that is come upon us for our evil deeds, and for our great trespass, seeing that thou our God hast punished us less than our iniquities deserve, and hast given us such deliverance as this. — Rejoice not against me, O mine enemy: when I fall, I shall arise; when I sit in darkness, the Lord shall be a light unto me. He will bring me forth to the light, and I shall behold his righteousness.

Isaiah 42:3   Psalm 23:3 2   Corinthians 7:10
Hebrews 12:11   Psalm 119:67   Ezra 9:13   Micah 7:8,9

NOVEMBER 23 MORNING

*Whoso hearkeneth unto me shall dwell safely,
and shall be quiet from fear of evil.*
— PROVERBS 1:33

Lord, thou hast been our dwelling place in all generations. — He that dwelleth in the secret place of the most High shall abide under the shadow of the Almighty. — His truth shall be thy shield and buckler. — Your life is hid with Christ in God. — He that toucheth you toucheth the apple of his eye. — Fear ye not, stand still, and see the salvation of the Lord. The Lord shall fight for you, and ye shall hold your peace. — God is our refuge and strength, a very present help in trouble. Therefore will not we fear. — Jesus spake unto them, saying, Be of good cheer; it is I; be not afraid. — Why are ye troubled? and why do thoughts arise in your hearts? Behold my hands and my feet, that it is I myself: handle me, and see ; for a spirit hath not flesh and bones, as ye see me have. — I know whom I have believed, and am persuaded that he is able to keep that which I have committed unto him against that day.

Psalms 90:1, 91:1,4   Colossians 3:3   Zechariah 2:8   Exodus 14:13,14
Psalm 46:1,2   Matthew 14:27   Luke 24:38,39 2   Timothy 1:12

NOVEMBER 23 EVENING

My kingdom is not of this world.
— JOHN 18:36

This man, after he had offered one sacrifice for sins for ever, sat down on the right hand of God; from henceforth expecting till his enemies may be made his footstool. — Hereafter shall ye see the Son of man sitting on the right hand of power, and coming in the clouds of heaven. — He must reign, till he hath put all enemies under his feet. — Thanks be to God, which giveth us the victory through our Lord Jesus Christ. — He raised him from the dead, and set him at his own right hand in the heavenly places, far above all principality, and power, and might, and dominion, and every name that is named, not only in this world, but also in that which is to come: and hath put all things under his feet, and gave him to be the head over all things to the church, which is his body, the fulness of him that filleth all in all. — He shall shew who is the blessed and only Potentate, the King of kings, and Lord of lords.

Hebrews 10:12,13   Matthew 26:64 1   Corinthians 15:25,57
Ephesians 1:20-23 1   Timothy 6:15

NOVEMBER 24 MORNING

*My mother and my brethren are
these which hear the word of God, and do it.*
— LUKE 8:21

Both he that sanctifieth and they who are sanctified are all of one: for which cause he is not ashamed to call them brethren: saying, I will declare thy name unto my brethren; in the midst of the church will I sing praise unto thee. — In Jesus Christ neither circumcision availeth any thing, nor uncircumcision; but faith which worketh by love. — Ye are my friends, if ye do whatsoever I command you. — Blessed are they that hear the word of God, and keep it. — Not every one that saith unto me, Lord, Lord, shall enter into the kingdom of heaven; but he that doeth the will of my Father which is in heaven. — My meat is to do the will of him that sent me. — If we say that we have fellowship with him, and walk in darkness, we lie, and do not the truth. — Whoso keepeth his word, in him verily is the love of God perfected; hereby know we that we are in him.

Hebrews 2:11,12   Galatians 5:6   John 15:14
Luke. 11:28   Matthew 7:21   John 4:34 1   John 1:6, 2:5

NOVEMBER 24 EVENING

What doest thou here, Elijah?
— 1 KINGS 19:9

He knoweth the way that I take. — O Lord, thou hast searched me, and known me. Thou knowest my downsitting, and mine uprising; thou understandest my thought afar off. Thou compassest my path, and my lying down, and art acquainted with all my ways. Whither shall I go from thy spirit? or whither shall I flee from thy presence? If I take the wings of the morning, and dwell in the uttermost parts of the sea; even there shall thy hand lead me, and thy right hand shall hold me. — Elias was a man subject to like passions as we are. — The fear of man bringeth a snare: but whoso putteth his trust in the Lord shall be safe. — Though he fall, he shall not be utterly cast down: for the Lord upholdeth him with his hand. — A just man falleth seven times, and riseth up again. — Let us not be weary in well doing: for in due season we shall reap, if we faint not. — The spirit indeed is willing, but the flesh is weak. — Like as a father pitieth his children, so the Lord pitieth them that fear him.

Job 23:10   Psalm 139:1-3,7,9,10   James 5:17   Proverbs 29:25   Psalm 37:24
Proverbs 24:16   Galatians 6:9   Matthew 26:41   Psalm 103:13,14

NOVEMBER 25 MORNING

*Being made free from sin,
ye became the servants of righteousness.*
— ROMANS 6:18

Ye cannot serve God and Mammon. — When ye were the servants of sin, ye were free from righteousness. What fruit had ye then in those things whereof ye are now ashamed? for the end of those things is death. But now being made free from sin, and become servants to God, ye have your fruit unto holiness, and the end everlasting life. — Christ is the end of the law for righteousness to every one that believeth. — If any man serve me, let him follow me; and where I am, there shall also my servant be: if any man serve me, him will my Father honour. — Take my yoke upon you, and learn of me: for I am meek and lowly in heart: and ye shall find rest unto your souls. For my yoke is easy, and my burden is light. — O Lord our God, other lords beside thee have had dominion over us: but by thee only will we make mention of thy name. — I will run the way of thy commandments, when thou shalt enlarge my heart.

Matthew 6:24   Romans 6:20-22, 10:4   John 12:26
Matthew 11:29,30   Isaiah 26:13   Psalm 119:32

NOVEMBER 25 EVENING

*Whosoever shall call on the name of the Lord
shall he saved.*
— ACTS 2:21

Manasseh did that which was evil in the sight of the Lord, after the abominations of the heathen, and he reared up altars for Baal. And he built altars for all the host of heaven in the two courts of the house of the Lord. And he made his son pass through the fire, and observed times, and used enchantments, and dealt with familiar spirits and wizards: he wrought much wickedness in the sight of the Lord, to provoke him to anger. — And when he was in affliction, he besought the Lord his God, and humbled himself greatly before the God of his fathers, and prayed unto him: and he was intreated of him, and heard his supplication. — Come now, and let us reason together, saith the Lord: though your sins be as scarlet, they shall be as white as snow; though they be red like crimson, they shall be as wool. — The Lord is longsuffering to us-ward, not willing that any should perish.

2 Kings 21:1-3,5,6 2   Chronicles 33:12,13   Isaiah 1:18 2   Peter 3:9

NOVEMBER 26 MORNING

The Lord delighteth in thee.
— ISAIAH 62:4

Thus saith the Lord that created thee…Fear not: for I have redeemed thee, I have called thee by thy name; thou art mine. — Can a woman forget her sucking child, that she should not have compassion on the son of her womb? yea, they may forget, yet will I not forget thee. Behold, I have graven thee upon the palms of mine hands: thy walls are continually before me. — The steps of a good man are ordered by the Lord: and he delighteth in his way. — My delights were with the sons of men. — The Lord taketh pleasure in them that fear him, in those that hope in his mercy. — They shall be mine, saith the Lord of hosts, in that day when I make up my jewels; and I will spare them, as a man spareth his own son that serveth him. — You, that were sometime alienated and enemies in your mind by wicked works, yet now hath he reconciled in the body of his flesh through death, to present you holy and unblameable and unreproveable in his sight.

Isaiah 43:1, 49:15,16   Psalm 37:23   Proverbs 8:31
Psalm 147:11   Malachi 3:17   Colossians 1:21,22

NOVEMBER 26 EVENING

The sorrow of the world worketh death.
— 2 CORINTHIANS 7:10

When Ahithophel saw that his counsel was not followed, he saddled his ass, and arose, and gat him home to his house, to his city, and put his household in order, and hanged himself, and died. — A wounded spirit who can bear? . — Is there no balm in Gilead? is there no physician there? why then is not the health of the daughter of my people recovered?— The Lord hath anointed me to preach good tidings unto the meek: he hath sent me to bind up the broken-hearted, to comfort all that mourn; to appoint unto them that mourn in Zion, to give unto them beauty for ashes, the oil of joy for mourning, the garment of praise for the spirit of heaviness. — Come unto me, all ye that labour and are heavy laden, and I will give you rest. Take my yoke upon you, and learn of me; for I am meek and lowly in heart: and ye shall find rest unto your souls. For my yoke is easy, and my burden is light. — Philip preached unto him Jesus. — He healeth the broken in heart, and bindeth up their wounds.

2 Samuel 17:23   Proverbs 18:14   Jeremiah 8:22
Isaiah 61:1-3   Matthew 11:28-30   Acts 8:35   Psalm 147:3

NOVEMBER 27 MORNING

The glory which thou gavest me I have given them.
— JOHN 17:22

I saw...the Lord sitting upon a throne, high and lifted up, and his train filled the temple. Above it stood the seraphims. And one cried unto another, and said, Holy, holy, holy, is the Lord of hosts; the whole earth is full of his glory. — These things said Esaias, when he saw his glory, and spake of him. — Upon the likeness of the throne was the likeness...of a man above upon it. As the appearance of the bow that is in the cloud in the day of rain, so was the appearance of the brightness round about. This was the appearance of the likeness of the glory of the Lord. — I beseech thee, shew me thy glory. And he said, Thou canst not see my face: for there shall no man see me, and live. — No man hath seen God at any time; the only begotten Son, which is in the bosom of the Father, he hath declared him. — God, who commanded the light to shine out of darkness, hath shined in our hearts, to give the light of the knowledge of the glory of God in the face of Jesus Christ.

Isaiah 6:1-3   John 12:41   Ezekiel 1:26,28
Exodus 33:18,20   John 1:18 2   Corinthians 4:6

NOVEMBER 27 EVENING

My son, if sinners entice thee, consent thou not.
— PROVERBS 1:10

She took of the fruit thereof, and did eat, and gave also unto her husband with her; and he did eat. — Did not Achan the son of Zerah commit a trespass in the accursed thing, and wrath fell on all the congregation of Israel? and that man perished not alone in his iniquity. — Thou shalt not follow a multitude to do evil. — Wide is the gate, and broad is the way, that leadeth to destruction, and many there be which go in thereat. — None of us liveth to himself. — Brethren, ye have been called unto liberty; only use not liberty for an occasion to the flesh, but by love serve one another. — Take heed lest by any means this liberty of yours become a stumblingblock to them that are weak. When ye sin so against the brethren, and wound their weak conscience, ye sin against Christ. — All we, like sheep, have gone astray; we have turned every one to his own way; and the Lord hath laid on him the iniquity of us all.

Genesis 3:6   Joshua 22:20   Exodus 23:2   Matthew 7:13
Romans 14:7   Galatians 5:13 1   Corinthians 8:9,12   Isaiah 53:6

NOVEMBER 28 MORNING

As the body without the spirit is dead,
so faith without works is dead also.
— *JAMES 2:26*

Not every one that saith...Lord, Lord, shall enter into the kingdom of heaven; but he that doeth the will of my Father which is in heaven. — Holiness, without which no man shall see the Lord. — Add to your faith virtue; and to virtue knowledge; and to knowledge temperance; and to temperance patience; and to patience godliness; and to godliness brotherly kindness; and to brotherly kindness charity. For if these things be in you, and abound, they make you that ye shall neither be barren nor unfruitful in the knowledge of our Lord Jesus Christ. But he that lacketh these things is blind, and cannot see afar off, and hath forgotten that he was purged from his old sins. Wherefore the rather, brethren, give diligence to make your calling and election sure: for if ye do these things, ye shall never fall. — By grace are ye saved through faith; and that not of yourselves; it is the gift of God: not of works, lest any man should boast.

Matthew 7:21   Hebrews 12:14   2 Peter 1:5-10   Ephesians 2:8,9

NOVEMBER 28 EVENING

As the children are partakers of flesh and blood,
he also himself likewise took part of the same;
that he might deliver them who through fear of death
were all their lifetime subject to bondage.
— *HEBREWS 2:14,15*

O death, where is thy sting? O grave, where is thy victory? Thanks be to God, which giveth us the victory through our Lord Jesus Christ. — For which cause we faint not; but though our outward man perish, yet the inward man is renewed day by day. — We know that if our earthly house of this tabernacle were dissolved, we have a building of God, an house not made with hands, eternal in the heavens. Therefore we are always confident, knowing that, whilst we are at home in the body, we are absent from the Lord. We are willing rather to be absent from the body, and to be present with the Lord. — Let not your heart be troubled: ye believe in God, believe also in me. In my Father's house are many mansions: if it were not so, I would have told you. I go to prepare a place for you.

1 Corinthians 15:55,57   2 Corinthians 4:16, 5:1,6-8   John 14:1-3

NOVEMBER 29 MORNING

We shall be satisfied with the goodness of thy house.
— PSALM 65:4

One thing have I desired of the Lord, that will I seek after; that I may dwell in the house of the Lord all the days of my life, to behold the beauty of the Lord, and to enquire in his temple. — Blessed are they which do hunger and thirst after righteousness: for they shall be filled. — He hath filled the hungry with good things; and the rich he hath sent empty away. — He satisfieth the longing soul, and filleth the hungry soul with goodness. — I am the bread of life: he that cometh to me shall never hunger; and he that believeth on me shall never thirst. — How excellent is thy lovingkindness, O God! therefore the children of men put their trust under the shadow of thy wings. They shall be abundantly satisfied with the fatness of thy house; and thou shalt make them drink of the river of thy pleasures. For with thee is the fountain of life: in thy light shall we see light.

Psalm 27:4   Matthew 5:6   Luke 1:53   Psalm 107:9   John 6:35   Psalm 36:7-9

NOVEMBER 29 EVENING

Do ye now believe?
— JOHN 16:31

What doth it profit, my brethren, though a man say he hath faith, and have not works? can faith save him? Faith, if it hath not works, is dead, being alone. — By faith Abraham, when he was tried, offered up Isaac: and he that had received the promises offered up his only begotten son. Accounting that God was able to raise him up, even from the dead. — Was not Abraham our father justified by works, when he had offered Isaac his son upon the altar? Ye see then how that by works a man is justified, and not by faith only. — Whoso looketh into the perfect law of liberty, and continueth therein, he being not a forgetful hearer, but a doer of the work, this man shall be blessed in his deed. — By their fruits ye shall know them. Not every one that saith unto me, Lord, Lord, shall enter into the kingdom of heaven; but he that doeth the will of my Father which is in heaven. — If ye know these things, happy are ye if ye do them.

James 2:14,17   Hebrews 11:17-19   James 2:21,24, 1:25
Matthew 7:20,21   John 13:17

NOVEMBER 30 MORNING

*The Lord of peace himself give you peace
always by all means.
The Lord be with you all.
— 2 THESSALONIANS 3:16*

Peace, from him which is, and which was, and which is to come. — The peace of God, which passeth all understanding, shall keep your hearts and minds through Christ Jesus. — Jesus himself stood in the midst of them, and saith unto them, Peace be unto you. — Peace I leave with you, my peace I give unto you: not as the world giveth, give I unto you. Let not your heart be troubled, neither let it be afraid. — The Comforter...even the Spirit of truth. — The fruit of the Spirit is love, joy, peace. — The Spirit itself beareth witness with our spirit, that we are the children of God. — My presence shall go with thee and I will give thee rest. And he said unto him, If thy presence go not with me, carry us not up hence. For wherein shall it be known here that I and thy people have found grace in thy sight? is it not in that thou goest with us?

Revelation 1:4   Philippians 4:7   Luke 24:36
John 14:27, 15:26   Galatians 5:22   Romans 8:16   Exodus 33:14-16

NOVEMBER 30 EVENING

*We glory in tribulations.
— ROMANS 5:3*

If in this life only we have hope in Christ, we are of all men most miserable. — Beloved, think it not strange concerning the fiery trial which is to try you, as though some strange thing happened unto you: but rejoice, inasmuch as ye are partakers of Christ's sufferings; that, when his glory shall be revealed, ye may be glad also with exceeding joy. — Sorrowful, yet alway rejoicing. — Rejoice in the Lord alway: and again I say, rejoice. — They departed from the presence of the council, rejoicing that they were counted worthy to suffer shame for his name. — The God of hope fill you with all joy and peace in believing. — Although the fig tree shall not blossom, neither shall fruit be in the vines; the labour of the olive shall fail, and the fields shall yield no meat; the flock shall be cut off from the fold, and there shall be no herd in the stalls: Yet I will rejoice in the Lord, I will joy in the God of my salvation.

1 Corinthians 15:19 1   Peter 4:12,13 2   Corinthians 6:10
Philippians 4:4   Acts 5:41   Romans 15:13   Habakkuk 3:17,18

DECEMBER 1 MORNING

A man shall be as a hiding place from the wind,
and a covert from the tempest.
— ISAIAH 32:2

Forasmuch...as the children are partakers of flesh and blood, he also himself likewise took part of the same. — The man that is my fellow, saith the Lord of hosts. — I and my Father are one. — He that dwelleth in the secret place of the most High shall abide under the shadow of the Almighty. — There shall be a tabernacle for a shadow in the daytime from the heat, and for a place of refuge, and for a covert from storm and from rain. — The Lord is thy shade upon thy right hand. The sun shall not smite thee by day, nor the moon by night. — When my heart is overwhelmed: lead me to the rock that is higher than I. — Thou art my hiding place; thou shalt preserve me from trouble. — Thou hast been a strength to the poor, a strength to the needy in his distress, a refuge from the storm, a shadow from the heat, when the blast of the terrible ones is as a storm against the wall.

Hebrews 2:14   Zechariah 13:7   John 10:30   Psalm 91:1
Isaiah 4:6   Psalms 121:5,6, 61:2, 32:7   Isaiah 25:4

DECEMBER 1 EVENING

Behold, I create new heavens and a new earth.
— ISAIAH 65:17

The new heavens and the new earth, which I will make, shall remain before me...so shall your seed and your name remain. — We, according to his promise, look for new heavens and a new earth, wherein dwelleth righteousness. — I saw a new heaven and a new earth: for the first heaven and the first earth were passed away; and there was no more sea. And 1 John saw the holy city, new Jerusalem, coming down from God out of heaven, prepared as a bride adorned for her husband. And I heard a great voice out of heaven saying, Behold, the tabernacle of God is with men, and he will dwell with them, and they shall be his people, and God himself shall be with them, and be their God. And God shall wipe away all tears from their eyes; and there shall be no more death, neither sorrow, nor crying, neither shall there be any more pain: for the former things are passed away. And he that sat upon the throne said, Behold, I make all things new.

Isaiah 66:22   2 Peter 3:13   Revelation 21:1-5

DECEMBER 2 MORNING

Ye have an unction from the Holy One,
and ye know all things.
— 1 JOHN 2:20

God anointed Jesus of Nazareth with the Holy Ghost and with power. — It pleased the Father that in him should all fulness dwell. — Of his fulness have all we received, and grace for grace. — Thou anointest my head with oil. — The anointing which ye have received of him abideth in you, and ye need not that any man teach you: but as the same anointing teacheth you of all things, and is truth, and is no lie, and even as it hath taught you, ye shall abide in him. — The Comforter, which is the Holy Ghost, whom the Father will send in my name, he shall teach you all things, and bring all things to your remembrance, whatsoever I have said unto you. — The Spirit also helpeth our infirmities: for we know not what we should pray for as we ought: but the Spirit itself maketh intercession for us with groanings which cannot be uttered.

Acts 10:38   Colossians 1:19   John 1:16
Psalm 23:5   1 John 2:27   John 14:26   Romans 8:26

DECEMBER 2 EVENING

Having our hearts sprinkled from an evil conscience.
— HEBREWS 10:22

If the blood of bulls and of goats, and the ashes of an heifer sprinkling the unclean, sanctifieth to the purifying of the flesh: How much more shall the blood of Christ, who through the eternal Spirit offered himself without spot to God, purge your conscience from dead works to serve the living God. — The blood of sprinkling, that speaketh better things than that of Abel. — We have redemption through his blood, the forgiveness of sins, according to the riches of his grace. — When Moses had spoken every precept to all the people according to the law, he took the blood of calves and of goats, with water, and scarlet wool, and hyssop, and sprinkled both the book, and all the people. Moreover he sprinkled...with blood both the tabernacle, and all the vessels of the ministry. And almost all things are by the law purged with blood; and without shedding of blood is no remission.

Hebrews 9:13,14, 12:24   Ephesians 1:7   Hebrews 9:19,21,22

DECEMBER 3 MORNING

I would seek unto God,
and unto God would I commit my cause.
— JOB 5:8

Is anything too hard for the Lord? — Commit thy way unto the Lord; trust also in him; and he shall bring it to pass. — Be careful for nothing; but in every thing by prayer and supplication, with thanksgiving, let your requests be made known unto God. — Casting all your care upon him, for he careth for you. — Hezekiah received the letter from the hand of the messengers, and read it: and Hezekiah went up unto the house of the Lord, and spread it before the Lord. And Hezekiah prayed unto the Lord. — It shall come to pass, that before they call, I will answer; and while they are yet speaking, I will hear. — The effectual fervent prayer of a righteous man availeth much. — I love the Lord, because he hath heard my voice and my supplications. Because he hath inclined his ear unto me, therefore will I call upon him as long as I live.

Genesis 18:14   Psalm 37:5   Philippians 4:6 1   Peter 5:7
Isaiah 37:14,15, 65:24   James 5:16   Psalm 116:1,2

DECEMBER 3 EVENING

Our bodies washed with pure water.
— HEBREWS 10:22

Thou shalt...make a laver of brass...and thou shalt put it between the tabernacle of the congregation and the altar, and thou shalt put water therein. For Aaron and his sons shall wash their hands and their feet thereat: when they go into the tabernacle of the congregation, they shall wash with water, that they die not;...they shall wash their hands and their feet, that they die not. — Your body is the temple of the Holy Ghost which is in you. — If any man defile the temple of God, him shall God destroy; for the temple of God is holy, which temple ye are. — In my flesh shall I see God: whom I shall see for myself, and mine eyes shall behold, and not another. — There shall in no wise enter into it any thing that defileth. — Thou art of purer eyes than to behold evil, and canst not look on iniquity. — I beseech you, therefore, brethren, by the mercies of God, that ye present your bodies a living sacrifice, holy, acceptable unto God, which is your reasonable service.

Exodus 30:18-21 1   Corinthians 6:19, 3:17   Job 19:26,27
Revelation 21:27   Habakkuk 1:13   Romans 12:1

DECEMBER 4 MORNING

Where shall wisdom be found?
— JOB 28:12

If any of you lack wisdom, let him ask of God, that giveth to all men liberally, and upbraideth not; and it shall be given him. But let him ask in faith, nothing wavering. — Trust in the Lord with all thine heart; and lean not unto thine own understanding. In all thy ways acknowledge him, and he shall direct thy paths. — The only wise God. — Be not wise in thine own eyes. — Ah, Lord God! Behold, I cannot speak: for I am a child. But the Lord said unto me, Say not, I am a child: for thou shalt go to all that I shall send thee, and whatsoever I command thee thou shalt speak. Be not afraid of their faces: for I am with thee to deliver thee, saith the Lord. — Whatsoever ye shall ask the Father in my name, he will give it you. Hitherto have ye asked nothing in my name: ask, and ye shall receive, that your joy may be full. — All things whatsoever ye shall ask in prayer, believing, ye shall receive.

James 1:5,6   Proverbs 3:5,6   1 Timothy 1:17   Proverbs 3:7
Jeremiah 1:6-8   John 16:23,24   Matthew 21:22

DECEMBER 4 EVENING

I would not live alway.
— JOB 7:16

And I said, O that I had wings like a dove, for then would I fly away, and be at rest. I would hasten my escape from the windy storm and tempest. — In this we groan, earnestly desiring to be clothed upon with our house which is from heaven. For we that are in this tabernacle do groan, being burdened: not for that we would be unclothed, but clothed upon, that mortality might be swallowed up of life. — Having a desire to depart, and to be with Christ; which is far better. — Let us run with patience the race that is set before us. Looking unto Jesus the author and finisher of our faith; who, for the joy that was set before him, endured the cross, despising the shame, and is set down at the right hand of the throne of God. For consider him that endured such contradiction of sinners against himself, lest ye be wearied and faint in your minds. — Let not your heart be troubled, neither let it be afraid.

Psalm 55:6,8   2 Corinthians 5:2,4   Philippians 1:23   Hebrews 12:1-3   John 14:27

DECEMBER 5 MORNING

*It is good for me that I have been afflicted;
that I might learn thy statutes.*
— PSALM 119:71

Though he were a Son, yet learned he obedience by the things which he suffered. — We suffer with him, that we may be also glorified together. — For I reckon that the sufferings of this present time are not worthy to be compared with the glory which shall be revealed in us. — He knoweth the way that I take: when he hath tried me, I shall come forth as gold. My foot hath held his steps, his way have I kept, and not declined. — Thou shalt remember all the way which the Lord thy God led thee these forty years in the wilderness, to humble thee, and to prove thee, to know what was in thine heart, whether thou wouldest keep his commandments, or no. Thou shalt also consider in thine heart, that, as a man chasteneth his son, so the Lord thy God chasteneth thee. Therefore thou shalt keep the commandments of the Lord thy God, to walk in his ways, and to fear him.

Hebrews 5:8   Romans 8:17,18   Job 23:10,11   Deuteronomy 8:2,5,6

DECEMBER 5 EVENING

By strength shall no man prevail.
— 1 SAMUEL 2:9

Then said David to the Philistine, Thou comest to me with a sword, and with a spear, and with a shield: but I come to thee in the name of the Lord of hosts, the God of the armies of Israel, whom thou hast defied. And David put his hand in his bag, and took thence a stone, and slang it. So David prevailed over the Philistine with a sling and with a stone. — There is no king saved by the multitude of an host: a mighty man is not delivered by much strength. Behold, the eye of the Lord is upon them that fear him, upon them that hope in his mercy. — Both riches and honour come of thee, and thou reignest over all; and in thine hand is power and might; and in thine hand it is to make great, and to give strength unto all. — I glory in my infirmities, that the power of Christ may rest upon me. Therefore I take pleasure in infirmities, in reproaches, in necessities, in persecutions, in distresses for Christ's sake: for when I am weak, then am I strong.

1 Samuel 17:45,49,50   Psalm 33:16,18 1   Chronicles 29:12 2   Corinthians 12:9,10

DECEMBER 6 MORNING

It is God which worketh in you.
— PHILIPPIANS 2:13

Not that we are sufficient of ourselves to think any thing as of ourselves; but our sufficiency is of God. — A man can receive nothing, except it be given him from heaven. — No man can come to me, except the Father which hath sent me draw him: and I will raise him up at the last day. — And I will give them one heart, and one way, that they may fear me for ever. — Do not err, my beloved brethren. Every good gift and every perfect gift is from above, and cometh down from the Father of lights, with whom is no variableness, neither shadow of turning. Of his own will begat he us with the word of truth, that we should be a kind of firstfruits of his creatures. — For we are his workmanship, created in Christ Jesus unto good works, which God hath before ordained that we should walk in them. — Lord, thou wilt ordain peace for us: for thou also hast wrought all our works in us.

2 Corinthians 3:5   John 3:27, 6:44   Jeremiah 32:39
James 1:16-18   Ephesians 2:10   Isaiah 26:12

DECEMBER 6 EVENING

The spirit indeed is willing, but the flesh is weak.
— MATTHEW 26:41

In the way of thy judgments, O Lord, have we waited for thee; the desire of our soul is to thy name, and to the remembrance of thee. With my soul have I desired thee in the night; yea, with my spirit within me will I seek thee early. — I know that in me, (that is, in my flesh) dwelleth no good thing: for to will is present with me; but how to perform that which is good I find not. For I delight in the law of God after the inward man: but I see another law in my members, warring against the law of my mind, and bringing me into captivity to the law of sin which is in my members. — The flesh lusteth against the Spirit, and the Spirit against the flesh: and these are contrary the one to the other: so that ye cannot do the things that ye would. — I can do all things through Christ which strengtheneth me. — Our sufficiency is of God. — My grace is sufficient for thee.

Isaiah 26:8,9   Romans 7:18,22,23   Galatians 5:17
Philippians 4:13 2 Corinthians 3:5, 12:9

DECEMBER 7 MORNING

He hath made him to be sin for us, who knew no sin;
that we might be made the righteousness of God in him.
— 2 CORINTHIANS 5:21

The Lord hath laid on him the iniquity of us all. — Who his own self bare our sins in his own body on the tree, that we, being dead to sins, should live unto righteousness: by whose stripes ye were healed. — As by one man's disobedience many were made sinners, so by the obedience of one shall many be made righteous. — After that the kindness and love of God our Saviour toward man appeared, not by works of righteousness which we have done, but according to his mercy he saved us, by the washing of regeneration, and renewing of the Holy Ghost; which he shed on us abundantly through Jesus Christ our Saviour; that being justified by his grace, we should be made heirs according to the hope of eternal life. — There is therefore now no condemnation to them which are in Christ Jesus, who walk not after the flesh, but after the Spirit. — The Lord our Righteousness.

Isaiah 53:6 1 Peter 2:24 Romans 5:19 Titus 3:4-7 Romans 8:1 Jeremiah 23:6

DECEMBER 7 EVENING

I will be as the dew unto Israel.
— HOSEA 14:5

The meekness and gentleness of Christ. — A bruised reed shall he not break, and the smoking flax shall he not quench. — The Spirit of the Lord is upon me, because he hath anointed me to preach the gospel to the poor; he hath sent me to heal the brokenhearted, to preach deliverance to the captives, and recovering of sight to the blind, to set at liberty them that are bruised, to preach the acceptable year of the Lord. And he began to say unto them, This day is this scripture fulfilled in your ears. And all bare him witness, and wondered at the gracious words which proceeded out of his mouth. — And the Lord turned, and looked upon Peter, and Peter remembered the word of the Lord, how he had said unto him, Before the cock crow, thou shalt deny me thrice. And Peter went out and wept bitterly. — He shall feed his flock like a shepherd: he shall gather the lambs with his arm, and carry them in his bosom, and shall gently lead those that are with young.

2 Corinthians 10:1 Isaiah 42:3 Luke 4:18,19,21,22, 22:61,62 Isaiah 40:11

DECEMBER 8 MORNING

By love serve one another.
— GALATIANS 5:13

Brethren, if a man be overtaken in a fault, ye which are spiritual, restore such an one in the spirit of meekness; considering thyself, lest thou also be tempted. Bear ye one another's burdens, and so fulfil the law of Christ. — Brethren, if any of you do err from the truth, and one convert him; let him know, that he which converteth the sinner from the error of his way shall save a soul from death, and shall hide a multitude of sins. — Seeing ye have purified your souls in obeying the truth through the Spirit unto unfeigned love of the brethren, see that ye love one another with a pure heart fervently. — Owe no man any thing, but to love one another: for he that loveth another hath fulfilled the law. — Be kindly affectioned one to another in brotherly love; in honour preferring one another. — Yea, all of you be subject one to another, and be clothed with humility: for God resisteth the proud, and giveth grace to the humble. — We...that are strong ought to bear the infirmities of the weak, and not to please ourselves.

Galatians 6:1,2   James 5:19,20   1 Peter 1:22
Romans 13:8, 12:10   1 Peter 5:5   Romans 15:1

DECEMBER 8 EVENING

The dust shall return to the earth as it was.
— ECCLESIASTES 12:7

It is sown in corruption; it is sown in dishonour; it is sown in weakness; it is sown a natural body. — The first man is of the earth, earthy. — Dust thou art, and unto dust shalt thou return. — One dieth in his full strength, being wholly at ease and quiet. And another dieth in the bitterness of his soul, and never eateth with pleasure. They shall lie down alike in the dust, and the worms shall cover them. — My flesh...shall rest in hope. — Though after my skin worms destroy this body, yet in my flesh shall I see God. — The Lord Jesus Christ shall change our vile body, that it may be fashioned like unto his glorious body, according to the working whereby he is able even to subdue all things unto himself. — Lord, make me to know mine end, and the measure of my days, what it is; that I may know how frail I am. — So teach us to number our days, that we may apply our hearts unto wisdom.

1 Corinthians 15:42-44,47   Genesis 3:19   Job 21:23,25,26   Psalm 16:9
Job 19:26   Philippians 3:20,21   Psalms 39:4, 90:12

DECEMBER 9 MORNING

*To do justice and judgment
is more acceptable to the Lord than sacrifice.*
— PROVERBS 21:3

He hath shewed thee, O man, what is good; and what doth the Lord require of thee, but to do justly, and to love mercy, and to walk humbly with thy God?— Hath the Lord as great delight in burnt offerings and sacrifices, as in obeying the voice of the Lord? Behold, to obey is better than sacrifice, and to hearken than the fat of rams. — To love him with all the heart, and with all the understanding, and with all the soul, and with all the strength, and to love his neighbour as himself, is more than all whole burnt offerings and sacrifices. — Therefore turn thou to thy God: keep mercy and judgment, and wait on thy God continually. — Mary...sat at Jesus' feet, and heard his word. One thing is needful: and Mary hath chosen that good part, which shall not be taken away from her. — It is God which worketh in you both to will and to do of his good pleasure.

Micah 6:8 1 Samuel 15:22 Mark 12:33
Hosea 12:6 Luke 10:39,42 Philippians 2:13

DECEMBER 9 EVENING

The spirit shall return unto God who gave it.
— ECCLESIASTES 12:7

The Lord God formed man of the dust of the ground, and breathed into his nostrils the breath of life; and man became a living soul. — There is a spirit in man; and the inspiration of the Almighty giveth them understanding. — The first man Adam was made a living soul. — The spirit of man that goeth upward. — Whilst we are at home in the body, we are absent from the Lord. We are confident...and willing rather to be absent from the body, and to be present with the Lord. — With Christ; which is far better. — I would not have you to be ignorant, brethren, concerning them which are asleep, that ye sorrow not, even as others which have no hope. For if we believe that Jesus died and rose again, even so them also which sleep in Jesus will God bring with him. — I go to prepare a place for you. And if I go and prepare a place for you, I will come again, and receive you unto myself; that where I am, there ye may be also.

Genesis 2:7 Job 32:8 1 Corinthians 15:45 Ecclesiastes 3:21 2 Corinthians 5:6,8
Philippians 1:23 1 Thessalonians 4:13,14 John 14:2,3

DECEMBER 10 MORNING

No man is able to pluck them out of my Father's hand.
— JOHN 10:29

I know whom I have believed, and am persuaded that he is able to keep that which I have committed unto him against that day. — The Lord shall deliver me from every evil work, and will preserve me unto his heavenly kingdom. — We are more than conquerors through him that loved us. For I am persuaded, that neither death, nor life, nor angels, nor principalities, nor powers, nor things present, nor things to come, nor height, nor depth, nor any other creature, shall be able to separate us from the love of God, which is in Christ Jesus our Lord. — Your life is hid with Christ in God. — Hath not God chosen the poor of this world rich in faith, and heirs of the kingdom which he hath promised to them that love him? — Our Lord Jesus Christ himself, and God, even our Father, which hath loved us, and hath given us everlasting consolation and good hope through grace, comfort your hearts, and stablish you in every good word and work.

2 Timothy 1:12, 4:18   Romans 8:37-39   Colossians 3:3
James 2:5   2 Thessalonians 2:16,17

DECEMBER 10 EVENING

The perfect law of liberty.
— JAMES 1:25

Ye shall know the truth, and the truth shall make you free. Verily, verily, I say unto you, Whosoever committeth sin is the servant of sin. — If the Son therefore shall make you free, ye shall be free indeed. — Stand fast therefore in the liberty wherewith Christ hath made us free, and be not entangled again with the yoke of bondage. For, brethren, ye have been called unto liberty; only use not liberty for an occasion to the flesh, but by love serve one another. For all the law is fulfilled in one word, even in this; Thou shalt love thy neighbour as thyself. — Being then made free from sin, ye became the servants of righteousness. — For the woman which hath an husband is bound by the law to her husband so long as he liveth; but if the husband be dead, she is loosed from the law of her husband. — The law of the Spirit of life in Christ Jesus hath made me free from the law of sin and death. — I will walk at liberty, for I seek thy precepts.

John 8:32-34,36   Galatians 5:1,13,14   Romans 6:18, 7:2, 8:2   Psalm 119:45

DECEMBER 11 MORNING

Let not your good be evil spoken of.
— ROMANS 14:16

Abstain from all appearance of evil. — Providing for honest things, not only in the sight of the Lord, but also in the sight of men. — For so is the will of God, that with well doing ye may put to silence the ignorance of foolish men. — But let none of you suffer as a murderer, or as a thief, or as an evildoer, or as a busybody in other men's matters. Yet if any man suffer as a Christian, let him not be ashamed; but let him glorify God on this behalf. — Brethren, ye have been called unto liberty; only use not liberty for an occasion to the flesh, but by love serve one another. — Take heed lest by any means this liberty of yours become a stumblingblock to them that are weak. — Whoso shall offend one of these little ones which believe in me, it were better for him that a millstone were hanged about his neck, and that he were drowned in the depth of the sea. — Inasmuch as ye have done it unto one of the least of these my brethren, ye have done it unto me.

1 Thessalonians 5:22   2 Corinthians 8:21   1 Peter 2:15, 4:15,16
Galatians 5:13   1 Corinthians 8:9   Matthew 18:6, 25:40

DECEMBER 11 EVENING

Awake thou that sleepest,
and arise from the dead,
and Christ shall give thee light.
— EPHESIANS 5:14

It is high time to awake out of sleep: for now is our salvation nearer than when we believed. — Therefore let us not sleep, as do others; but let us watch and be sober. For they that sleep in the night: and they that be drunken are drunken in the night. But let us, who are of the day, be sober, putting on the breastplate of faith and love; and for an helmet, the hope of salvation. — Arise, shine; for thy light is come, and the glory of the Lord is risen upon thee. For behold darkness shall cover the earth, and gross darkness the people, but the Lord shall arise upon thee, and his glory shall be seen upon thee. — Wherefore gird up the loins of your mind, be sober, and hope to the end for the grace that is to be brought unto you at the revelation of Jesus Christ. — Let your loins be girded about, and your lights burning; and ye yourselves like unto men that wait for their lord.

Romans 13:11   1 Thessalonians 5:6-8   Isaiah 60:1,2   1 Peter 1:13   Luke 12:35,36

DECEMBER 12 MORNING

The Lord is in the midst of thee.
— ZEPHANIAH 3:15

Fear thou not; for I am with thee: be not dismayed; for I am thy God: I will strengthen thee; yea, I will help thee; yea, I will uphold thee with the right hand of my righteousness. — Strengthen ye the weak hands, and confirm the feeble knees. Say to them that are of a fearful heart, Be strong, fear not: behold, your God will come with vengeance, even God with a recompence; He will come and save you. — The Lord thy God in the midst of thee is mighty; he will save, he will rejoice over thee with joy; he will rest in his love, he will joy over thee with singing. — Wait on the Lord: be of good courage, and he shall strengthen thine heart. — I heard a great voice out of heaven, saying, Behold, the tabernacle of God is with men, and he will dwell with them, and they shall be his people, and God himself shall be with them, and be their God. And God shall wipe away all tears from their eyes; and there shall be no more death, neither sorrow, nor crying, neither shall there be any more pain.

Isaiah 41:10, 35:3,4   Zephaniah 3:17   Psalm 27:14   Revelation 21:3,4

DECEMBER 12 EVENING

Wherefore criest thou unto me?
Speak unto the children of Israel, that they go forward.
— EXODUS 14:15

Be of good courage, and let us behave ourselves valiantly for our people, and for the cities of our God: and let the Lord do that which is good in his sight. — We made our prayer unto our God, and set a watch against them day and night. — Not every one that saith unto me, Lord, Lord, shall enter into the kingdom of heaven; but he that doeth the will of my Father which is in heaven. — If any man will do his will, he shall know of the doctrine, whether it be of God. — Then shall we know, if we follow on to know the Lord. — Watch and pray, that ye enter not into temptation. — Watch ye, stand fast in the faith, quit you like men, be strong. — Not slothful in business; fervent in spirit; serving the Lord. — Strengthen ye the weak hands, and confirm the feeble knees. Say to them that are of a fearful heart, Be strong, fear not.

1 Chronicles 19:13   Nehemiah 4:9   Matthew 7:21   John 7:17   Hosea 6:3   Matthew 26:41   1 Corinthians 16:13   Romans 12:11   Isaiah 35:3,4

DECEMBER 13 MORNING

Be strong in the grace that is in Christ Jesus.
— 2 TIMOTHY 2:1

Strengthened with all might, according to his glorious power. — As ye have therefore received Christ Jesus the Lord, so walk ye in him: rooted and built up in him, and stablished in the faith, as ye have been taught, abounding therein with thanksgiving. — Trees of righteousness, the planting of the Lord, that he might be glorified. — Built upon the foundation of the apostles and prophets, Jesus Christ himself being the chief corner stone; in whom all the building fitly framed together groweth unto a holy temple in the Lord: in whom ye also are builded together for a habitation of God through the Spirit. — I commend you to God, and to the word of his grace, which is able to build you up, and to give you an inheritance among all them which are sanctified. — Being filled with the fruits of righteousness, which are by Jesus Christ, unto the glory and praise of God. — Fight the good fight of faith. — In nothing terrified by your adversaries.

Colossians 1:11, 2:6,7   Isaiah 61:3   Ephesians 2:20,22
Acts 20:32   Philippians 1:11 1 Timothy 6:12   Philippians 1:28

DECEMBER 13 EVENING

Thou renderest to every man according to his work.
— PSALM 62:12

Other foundation can no man lay than that is laid, which is Jesus Christ. If any man's work abide which he hath built thereupon, he shall receive a reward. If any man's work shall be burned, he shall suffer loss: but he himself shall be saved; yet so as by fire. — We must all appear before the judgment seat of Christ; that every one may receive the things done in his body, according to that he hath done, whether it be good or bad. — When thou doest alms, let not thy left hand know what thy right hand doeth: that thine alms may be in secret: and thy Father which seeth in secret himself shall reward thee openly. — After a long time the lord of those servants cometh, and reckoneth with them. — Not that we are sufficient of ourselves to think any thing as of ourselves; but our sufficiency is of God. — Lord, thou wilt ordain peace for us: for thou also hast wrought all our works in us.

1 Corinthians 3:11,14,15 2 Corinthians 5:10
Matthew 6:3,4, 25:19 2 Corinthians 3:5   Isaiah 26:12

DECEMBER 14 MORNING

Make his praise glorious.
— PSALM 66:2

This people have I formed for myself; they shall shew forth my praise. — I will cleanse them from all their iniquity, whereby they have sinned against me; and I will pardon all their iniquities, whereby they have sinned, and whereby they have transgressed against me. And it shall be to me a name of joy, a praise and an honour before all the nations of the earth. — By him therefore let us offer the sacrifice of praise to God continually, that is, the fruit of our lips giving thanks to his name. — I will praise thee, O Lord my God, with all my heart: and I will glorify thy name for evermore. For great is thy mercy toward me: and thou hast delivered my soul from the lowest hell. — Who is like unto thee, O Lord... glorious in holiness, fearful in praises, doing wonders?— I will praise the name of God with a song, and will magnify him with thanksgiving. — They sing the song of Moses the servant of God and the song of the Lamb, saying, Great and marvellous are thy works, Lord God Almighty.

Isaiah 43:21   Jeremiah 33:8,9   Hebrews 13:15   Psalm 86:12,13
Exodus 15:11   Psalm 69:30   Revelation 15:3

DECEMBER 14 EVENING

By nature the children of wrath, even as others.
— EPHESIANS 2:3

We ourselves also were sometime foolish, disobedient, deceived, serving divers lusts and pleasures, living in malice and envy, hateful, and hating one another. — Marvel not that I said unto thee, Ye must be born again. — Job answered the Lord, and said, Behold, I am vile: what shall I answer thee? I will lay mine hand upon my mouth. — The Lord said unto Satan, Hast thou considered my servant Job, that there is none like him in the earth, a perfect and an upright man, one that feareth God, and escheweth evil? — Behold, I was shapen in iniquity; and in sin did my mother conceive me. — David...to whom also he gave testimony, and said, I have found David the son of Jesse, a man after mine own heart, which shall fulfil all my will. — I obtained mercy...who was before a blasphemer, and a persecutor, and injurious. — That which is born of the flesh is flesh; and that which is born of the Spirit is spirit.

Titus 3:3   John 3:7   Job 40:3,4, 1:8   Psalm 51:5
Acts 13:22   1 Timothy 1:13   John 3:6

DECEMBER 15 MORNING

Bear ye one another's burdens,
and so fulfil the law of Christ.
— GALATIANS 6:2

Look not every man on his own things, but every man also on the things of others. Let this mind be in you, which was also in Christ Jesus: who...took upon him the form of a servant. — Even the Son of man came not to be ministered unto, but to minister, and to give his life a ransom for many. — He died for all, that they which live should not henceforth live unto themselves, but unto him which died for them, and rose again. — When Jesus...saw her weeping, and the Jews also weeping which came with her, he groaned in the spirit, and was troubled. — Jesus wept. — Rejoice with them that do rejoice, and weep with them that weep. — Be ye all of one mind, having compassion one of another, love as brethren, be pitiful, be courteous: not rendering evil for evil or railing for railing: but contrariwise blessing; knowing that ye are thereunto called, that ye should inherit a blessing.

Philippians 2:4,5,7   Mark 10:45 2   Corinthians 5:15
John 11:33,35   Romans 12:15 1   Peter 3:8,9

DECEMBER 15 EVENING

Son, go work today in my vineyard.
— MATTHEW 21:28

Thou are no more a servant, but a son; and if a son, then an heir of God through Christ. — Reckon ye...yourselves to be dead indeed unto sin, but alive unto God through Jesus Christ our Lord. Let not sin therefore reign in your mortal body, that ye should obey it in the lusts thereof. Neither yield ye your members as instruments of unrighteousness unto sin; but yield yourselves unto God, as those that are alive from the dead, and your members as instruments of righteousness unto God. — As obedient children, not fashioning yourselves according to the former lusts in your ignorance: but as he which hath called you is holy, so be ye holy in all manner of conversation; because it is written, Be ye holy; for I am holy. — Sanctified, and meet for the master's use, and prepared unto every good work. — Therefore, my beloved brethren, be ye steadfast, unmovable, always abounding in the work of the Lord, forasmuch as ye know that your labour is not in vain in the Lord.

Galatians 4:7   Romans 6:11-13 1   Peter 1:14-16
2 Timothy 2:21 1   Corinthians 15:58

DECEMBER 16 MORNING

Having loved his own which were in the world,
he loved them unto the end.
— JOHN 13:1

I pray for them: I pray not for the world, but for them which thou hast given me; for they are thine. And all mine are thine, and thine are mine; and I am glorified in them. I pray not that thou shouldest take them out of the world, but that thou shouldest keep them from the evil. They are not of the world, even as I am not of the world. — As the Father hath loved me, so have I loved you: continue ye in my love. — Greater love hath no man than this, that a man lay down his life for his friends. Ye are my friends, if ye do whatsoever I command you. — A new commandment I give unto you, That ye love one another; as I have loved you, that ye also love one another. — He which hath begun a good work in you will perform it until the day of Jesus Christ. — Christ...loved the church, and gave himself for it; that he might sanctify and cleanse it with the washing of water by the word.

John 17:9,10,15,16, 15:9,13,14, 13:34   Philippians 1:6   Ephesians 5:25,26

DECEMBER 16 EVENING

The deep things of God.
— 1 CORINTHIANS 2:10

Henceforth I call you not servants; for the servant knoweth not what his lord doeth; but I have called you friends; for all things that I have heard of my Father I have made known unto you. — It is given unto you to know the mysteries of the kingdom of heaven. — We have received, not the spirit of the world, but the Spirit which is of God; that we might know the things that are freely given to us of God. — For this cause I bow my knees unto the Father of our Lord Jesus Christ, of whom the whole family in heaven and earth is named, that he would grant you, according to the riches of his glory, to be strengthened with might by his Spirit in the inner man; that ye, being rooted and grounded in love, may be able to comprehend with all saints what is the breadth, and length, and depth, and height; and to know the love of Christ, which passeth knowledge, that ye might be filled with all the fulness of God.

John 15:15   Matthew 13:11   1 Corinthians 2:12   Ephesians 3:14-19

DECEMBER 17 MORNING

Quicken us, and we will call upon thy name.
— PSALM 80:18

It is the Spirit that quickeneth. — The Spirit also helpeth our infirmities: for we know not what we should pray for as we ought: but the Spirit itself maketh intercession for us with groanings which cannot be uttered. And he that searcheth the hearts knoweth what is the mind of the Spirit, because he maketh intercession for the saints according to the will of God. — Praying always with all prayer and supplication in the Spirit, and watching thereunto with all perseverance. — I will never forget thy precepts: for with them thou hast quickened me. — The words that I speak unto you, they are spirit, and they are life. — The letter killeth, but the spirit giveth life. — If ye abide in me, and my words abide in you, ye shall ask what ye will, and it shall be done unto you. — This is the confidence that we have in him, that, if we ask any thing according to his will, he heareth us. — No man can say that Jesus is the Lord, but by the Holy Ghost.

John 6:63   Romans 8:26,27   Ephesians 6:18   Psalm 119:93   John 6:63
2 Corinthians 3:6   John 15:7   1 John 5:14   1 Corinthians 12:3

DECEMBER 17 EVENING

Have no fellowship with the unfruitful works of darkness,
but rather reprove them.
— EPHESIANS 5:11

Be not deceived: evil communications corrupt good manners. — Know ye not that a little leaven leaveneth the whole lump? Purge out therefore the old leaven. I wrote unto you in an epistle not to company with fornicators. Yet not altogether with the fornicators of this world, or with the covetous, or extortioners, or with idolaters; for then must we needs go out of the world. I have written unto you not to keep company, if any man that is called a brother be a fornicator, or covetous, or an idolater, or a railer, or a drunkard, or an extortioner; with such an one no not to eat. — That ye may be blameless and harmless, the sons of God, without rebuke, in the midst of a crooked and perverse nation, among whom ye shine as lights in the world. — In a great house there are not only vessels of gold and of silver, but also of wood and of earth; and some to honour, and some to dishonour.

1 Corinthians 15:33, 5:6,7,9-11   Philippians 2:15   2 Timothy 2:20

DECEMBER 18 MORNING

*Let us come boldly unto the throne of grace
that we may obtain mercy,
and find grace to help in time of need.*
— HEBREWS 4:16

Be careful for nothing; but in every thing by prayer and supplication with thanksgiving let your requests be made known unto God. And the peace of God, which passeth all understanding, shall keep your hearts and minds through Christ Jesus. — Ye have not received the spirit of bondage again to fear; but ye have received the Spirit of adoption, whereby we cry, Abba, Father. — I said not unto the seed of Jacob, Seek ye me in vain. — Having therefore...boldness to enter into the holiest by the blood of Jesus, by a new and living way, which he hath consecrated for us, through the veil, that is to say, his flesh; and having an high priest over the house of God; let us draw near with a true heart in full assurance of faith, having our hearts sprinkled from an evil conscience, and our bodies washed with pure water. — We may boldly say, The Lord is my helper, and I will not fear what man shall do unto me.

Philippians 4:6,7   Romans 8:15   Isaiah 45:19   Hebrews 10:19,22, 13:6

DECEMBER 18 EVENING

Ye shall know the truth, and the truth shall make you free.
— JOHN 8:32

Where the Spirit of the Lord is, there is liberty. — The law of the Spirit of life in Christ Jesus hath made me free from the law of sin and death. — If the Son...shall make you free, ye shall be free indeed. — Brethren, we are not children of the bondwoman, but of the free. — Knowing that a man is not justified by the works of the law, but by the faith of Jesus Christ, even we have believed in Jesus Christ, that we might be justified by the faith of Christ, and not by the works of the law: for by the works of the law shall no flesh be justified. — Whoso looketh into the perfect law of liberty, and continueth therein, he being not a forgetful hearer, but a doer of the work, this man shall be blessed in his deed. — Stand fast therefore in the liberty wherewith Christ hath made us free, and be not entangled again with the yoke of bondage.

2 Corinthians 3:17   Romans 8:2   John 8:36
Galatians 4:31, 2:16   James 1:25   Galatians 5:1

DECEMBER 19 MORNING

Unto the upright there ariseth light in the darkness.
— PSALM 112:4

Who is among you that feareth the Lord, that obeyeth the voice of his servant, that walketh in darkness, and hath no light? let him trust in the name of the Lord, and stay upon his God. — Though he fall, he shall not be utterly cast down: for the Lord upholdeth him with his hand. — The commandment is a lamp, and the law is light. — Rejoice not against me, O mine enemy: when I fall, I shall arise; when I sit in darkness, the Lord shall be a light unto me. I will bear the indignation of the Lord, because I have sinned against him, until he plead my cause, and execute judgment for me: he will bring me forth to the light, and I shall behold his righteousness. — The light of the body is the eye: if therefore thine eye be single, thy whole body shall be full of light. But if thine eye be evil, thy whole body shall be full of darkness. If therefore the light that is in thee be darkness, how great is that darkness!

Isaiah 50:10   Psalm 37:24   Proverbs 6:23   Micah 7:8,9   Matthew 6:22,23

DECEMBER 19 EVENING

He shall feed his flock like a shepherd:
he shall gather the lambs with his arm,
and carry them in his bosom,
and shall gently lend those that are with young.
— ISAIAH 40:11

I have compassion on the multitude, because they continue with me now three days, and have nothing to eat:...I will not send them away fasting, lest they faint in the way. — We have not an high priest which cannot be touched with the feeling of our infirmities. — They brought young children to him, and he took them up in his arms, put his hands upon them, and blessed them. — I have gone astray like a lost sheep; seek thy servant. — The Son of man is come to seek and to save that which was lost. — Ye were as sheep going astray; but are now returned unto the Shepherd and Bishop of your souls. — Fear not, little flock; for it is your Father's good pleasure to give you the kingdom. — I will feed my flock, and I will cause them to lie down, saith the Lord God.

Matthew 15:32   Hebrews 4:15   Mark 10:13,16   Psalm 119:176
Luke 19:10   1 Peter 2:25   Luke 12:32   Ezekiel 34:15

DECEMBER 20 MORNING

*He hath chosen us in Him
before the foundation of the world.
— EPHESIANS 1:4*

That we should be holy and without blame before him in love. — God hath from the beginning chosen you to salvation through sanctification of the Spirit and belief of the truth: whereunto he called you...to the obtaining of the glory of our Lord Jesus Christ. — Whom he did foreknow, he also did predestinate to be conformed to the image of his Son, that he might be the firstborn among many brethren. Moreover whom he did predestinate, them he also called: and whom he called, them he also justified: and whom he justified, them he also glorified. — Elect according to the foreknowledge of God the Father, through sanctification of the Spirit, unto obedience and sprinkling of the blood of Jesus Christ. — A new heart also will I give you, and a new spirit will I put within you: and I will take away the stony heart out of your flesh, and I will give you a heart of flesh. — God hath not called us unto uncleanness, but unto holiness.

Ephesians 1:4 2 Thessalonians 2:13,14 Romans 8:29,30
1 Peter 1:2 Ezekiel 36:26 1 Thessalonians 4:7

DECEMBER 20 EVENING

*If the Lord would make windows in heaven
might this thing be?
— 2 KINGS 7:2*

Have faith in God. — Without faith it is impossible to please God. — With God all things are possible. — Is my hand shortened at all, that it cannot redeem? Or have I no power to deliver? — My thoughts are not your thoughts, neither are your ways my ways, saith the Lord. For as the heavens are higher than the earth, so are my ways higher than your ways, and my thoughts than your thoughts. — Prove me now herewith, saith the Lord of hosts, if I will not open you the windows of heaven, and pour you out a blessing, that there shall not be room enough to receive it. — Behold, the Lord's hand is not shortened, that it cannot save; neither his ear heavy, that it cannot hear. — Lord, it is nothing with thee to help, whether with many or with them that have no power. — We should not trust in ourselves, but in God which raiseth the dead.

Mark 11:22 Hebrews 11:6 Matthew 19:26 Isaiah 50:2, 55:8,9
Malachi 3:10 Isaiah 59:1 2 Chronicles 14:11 2 Corinthians 1:9

DECEMBER 21 MORNING

The days of thy mourning shall be ended.
— ISAIAH 60:20

In the world ye shall have tribulation. — The whole creation groaneth and travaileth in pain together until now. And not only they, but ourselves also, which have the first fruits of the Spirit, even we ourselves groan within ourselves, waiting for the adoption, to wit, the redemption of our body. — We that are in this tabernacle do groan, being burdened: not for that we would be unclothed, but clothed upon, that mortality might be swallowed up of life. — These are they which came out of great tribulation, and have washed their robes, and made them white in the blood of the Lamb, Therefore are they before the throne of God, and serve him day and night in his temple: and he that sitteth on the throne shall dwell among them. They shall hunger no more, neither thirst any more; neither shall the sun light on them, nor any heat. For the Lamb which is in the midst of the throne shall feed them, and shall lead them unto living fountains of waters; and God shall wipe away all tears from their eyes.

John 16:33   Romans 8:22,23 2   Corinthians 5:4   Revelation 7:14-17

DECEMBER 21 EVENING

Master, carest thou not that we perish?
— MARK 4:38

The Lord is good to all: and his tender mercies are over all his works. — Every moving thing that liveth shall be meat for you; even as the green herb have I given you all things. — While the earth remaineth, seedtime and harvest, and cold and heat, and summer and winter, and day and night, shall not cease. — The Lord is good, a strong hold in the day of trouble; and he knoweth them that trust in him. — God heard the voice of the lad: and the angel of God called to Hagar out of heaven, and said unto her, What aileth thee, Hagar? fear not; for God hath heard the voice of the lad where he is. And God opened her eyes, and she saw a well of water; and she went, and filled the bottle with water, and gave the lad drink. — Take no thought, saying, What shall we eat? or, what shall we drink? for your heavenly Father knoweth that ye have need of all these things. — Trust...in the living God, who giveth us richly all things to enjoy.

Psalm 145:9   Genesis 9:3, 8:22   Nahum 1:7
Genesis 21:17,19   Matthew 6:31,32 1   Timothy 6:17

DECEMBER 22 MORNING

Your work of faith.
— 1 THESSALONIANS 1:3

This is the work of God, that ye believe on him whom he hath sent. — Faith, if it hath not works, is dead, being alone. — Faith worketh by love. — He that soweth to his flesh, shall of the flesh reap corruption; but he that soweth to the Spirit shall of the Spirit reap life everlasting. — We are his workmanship, created in Christ Jesus unto good works, which God hath before ordained that we should walk in them. — Who gave himself for us, that he might redeem us from all iniquity, and purify unto himself a peculiar people, zealous of good works. — We are bound to thank God always for you, brethren, as it is meet, because that your faith groweth exceedingly, and the charity of every one of you all toward each other aboundeth. Wherefore also we pray always for you, that our God would count you worthy of this calling, and fulfil all the good pleasure of his goodness, and the work of faith with power. — It is God which worketh in you both to will and to do of his good pleasure.

John 6:29   James 2:17   Galatians 5:6, 6:8   Ephesians 2:10
Titus 2:14 2 Thessalonians 1:3,11   Philippians 2:13

DECEMBER 22 EVENING

Where is the promise of his coming?
— 2 PETER 3:4

Enoch...the seventh from Adam, prophesied of these, saying, Behold, the Lord cometh with ten thousands of his saints, to execute judgment upon all. — Behold, he cometh with clouds; and every eye shall see him, and they also which pierced him; and all kindreds of the earth shall wail because of him. — The Lord himself shall descend from heaven with a shout, with the voice of the archangel, and with the trump of God: and the dead in Christ shall rise first: then we which are alive and remain shall be caught up together with them in the clouds, to meet the Lord in the air: and so shall we ever be with the Lord. — The grace of God that bringeth salvation hath appeared to all men, teaching us that, denying ungodliness and worldly lusts, we should live soberly, righteously, and godly, in this present world; looking for that blessed hope, and the glorious appearing of the great God and our Saviour Jesus Christ.

Jude 14,15   Revelation 1:7 1 Thessalonians 4:16,17   Titus 2:11-13

DECEMBER 23 MORNING

Let him take hold of my strength,
that he may make peace with me.
— ISAIAH 27:5

I know the thoughts that I think toward you, saith the Lord, thoughts of peace, and not of evil. — There is no peace, saith the Lord, unto the wicked. — In Christ Jesus ye who sometime were far off are made nigh by the blood of Christ. For he is our peace. — It pleased the Father that in him should all fulness dwell: and having made peace through the blood of his cross, by him to reconcile all things unto himself. — Christ Jesus: whom God hath set forth to be a propitiation through faith in his blood, to declare his righteousness for the remission of sins that are past:...that he might be just, and the justifier of him which believeth in Jesus. — If we confess our sins, he is faithful and just to forgive us our sins, and to cleanse us from all unrighteousness. — Trust ye in the Lord for ever, for in the Lord Jehovah is everlasting strength.

Jeremiah 29:11   Isaiah 48:22   Ephesians 2:13,14
Colossians 1:19,20   Romans 3:24-26 1 John 1:9   Isaiah 26:4

DECEMBER 23 EVENING

God hath given to us eternal life,
and this life is in his Son.
— 1 JOHN 5:11

As the Father hath life in himself; so hath he given to the Son to have life in himself. As the Father raiseth up the dead, and quickeneth them; even so the Son quickeneth whom he will. — I am the resurrection, and the life: he that believeth in me, though he were dead, yet shall he live: and whosoever liveth and believeth in me shall never die. — I am the good shepherd: the good shepherd giveth his life for the sheep. I lay down my life, that I might take it again. No man taketh it from me, but I lay it down of myself. I have power to lay it down, and I have power to take it again. This commandment have I received of my Father. — No man cometh unto the Father, but by me. — He that hath the Son, hath life; and he that hath not the Son of God, hath not life. — For ye are dead and your life is hid with Christ in God. When Christ, who is our life, shall appear, then shall ye also appear with him in glory.

John 5:26,21, 11:25,26, 10:11,17,18, 14:6 1 John 5:12   Colossians 3:3,4

DECEMBER 24 MORNING

*If ye live after the flesh, ye shall die:
but if ye through the Spirit
do mortify the deeds of the body,
ye shall live.*
— ROMANS 8:13

Now the works of the flesh are manifest which are these; adultery, fornication and such like: of the which I tell you before, as I have also told you in time past, that they which do such things shall not inherit the kingdom of God. But the fruit of the Spirit is love, joy, peace, longsuffering, gentleness, goodness, faith, meekness, temperance: against such there is no law. And they that are Christ's have crucified the flesh with the affections and lusts. If we live in the Spirit, let us also walk in the Spirit. — The grace of God that bringeth salvation hath appeared to all men, teaching us that, denying ungodliness and worldly lusts, we should live soberly, righteously, and godly, in this present world; looking for that blessed hope, and the glorious appearing of the great God and our Saviour Jesus Christ; who gave himself for us, that he might redeem us from all iniquity.

Galatians 5:19,21-25   Titus 2:11-14

DECEMBER 24 EVENING

*Then said the princes of the Philistines,
What do these Hebrews here?*
— 1 SAMUEL 29:3

If ye be reproached for the name of Christ, happy are ye: for the spirit of glory and of God resteth upon you: on their part he is evil spoken of, but on your part he is glorified. But let none of you suffer as a murderer, or as a thief...or as a busybody in other men's matters. — Let not...your good be evil spoken of. — Having your conversation honest among the Gentiles. — Be ye not unequally yoked together with unbelievers: for what fellowship hath righteousness with unrighteousness? And what communion hath light with darkness? Ye are the temple of the living God. Wherefore come out from among them, and be ye separate, saith the Lord, and touch not the unclean thing. — Ye are a chosen generation, a royal priesthood, an holy nation, a peculiar people: that ye should shew forth the praises of him who hath called you out of darkness into his marvellous light.

1 Peter 4:14,15   Romans 14:16   1 Peter 2:12
2 Corinthians 6:14,16,17   1 Peter 2:9

DECEMBER 25 MORNING

The kindness and love of God our Saviour
toward man appeared.
— TITUS 3:4

    I have loved thee with an everlasting love. — In this was manifested the love of God toward us, because that God sent his only begotten Son into the world, that we might live through him. — Herein is love, not that we loved God, but that he loved us, and sent his Son to be the propitiation for our sins. — When the fulness of the time was come, God sent forth his Son, made of a woman, made under the law, to redeem them that were under the law, that we might receive the adoption of sons. — The Word was made flesh, and dwelt among us, (and we beheld his glory, the glory as of the only begotten of the Father) full of grace and truth. — Great is the mystery of godliness: God was manifest in the flesh. — As the children are partakers of flesh and blood, he also himself likewise took part of the same; that through death he might destroy him that had the power of death, that is, the devil.

    Jeremiah 31:3 1   John 4:9,10   Galatians 4:4,5
    John 1:14 1   Timothy 3:16   Hebrews 2:14

DECEMBER 25 EVENING

Thanks be unto God for his unspeakable gift.
— 2 CORINTHIANS 9:15

    Make a joyful noise unto the Lord, all ye lands. Serve the Lord with gladness; come before his presence with singing. Enter into his gates with thanksgiving, and into his courts with praise: be thankful unto him, and bless his name. — For unto us a child is born, unto us a son is given: and the government shall be upon his shoulder: and his name shall be called Wonderful, Counsellor, The mighty God, The everlasting Father, The Prince of Peace. — He...spared not his own Son, but delivered him up for us all. — Having yet...one son, his well beloved, he sent him. — Oh that men would praise the Lord for his goodness, and for his wonderful works to the children of men!— Bless the Lord, O my soul: and all that is within me, bless his holy name. — My soul doth magnify the Lord, and my spirit hath rejoiced in God my Saviour.

    Psalm 100:1,2,4   Isaiah 9:6   Romans 8:32
    Mark 12:6   Psalms 107:21, 103:1   Luke 1:46,47

DECEMBER 26 MORNING

Be ye stedfast, unmoveable,
always abounding in the work of the Lord.
— 1 CORINTHIANS 15:58a

Ye know that your labour is not in vain in the Lord. — As ye have... received Christ Jesus the Lord, so walk ye in him: rooted and built up in him, and stablished in the faith, as ye have been taught, abounding therein with thanksgiving. — He that shall endure unto the end, the same shall be saved. — That on the good ground are they, which in an honest and good heart, having heard the word, keep it, and bring forth fruit with patience. — By faith ye stand. — I must work the works of him that sent me, while it is day: the night cometh, when no man can work. — He that soweth to his flesh shall of the flesh reap corruption; but he that soweth to the Spirit shall of the Spirit reap life everlasting. And let us not be weary in well doing: for in due season we shall reap, if we faint not. As we have therefore opportunity, let us do good unto all men, especially unto them who are of the household of faith.

1 Corinthians 15:58b   Colossians 2:6,7   Matthew 24:13   Luke 8:15
2 Corinthians 1:24   John 9:4   Galatians 6:8-10

DECEMBER 26 EVENING

He is able...to save them to the uttermost
that come unto God by him.
— HEBREWS 7:25

I am the way, the truth, and the life: no man cometh unto the Father, but by me. — Neither is there salvation in any other: for there is none other name under heaven given among men, whereby we must be saved. — My sheep hear my voice, and I know them, and they follow me: and I give unto them eternal life; and they shall never perish, neither shall any man pluck them out of my hand. — He which hath begun a good work in you will perform it until the day of Jesus Christ. — Is any thing too hard for the Lord! — Now unto him that is able to keep you from falling, and to present you faultless before the presence of his glory with exceeding joy, to the only wise God our Saviour, be glory and majesty, dominion and power, both now and ever. Amen.

John 14:6   Acts 4:12   John 10:27,28
Philippians 1:6   Genesis 18:14   Jude 24,25

DECEMBER 27 MORNING

*We look not at the things which are seen,
but at the things which are not seen:
for the things which are seen are temporal;
but the things which are not seen are eternal.*
— 2 CORINTHIANS 4:18

Here have we no continuing city. — Ye have in heaven a better and an enduring substance. — Fear not, little flock; for it is your Father's good pleasure to give you the kingdom. — Now for a season, if need be, ye are in heaviness through manifold temptations. — There the wicked cease from troubling; and there the weary be at rest. — We that are in this tabernacle do groan, being burdened. — God shall wipe away all tears from their eyes; and there shall be no more death, neither sorrow, nor crying, neither shall there be any more pain: for the former things are passed away. — The sufferings of this present time are not worthy to be compared with the glory which shall be revealed in us. — Our light affliction, which is but for a moment, worketh for us a far more exceeding and eternal weight of glory.

Hebrews 13:14, 10:34   Luke 12:32 1   Peter 1:6   Job 3:17
2 Corinthians 5:4   Revelation 21:4   Romans 8:18 2   Corinthians 4:17

DECEMBER 27 EVENING

He is our peace.
— EPHESIANS 2:14

God was in Christ, reconciling the world unto himself, not imputing their trespasses unto them; for he hath made him to be sin for us, who knew no sin; that we might be made the righteousness of God in him. — Having made peace through the blood of his cross, by him to reconcile all things unto himself. And you that were sometime alienated and enemies in your mind by wicked works, yet now hath he reconciled in the body of his flesh through death, to present you holy and unblameable and unreproveable in his sight. — Blotting out the handwriting of ordinances that was against us, which was contrary to us, and took it out of the way, nailing it to his cross. — Having abolished in his flesh the enmity, even the law of commandments contained in ordinances; for to make in himself of twain one new man, so making peace. — Peace I leave with you, my peace I give unto you: not as the world giveth, give I unto you. Let not your heart be troubled, neither let it be afraid.

2 Corinthians 5:19,21   Colossians 1:20-22, 2:14   Ephesians 2:15   John 14:27

DECEMBER 28 MORNING

Thy sins be forgiven thee.
— *MARK 2:5*

I will forgive their iniquity, and I will remember their sin no more. — Who can forgive sins but God only? — I, even I, am he that blotteth out thy transgressions for mine own sake, and will not remember thy sins. — Blessed is he whose transgression is forgiven, whose sin is covered. Blessed is the man unto whom the Lord imputeth not iniquity. — Who is a God like unto thee, that pardoneth iniquity? — God for Christ's sake hath forgiven you. — The blood of Jesus Christ his Son cleanseth us from all sin. If we say that we have no sin, we deceive ourselves, and the truth is not in us. If we confess our sins, he is faithful and just to forgive us our sins, and to cleanse us from all unrighteousness. — As far as the east is from the west, so far hath he removed our transgressions from us. — Sin shall not have dominion over you: for ye are not under the law, but under grace. Being then made free from sin, ye became the servants of righteousness.

Jeremiah 31:34 Mark 2.7 Isaiah 43:25 Psalm 32:1,2 Micah 7:18
Ephesians 4:32 1 John 1:7-9 Psalm 103:12 Romans 6:14,18

DECEMBER 28 EVENING

We would see Jesus.
— *JOHN 12:21*

O Lord, we have waited for thee; the desire of our soul is to thy name, and to the remembrance of thee. — The Lord is nigh unto all them that call upon him, to all that call upon him in truth. — Where two or three are gathered together in my name, there am I in the midst of them. — I will not leave you comfortless: I will come to you. — Lo, I am with you alway, even unto the end of the world. — Let us run with patience the race that is set before us, looking unto Jesus the author and finisher of our faith. — Now we see through a glass, darkly; but then face to face. — Having a desire to depart, and to be with Christ; which is far better. — Beloved, now are we the sons of God; and it doth not yet appear what we shall be: but we know that, when he shall appear, we shall be like him; for we shall see him as he is. And every man that hath this hope in him purifieth himself, even as he is pure.

Isaiah 26:8 Psalm 145:18 Matthew 18:20 John 14:18 Matthew 28:20
Hebrews 12:1,2 1 Corinthians 13:12 Philippians 1:23 1 John 3:2,3

DECEMBER 29 MORNING

Understanding what the will of the Lord is.
— EPHESIANS 5:17

This is the will of God, even your sanctification. — Acquaint now thyself with him, and be at peace: thereby good shall come unto thee. — This is life eternal, that they might know thee the only true God, and Jesus Christ, whom thou hast sent. — We know that the Son of God is come, and hath given us an understanding, that we may know him that is true, and we are in him that is true, even in his Son Jesus Christ. This is the true God, and eternal life. — We...do not cease to pray for you, and to desire that ye might be filled with the knowledge of his will in all wisdom and spiritual understanding. — The God of our Lord Jesus Christ, the Father of glory, give unto you the spirit of wisdom and revelation in the knowledge of him: the eyes of your understanding being enlightened; that ye may know what is the hope of his calling, and what the riches of the glory of his inheritance in the saints, and what is the exceeding greatness of his power to us-ward who believe.

1 Thessalonians 4:3   Job 22:21   John 17:3
1 John 5:20   Colossians 1:9   Ephesians 1:17-19

DECEMBER 29 EVENING

Draw nigh to God, and he will draw nigh to you.
— JAMES 4:8

Enoch walked with God. — Can two walk together, except they be agreed?— It is good for me to draw near to God. — The Lord is with you, while ye be with him: and if ye seek him, he will be found of you: but if ye forsake him, he will forsake you. When they in their trouble did turn unto the Lord God of Israel, and sought him, he was found of them. — For I know the thoughts that I think toward you, saith the Lord, thoughts of peace, and not of evil, to give you an expected end. Then shall ye call upon me, and ye shall go and pray unto me, and I will hearken unto you. And ye shall seek me, and find me, when ye shall search for me with all your heart. — Having therefore, brethren, boldness to enter into the holiest by the blood of Jesus, by a new and living way...and having an high priest over the house of God; let us draw near with a true heart in full assurance of faith.

Genesis 5:24   Amos 3:3   Psalm 73:28
2 Chronicles 15:2,4   Jeremiah 29:11-13   Hebrews 10:19-22

DECEMBER 30 MORNING

Blameless in the day of our Lord Jesus Christ.
— 1 CORINTHIANS 1:8

You, that were sometime alienated and enemies in your mind by wicked works, yet now hath he reconciled in the body of his flesh through death, to present you holy and unblameable and unreproveable in his sight: if ye continue in the faith grounded and settled, and be not moved away from the hope of the gospel. — That ye may be blameless and harmless, the sons of God, without rebuke, in the midst of a crooked and perverse nation, among whom ye shine as lights in the world. — Wherefore, beloved, seeing that ye look for such things, be diligent that ye may be found of him in peace, without spot, and blameless. — Sincere and without offence till the day of Christ. — Now unto him that is able to keep you from falling, and to present you faultless before the presence of his glory with exceeding joy, to the only wise God our Saviour, be glory and majesty, dominion and power, both now and ever.

Colossians 1:21-23   Philippians 2:15   2 Peter 3:14   Philippians 1:10   Jude 24,25

DECEMBER 30 EVENING

He will keep the feet of his saints.
— 1 SAMUEL 2:9

If we say that we have fellowship with him, and walk in darkness, we lie, and do not the truth: but if we walk in the light, as he is in the light, we have fellowship one with another, and the blood of Jesus Christ his Son cleanseth us from all sin. — He that is washed needeth not save to wash his feet, but is clean every whit. — I have taught thee in the way of wisdom; I have led thee in right paths. When thou goest, thy steps shall not be straitened; and when thou runnest, thou shalt not stumble. Enter not into the path of the wicked, and go not in the way of evil men. Avoid it, pass not by it, turn from it, and pass away. Let thine eyes look right on, and let thine eyelids look straight before thee. Ponder the path of thy feet, and let all thy ways be established. Turn not to the right hand nor to the left: remove thy foot from evil. — The Lord shall deliver me from every evil work, and will preserve me unto his heavenly kingdom: to whom be glory for ever and ever. Amen.

1 John 1:6,7   John 13:10   Proverbs 4:11,12,14,15,25-27   2 Timothy 4:18

DECEMBER 31 MORNING

*The Lord thy God bare thee, as a man doth bear his son,
in all the way that ye went, until ye came into this place.*
— DEUTERONOMY 1:31

I bare you on eagles' wings, and brought you unto myself. — In his love and in his pity he redeemed them; and he bare them, and carried them all the days of old. — As an eagle stirreth up her nest, fluttereth over her young, spreadeth abroad her wings, taketh them, beareth them on her wings: so the Lord alone did lead him. — Even to your old age I am he; and even to hoar hairs will I carry you: I have made, and I will bear; even I will carry, and will deliver you. — This God is our God for ever and ever: he will be our guide even unto death. — Cast thy burden upon the Lord, and he shall sustain thee. — Take no thought for your life, what ye shall eat, or what ye shall drink; nor yet for your body, what ye shall put on. For your heavenly Father knoweth that ye have need of all these things. — Hitherto hath the Lord helped us.

Exodus 19:4   Isaiah 63:9   Deuteronomy 32:11,12   Isaiah 46:4
Psalms 48:14, 55:22   Matthew 6:25,32 1   Samuel 7:12

DECEMBER 31 EVENING

There remaineth yet very much land to be possessed.
— JOSHUA 13:1

Not as though I had already attained, either were already perfect: but I follow after, if that I may apprehend that for which also I am apprehended of Christ Jesus. — Be ye therefore perfect. Giving all diligence, add to your faith virtue; and to virtue knowledge; and to knowledge temperance; and to temperance patience; and to patience godliness; and to godliness brotherly kindness; and to brotherly kindness charity. — I pray that your love may abound yet more and more in knowledge and in all judgment. — Eye hath not seen, nor ear heard, neither have entered into the heart of man, the things which God hath prepared for them that love him. But God hath revealed them unto us by his Spirit. — There remaineth...a rest for the people of God. — Thine eyes shall see the king in his beauty: they shall behold the land that is very far off.

Philippians 3:12   Matthew 5:48 2   Peter 1:5-7
Philippians 1:9 1   Corinthians 2:9,10   Hebrews 4:9   Isaiah 33:17

SICKNESS

HAVE MERCY UPON ME, O Lord, for I am weak. O Lord, heal me. — When my heart is overwhelmed, lead me to the rock that is higher than I. — He giveth power to the faint, and to them that have no might he increaseth strength. — The Lord is the strength of my life. — Be not far from me, for trouble is near. — Thou art near, O Lord. — Thou hast heard my voice. Thou drewest near in the day that I called upon thee: thou saidst, Fear not. — A very present help. — O Lord, I am oppressed; undertake for me. — A bruised reed shall he not break. — Yea, though I walk through the valley of the shadow of death I will fear no evil: for thou art with me. — Underneath are the everlasting arms. — Now our Lord Jesus Christ himself, and God, even our Father, which hath loved us and hath given us everlasting consolation and good hope through grace, comfort your hearts.

Psalms 6:2, 61:2 Isaiah 40:29
Psalms 27:1, 22:11, 119:151
Lamentations 3:56,57 Psalm 46:1 Isaiah 38:14
Matthew 12:20 Psalm 23:4
Deuteronomy 33:27 2 Thessalonians 2:16,17

SICKNESS

LORD, BEHOLD, he whom thou lovest is sick. — Surely he hath borne our griefs, and carried our sorrows. — Himself took our infirmities, and bare our sicknesses. — He, being full of compassion. — Like as a father pitieth his children, so the Lord pitieth them that fear him. — For he knoweth our frame. — Who shall separate us from the love of Christ? Shall tribulation, or distress? — Whom the Lord loveth he chasteneth. —Now no chastening for the present seemeth to be joyous, but grievous: nevertheless afterward it yieldeth the peaceable fruit of righteousness unto them which are exercised thereby. —We know that all things work together for good to them that love God. —The Lord said unto me, my grace is sufficient for thee: for my strength is made perfect in weakness. Most gladly therefore will I rather glory in my infirmities, that the power of Christ may rest upon me.

John 11:3 Isaiah 53:4 Matthew 8:17
Psalms 78:38, 103:13,14
Romans 8:35 Hebrews 12:6,11
Romans 8:28 2 Corinthians 12:9

ANXIETY

FEAR NOT; I will help thee. — Come unto me, all ye that labour and are heavy laden, and I will give you rest. — All the promises of God in him are Yea, and in him Amen. — He shall call upon me, and I will answer him: I will be with him in trouble. — I have made and I will bear; even I will carry and will deliver you. — I will be with thee. — Be careful for nothing, but in everything by prayer and supplication, with thanksgiving, let your requests be made known unto God. And the peace of God, which passeth all understanding, shall keep your hearts and minds through Christ Jesus. — I will instruct thee and teach thee in the way which thou shalt go. I will guide thee with mine eye. — I will never leave thee nor forsake thee. — Lo, I am with you alway, even unto the end of the world. — Fear not; I am the first and the last.

Isaiah 41:13 Matthew 11:28 2 Corinthians 1:20
Psalm 91:15 Isaiah 46:4, 43:2 Philippians 4:6,7
Psalm 32:8 Hebrews 13:5 Matthew 28:20
Revelation 1:17

ANXIETY

NEITHER KNOW WE what to do: but our eyes are upon thee. — O God, thou knowest my foolishness; and my sins are not hid from thee. — Teach me to do thy will; for thou art my God. — Lead me, O Lord, in they righteousness, make thy way straight before my face. — My times are in they hand. — If any of you lack wisdom, let him ask of God, that giveth to all men liberally, and upbraideth not; and it shall be given him. — But let him ask in faith, nothing wavering. — Who is among you that feareth the Lord, that walketh in darkness, and hath no light? Let him trust in the name of the Lord, and stay upon his God. — In the multitude of my thoughts within me, thy comforts delight my soul. — Why art thou cast down, O my soul? And why art thou disquieted within me? Hope thou in God. — Jesus…saith unto them, Why are ye so fearful? How is it that ye have no faith? — Now faith is the evidence of things not seen.

2 Chronicles 20:12 Psalms 69:5, 143:10, 5:8, 31:15
James 1:5,6 Isaiah 50:10 Psalms 94:19, 42:5 Mark 4:40 Hebrews 11:1

AFFLICTION

I, EVEN I, am he that comforteth you. — His compassions fail not. For he doth not afflict willingly nor grieve the children of men. — What I do thou knowest not now, but thou shalt know hereafter. — Lo, these are parts of his ways: but how little a portion is heard of him? — The Lord is very pitiful and of tender mercy. — The Father of mercies and the God of all comfort, who comforteth us in all our tribulation, that we may be able to comfort them which are in any trouble, by the comfort wherewith we ourselves are comforted of God. — He hath sent me to bind up the brokenhearted. — A man of sorrows and acquainted with grief. — I will not leave you comfortless. — Another Comforter, even the Spirit of truth. — The eternal God is thy refuge, and underneath are the everlasting arms. — As one whom his mother comforteth, so will I comfort you.

Isaiah 51:12 Lamentations 3:22,33 John 13:7
Job 26:44 James 5:11 2 18,16,17
Deuteronomy 33:27 Corinthians 1:3,4
Isaiah 61:1, 53:3 John 14: Isaiah 66:13

AFFLICTION

SAVE ME, O God; for the waters are come in unto my soul. — O my father, if it be possible, let this cup pass from me: nevertheless not as I will, but as thou wilt. — Being in an agony. — Jesus wept. — Surely he hath borne our griefs and carried our sorrows. — We have not an high priest which cannot be touched with the feeling of our infirmities; but was in all points tempted like as we are, yet without sin. — Let us therefore come boldly unto the throne of grace, that we may find grace to help in time of need. — He careth for you. — I have called thee by thy name; thou art mine. — When thou passest through the waters, I will be with thee; and through the rivers, they shall not overflow thee. — I will never leave thee, nor forsake thee. — Though he slay me, yet will I trust in him. — My flesh and my heart faileth: but God is the strength of my hear, and my portion forever.

Psalm 69:1 Matthew 26:39 Luke 22:44 John 11:35
Isaiah 53:4 Hebrews 4:15,16 1 Peter 5:7
Isaiah 43:1,2 Hebrews 13:5 Job 13:15 Psalm 73:26

BEREAVEMENT

ASLEEP. — Fallen asleep. — Them which sleep in Jesus. — Asleep in Christ. — Our friend sleepeth. — Howbeit Jesus spake of his death. — They stoned Stephen; and…he fell asleep. — So he giveth his beloved sleep. — Our Saviour Jesus Christ hath abolished death. — That through death he might deliver them who through fear of death were all their lifetime subject to bondage. — That he by the grace of God should taste death for every man. — Death is swallowed up in victory. O death, where is thy sting? O grave, where is thy victory? The sting of death is sin; and the strength of sin is the law. But thanks be to God, which giveth us the victory through our Lord Jesus Christ. Therefore, my beloved brethren, be ye stedfast, unmovable, always abounding in the work of the Lord, forasmuch as ye know that your labour is not in vain in the Lord.

1 Thessalonians 4:13 1 Corinthians 15:6
1 Thessalonians 4:14 John 11:11,13 Acts 7:59,60
Psalm 127:2 2 Timothy 1:10 Hebrews 2:14,15,9
1 Corinthians 15:54-58

BEREAVEMENT

FATHER, I will that they also, whom thou has given me, be with me where I am. — He shall return no more to his house, neither shall his place know him any more. — Whilst we are at home in the body, we are absent from the Lord: we are willing rather to be absent from the body, and to be present with the Lord. — I am in a strait betwixt two, having a desire to depart, and to be with Christ; which is far better. — Whether we live or die, we are the Lord's. — Ye have in heaven a better and an enduring substance. — It doth not yet appear what we shall be: but we know that, when he shall appear, we shall be like him; for we shall see him as he is. — Now we see through a glass, darkly; but then face to face. — I will behold thy face in righteousness: I shall be satisfied, when I awake, with thy likeness. — So shall we ever be with the Lord. Wherefore comfort one another with these words.

John 17:24 Job 7:10 2 Corinthians 5:6-8
Philippians 1:23 Romans 14:8 Hebrews 10:34
1 John 3:2 1 Corinthians 13:12 Psalm 17:15
1 Thessalonians 4:17,18

FOR A BIRTHDAY

THE LORD thy God is with thee whithersoever thou goest. Every place that the sole of your foot shall tread upon, that have I given unto you.... There shall not any man be able to stand before thee all the days of thy life. As I was with Moses, so I will be with thee: I will not fail thee nor forsake thee. — The land whither ye go to possess it is a land of hills and valleys.... A land which the LORD thy God careth for: the eyes of the LORD thy God are always upon it, from the beginning of the year even unto the end of the year. — Ye are God's husbandry. — Created in Christ Jesus unto good works, which God hath before ordained that we should walk in them. — Oh, how great is thy goodness which thou hast laid up for them that fear thee! Thou shalt hide them in the secret of thy presence from the pride of man; thou shalt keep them secretly in a pavilion from the strife of tongues. — He that dwelleth in the secret place of the Most High shall abide under the shadow of the Almighty.

Joshua 1:9,3,5 Deuteronomy 11:11,12 1 Corinthians 3:9
Ephesians 2:10 Psalms 31:19,20, 91:1

FOR A BIRTHDAY

THE LORD bless thee, and keep thee. —The Lord that made heaven and earth bless thee. —God, even our Father. —The living God, who giveth us richly all things to enjoy. — Your heavenly Father knoweth that you have need of all these things. — For the Father himself loveth you. — No good thing will he withhold from them that walk uprightly. — Blessed are they that keep his testimonies, and that seek him with the whole heart. — He that keepeth thee will not slumber. Behold, he that keepeth Israel shall neither slumber nor sleep. — The Lord shall be they confidence, and shall keep they foot from being taken. — Thou wilt keep him in perfect peace whose mind is stayed on thee, because he trusteth in thee. — The Lord of peace himself give you peace always by all means.

Numbers 6:24 Psalm 134:3 2 Thessalonians 2:16 1 Timothy 6:17
Matthew 6:32 John 16:27 Proverbs 2:7 Psalms 119:2, 121:3,4
Proverbs 3:26 Isaiah 26:3 2 Thessalonians 3:16

THANKSGIVING

THEY CRY unto the Lord in their trouble, and he saveth them out of their distresses. Oh that men would praise the Lord for his goodness, and for his wonderful works to the children of men! — Were there not ten cleansed? But where are the nine? — Forget not all his benefits. — God, who answered me in the day of my distress. — I sought the Lord, and he heard me, and delivered me from all my fears. — I love the Lord, because he hath heard my voice, and my supplications. Because he hath inclined his ear unto me, therefore will I call upon him as long as I live. — My heart trusted in him, and I am helped: therefore my heart greatly rejoiceth; and with my song will I praise thee. — Call upon me in the day of trouble: I will deliver thee, and thou shalt glorify me. — Whoso offereth praise glorifieth me. — Giving thanks for all things unto God and the Father in the name of our Lord Jesus Christ.

Psalm 107:19,21 Luke 17:17 Psalm 103:2
Genesis 35:3 Psalms 34:4, 116:1-2, 28:7, 50:15,23 Ephesians 5:20

THANKSGIVING

THEY SHALL NOT be ashamed that wait for Me. — Said I not unto thee that, if thou wouldest believe, thou shouldest see the glory of God? — O Daniel, servant of the living God, is thy God, whom thou servest continually, able to deliver thee? No manner of hurt was found upon him, because he believed in his God. — I prayed; and the Lord hath given me my petition which I asked of him. — My heart rejoiceth in the LORD. — Come and hear, all ye that fear God, and I will declare what he hath done for my soul. — Blessed be God, which hath not turned away my prayer nor his mercy from me. I thank thee and praise thee, O thou God of my fathers, who hast given me wisdom and might. — When the waves arise thou stillest them. — He maketh the storm a calm, so that the waves thereof are still. — So he bringeth them unto their desired haven. — Oh that men would praise the Lord for his goodness. — Blessed is the man that trusteth in him.

Isaiah 49:23 John 11:40 Daniel 6:20,23 1 Samuel 1:27, 2:1
Psalm 66:16,20 Daniel 2:23 Psalms 89:9, 107: 29-31, 34:8

I'm Still in a Gang

As a new Christian, your membership in a violent prison gang presents a conflict. Becoming a follower of Jesus doesn't change your identity overnight in the sight of your gang or the system (especially if you're a validated STG member).

If you're an officer, a shot caller or run the yard, you're expected to enforce discipline and occasionally order hits. If you're an ordinary member, you're still expected to support illicit activities and put in work against others, if so ordered.

Obviously, none of that is compatible with being a Christian.

Follow peace with all men, and holiness, without which no man shall see the Lord (Hebrews 12:14).

So, should you drop your flag, debrief, and disappear as fast as you can?

God knows what's going on. Lean hard on his promises and ask the Holy Spirit to guide you as to whether, when and how to renounce your gangstership.

You may be in a facility where rigid racial and gang separations are part of the system, resulting in forced associations that no one can avoid. In that case, trust God to protect you, carefully follow his leading and let him engineer your circumstances. Meanwhile, don't do anything stupid that might annoy or anger members of your gang family (see Matthew 10:16).

They think it strange that ye run not with them to the same excess of riot, speaking evil of you (1 Peter 4:4).

If your gang's constitution prohibits you from leaving, or if your reputation is already shaky, dropping out suddenly might get you viewed as a traitor. That could mean bad news for you and/or loved ones on the outside. It might be wiser to just stay put, pray hard and expect God to work things out (see Psalm 37:3-9).

If leaving the gang is dangerous only for you, consider getting a transfer. If your institution has something like a "Sensitive Needs Unit" for former gangbangers, disappearing from mainline won't be too complicated. If not, your only option may be to check yourself in to protective custody for a while. In either case, trust that God's presence will still be with you, safely leading you along the right path. He promises to be faithful and to never abandon you (see Deuteronomy 31:8).

On the other hand, if you have a solid reputation with your gang as a stand-up guy, you may be able to remain where you are without too much hassle. Your gang leaders might not treat you too harshly if you can stay on friendly terms with everyone while gradually scaling back your activities with them.

Keep thanking God (out loud, if possible) for going before you as your "vanguard" and behind you as your "rearguard" (see Isaiah 52:12).

The best way to avoid possible gang retribution is to keep trusting in your Father's favor and goodness towards you while sincerely asking him to bless your fellow gang members (however he chooses to do that) and demonstrating to them the genuineness of your new faith by the new ways you walk, talk and react.

They're watching closely to see if that faith – and the new you – are for real. In time, some of them might even come to you (privately) for help.

Recommended Readings

God Don't Lie: A Memoir by a Former Racist Gang Member and All-Around Miscreant, Richard Smith (Christian Faith). Convicted of murder at 17 and sentenced to Texas prisons for 99 years, Smith eventually became an Aryan Brotherhood captain, then endured 13 years in solitary before deciding to accept God's forgiveness and be restored. Today, instead of hatefully preaching racial pride and intimidation, Smith promotes God's mercy and redemption to other receptive inmates.

The Tommie Scott Story: From Gangs, Drugs, and Crime to Soldier for Christ, Tommie Scott (Innovo). How a violent gangbanger – an East Los Angeles gang enforcer – dramatically met the Lord in a California state prison Bible study.

The Cross and the Switchblade, David Wilkerson with John & Elizabeth Sherrill (Chosen). This old school classic tells how warlord Nicky Cruz, leader of NYC's most-feared Puerto Rican street gang, became a Christian and successfully walked away from his old life unharmed, thanks to God's divine protection.

The Devil Has No Mother: Why He's Worse Than You Think – But God is Greater, Nicky Cruz (Worth). The same Nicky Cruz tells how Satan uses every possible means to prevent us from turning to God, drawing on examples from his own spiritualist childhood, the murder of his brother, and his encounters today with gangbangers in the world's highest security prisons.

Lord, how many adversaries I have!
How many there be who rise up against me!

Many there be who say of me,
"There is no help for him in God."
But thou, O Lord, are a shield for me,
my glory and the lifter of my head.

I cried unto the Lord with my voice,
and he heard me out of his holy hill.

I lay down and slept; I awoke;
For the Lord sustained me.

I will not be afraid of those around me
who have set themselves against me.
— Psalm 3:1-6

I'm Stuck in Solitary

Being forced to subsist in a storage bin 23 hours a day, deprived of almost all outside contact, over weeks, months or years, drives some men insane.

Whether you're in a supermax prison, in administrative segregation, are being punished in the hole or have checked yourself in to protective custody, the effects are the same: relentless boredom, frustration and restlessness. You can try sleeping your way through it but may eventually fall into depression and a mind-numbing haze after losing so much touch with time and reality.

At the very least, feeling so all alone is psychologically disorienting. But you need to know that you are not so all alone, nor have you lost touch with reality: Your reality is just personal confinement while enduring near-total rejection.

But God hasn't rejected you!

He is here, and if you won't reject him, his real presence can change your life.

Solitary is not divine punishment.

God may be permitting it, though, because – if you will pay attention to him – he can bless you in this tight space. Getting out now might just make you run off like a wild animal sprung free from a trap – straight back to your bad old habits and hang-ups. God can't bless that.

> **Every promise in this book (and the Recommended Readings) can become true for you.**
> **Your isolation cell can become a private sanctuary of study, prayer, praise, faith, hope and restoration.**

In offering you his real presence God doesn't just want to keep you company. He wants to give you some divine enlightenment and real inner restoration.

Instead of making you go crazy, your time in solitary can be spent making yourself saner, smarter and stronger.

Would you like that to happen?

If you've grown up wrapped in the surround sound of radios, TVs, Walkmen, boomboxes, iPods, AirPods, Instagram, smartphones, street life and non-stop partying, being left all alone can feel totally unnatural. That's why solitary is so hard: you're just not used to being left all alone with your own thoughts.

Banging your head against the door, trashing your cell, going on a hunger strike, cutting yourself to get attention or acting out with a dramatic suicide attempt won't do anything for you.

Right now, the Father is offering you a better option.

Hear God's "still small voice" (see 1 Kings 19:12).
The only positive way to get through solitary is to do your time constructively: Get close to God, hear what he has to tell you and respond to it.

Read and meditate on (think about) his written Word, using these daily scriptures (and a Bible-reading devotional, if you can get one); ask the Holy Spirit to give you understanding. Try to get some of the Recommended Readings.

Ask Jesus to make himself real to you right now. He will do it!

Ask, and it shall be given you; seek and ye shall find; knock, and it shall be opened unto you: For every one that asketh receiveth; and be that seeketh findeth and to him that knocketh it shall be opened (Matthew 7:7-8).

God will prove to you that you are not too far gone to be worthy of his mercy and forgiveness, his inspiration and a new mind and heart – even in solitary.

Actually, this might be a better place for you to be transformed and restored by God's grace than general population, with all of its distractions and temptations.

Now is your chance to find out.

There are some defeats more triumphant than victories.
—*Michael de Montaigne*

Psalm 40

(vv. 1-4)
I waited patiently for the Lord;
and he inclined unto me,
and heard my cry.
He brought me up also
out of an horrible pit,
out of the miry clay,
and set my feet upon a rock,
and established my goings.
He hath put a new song in my mouth,
even praise unto our God:
Many shall see it, and fear,
and shall trust in the Lord.
Blessed is that man
that maketh the Lord his trust,
and respecteth not the proud,
nor such as turn aside to lies.

No One Asked

I am so tired of crying!
But if the tears should cease...only rage will remain.
The anger was not born within me, it was given.
I crave the wandering time-kill of sleep,
For my nightmares are in wakefulness:
    The indignity of the cold steel cage;
    The cruel mockery of abused authority;
    The ruthless, grinding destruction of the will;
Humanity taken, stomped and torn...methodical soul-kill.
Living relentlessly in frozen-framed past (for no future is offered).
Only a blind, scented march toward oblivion.
Wasting mind-games challenge rambling sanity
(I feel the slippage).
Memories separated from reality,
    rebuilding again, and again, and again;
    indigo speculations of "what might have been."
Yet fantasy can never paint over pained regret.
Escape and rest come only through tear-faded dreams.
No, I am not a quitter (there is nothing left for me to quit...
    and nothing left for me not to quit).
I have nothing...nothing at all, but
    this burdensome breath,
    this useless heartbeat,
    this non-life.
No one asked why.
They just mindlessly ruled, "no more chances."
Mystic powers of circumstance could have given them reasons
(not excuses). But no one asked.
Oh, no, don't let me out now! No, it's too late!
Too many stained years have slipped by,
    killing desire, robbing need.
This dog has been beaten too much.
Some can now recognize the dull red grazed shadow in my eyes.
They fear me (they should); I need to be left alone.
But I am not evil, just spent.
Punishment extended too long simply destroys.
I know I am no longer human.

    —*Robert L. Hambrick (2014), age 57*
    Texas DCJ Lubbock

I'm Down for Life

Have you noticed? Most lifers do better time than most short timers. It's true that some lifers let unrelenting sadness wear them down with despair, or let angry bitterness turn them into monsters, but most come to terms with reality.

While none of them should be called happy, more than a few lifers exhibit an inner calm and ability to get along with others that is remarkable, considering the grisly offenses that may have earned them their lifetime bids.

Life on the Installment Plan

Most short timers do their time feeling angry and frustrated, especially if they've been ratted out or lied about. Itching to prove the world wrong about its opinion of them, they spend their time fantasizing about how they'll settle old scores and make even bigger ones as soon as they get back on the street.

Young short timers often act out, trying to show off how slick they think they are. Mainly, they just annoy the older convicts, who dismiss them as loudmouthed knuckleheads in need of impulse control (see Proverbs 29:9). Even so, respected old heads can often befriend, mentor and even straighten out the few sweet kids ready to be schooled in a little wisdom and accept guidance from mature convicts willing to take a sincere (non-predatory) interest in them (see Proverbs 9:8-9).

> **Ironically, chronic offenders can end up doing as much time behind bars as lifers. They keep violating their release conditions and getting sent back inside. They never come to terms with reality, enjoy God's blessings or correct their downward spiral towards eventual destruction.**

Smart lifers work through their hard feelings and move on – not just because they mellow into middle age or lose their fighting spirit, but because they eventually accept the hard truth that "it is what it is." For some it might take a six-month stretch in the SHU. Others realize right away that long-term prisoners really do seem to cope better, and so decide to "go with the flow."

The Lord will not cast off for ever:
But though he cause grief, yet will he have compassion
according to the multitude of his mercies.
For he doth not afflict willingly nor grieve the children of men.
To crush under his feet all the prisoners of the earth.
To turn aside the right of a man before the face of the most High,
To subvert a man in his cause, the Lord approveth not.
— Lamentations 3:31-36

Permanent confinement is never enjoyable.

It need not be a dead end, though. Whether or not you ever get released, you can still enjoy a positive outlook, sense of purpose and eternal destiny. You can still enjoy a place of sonship, blessing and comfortable intimacy with the Father.

You really can have all of that – even as a lifer.

Do you really want it?

One of every nine US prisoners is serving life.

With God's help you can choose to stop fighting your fate (while continuing your appeals) and instead experience a relatively peaceful and low-stress confinement.

To quit agonizing over a life sentence (or having to spend any time inside), believe that what the Bible says is true:

1) No matter how badly you have sinned, you can become a righteous son of the Father worthy to receive all of his blessings as you trust in him and respond obediently to his written Word.

2) God can enable you to forgive all of your enemies, no matter the injustices committed against you.

3) The Father is willing to take up your cause.

Must life always mean life?

Having renounced evil and been restored as beloved sons or daughters of the Father being gradually set free from the control of their sinful pasts, many Christian lifers hope and pray to God to get them pardoned, paroled, deported or otherwise set free, indeed (see John 8:36). After all, aren't Christians promised that God works everything together for their good (see Romans 8:28, Psalm 37:4)?

The problem is that we don't always know what that "good" is or how long it may take to be realized. (Read the story of Joseph, who as a teenager was unjustly enslaved and later imprisoned for years before getting released and eventually realizing what "good" it had all been for (Genesis 37-50).)

Disappointment can hit hard if things aren't working out the way you've been hoping and praying for. Your belief in the Father's favor and goodness can start to wobble. At that point you must again choose to trust God anyway – despite your frustration with him, the system and your seemingly endless predicament.

Nazi labor camp survivor Corrie ten Boom finally decided to trust God by saying, "Don't wrestle, just nestle."

Give God the desires of your heart.

Grieve (you *have* lost a lot), but don't despair. Believe that your life is not being totally wasted because of indefinite (or permanent) incarceration. Ask God what he wants to do in and through you right now. Ask him for the joy of being a child who resolutely trusts in the Father's favor and goodness – and justice.

God knows the hard facts of your case. In the fullness of time he will either get you out or give you more grace to stay in and be a blessing to others with a peace "that passes all understanding" (see Philippians 4:7, Colossians 1:10-14).

Meanwhile, instead of questioning God's fairness, put yourself back in the hands of Him who knows all of your sorrows and griefs (see Isaiah 53:3-4, Hebrews 4:15-16).

Recommended Readings

Lessons from San Quentin: Everything I Needed to Know about Life I Learned in Prison, Bill Dallas (Tyndale House). Invaluable truths passed on by the lifers who mentored Dallas inside California's notorious state prison, where God led him from being "a narcissistic playboy to suicidal inmate to spiritual apprentice."

Young Man Arise!, Brian V. Warth (Xulon Press). Sentenced at 16 to 16-to-life, Warth spent 16 years in California prisons before being paroled...as a new man.

Just Mercy: A Story of Justice and Redemption, Bryan Stevenson (Spiegel & Grau). The black founder of Alabama's Equal Justice Initiative overcame childhood segregation to earn a Harvard law degree and professorship at NYU Law School. He's won relief for *dozens* of condemned prisoners and argued five times before the US Supreme Court while vigorously challenging legal biases against the poor.

The Serenity Prayer

God grant me the serenity
to accept the things I cannot change,
courage to change the things I can
and wisdom to know the difference;
living one moment at a time,
enjoying one day at a time and
accepting hardships as the pathway to peace;
taking, as He did, this sinful world
as it is, not as I would have it;
trusting that He will make all things right
if I surrender to His will,
that I may be reasonably happy in this life
and supremely happy with Him
forever in the next.
Amen.

—*Reinhold Niebuhr*

Who Am I?

They often tell me
I would step from my cell's confinement
calmly, cheerfully, firmly,
like a squire from his country-house.

Who am I? They often tell me
I would talk to my warders
freely and friendly and clearly,
as though it were mine to command.

Who am I? They also tell me
I would bear the days of misfortune
equably, smilingly, proudly,
like one accustomed to win.

Am I then really all that which other men tell of?
Or am I only what I know of myself?
Restless and longing and sick, like a bird in a cage,
struggling for breath, as though
hands were compressing my throat,
yearning for colours, for flowers,
for the voices of birds,

thirsting for words of kindness, for neighbourliness,
trembling with anger at despotisms
and petty humiliation,
tossing in expectation of great events,
powerlessly trembling for friends
at an infinite distance,
weary and empty at praying, at thinking, at making,
faint, and ready to say farewell to it all?

Who am I? This or the other?
Am I one person today and tomorrow another?
Am I both at once?
A hypocrite before others,
and before myself a contemptibly
woebegone weakling?
Or is something within me still like a beaten army,
fleeing in disorder from victory already achieved?

Who am I? They mock me,
these lonely questions of mine.
Whoever I am, thou knowest, O God, I am thine!

—Dietrich Bonhoeffer (1944), age 38

Can I Lose My Salvation?

Your relationship with the Father is a covenant (a spiritual contract I call a divine plea agreement): You agree to keep confessing and turning away from sinful desires and behaviors and follow Jesus as your Lord, with help from the Holy Spirit. The Father agrees to always restore you when you confess and repent, to maintain your adoption in his eternal family, and to keep renewing your heart and mind so you can enjoy a life of integrity and godliness that honors him.

The Father promises to keep his part of the covenant and to never walk away from it (see Joshua 1:5, Hebrews 13:5). Jesus promises to do the same by keeping others from snatching you out of the Father's protective hand (see John 10:28-30).

That doesn't mean you cannot void the contract by wriggling out of his hand yourself and walking away forever. God won't stop you.

Even after you have truly been born-again, you can still decide to turn your back on God and the church, disavow your Christian beliefs (or just pretend to believe them (see Titus 1:16)), ignore God's Word and the Holy Spirit, quit confessing and repenting of any new sins and just go your own way as you please.

God will let you do all of that – but with eternal consequences:

Now the just shall live by faith: but if any man draw back, my soul shall have no pleasure in him (Hebrews 10:38).

That sounds harsh but God has not bound up your free will so that you cannot disagree with him or choose to permanently break off relations with him. If you do that, though, Jesus says you will lose your covenant blessings:

No man, having put his hand to the plough, and looking back, is fit for the kingdom of God (Luke 9:62).

He that believeth on the Son hath everlasting life: and he that believeth not the Son shall not see life; but the wrath of God abideth on him (John 3:36).

Quenching (stifling) the Holy Spirit's influence and going back to being a natural-born sinner instead of remaining a saved son or daughter is bad news (see Romans 8:13-14). If you should die in that state of willful rejection and rebellion against God, after having experienced his presence, received his divine help and even operated in signs and wonders, you will have to face divine judgment by Jesus as an unrepentant sinner (see 1 Peter 2:20-22).

Why would anyone *choose* that fate?

It is impossible for those who were once enlightened, and have tasted of the heavenly gift, and were made partakers of the Holy Ghost, and have tasted the good word of God, and the powers of the world to come, if they shall fall away, to renew them again unto repentance (Hebrews 6:4-5).

Now, here's the good news: Very few unhappy Christians ever take it that far by *totally* falling away and *permanently* terminating their plea agreement with the Father.

After all, who wants to end up like Lucifer (see Isaiah 14:12-21)?

Backsliding into former sins, addictions or immoral thinking is not the same as "losing your salvation." It's a very serious condition that can deafen you to God's voice, cripple you spiritually and expose you to future judgment, but it does not mean you may never again be restored to a right relationship with the Father.

As long as you live, you may always return – even if you have deliberately sinned big-time (see Psalm 103:8-14). Here's proof:

Jesus warned his disciples that if they ever publicly denied having a relationship with him, he would tell the Father that he had no relationship with them (see Matthew 10:32-33, Mark 8:38). Twice afterwards, Jesus personally cautioned his first disciple, Peter, against doing that. Peter swore it would never happen (see Luke 22:31-33, Matthew 26:33-35) but just hours after Jesus was taken into late-night custody Peter was pointed out in a public crowd as one of Jesus' companions.

Just as Jesus had predicted, Peter swore he didn't know Jesus – three times!

Did Peter lose his salvation for doing that? He might have, had he imitated his fellow disciple, Judas, who killed himself after betraying Jesus earlier that night.

But instead of disowning Peter *right away*, Jesus offered to restore him, and Peter took it (see John 21:1-19). That made all the difference in his eternal destiny.

Until you die, the Father will always offer restoration to you, too (see Isaiah 55:7).

It's yours to accept or reject…until it's too late (see Hebrews 9:27).

The only way to become a truly hellbound apostate or reprobate is to refuse *ever again* to confess, repent and be restored by God, perhaps out of bitter anger. But if you ever get that upset with the Father, don't walk away – *talk* away!

Many psalmists direct angry complaints to God, but then end up recognizing his faithfulness and goodness to them (see Psalm 77, for example). That's why the psalmist David was "a man after God's own heart" (see 1 Samuel 13:14, Acts 13:22).

When you're suffering and it seems like the Father is ignoring your prayers, he isn't punishing you, amusing himself by playing hard to get, or rejecting you as an unloved loser (that's what Satan will try to make you think (see Job 2:9)). Rather, the Bible tells us that God uses suffering as a means to make us more dependent on himself and thus more resolute (strong) in our belief that God *does* love and care for us, come what may (see Romans 5:3-4, James 1:2-4, 1 Peter 1:6-7).

That's a big reason to keep going to Chapel each week: so you can stay encouraged to "keep the faith" (see Hebrews 10:25, Matthew 24:13, 1 Corinthians 16:13).

The only way to "lose" your salvation is to forever reject it yourself. Instead, humble yourself, enjoy God's generous mercy by again seeking and receiving his full forgiveness. Then step back onto the safe path of faith, hope and restoration.

If Thou But Suffer God to Guide Thee

And hope in him through all thy ways,
He'll give thee strength, whate'er betide thee,
And bear thee through the evil days.
Who trusts in God's unchanging love
Builds on the Rock that naught can move.

What can these anxious cares avail thee,
These never-ceasing moans and sighs?
What can it help, if thou bewail thee
O'er each dark moment as it flies?
Our cross and trials do but press
The heavier for our bitterness.

Only be still and wait his leisure
In cheerful hope, with heart content
To take whate'er thy Father's pleasure
And all-deserving love hath sent,
Nor doubt our inmost wants are known
To Him who chose us for his own.

Sing, pray, and keep his ways unswerving;
So do thine own part faithfully,
And trust his Word, though undeserving;
Thou yet shalt find it true for thee.
God never yet forsook in need
The soul that trusted him indeed.

—*Georg Neumark (1641), age 20*

Get Me Outta Here!

Having to live locked inside a secret, secluded, self-contained, overcrowded, unhealthy, unpredictable and often-dangerous world of weirdoes, with no realistic hope of escape, can make anyone seriously unhappy and resentful.

O God, where's my comfort zone?

You may frequently get fed up with trying to maintain a positive Christian attitude while having to put up with everyone and everything around you.

Having to get along with strangers so very different from yourself can soon become less of a fascination and more of an annoyance.

Having to silently submit to stand-up counts, controlled movements, lockdowns, shakedowns, pat downs (or worse), petty rules, cramped quarters, loudspeaker blasts, monotonous meals and non-stop noise can wear you down.

Having to stay on guard against assaults can make you sick from stress.

Family crises or disturbing news from home can trigger resentment and rage at being so isolated and unable to immediately manage things (see Psalm 88:8,18).

At the very least, the system's outright indifference to so much routine suffering and neglect can make you downright disgusted.

You just want to get this over with, get out and get on with your life.

To relieve such frustrations, many inmates act out, overeat, overexercise, oversleep or get high. What should a Christian do?

Be honest about your feelings (see Psalm 55).

Go walk the track, if you have one, and talk with your Father. Don't think you are being faithless when you feel like complaining to him about your anger, anxiety, frustration, fear or other kinds of upsets (see Psalm 62:5-8).

Just don't accuse him of being responsible for your unhappiness.

Instead, thank God for his good plans for you and that in the fullness of time he *will* bring you safely through to accomplish them. Thank him for his promises (see Psalm 63:5-6 and pp. 68-71). Continue meditating on these morning and evening scriptures, reading them as your Father's personal assurances to you.

Talk things over (or correspond) with other Christians; pray for them and what they too are going through (see 1 Corinthians 10:3); seek new insights and wisdom.

Whenever you feel disconsolate, tell all your troubles to God and thank him for his promises to help you (see Psalms 43:5, 55:22, 1 Peter 5:7). He really can calm you down, give you peace and joy in believing, and a welcome sense of detachment from all your worries (read Hebrews 10:35-36, Psalm 142, Isaiah 26:3, Lamentations 3:54-57, Micah 7:2-10,18-19, John 14:27, Colossians 1:10-14).

Whate'er My God Ordains is Right,

His holy will abideth;
I will be still whate'er he doth;
And follow where he guideth;
He is my God; though dark my road,
He holds me that I shall not fall:
Wherefore to him I leave it all.

Whate'er my God ordains is right:
He never will deceive me;
He leads me by the proper path:
I know he will not leave me.
I take, content, what he hath sent;
His hand can turn my griefs away,
And patiently I wait his day.

Whate'er my God ordains is right:
His loving thought attends me;
No poison can be in the cup
That my Physician sends me.
My God is true; each morn anew
I'll trust his grace unending,
My life to him commending.

Whate'er my God ordains is right:
He is my Friend and Father;
He suffers naught to do me harm,
Though many storms may gather,
Now I may know both joy and woe,
Some day I shall see clearly
That he hath loved me dearly.

Whate'er my God ordains is right:
Though now this cup, in drinking,
May bitter seem to my faint heart,
I take it all, unshrinking.
My God is true; each morn anew.
Sweet comfort yet shall fill my heart,
And pain and sorrow shall depart.

Whate'er my God ordains is right:
Here shall my stand be taken;
Though sorrow, need, or death be mine,
Yet I am not forsaken.
My Father's care is round me there;
He holds me that I shall not fall:
And so to him I leave it all.

—*Samuel Rodigast (1676), age 27*

> **Anxiety is apt to arise from remembering [our] yesterdays. Our present enjoyment of God's grace is apt to be checked by the memory of yesterday's sins and blunders.**
>
> **But God is the God of our yesterdays...**
>
> **Our yesterdays present irreparable things to us.**
>
> **It is true that we have lost opportunities that will never return, but God can transform this destructive anxiety into a constructive thoughtfulness for the future.**
>
> **Leave the Irreparable Past in His hands, and step out into the Irresistible Future with Him.**
> **—Oswald Chambers**

You, O God, have proved us;
You have tried us as silver is tried.
You have brought us into the snare;
You have laid heavy burdens on our backs.
You let enemies run over our heads;
We went through fire and water;
But you brought us out into a place of refreshment.
— Psalm 66:9-11

The path of the just is as the shining light,
that shineth more and more unto the perfect day.
— Proverbs 4:18

This one thing I do,
forgetting those things which are behind,
and reaching forth unto those things which are before,
I press toward the mark for the prize of
the high calling of God in Christ Jesus.
— Philippians 3:13-14

When It's Finally Time to Leave

Unless you are truly serving a natural life sentence, in the fullness of time you probably will be released back to the streets. O happy day!

Real Air! Real Food! Real Clothes! Real Women!

How is it, then, that within just three years more than a third of all ex-offenders get re-arrested and returned to custody? Maybe that's where they prefer to be.

Correctional systems only produce inmates.

They don't correct anything (especially bad character) or restore you to good standing in the community. If you've become institutionalized by a long stretch, used to floating along on a highly regimented prison routine, getting suddenly thrown back into the public mainstream as an independent swimmer can make you feel like a drowning victim. You've probably met more than a few folks who couldn't make it on the outside because of using poor judgment about decisions and adjustments they needed to make or temptations they needed to resist.

You are now a second-class citizen.

While on supervised release you'll get your street clothes back but not your full freedom. You may have to submit to involuntary treatment (including polygraphs), regular drug and/or alcohol testing, GPS tracking, a curfew and no contact with certain people, places or activities deemed out of bounds for you.

If you must register as a sex offender, you will have to endure years (perhaps even a lifetime) of public shaming on numerous Web sites.

Because you can be revoked easily for all kinds of technical violations, you must get along with your probation/parole officer, who will make your supervision either manageable or miserable, depending on how you behave and how you are perceived. Always keep Matthew 10:16 in mind.

Rather than being liberating, the terms of your release can feel restrictive, unfair and frustrating. But as one who has learned to walk in divine forgiveness, wisdom and power, you can expect to do better than most (see Colossians 1:10-14).

Some churches want to help you.

At least a few months before your release, ask your chaplain or a friend on the outside to do an Internet search for the names and addresses of churches or Christian social service groups in your release area that run re-entry ministries.

Write letters to them describing yourself and your conviction(s), and why you would like to participate in their program. If possible, include a separate note written by your chaplain telling of your sincere efforts toward personal restoration and Christian maturity.

Satan wants to rob you (see John 10:10a).

Depending on your offense(s) and where you live, your criminal record may deny you food stamps (SNAP), public housing, scholarship and tuition aid, personal and business loans, a professional license, voting rights, election to public office, jury duty, gun ownership, entry to some countries, and access to US citizenship.

The military and most large corporations probably won't hire you.

Don't be dismayed if your faith in God's ability to meet all of your needs is challenged by sudden setbacks or intense temptations (see Psalm 73, Philippians 4:19). When that happens, you might feel a very strong urge to violate your release conditions for a free ride back to where things are predictable and where you know the ropes, even though only your basic needs, not all of them, will be met there.

Don't let Satan sabotage you like that! Double down on your warrior praying!

Keep believing that God will come through for you as you persistently praise him, thank him, and trust him, come what may (see Deuteronomy 4:9, Jeremiah 17:7, Isaiah 41:10,13, 1 Thessalonians 5:16-18).

God wants to bring you through (see John 10:10b).

As soon as possible, join a church where God's supernatural power is at work and where you can form solid friendships with other Christians happy to have fellowship with you as an ex-offender (although perhaps with some restrictions).

If you must spend time in a halfway house before ending your confinement, take full advantage of every resource that's offered.

If you may be with family, prove by your godly behavior that you've changed.

Don't let pride or shame keep you from getting help staying straight and clean. For your first six months (at least) meet once or more each week, rain or shine, with two or three confidential prayer partners and/or a Christian counselor. Be accountable to them with 100% honesty, respecting their spiritual maturity and practical advice. They will help you overcome discouragement and resist heavy pressures to relapse into old addictions or sin patterns (see Hebrews 10:25).

No matter how challenging things may get, as you continue praising, thanking and trusting God, come what may, he will give you favor with others, peace with your enemies, and opportunities or ideas for making honest money.

God *is* faithful in keeping all of his promises, so stay safely on the path of faith, hope and restoration.

You will remain happy, whole – and fully free – forever!

Thank You, God

For all You have given,
Thank you, God.

For all You have withheld,
Thank you, God.

For all You have withdrawn,
Thank you, God.

For all You have permitted,
Thank you, God.

For all You have prevented,
Thank you, God.

For all You have forgiven me,
Thank you, God.

For all You have prepared for me,
Thank you, God.

For the place You are keeping for me,
Thank you, God.

For the death You have chosen for me,
Thank you, God.

For having created me to love You for all eternity,
Thank you, God,
Thank you, God,
Thank you, God.

—A Benedictine prayer

About the Author

J. R. Woodgates graduated from Northwestern University in 1975 with a degree in broadcast journalism. He enjoyed a professional career in Washington, DC, both as an international radio broadcaster for 27 years at the Voice of America and as a local part-time public radio announcer for 13 years at WETA-FM.

In 2006 Woodgates pleaded guilty in federal court to having had child pornography on his office computer in 2002. He was sentenced to a year and a day in federal prison. The formal process of church discipline and restoration he had already gone through by then, coupled with the surprising depth of Christian fellowship he soon found among his fellow inmates, was life changing.

Afterwards, he successfully completed a five-year period of supervised release and a 10-year stint on the sex offender registry.

Today, Woodgates continues enjoying the Father's favor and goodness, as well as the love and support of his family, friends and church.

He wants all those living in confinement to learn about and experience the relief, restoration and empowerment they too can enjoy as repentant, forgiven and blessed sons (and daughters) of the Father.

Until 2009 Woodgates was a lifelong Episcopalian (a "preacher's kid"). Today, he is a founding member of the Anglican Church in North America.

**Ask someone to purchase this book
for you or a friend for $14.99
via
DLPP.INFO**

A Note to Prison Ministers and Chaplains

Case lot discounts are available for bulk purchases of this book. For details, send inquiries with direct telephone and email contact information to this address. Prisoner correspondence is always welcome.

Prisoner's Path Books
Post Office Box 32014
Washington, DC 20007